W9-AUP-824

ZAGAT

Long Island Restaurants
2012/13

LOCAL EDITOR
Suzi Forbes Chase with Phil Carlucci
and Donna Marino Wilkins
STAFF EDITOR
Cynthia Kilian

Published and distributed by
Zagat Survey, LLC
76 Ninth Avenue
New York, NY 10011
T: 212.977.6000
E: longisland@zagat.com
www.zagat.com

ACKNOWLEDGMENTS

We thank Mike Lima and Bernard Onken, as well as the following members of our staff: Aynsley Karps (editor), Brian Albert, Sean Beachell, Maryanne Bertollo, Danielle Borovoy, Reni Chin, Larry Cohn, Nicole Diaz, Kelly Dobkin, Kara Freewind, Jeff Freier, Alison Gainor, Matthew Hamm, Justin Hartung, Marc Henson, Karen Hudes, Ryutaro Ishikane, Natalie Lebert, Mike Liao, Vivian Ma, James Mulcahy, Polina Paley, Amanda Spurlock, Stefanie Tuder, Chris Walsh, Jacqueline Wasilczyk, Sharon Yates, Samantha Zalaznick, Anna Zappia and Kyle Zolner.

The reviews in this guide are based on public opinion surveys. The ratings reflect the average scores given by the survey participants who voted on each establishment. The text is based on quotes from, or paraphrasings of, the surveyors' comments. Phone numbers, addresses and other factual data were correct to the best of our knowledge when published in this guide.

Our guides are printed using environmentally preferable inks containing 20%, by weight, renewable resources on papers sourced from well-managed forests. Deluxe editions are covered with Skivertex Recover® Double containing a minimum of 30% post-consumer waste fiber.

© 2012 Zagat Survey, LLC
ISBN-13: 978-1-60478-448-0
ISBN-10: 1-60478-448-2
Printed in the
United States of America

Contents

Ratings & Symbols

Zagat Top Spot	Name	Symbols	Cuisine	Zagat Ratings			
				FOOD	DECOR	SERVICE	COST

Area, Address & Contact

Z Tim & Nina's ◗ *American*   ▽ 23 | 9 | 13 | $15

East Hampton | 1 Main St. (Maidendive Ln.) |
631-555-1212 | www.zagat.com

Review, surveyor comments in quotes

Locals, "celebrities" and "congenial drifters" alike "storm the hedgerows" for a taste of the "haute campground grub" at this East Hampton American; while cognoscenti crow over the "classy" yet "comforting", "cheap" cuisine, aesthetes object to "eating in a trailer" "without air-conditioning or even a fan", and suggest the "surly" staff "should be used as fish bait."

Ratings   **Food, Decor** & **Service** are rated on a 30-point scale.

0 – 9	poor to fair
10 – 15	fair to good
16 – 19	good to very good
20 – 25	very good to excellent
26 – 30	extraordinary to perfection
▽	low response | less reliable

Cost   The price of dinner with a drink and tip; lunch is usually 25% to 30% less. For unrated **newcomers** or **write-ins,** the price range is as follows:

I	$25 and below	E	$41 to $65
M	$26 to $40	VE	$66 or above

Symbols

Z	highest ratings, popularity and importance
◗	serves after 11 PM
S M	closed on Sunday or Monday
⊘	no credit cards accepted

About This Survey

This **2012/13 Long Island Restaurants Survey** is an update reflecting significant developments since our last Survey was published. It covers 951 restaurants on Long Island, including 99 important additions. We've also indicated new addresses, phone numbers and other major changes. Like all our guides, this one is based on input from avid local diners – 6,217 all told. Our editors have synopsized this feedback, including representative comments (in quotation marks within each review). To read full surveyor comments – and share your own opinions – visit **zagat.com,** where you will also find the latest restaurant news, special events, deals, reservations, menus, photos and lots more, **all for free.**

ABOUT ZAGAT: In 1979, we started asking friends to rate and review restaurants purely for fun. The term "user-generated content" had yet to be coined. That hobby grew into Zagat Survey; 33 years later, we have over 375,000 surveyors and cover airlines, bars, dining, fast food, entertaining, golf, hotels, movies, music, resorts, shopping, spas, theater and tourist attractions in over 100 countries. Along the way, we evolved from being a print publisher to a digital content provider, e.g. **zagat.com** and Zagat mobile apps (for Android, iPad, iPhone, BlackBerry, Windows Phone 7 and Palm webOS). We also produce marketing tools for a wide range of blue-chip corporate clients. And you can find us on Google+ and just about any other social media network.

UNDERLYING PREMISES: Three simple ideas underlie our ratings and reviews. First, we believe that the collective opinions of large numbers of consumers are more accurate than those of any single person. (Consider that our surveyors bring some 906,000 annual meals' worth of experience to this survey, visiting restaurants regularly year-round, anonymously – and on their own dime.) Second, food quality is only part of the equation when choosing a restaurant, thus we ask our surveyors to rate food, decor and service separately and then report on cost. Third, since people need reliable information in an easy-to-digest format, we strive to be concise and we offer our content on every platform – print, online and mobile.

THANKS: We're grateful to our editor, Suzi Forbes Chase, author of *The Hamptons, A Great Destination* as well as other travel guides and cookbooks. We also thank Phil Carlucci, a food- and golf-focused freelance writer and the creator of Golf On Long Island online, and Donna Marino Wilkins, a food, travel and lifestyle journalist. We also sincerely thank the thousands of people who participated in this survey – this guide is really "theirs."

JOIN IN: To improve our guides, we solicit your comments – positive or negative; it's vital that we hear your opinions. Just contact us at **nina-tim@zagat.com.** We also invite you to join our surveys at **zagat.com.** Do so and you'll receive a choice of rewards in exchange.

New York, NY
April 25, 2012

Nina and Tim

Nina and Tim Zagat

What's New

The economy took its toll on Long Island again this year, with many restaurants closing. On the upside, a crop of high-profile newcomers debuted with pricey fare and eye-candy decor. But it wasn't all upscale steakhouses and hot spots, as casual pizzerias and burger joints also materialized in a nod to those still guarding their wallets.

 BUZZ MAKERS: Insignia, the flashy sibling of **Blackstone Steakhouse,** swaggered into Smithtown with 20-ft. ceilings and a 700-bottle wine display; **Jewel,** a Contemporary American from Tom Schaudel (**A Mano, Coolfish**), opened in a splashy Melville setting; and classy cantina **K·Pacho** from the **Four Food Studio** team added gusto to New Hyde Park. **Mint** hit Garden City with upscale Asian fare and a roof-garden lounge, and Pan-Asian **Monsoon** blew into a hip, bi-level Babylon setting via the Bohlsen Group (**Tellers, Prime**). Chefs spiced up the scene too, with **Orto,** an Italian from Eric Lomando (**Kitchen A Bistro** and **Kitchen A Trattoria**), opening in Miller place, and **MP Taverna,** a casual Greek from chef Michael Psilakis (NYC's **Kefi**), debuting in Roslyn.

HOLY COW: Islanders love beef. And steakhouses – led by perennial Most Popular winner **Peter Luger** in Great Neck – are local fixtures. But there's always room for more. Enter **Grill 454** in Commack, **Jake's Steakhouse** in East Meadow, **J. Michaels Tuscan Steakhouse** in Northport and **Spiro's** in Rocky Point. More casual burger joints also popped up. In addition to two **Five Guys** chain links, new patty purveyors include **Banzai Burger** in Amagansett, a Garden City branch of **Bobby's Burger Palace, Jack's Shack** in Glen Head, **Prime Burger** in Albertson and **Smashburger** in Hicksville.

PIE-EYED: The bottom line inspired more than just burgers. A cache of affordable new pizzerias includes **Angelina's Fireshack** in New Hyde Park, **Anthony's Coal Fired Pizza** (Woodbury), **Primo Piatto** in Huntington and **Red Tomato** in East Norwich.

CLOSING TIME: Sadly, lots of favorite eateries shuttered. Among them are **Branzino, Da Ugo, Della Femina, Epiphany, Farmhouse, Meritage, Oasis, Oevo, Osteria Toscana, Philippe, Planet Bliss, Rock 'n Sake, Roots, Rugosa, Table 9, Trata** and **Turtle Crossing.**

GO EAST: The ever-changing Twin Forks welcomed Tom Schaudel's **A Lure,** a chic seafooder in Southold, and the reopened **Almond** in larger Bridgehampton quarters. California-based Hillstone Group hatched **East Hampton Grill** at the former Della Femina address; ex-Bayville Italian **18 Bay** resurfaced on Shelter Island; and Matthew Guiffrida moved from Water Mill to Sag Harbor with renamed **Muse in the Harbor.** Dennis McDermott (ex Greenport's **Frisky Oyster**) brought the classy **Riverhead Project** to the namesake town and **Southampton Social Club** entered the fray as a new Hamptons hot spot. Hampton Bays sprouted **TR Restaurant,** a seafooder from Tom Rutyna (ex **Coast Grill**), and a seasonal branch of trendy Japanese **Nobu** opened in Southampton.

Long Island, NY
April 25, 2012

Suzi Forbes Chase

Most Popular

This list is plotted on the map at the back of this book.

1	Peter Luger	*Steak*	
2	Besito	*Mexican*	
3	Kotobuki	*Japanese*	
4	Bryant & Cooper	*Steak*	
5	West End Cafe	*American*	
6	North Fork Table	*American*	
7	Il Mulino NY	*Italian*	
8	Cheesecake Factory	*American*	
9	Kitchen A Bistro	*French*	
10	Smokin' Al's BBQ	*BBQ*	
11	American Hotel	*Amer./French*	
12	Waterzooi	*Belgian*	
13	Butera's	*Italian*	
14	Blackstone Steak	*Steak*	
15	Prime	*American*	
16	Bistro Cassis	*French*	
17	Lake House	*American*	
18	Tellers Chophouse	*Steak*	
19	Coolfish	*Seafood*	
20	Maroni	*Eclectic/Italian*	
21	Morton's	*Steak*	
22	Ruth's Chris	*Steak*	
23	Cafe Baci	*Italian*	
24	Matteo's	*Italian*	
25	La Parma	*Italian*	
26	Palm	*Seafood/Steak*	
27	Riverbay	*Seafood*	
28	Limani	*Med./Seafood*	
29	Sage Bistro	*French*	
30	Nick & Toni's	*Italian/Med.*	
31	Ben's Kosher Deli	*Deli*	
32	Rothmann's Steak	*Steak*	
33	Harvest/Ft. Pond	*Italian/Med.*	
34	1770 House	*Amer.*	
35	Stone Creek	*French/Med.*	
36	Five Guys	*Burgers*	
37	Legal Sea Foods	*Seafood*	
38	Mirabelle	*French*	
39	Umberto's	*Italian/Pizza*	
40	Solé	*Italian*	
41	H2O Seafood	*Seafood*	
42	Ayhan's Shish	*Med./Turkish*	
43	Chachama Grill	*American*	
44	Piccolo*	*American/Italian*	
45	Bobby Van's	*Steak*	
46	Jimmy Hays*	*Steak*	
47	City Cellar	*American*	
48	Jolly Fisherman	*Seafood/Steak*	
49	Wild Ginger	*Asian*	
50	Millpond House	*Seafood/Steak*	

Many of the above restaurants are among Long Island's most expensive, but if popularity were calibrated to price, a number of other restaurants would surely join their ranks. To illustrate this, we have added two lists comprising 94 Best Buys on page 15 as well as Prix Fixe Dinner Deals on page 16.

* Indicates a tie with restaurant above

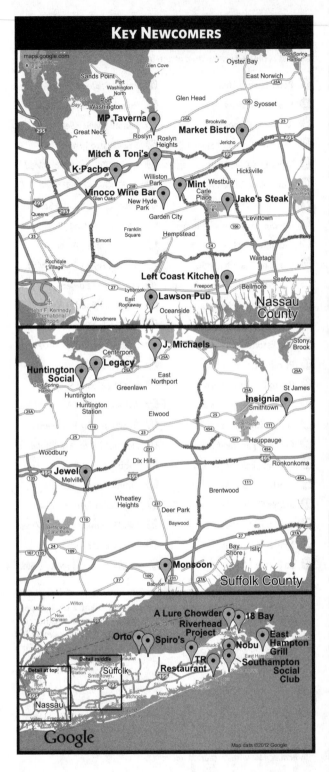

KEY NEWCOMERS

maps.google.com

MP Taverna

Market Bistro

Mitch & Toni's

K-Pacho

Vinoco Wine Bar

Mint

Jake's Steak

Left Coast Kitchen

Lawson Pub

Nassau County

J. Michaels

Legacy

Huntington Social

Insignia

Jewel

Monsoon

Suffolk County

A Lure Chowder

18 Bay

Riverhead Project

Orto

Spiro's

Nobu

East Hampton Grill

TR Restaurant

Southampton Social Club

Detail at top

Detail middle

Suffolk

Nassau

Google

Map data ©2012 Google

8

Key Newcomers

Our editors' picks among this year's arrivals. See full list at p. 202.

A Lure Chowder House | *Seafood* | Tom Schaudel's waterfront Southolder

East Hampton Grill | *American* | Hillstone Group takes East Hampton

18 Bay | *Italian* | Shelter Island market-menu specialist

Huntington Social | *American* | Huntington quasi 1920s speakeasy

Insignia | *Seafood/Steak* | Chops and sushi in splashy Smithtown digs

Jake's Steakhouse | *Steak* | East Meadow cousin of Bronx chophouse

Jewel | *American* | Big and stylish Melville multitasker

J. Michaels Tuscan Steakhouse | *Steak* | Beef in vintage Northport house

K·Pacho Cocina & Tequila | *Mexican* | Upscale New Hyde Park cantina

Lawson Pub | *American* | Historic setting at Oceanside train station

Left Coast Kitchen | *American* | Merrick gastropub with regional bent

Legacy Asian Fusion | *Asian* | Fusion in a striking Huntington setting

Market Bistro | *American* | Jericho sibling of West End Cafe

Mint | *Asian* | Flashy Garden City hot spot for fusion fare

Mitch & Toni's American Bistro | *American* | New home of Bistro M team

Monsoon | *Asian* | Hip, bi-level setting in a former Babylon bank

MP Taverna | *Greek* | Chef Michael Psilakis comes to Roslyn

Nobu at Capri | *Japanese* | Trendy chain link in Southampton

Orto | *Italian* | Eric Lomando's quaint Miller Place hideaway

Riverhead Project | *American* | Sleek and classy in Riverhead

Ruschmeyer's | *American* | Summer-camp theme in Montauk

Southampton Social Club | *American* | Southampton hot spot

Spiro's | *Steak* | Martinis and meat in Rocky Point

TR Restaurant & Bar | *Seafood* | Fisherman chef in Hampton Bays

Vinoco Wine Bar & Tapas | *Eclectic* | Globe-trotting tapas in Mineola

---

Looking ahead, the Poll brothers (**Bryant & Cooper**) are remaking Roslyn's **GW** (aka George Washington Manor – the first POTUS had breakfast there in 1790) as **Hendrick's Tavern**. Named in honor of Washington's host and serving American fare, it's scheduled to open at press time. Centerport's long-anticipated **Jellyfish** is also set to debut, with a seafood-centric menu that, yes, may include jellyfish, by *Hell's Kitchen* winner Heather West. A Westbury branch of **Shake Shack,** Danny Meyer's popular burger chain, is slated for late 2012.

The East End expects seafooder **The Anchor** from the **Beacon** team in the shuttered Sag Harbor **Oasis** space, while the **Rumba** folks are making the former **Indian Cove** into steak, seafood and blues spot **Cowfish** in Hampton Bays. Huntington's **Swallow** plans a Montauk sibling by summer, and celebrity chef Tom Colicchio is aiming to open a restaurant in Bridgehampton's historic Topping Rose House by summer's end.

Top Food

29 North Fork Table | *American*

28 Siam Lotus | *Thai*
Mosaic | *American*
Kitchen A Trattoria | *Italian*
Maroni | *Eclectic/Italian*
Nagahama | *Japanese*
Lake House | *American*

27 Chachama Grill | *American*
La Piccola Liguria | *Italian*
Le Soir | *French*
Kitchen A Bistro | *French*
Kotobuki | *Japanese*
Peter Luger | *Steak*
La Plage | *Eclectic*
Orient | *Chinese*
Chez Noëlle | *French*
Sempre Vivolo | *Italian*
Aji 53 | *Japanese*
Dave's | *Continental/Seafood*
Il Mulino NY | *Italian*
Piccolo | *American/Italian*

26 Bryant & Cooper | *Steak*
Starr Boggs | *Amer./Seafood*
Mirko's | *Eclectic*
Barney's | *American/French*

Plaza Café | *Seafood*
Stone Creek | *French/Med.*
Dario's | *Italian*
Tellers Chophouse | *Steak*
Limani | *Med./Seafood*
Noah's | *American*
Snaps American | *American*
San Marco | *Italian*
Verace | *Italian*
Rialto | *Italian*
Thai Gourmet | *Thai*
Galleria Ristorante | *Italian*
PeraBell | *American/Eclectic*
Harvest/Ft. Pond | *Italian/Med.*
Palm | *Seafood/Steak*
Franina | *Italian*
Fifth Season | *American*
Solé | *Italian*

25 Maureen/Daughters' | *Amer.*
Living Rm. | *American*
Frisky Oyster | *Eclectic*
Robert's | *Italian*
Kumo Sushi | *Japanese*
Vittorio's | *Amer./Italian*
Casa Rustica | *Italian*

BY CUISINE

AMERICAN (NEW)

29 North Fork Table
28 Mosaic
Lake House
27 Chachama Grill
26 Starr Boggs

AMERICAN (TRAD.)

26 PeraBell
25 Maureen/Daughters'
Vittorio's
Vine Street
American Hotel

ASIAN

25 West East Bistro
Toku
24 Taiko
Haiku Bistro
20 Thom Thom

BBQ/SOUTHWESTERN

24 Big Daddy's
23 Smokin' Al's BBQ

Swingbelly's Beachside
22 RS Jones
21 BobbiQue

CAJUN/SOUTHERN

24 Big Daddy's
23 Bayou
LL Dent
20 Blackbirds' Grille
18 B. Smith's

CHINESE

27 Orient
23 Orchid
Pearl East
22 Fortune Wheel
Hunan Taste

CONTINENTAL

27 Dave's
25 Barolo
24 Palm Court

Excludes places with low votes

23 Irish Coffee
Frederick's

ECLECTIC
28 Maroni
27 La Plage
26 Mirko's
PeraBell
25 Frisky Oyster

FRENCH
27 Le Soir
Chez Noëlle
26 Barney's
Stone Creek
25 Mirabelle

FRENCH (BISTRO)
27 Kitchen A Bistro
25 Aperitif
24 Voila!
Sage Bistro
Bistro Cassis

GREEK
23 Alexandros
22 Trata
Med. Snack
21 Chicken Kebab
Ethos

INDIAN
25 House of Dosas
24 Kiran Palace
23 Rangmahal
Dosa Diner
22 Hampton Chutney

ITALIAN
28 Kitchen A Trattoria
Maroni
27 Sempre Vivolo
Piccolo
26 Verace
Franina

ITALIAN (NORTHERN)
27 La Piccola Liguria
Il Mulino NY
26 Dario's
San Marco
Rialto

ITALIAN (SOUTHERN)
25 La Ginestra
24 Bravo! Nader
23 Mamma Lombardi's
Matteo's
La Parma

JAPANESE
28 Nagahama
27 Kotobuki
Aji 53
25 Kumo Sushi
Nisen Sushi

MEDITERRANEAN
26 Stone Creek
Limani
Harvest/Ft. Pond
24 Pier 95
Nick & Toni's

MEXICAN
24 Besito
23 Oaxaca Mexican
Salsa Salsa
22 Zim Zari
20 Chipotle

MIDDLE EASTERN
23 Kabul Afghani
22 Pita House
Azerbaijan Grill
21 Colbeh
20 Ariana

PIZZA
25 Salvatore's
23 Emilio's
Nick's
Grimaldi's
King Umberto

SEAFOOD
26 Dave's
Starr Boggs
Plaza Café
Limani
25 Mill Pond House
24 Nautilus Cafe

STEAKHOUSES
27 Peter Luger
26 Bryant & Cooper
Tellers Chophouse
Palm
25 Jimmy Hays
Morton's

THAI
28 Siam Lotus
26 Thai Gourmet
25 Sripraphai
24 Onzon Thai
Thai House*

BY SPECIAL FEATURE

BREAKFAST

- 25 Maureen/Daughters'
- 24 Toast
- 23 Estia's Kitchen
- Rein
- Love Lane Kitchen

BRUNCH

- 26 Limani
- 25 Rothmann's Steak
- 24 Palm Court
- Waterzooi
- Bistro Cassis

BYO

- 28 Kitchen A Trattoria
- 27 Kitchen A Bistro
- 26 Thai Gourmet
- 24 Onzon Thai
- Kiran Palace

HOTEL DINING

- 29 North Fork Table
  (North Fork Table & Inn)
- 26 Palm (Huntting Inn)
- 25 Living Rm. (c/o Maidstone)
- Mirabelle (Three Village)
- Luce & Hawkins
  (Jedediah Hawkins Inn)

PEOPLE-WATCHING

- 27 Peter Luger
- Il Mulino NY
- 26 Starr Boggs
- Barney's
- Stone Creek

SINGLES SCENES

- 26 Bryant & Cooper
- Tellers Chophouse
- Limani
- Verace
- 25 Nisen Sushi

VIEWS

- 28 Lake House
- 26 Harvest/Ft. Pond
- 25 Amarelle
- Mill Pond House
- 24 Nautilus Cafe

WINNING WINE LISTS

- 27 La Piccola
- Le Soir
- La Plage
- Chez Noëlle
- Sempre Vivolo

BY LOCATION

EAST HAMPTON

- 26 Palm
- 25 Living Rm.
- 1770 House
- 24 Nick & Toni's
- 23 Cafe Max

NASSAU COUNTY

- 28 Nagahama
- 27 La Piccola Liguria
- Kotobuki
- Peter Luger
- Orient

N. FORK & SHELTER IS.

- 29 North Fork Table
- 27 La Plage

- 26 Noah's
- 25 Frisky Oyster
- Luce & Hawkins

SOUTHAMPTON

- 26 Plaza Café
- 24 Sant Ambroeus
- 23 Silver's
- 22 La Parmigiana
- Red Bar

SUFFOLK COUNTY

- 29 North Fork Table
- 28 Siam Lotus
- Mosaic
- Kitchen A Trattoria
- Maroni

Top Decor

28 Palm Court	Amarelle
27 Limani	Honu Kitchen
Atlantica	Living Rm.
Luce & Hawkins	24 Lombardi's on the Bay
Prime	Rein
Tellers Chophouse	Nonnina
26 Toku	Rare 650
Country House	Sunset Beach
East Hampton Point	American Hotel
Verace	Nisen Sushi
25 North Fork Table	Stone Creek
Trumpets	Dockers Waterside
Jamesport Manor	Four Food Studio
Barrique Kitchen & Wine Bar	Besito
Porto Vivo*	Milk & Sugar Café*
Aperitif	Aji 53
Pine Island*	Rist. Gemelli
Blackwells	Blackstone Steak
Tula Kitchen	Ram's Head
1770 House	Lake House

OUTDOORS

Cipollini	Pop's Seafood Shack
East Hampton Point	Ram's Head
Fork & Vine	Riverhead Project
Harvest/Ft. Pond	Savanna's
Maroni	Starr Boggs

ROMANCE

American Hotel	Palm Court
Barney's	Ram's Head
Country House	Robert's
Lake House	1770 House
Luce & Hawkins	Stone Creek

ROOMS

Atlantica	Limani
Four Food Studio	Palm Court
Insignia	1770 House
Jewel	Tellers Chophouse
K·Pacho	Toku

VIEWS

Dockers Waterside	Prime
East Hampton Point	Sunset Beach
Harvest/Ft. Pond	Trumpets
Oakland's	View
Pine Island Grill	Wall's Wharf

Top Service

27
- North Fork Table
- Sempre Vivolo
- Chachama Grill
- La Piccola Liguria
- Mosaic

26
- Luce & Hawkins
- Siam Lotus
- San Marco
- Lake House
- Maroni
- Dario's
- Voila!

25
- Galleria Ristorante
- Rialto
- Chez Noëlle
- Palm Court
- Tellers Chophouse
- Vittorio's
- Verace
- Tula Kitchen

- Casa Rustica
- Café Capriccio
- Mario
- Le Soir
- Piccolo
- Il Mulino NY
- La Pace
- Red Restaurant
- Grey Horse Tavern
- Kitchen A Trattoria

24
- Franina
- Crew Kitchen
- Mirabelle
- Bevanda
- La Marmite
- American Hotel
- Limani
- Barney's
- Stone Creek
- Morton's

Best Buys

In order of Bang for the Buck rating.

1. Five Guys
2. Chipotle
3. American Roadside
4. Maureen/Daughters'
5. Fresco Crêperie
6. Salsa Salsa
7. Bobby's Burger
8. Green Cactus
9. Baja Fresh
10. Zim Zari
11. Thomas's Eggery
12. Robinson's Tea
13. Tricia's Café
14. House of Dosas
15. Toast
16. Salvatore's
17. Hampton Coffee
18. Thai Gourmet
19. Dosa Diner
20. Massa's
21. Hampton Chutney
22. Grimaldi's
23. Bay Burger
24. La Bottega
25. Hildebrandt's
26. Baja Grill
27. Sweet Mama's
28. Thai Table
29. Bigelow's
30. Ancient Ginger
31. Nick's
32. Pie
33. Kiran Palace
34. Oaxaca Mexican
35. Thai House
36. Lemonleaf Grill
37. International Delight
38. Tula Kitchen
39. Galangal
40. Chat Noir

OTHER GOOD VALUES

Afghan Grill
Asian Moon
Azuma Sushi
Batata Café
Benkei Japanese
Ben's Kosher Deli
Blue Moon
BobbiQue
Bozena Polish-European
Bridgehampton Candy
California Pizza Kitchen
Chat Noir
Chefs of New York
Cookroom
Crave 11025
Declan Quinn's
Dynasty
Eddie's Pizza
Emilio's
Golden Pear Café
Goldmine Mexican Grill
Gonzalo's American Café
Greek Village
Harbor-Q
Itgen's
Jean Marie Patisserie
JT's Corner Cafe

La Panchita
Long River
Los Compadres
Madras Woodlands
Milk & Sugar Café
Minami
New Chilli & Curry
Onzon Thai House
Orient
Panini Café at Diane's
Perfecto Mundo
Pizza Place
Relish
Roe's Casa Dolce
Sabai Thai Bistro
Salamander's General Store
Siam Lotus
Souvlaki Palace
Spicy's Barbecue
Sripraphai
Sri Thai
Star Confectionary
Sundried Tomato Cafe
Sushi Palace
Toast & Co.
Torcellos
Zorba the Greek

PRIX FIXE DINNER DEALS

Since hours and prices may vary, please call ahead.

$26-$30

Arturo's	$30	Jonathan's	26
Barney's	29	Le Chef	30
Bistro Citron	27	Matsulin	26
Bobby Van's	27	Patio at 54 Main	26
Cafe Capriccio	24	Ruvo	29
Chachama Grill	26	Snaps American	30
Chez Noëlle	28	Stone Creek	30
Coast Grill	27	Thyme	28
Fifth Season	28	Tratt. Diane	30
Fresno	28	Uncle Bacala's	28
Garden Grill	27	View	27
Harbor Bistro	29	Wild Honey	27

$25 AND UNDER

Angelina's	$25	Grill on Pantigo	24
Azerbaijan Grill	13	Hemingway's	25
Babylon Carriage	25	Hudson's Mill	25
Bellport	22	Lola's Kitchen	20
Blackbirds' Grille	25	Mama's	14
Blackwells	25	Nicholas James	24
Bliss	25	Page One	24
Brasserie Persil	25	Palmer's American Grille	22
Brasserie 214	22	Peppercorns	22
Brio	23	Phao Thai Kitchen	25
Butera's	25	Pierre's	24
Butterfields	25	Red Fish	25
Cafe Joelle	25	RS Jones	20
Cafe Max	25	San Marco	23
Chop Shop	25	Sea Basin	23
Cho-Sen Island	24	75 Main	14
Cielo	25	Shagwong	22
Crossroads Cafe	22	34 New Street	22
Fisherman's Catch	25	Thom Thom	25
Georgica	25	Villa D'Este	25

RESTAURANT DIRECTORY

Absolutely Mario Ⓜ *Italian*
20 | 16 | 23 | $39

Farmingdale | 10 Allen Blvd. (Broad Hollow Rd.) | 631-694-7416 |
www.absolutelymario.com

The "charming" namesake chef-owner is "always on hand making you feel like family" at this Farmingdale "favorite" serving "good old Italian fare"; the "bustling" setting is "homey" and the staff "goes the extra mile", so a few reviewers feel "if Mario gets his food up to the level of his service, he'd be world-class"; P.S. there's live music during happy hour.

Afghan Grill
Kabob House *Afghan*
20 | 14 | 21 | $28

New Hyde Park | 1629 Hillside Ave. (New Hyde Park Rd.) |
516-998-4084 | www.afghangrill.ny.com

The namesake skewers are "fabulous" at this affordable, "family-run" Afghan, a "quaint" New Hyde Park "standout" delivering "tasty", "plentiful" dishes that even "delight" vegetarians; sure, the "run-down" digs could use some "personality", but the "welcoming" servers "try very hard to please" and the BYO policy is "a definite plus."

NEW Agave Bar &
Mexican Grill *Mexican*
- | - | - | M

Bridgehampton | 1970 Montauk Hwy. (bet. Hayground & Snake Hollow Rds.) | 631-237-1334 | www.agavethehamptons.com

Equal parts bar and restaurant, this midpriced Mexican Bridgehampton newcomer dishes out Tex-Mex standards with some 20 beers on tap to wash it down; the casual setting has brightly painted walls and multiple TVs, while a tequila bar and live music Friday nights fuel a lively Hamptons scene.

Ⓩ Aji 53 *Japanese*
27 | 24 | 23 | $43

Bay Shore | 53 E. Main St. (3rd Ave.) | 631-591-3107
NEW Smithtown | 1 Miller Pl. (E. Main St.) | 631-979-0697
www.aji53.com

An "all-around hit", this "chic", "modern" Japanese brings "NYC ambiance" to Bay Shore, with "stunning" decor, "incredible", "inventive" sushi and "charming" (if at times "almost too eager") service; the "cool vibe" and "martinis at the bar" make "waits worthwhile", while dishes like "to-die-for black miso cod" are so "artful" you'll "forget about the price tag" and the "noise" – just "don't even think of going on a weekend without reservations"; P.S. the Smithtown branch opened post-Survey.

Akbar *Indian*
22 | 19 | 20 | $35

Garden City | 2 South St. (Stewart Ave.) | 516-357-8300

A "reliable" outpost for "authentic" Indian with "just enough fire", this "upscale", "pleasant" Garden City veteran is a "perennial favorite" thanks to "abundant" lunch and Sunday dinner buffets presenting "well-seasoned specialties" at "bargain" prices; true, "the tab can add up if you order à la carte", but the "courteous" staff, offering advice about spice, is a plus.

	FOOD	DECOR	SERVICE	COST

NEW Alaine's *American*

| - | - | - | M |

Massapequa | 27 Carmans Rd. (E. Hemlock St.) | 516-809-7979 | www.alaines.com

Located across from the Sunrise Mall, this Massapequa eatery named for and run by a hometown native features a simple brick facade and an interior with tiny pink accent lights as a backdrop for midpriced American fare such as burgers, pasta and pizza, plus an array of cocktails including Long Island Iced Tea; a patio for warm-weather dining is tucked behind a high enclosure.

Albert's Mandarin Gourmet *Chinese*

| 20 | 15 | 20 | $29 |

Huntington | 269 New York Ave. (bet. Gerard St. & Union Pl.) | 631-673-8188

While there's "nothing new or exciting" about this "Huntington staple", the "always reliable" Mandarin fare and "prompt" service – helmed by "affable" owner Albert Leung – pleases "plenty" of long-time customers, who count on it for "large get-togethers"; some critics call for a "spruce-up" of the "frozen-in-time" decor and "clichéd cuisine", but if you're "looking for old-school Chinese, this is your restaurant."

Alexandros *Greek/Mediterranean*

| 23 | 19 | 23 | $43 |

Mount Sinai | 1060 Rte. 25A (Pipe Stave Hollow Rd.) | 631-928-8600 | www.alexandrosrestaurant.com

"Authentic" Greek-Mediterranean food (including "simply prepared but outstanding" fish and other "delicious" grilled specialties) entices eaters at this "cozy", slightly upscale Mount Sinai spot where "gracious" chef-owner Sam Constantis and his "warm, welcoming" family make the whole meal "special"; though the "small" room tends to get "loud", it's "wonderful" for outdoor dining in the summer.

Allison's Amalfi Ristorante *Italian/Mediterranean*

| 21 | 21 | 22 | $48 |

Sea Cliff | 400 Glen Cove Ave. (Glenola Ave.) | 516-656-4774 | www.allisonsamalfi.com

The winning team of "welcoming" co-owner and hostess Allison Izzo and her husband O'Michael Zara, a "fine" chef who "accommodates special orders", adds to the "charm" of this "sophisticated" Italian-Mediterranean "tucked away" in a Sea Cliff strip mall; prices are "a trifle high", but most "enjoy" the "beautifully prepared" dishes served in a "relaxing", "rarely crowded" locale; P.S. closed Tuesdays.

Almarco *Italian*

| 20 | 18 | 22 | $38 |

Huntington | 13 Wall St. (bet. Gerard & Main Sts.) | 631-935-1690

Many commend the "wonderful" staff at this "pleasant" Huntington Italian offering "good", "bountiful" plates and outdoor seating in back for "sunny days"; still, while the "step-above-basic" fare works for "family dining", a few naysayers knock the "plain"-Jane decor and dishes that "should be tastier" for the price.

	FOOD	DECOR	SERVICE	COST

Almond *French*

| 20 | - | 19 | $51 |

Bridgehampton | 1 Ocean Rd. (Main St.) | 631-537-5665 |
www.almondrestaurant.com

Eric Lemonides and Jason Weiner have relocated their popular bistro to another Bridgehampton location (there's also a Manhattan branch), which is welcome news to fans who enjoyed its "well-executed", "French-inspired cuisine", "attentive" service and "reasonable" prices; it has retained the ornate tin ceiling and dark wood floors from the space's former inhabitant, but added the red zebra wallpaper from its original home.

NEW A Lure Chowder House & Oyster-ia Ⓜ *Seafood*

| - | - | - | E |

Southold | Port of Egypt | 62300 Main Rd./Rte. 25 (bet. Albacore Dr. & Bay Home Rd.) | 631-876-5300 | www.alurenorthfork.com

At this seasonal Southold newcomer, Tom Schaudel (A Mano, Coolfish) dishes out an extensive, locally sourced menu of fresh fish and seafood served alongside specialty cocktails and wines from a Long Island–only list complete with difficult-to-find bottles; its rustic dining room has barn-wood walls and a fireplace and leads to a large summertime deck overlooking the marina.

A Mano *Italian*

| 24 | 20 | 22 | $47 |

Mattituck | 13550 Main Rd. (bet. Love Ln. & Wickam Ave.) | 631-298-4800 | www.amanorestaurant.com

Chef/co-owner Tom Schaudel crafts "fresh local" ingredients into "tantalizing" Italian dishes – including "terrific" wood-fired pizzas – matched by an "amazing wine selection" at this "hip", "not too expensive" Mattituck osteria where a "courteous" crew "plays to a packed house every night"; though nitpickers nag about the "noise level", most either revel in the "buzzy atmosphere" or choose to eat on the patio in warm weather.

Amarelle Ⓜ *American*

| 25 | 25 | 23 | $52 |

Wading River | 2028 N. Country Rd. (bet. N. Wading River & Sound Rds.) | 631-886-2242 | www.amarelle.net

An "innovative, clever menu" highlighting "local seasonal offerings" makes this "out-of-the-way" Wading River New American a "sublime" stop for foodies, while the "elegant" interior with a "large stone fireplace" and view of a duck pond provides a "lovely romantic atmosphere" (even if it's slightly "over-the-top for its country setting"); the service is "attentive but not obtrusive", and the "small plate option" for every entree is a "hit" too.

ⓩ American Hotel, The *American/French*

| 25 | 24 | 24 | $67 |

Sag Harbor | The American Hotel | 49 Main St. (bet. Bay & Washington Sts.) | 631-725-3535 | www.theamericanhotel.com

Ever "enchanting", this "quintessential" Sag Harbor haven brings together "sensational" American-French dishes and an "exceptional", "dizzying" wine list in a "gorgeous" 1846-vintage setting with "glittering tables" tended to by a "formal", "carefully trained" staff; you can sit by the "roaring fireplace" in winter or "on the porch" in summer and "watch the celebs go by", and while "you'll likely spend more than you originally thought", its "eternal popularity is well deserved."

American Roadside Burgers *Burgers*   18 | 12 | 15 | $13

Smithtown | 80 E. Main St. (bet. Landing & Lawrence Aves.) | 631-382-9500 | www.americanroadsideburgers.com

Those who "wouldn't be caught dead in a McDonald's" hail the "terrific", "juicy" hamburgers "made your way" "with just enough grease" at this Smithtown order-at-the-counter joint; sure, the "kinda cold" "motorcycle decor" isn't for everyone, and some dub the grub merely "so-so", but it's "better than the drive-thrus" – and if you eat the four-patty RoadStar "your name goes on the wall."

Amicale *Continental*   25 | 23 | 24 | $66
(fka Panama Hatties)

Huntington Station | Post Plaza | 872 E. Jericho Tpke. (bet. Cooper Ave. & Emerald Ln.) | 631-351-1727 | www.amicalerestaurant.com

This "truly top-drawer" Continental "hidden" in a Huntington Station "strip mall" "never fails to impress" with an "inspired menu" of "sensational" seasonal dishes presented by "experienced, unobtrusive" servers in "classy quarters"; it's "costly" but "worth the splurge", and on weekdays there's a "bargain" prix fixe lunch; P.S. a post-Survey chef change and renovation are not reflected in the Food and Decor ratings.

Ancient Ginger *Chinese*   21 | 17 | 22 | $26

St. James | 556 N. Country Rd. (Lake Ave.) | 631-584-8883 | www.ancientginger.com

Guests agree it's "always a pleasure" dining on the "light, fresh" and often "sumptuous" Chinese food ferried by a "gracious" staff at this "darn good" St. James option; the "cut-above" decor is "charming for a storefront", while the "bang-for-the-buck" menu keeps regulars returning "at least once a week."

NEW Andiamo *American/Italian*   - | - | - | E

Mineola | 149 Mineola Blvd. (Harrison Ave.) | 516-294-1715 | www.andiamo-mineola.com

George Echeverria (ex Amicale) mans the stove at this Mineola newcomer, already drawing a following for an American-Italian menu including housemade pastas; black-and-white tile floors and rattan Italian cafe chairs create a casual ambiance that's enhanced by light from tall windows.

Angelina's *Italian*   23 | 18 | 23 | $50

East Norwich | Christina's Shopping Ctr. | 1017 Oyster Bay Rd. (bet. Johnson Ct. & Northern Blvd.) | 516-922-0039 | www.angelinasofeastnorwich.com

Angelina's II *Italian*

Syosset | 30 Berry Hill Rd. (East St.) | 516-364-8234 | www.angelinas2.com

Fans of "down-home" Italian food flock to these "upscale neighborhood" trattorias for "generous portions" of all the classics, served by a "congenial" staff that's "well versed" in the "old-school" menu; the "dependable" East Norwich original with a Tuscan-style dining room serves dinner only, while the separately owned Syosset locale, set inside a "comfy" converted country house, offers popular lunch and prix fixe specials.

NEW Angelina's Fireshack & Pizzeria *Pizza*

| - | - | - | I |

New Hyde Park | 1300 Jericho Tpke. (Millers Ln.) | 516-326-0100 | www.angelinasfireshack.com

Hot and spicy defines many of the pizzas and other dishes at this small, informal, mostly take-out joint in New Hyde Park; but those not on a heat-seeking mission can choose from other items on the affordable American menu such as burgers, wraps and foot-long hot dogs, and all can slake their thirst with a craft beer or something from the wine bar.

Anthony's Coal Fired Pizza *Pizza*

| - | - | - | I |

Carle Place | 137 Old Country Rd. (Cherry Ln.) | 516-877-7750
NEW Woodbury | 8077 Jericho Tpke. (bet. Southwoods & Woodbury Rds.) | 516-367-2625
www.anthonyscoalfiredpizza.com

Anthony Bruno brings his Florida chain to his native Long Island with these affordable pizzerias in Carle Place and Woodbury turning out pies crisped in 900-degree coal-fired ovens; decor touches include tile floors, bars and walls covered with iconic photos of movie, theater, music and sports stars.

NEW Antonette's Classico M *Italian*

| - | - | - | VE |

Rockville Centre | 509 Merrick Rd. (bet. Long Beach Rd. & Montauk Ave.) | 516-764-1900

Italian fare is on the menu of this tiny Rockville Centre newcomer (in the quarters of defunct longtimer Da Ugo); an intimate setting featuring brown silk fabric gathered along one wall, gold booths and white tablecloths graced with fresh flowers befits the steep price tag.

Aperitif *French*

| 25 | 25 | 24 | $45 |

Rockville Centre | 242 Sunrise Hwy. (bet. Park & Village Aves.) | 516-594-3404 | www.aperitifbistro.com

From the owners of the Sage Bistro Restaurant Group comes this "hit" on the Rockville Centre scene – a "gorgeous" French bistro that pairs "enticing", slightly "eclectic" dishes (many available as part of an extensive small-plates menu) with an "excellent" 70-bottle wine list; embellished with pendant lights, red velvet and Moroccan tiles, it sets the stage for "memorable" meals, as well as late-night bites and colorful drinks from the "great bar staff."

NEW Arata Sushi *Japanese*

| - | - | - | M |

Syosset | 18 Cold Spring Rd. (Jackson Ave.) | 516-921-8154

An ex Nobu chef has taken over the former Syosset digs of Tsubo, offering a sushi selection including inventive rolls such as unagi Labyrinth – a combination of avocado, cucumber, eel, almond and sesame seeds – plus midpriced Japanese hot dishes such as Chilean sea bass tempura; the bright quarters feature a tile floor, wood tables and a wall painted to resemble a stand of bamboo.

	FOOD	DECOR	SERVICE	COST

Argyle Grill & Tavern *American*
| 22 | 21 | 21 | $37 |

Babylon | 90 Deer Park Ave. (bet. Grove Pl. & Main St.) |
631-321-4900 | www.theargylegrill.com

"Always packed", this "upscale pub" in Babylon attracts an avid
"after-work" crowd for its "meat-and-potatoes" New American
eats, happy-hour martinis and "swinging" scene; some warn the
"tight" quarters can get "too loud" and dub the dishes "not worth
the wait", but most find it "comfortable" and "dependable", and dig
the "specials during the week"; P.S. no reservations.

Ariana *Afghan/Vegetarian*
| 20 | 19 | 19 | $35 |

Huntington | 255 Main St. (bet. New St. & New York Ave.) |
631-421-2933 | www.arianacafe.com

"Sophisticated", "delicately seasoned" dishes with an "exotic" twist
(and plenty of options for "vegetarians and vegans") provide a
"new" experience for many at this midpriced, "family-owned"
Afghan eatery in Huntington; the service is generally "accommodating", and the "inviting" Persian-style atmosphere with "cozy pil-
lows" is just right "for a date" or "meeting friends."

Arthur Avenue ◐ *American*
| - | - | - | M |

Smithtown | 155 W. Main St. (Elliott Pl.) | 631-780-5969 |
www.arthuraveny.com

Sports fans watch multi screens at the double-sided bar while less-
boisterous types head for the separate glass-enclosed dining room
at this Smithtown American located beside the railroad tracks; the
midpriced menu ranges from wraps to entrees such as wild-caught
salmon Dijon, and live weekend entertainment varies from karaoke
to bands and dancing.

Arturo's *Italian*
| 22 | 18 | 22 | $48 |

Floral Park | 246-04 Jericho Tpke. (Colonial Rd.) | 516-352-7418 |
www.arturorestaurant.com

A Floral Park fixture for half a century, this "oldie but goodie" caters
to "special celebrations" with "terrific" Italian classics "just like
grandma used to cook", some of which are "prepared tableside" for
added "charm"; try to "save room" for "scrumptious" zabaglione,
and let the Saturday night "strolling guitarist" turn your attention
from the "dated" decor.

Asian Moon *Asian*
| 23 | 22 | 22 | $33 |

Garden City | 825 Franklin Ave. (bet. 9th St. & Stewart Ave.) |
516-248-6161
Massapequa Park | 4922 Merrick Rd. (bet. Southgate Circle &
Whitewood Dr.) | 516-799-8800
www.asianmoononline.com

Guests are "over the moon" for this "slightly upscale" yet "reasonable" Pan-Asian pair dishing up "light, flavorful" food that's a
"fresh", "eclectic" alternative to typical takeout; "pleasant" servers
keep the "calm", "cool vibe" flowing through the Garden City original and its Massapequa Park offshoot, which "rocks" with a sushi
menu and more fabulous "feng shui."

	FOOD	DECOR	SERVICE	COST

A Taberna *Portuguese*

23 | 15 | 19 | $38

Island Park | 4135 Austin Blvd. (bet. Saratoga & Trafalgar Blvds.) | 516-432-0455

"Beautifully presented", "authentic" Portuguese draws a lively "local crowd" to this "casual" Island Park spot where "conviviality flows like a good red"; critics complain that they often get "squeezed in" – and "wait and wait" despite reservations – but the "zesty" eats and sangria are usually "worth it", since you get "a lot for your money."

Athens Grill ☒ *Greek/Mediterranean*

- | - | - | E

Riverhead | 33 E. Main St. (bet. East & Roanoke Aves.) | 631-727-1301 | www.athensgyro.com

Chef-owner John Mantzopoulos expanded and upgraded this former Riverhead gyro joint into a casual yet elegant dining destination focusing on Greek-Mediterranean dishes that change daily depending on the East End markets; an upscale-romantic vibe comes via decor touches including bas-relief wall plaques, brown leather chairs, tablecloths and an elaborate brass-colored ceiling.

☑ Atlantica *American/Seafood*

20 | 27 | 19 | $55

Long Beach | Allegria Hotel | 80 W. Broadway (National Blvd.) | 516-992-3730 | www.allegriahotel.com

"Stunning views" of the Atlantic and "fabulous decor fit for Miami Beach" up the wow factor at this high-end Long Beach jewel in the Allegria Hotel that glimmers with beveled mirrors and jellyfish light fixtures; chef Todd Jacobs' seafood-focused New American menu is "still finding its way" among all the eye candy, and service "needs upgrading" too, so some recommend it just for "apps and drinks" (if you don't mind the "din" at the bar).

Ayhan's Fish Kebab *Seafood/Turkish*

19 | 17 | 18 | $34

Port Washington | 286 Main St. (bet. Carlton Ave. & Shore Rd.) | 516-883-1515 | www.ayhansrestaurants.com

Supporters of this Turkish seafooder in Port Washington appreciate the "large portions" of "reasonably priced" fare, particularly the "simple" but "excellent" whole grilled fish; the "pretty" brick-walled space in an 1898 bank building is "energetic" and the service "decent", though "disappointed" guests dub the meal a "mixed bag", declaring there's "nothing to do handstands over" here.

Ayhan's Mediterranean
Cafe & Marketplace *Mediterranean/Turkish*

18 | 16 | 17 | $28

Port Washington | 293 Main St. (bet. Bank St. & Carlton Ave.) | 516-767-1400

Ayhan's Shish
Kebab *Mediterranean/Turkish*

Baldwin | 550 Sunrise Hwy. (bet. Lancaster & Rockwood Aves.) | 516-223-1414

Plainview | Plainview Ctr. | 379 S. Oyster Bay Rd. (Woodbury Rd.) | 516-827-5300

Port Washington | 283 Main St. (bet. Bank St. & Carlton Ave.) | 516-883-9309

(continued)

Ayhan's Shish Kebab

Rockville Centre | 201 Sunrise Hwy. (N. Village Ave.) | 516-255-0005
www.ayhansrestaurants.com

"Go for the whole fish" or "tasty" kebabs at these Turkish-Med grills delivering "fast", "fairly priced" eats in a "family-friendly" setting; other items leave critics bemoaning a "mass-produced" feel, though "bargain hunters" swear by the "well-stocked" weekend brunch buffet; P.S. the Mediterranean Cafe in Port Washington has what may be the "best view per dollar on the North Shore."

Ayhan's Trodos
Mediterranean Restaurant *Mediterranean*

▽ 21 | 18 | 21 | $36

Westbury | 477 Old Country Rd. (Evelyn Ave.) | 516-222-8000 | www.ayhansrestaurants.com

Ayhan Hassan's latest brings the Mediterranean to Westbury with signature grilled whole fish "seasoned to perfection", complemented by "delicious" skewers and other "traditional" fare; while a few contend the familiar menu is "no better" than what's already found at the Shish Kebab chain, others view the "personable" service and "nice digs" – furnished with a granite bar and communal table – as an "upgrade."

Azerbaijan Grill *Mideastern*

22 | 15 | 21 | $30

Westbury | 1610 Old Country Rd. (Post Ave.) | 516-228-0001

Azerbaijan Grill II *Mideastern*

NEW **East Meadow** | 2320 Hempstead Tpke. (Prospect Ave.) | 516-644-2200
www.azerbaijangrill.com

"Flavorful" kebabs sizzle inside this "unassuming" Mideastern tucked away in a Westbury strip mall, a "find" for fans of "authentic" char-grilled dishes with Persian and Turkish influences; the "zest" is in the kitchen – not in the "bare-bones" decor – so it's the "generous" plates, "welcoming" staff and "great lunch specials" that "really make the experience"; P.S. an East Meadow sibling opened post-Survey.

Azuma Sushi
Asian Fusion *Asian/Japanese*

23 | 14 | 22 | $29

Greenlawn | 252 Broadway (Little Plains Rd.) | 631-262-7200 | www.azumasushiasianfusion.com

Loyalists "love the sushi, specialty salads" and extensive Asian fusion options at this "surprisingly good" Greenlawn Japanese that's definitely "better than it looks" since there's "no ambiance" to speak of; despite its shortcomings, the "wonderful hospitality" and affordable tabs keep customers "happy."

Babette's *Eclectic*

20 | 13 | 17 | $40

East Hampton | 66 Newtown Ln. (bet. Main St. & Osborne Ln.) | 631-329-5377 | www.babettesrestaurant.com

"Organic, health-conscious food" from a "creative, guilt-free menu" is the specialty at this often "packed" Eclectic where, along with your grass-fed beef burger and BBQ tofu, "you might get neck strain from seeing famous people"; so while the ambiance is "one step above a diner", the service is just "ok" and wallet-watchers protest that "no omelet is worth mortgaging your house for", it's still an "East Hampton classic."

Babylon Carriage House *Continental*

21 | 23 | 21 | $42

Babylon | 21 Fire Island Ave. (Main St.) | 631-422-5161 | www.babyloncarriagehouse.com

Regulars relish visits to this "refined" yet "friendly" Babylon Continental, set in a "romantic" 1865 carriage house with two fireplaces, a "happening" bar and a "classy stairway to the second floor" (sit upstairs "if you want a quiet meal"); while the "good", "varied" grub ("delicious" Thai calamari) and "happy-hour feeling" are a hit with most, a handful complains about "overpriced" eats and a "noisy" weekend "club" crowd that "hangs out" "looking for love the second time around"; P.S. the "Wednesday lobster bake" is a "bargain."

Baby Moon *Italian*

18 | 13 | 18 | $35

Westhampton Beach | 238 Montauk Hwy. (bet. Rogers Ave. & S. Country Rd.) | 631-288-6350 | www.babymoonrestaurant.com

A "go-to for locals" in Westhampton Beach, this "busy", "noisy" "red-sauce" Southern Italian offers "huge platters" of "reliable, if not memorable", "homestyle" fare, including "well-prepared" pizza, pasta and salads; still, some patrons protest it's "not worth the money" given the "uneven service" and "way too family-friendly" space that's "been around for a while, and it shows."

Backyard *Mediterranean*

▽ 23 | 23 | 21 | $49

Montauk | Solé East | 90 Second House Rd. (S. Eldert Ln.) | 631-668-9739 | www.soleeast.com

Montauk's Solé East hotel provides the "lovely setting" for this "laid-back" Mediterranean focusing on "market-fresh" ingredients sourced from local suppliers; with an indoor fireplace and a "wonderful" outdoor poolside terrace furnished with oversized mattresses, it's a "treat" for lounging over "creative cocktails" among a "so hip it hurts" crowd; P.S. frequent DJ sets and live music include reggae on Thursdays and Brazilian during Sunday brunch.

Baja Fresh
Mexican Grill *Mexican*

18 | 12 | 15 | $14

New Hyde Park | Lake Success Shopping Ctr. | 1468 Union Tpke. (bet. Lakeville & New Hyde Park Rds.) | 516-354-2252 | www.bajafresh.com

Fans find "everything fast food usually is not" at this "always fresh" Mexican chain link in New Hyde Park, where the "fish tacos are a highlight" and the "salsa bar is a hit"; though critics find it "under-spiced" with "hit-or-miss" service, most consider it "worthwhile" for a "cheap" meal "on the run."

Baja Grill *Mexican*

18 | 14 | 16 | $20

East Northport | Elwood Shopping Ctr. | 1920 Jericho Tpke. (Elwood Rd.) | 631-462-2252

(continued)

Baja Grill

Smithtown | Sleepys Shopping Plaza | 20 E. Main St. (bet. Hauppauge Rd. & Lawrence Ave.) | 631-979-2252
www.bajagrillny.com

When you're looking for an "affordable" "alternative to fast food", these East Northport and Smithtown siblings deliver "solid" Mexican fare that's big on "wraps, nachos and margaritas"; sure, they're a bit "lacking" when it comes to decor, but even if they don't "knock your socks off", they're "kid-friendly" and "handy for a quick bite."

NEW Banzai Burger *Burgers*

– – – M

Amagansett | 2095 Montauk Hwy. (Napeague Stretch) |
631-267-3175 | www.banzaiburger.com

This trendy addition to the laid-back seasonal eateries lining Amagansett's Napeague Stretch serves a burger lineup that includes vegan and foie gras variations, while a sushi menu fills the bill for raw-fish fans; a whitewashed interior decorated with red stripes and marine-blue accents leads to an outdoor bar that includes a ping-pong table, and a romantic, under-the-stars dining room is hidden behind lush plants and flowers; P.S. there's a DJ some nights.

Bar Frites *French*

18 21 18 $48

Greenvale | Wheatley Plaza | 400 Wheatley Plaza (Northern Blvd.) |
516-484-7500 | www.barfrites.com

A "lively scene" that "really hops on weekends" unfolds at this "bright, airy" French bistro in Greenvale's Wheatley Plaza run by George and Gillis Poll (Bryant & Cooper, Cipollini, Toku); admirers "love" the outdoor seating, "Parisian" atmosphere and "classic" cuisine, but a "disappointed" faction cites a "deafening din", a "frantic" pace and "expensive" tabs for "unimaginative" fare, calling it the "first chink in the Poll brothers' armor."

✚ Barney's Ⓜ *American/French*

26 23 24 $63

Locust Valley | 315 Buckram Rd. (Bayville Rd.) | 516-671-6300 |
www.barneyslv.com

"Excellent from start to finish" declare diners about this "romantic" "retreat" on a "hard-to-find" country byway in "tony Locust Valley", offering "first-rate" American-French dishes delivered by a "cordial" staff; the "chic, understated" setting "feels like a Vermont inn", especially in the "fireplace room" where a "log fire blazes and crackles" in winter, so while it can be "expensive", many consider it a "must-go"; P.S. a prix fixe is offered Sunday–Thursday and an early-bird on Friday.

Barolo Ⓩ *Continental/Italian*

25 20 24 $54

Melville | 1197 Walt Whitman Rd. (Sweet Hollow Rd.) | 631-421-3750

Expect "consistently delicious" Continental-Italian fare at this "classy" "local favorite" in Melville where the "fantastic" dishes are "impeccably prepared and served" by an "eager-to-please" staff; even if the "small", "dark" room "could use a little sprucing up", it's still "highly recommended" for "special occasions."

	FOOD	DECOR	SERVICE	COST

◪ Barrique Kitchen & Wine Bar *Mediterranean*

24 | 25 | 23 | $38

Babylon | 69 Deer Park Ave. (bet. Grove Pl. & Montauk Hwy.) | 631-321-1175 | www.barriquekitchenandwinebar.com

Delivering "delectable small plates" and a "serious" vino selection in a "cozy" wine cellar–style interior heavy on reclaimed wood (a barn door serves as a communal table), this "hopping" Babylon Med is a top pick for an evening "without the kids"; a staff with "knowledge and personality" "makes every night special", but since there are no rezzies, be ready to wait "over an hour" on the weekends.

Basil Leaf Café *Italian*

21 | 20 | 21 | $41

Locust Valley | Plaza Shoppes | 7 Birch Hill Rd. (bet. Elm St. & Underhill Rd.) | 516-676-6252 | www.thebasilleafrestaurant.com

This "neighborhood favorite" in a little shopping plaza in Locust Valley seems to have "improved" recently, offering regional Italian cuisine that's both "comforting" and "creatively prepared", delivered by an "accommodating" staff; the "quaint" surroundings open up to a "cheery terrace in the summer", attracting plenty of "ladies who lunch, local families and regulars"; P.S. reservations are recommended for the weekends.

Batata Café *Eclectic*

▽ 21 | 11 | 17 | $15

Northport | 847 Fort Salonga Rd. (bet. Layne Way & Waterside Ave.) | 631-754-4439 | www.batatacafe.com

"Well-thought-out panini", "soups with a twist" and morning burritos make this "cute", "counter-service" Eclectic Northport cafe a popular "gathering place" for breakfast or "moms' lunch out while the kids are at school"; the funky setting "showcases local artists' work", which provides a pleasant diversion when the service "takes a long time"; P.S. closes at 7 PM weekdays, 4 PM Saturdays and Sundays.

Bay Burger *Burgers*

21 | 11 | 15 | $19

Sag Harbor | 1742 Bridgehampton-Sag Harbor Tpke. (Carroll St.) | 631-899-3915 | www.bayburger.com

"They keep the formula simple" at this seasonal Sag Harbor joint – "freshly ground beef burgers" from "high-quality meat" served on a house-baked bun, accompanied by "a glass of wine" (or a bottle of beer), all topped off with "amazing" housemade ice cream; there's "zero ambiance" inside, but the nice patio is a summertime draw, and a "jazz group entertains a mellow crowd" on Thursday nights.

Bayou, The Ⓜ *Cajun/Creole*

23 | 19 | 20 | $35

North Bellmore | Omni Plaza | 2823 Jerusalem Ave. (Pea Pond Rd.) | 516-785-9263 | www.bayou4bigfun.com

It's "Mardi Gras every day" at this "funky", "festive" New Orleans outpost in North Bellmore, especially after you down one of the "signature Hurricanes" (careful, they "creep up on you") and some "spicy", "super-tasty" Cajun-Creole eats; sure, the strip-mall location "could be better", but once you get into the brazenly "tacky decor" and "party atmosphere", you "don't want to leave."

	FOOD	DECOR	SERVICE	COST

Bayview Inn & Restaurant ☒ *American/Continental*

| 22 | 19 | 22 | $47 |

South Jamesport | Bayview Inn | 10 Front St. (S. Jamesport Ave.) | 631-722-2659 | www.northforkmotels.com

"Pleasant, relaxed" repasts await at this "out-of-the-way" American-Continental in South Jamesport where there's fireside dining in winter and a "lovely" porch for "well-prepared" summer meals; it feels "like eating at home, but you can still get dessert if you don't finish your meal", and the Sunday–Thursday prix fixe appeals to recessionaires.

NEW Beach House *Seafood/Steak*

| - | - | - | E |

East Hampton | 103 Montauk Hwy. (Cove Hollow Rd.) | 631-604-5600 | www.ehbeachhouse.com

Fresh off his success with Boathouse, Michael Gluckman has debuted this upscale East Hampton steak and seafooder featuring a raw bar and lively bar area; stained-glass sconces and a reflecting pool stand out in the elegant space, and there's also covered patio seating.

Beacon *American*

| 22 | 23 | 20 | $59 |

Sag Harbor | 8 W. Water St. (Bridge St.) | 631-725-7088 | www.beaconsagharbor.com

"Incredible sunsets" and "top-notch" New American cuisine are a "hard combination to beat" at this "exquisite" waterside "favorite" in Sag Harbor; so while the tabs are "hefty" and the no-reservations policy a "real pain", many find the wait "worthwhile" since this "hot spot actually deserves its reputation"; P.S. open seasonally.

Bellissimo Ristorante *Italian*

| ∇ 23 | 24 | 24 | $36 |

Deer Park | 786 Grand Blvd. (Commack Rd.) | 631-274-3378 | www.grandmajosephine.com

"Wonderful Italian food" by a 60-year veteran chef impresses at this tiny, "romantic" Deer Park "staple" with just eight tables; it can be easily missed in its strip-mall location, but moderate prices and a staff that treats you like "family" ensure a loyal clientele.

Bellport, The *American/Continental*

| 22 | 19 | 19 | $44 |

Bellport | 159 S. Country Rd. (Woodruff St.) | 631-286-7550 | www.bellport.com

Regulars say it's "always a pleasure" to dine at this "arty" New American-Continental in Bellport by the married team of Taylor Alonso and Patricia Trainor, who complement "imaginative" dishes with a "quirky", "country-house vibe"; though a few find the luster has "faded" and cite inconsistent service, it "can feel like home on the right night", and the Monday 'recession special' is a plus; P.S. closed Tuesdays year-round and Wednesdays in the winter.

Benihana *Japanese/Steak*

| 19 | 18 | 20 | $38 |

Manhasset | Bed, Bath & Beyond Shopping Plaza | 2105 Northern Blvd. (Port Washington Blvd.) | 516-627-3400

Westbury | 920 Merchants Concourse (Privado Dr.) | 516-222-6091 | www.benihana.com

"Bring on the onion volcano" clamor customers who count on an "entertaining" "show" for "all ages" (even "jaded teenagers") at this

Japanese steakhouse chain in Manhasset and Westbury, where teppanyaki chefs perform tableside feats while delivering "reliable" eats, including sushi and other "updated" items; critics call it "tired", "tacky" and "overpriced", but it works as a place to "take the kids and still have an edible meal."

Benkei 🅜 *Japanese* ▽ 23 | 19 | 21 | $31

Northport | 16 Woodbine Ave. (bet. Main St. & Scudder Ave.) | 631-262-7100

A "warm greeting at the door" sets the tone at this "inviting" family-owned Japanese in Northport serving "creative" sushi and sashimi, plus a range of cooked dishes, for a "reasonable price"; it has a "nice location facing the harbor", and while it's "certainly not fancy", many feel it "stands out above the crowd."

Benny's Ristorante 🅩 *Italian* 25 | 19 | 24 | $52

Westbury | 199 Post Ave. (Maple Ave.) | 516-997-8111 | www.bennysristorante.com

"Still the ultimate" in "fine" Northern Italian dining, this "true classic" in Westbury "always delivers" a "superb" meal in an "old-fashioned", "formal atmosphere"; the "throwback" decor is "ornate" and "elegant" to some and a bit "tired" to others, but most commend the "first-class" service, helmed by "wonderful" hosts who "treat you like royalty."

🅩 Ben's Kosher Deli *Deli* 19 | 14 | 17 | $25

Carle Place | 59 Old Country Rd. (Glen Cove Rd.) | 516-742-3354
Greenvale | 140 Wheatley Plaza (bet. Glen Cove Rd. & Northern Blvd.) | 516-621-3340
Woodbury | 7971 Jericho Tpke. (S. Woods Rd.) | 516-496-4236
www.bensdeli.net

"When the craving strikes" for "flavorful" matzo ball soup, "tender" corned beef and "unbelievable pastrami on rye" ("never mind the cholesterol"), this "old-fashioned kosher deli" trio "fits the bill"; those who've "eaten here for over 20 years" say the "fair prices", "plain yet comfortable" digs and "loud" crowd work for "family dining", though a few wish the "brassy" staff "cared a little more."

Bertucci's *Italian* 17 | 16 | 17 | $26

Westbury | 795 Merrick Ave. (Corporate Dr.) | 516-683-8800
Hauppauge | 358 Vanderbilt Motor Pkwy. (bet. Kennedy Dr. & Marcus Blvd.) | 631-952-2100
Melville | 881 Walt Whitman Rd. (Gwynne Rd.) | 631-427-9700
www.bertuccis.com

It's "rug-rat heaven" at this "decent" Italian chain that's a "surefire thing" with the kids (who get to "play with dough" at the table); just "stick with" the brick-oven pies, "hot rolls" and "nice salads" (the rest can seem "processed"), and expect "predictable" fare for a "fair price."

🅩 Besito *Mexican* 24 | 24 | 22 | $45

Roslyn | Harborview Shoppes | 1516 Old Northern Blvd. (bet. Northern Blvd. & Remsen Ave.) | 516-484-3001

(continued)

Besito

Huntington | 402 New York Ave. (bet. Carver & Fairview Sts.) | 631-549-0100

www.besitomex.com

Fans indulge in a "fiesta of the senses" at this "attractive" Mexican twosome in Huntington and Roslyn where the "guac rocks", the "contemporary" *comida* is "different and delicious" and the "killer" margaritas lend extra zing to a "glowing" atmosphere that's "cool as the other side of a pillow"; though it can all add up to a "pricey night", most "shout '*arriba!*'" and come back for more.

Best Buffet   *Chinese/Eclectic*   18 | 12 | 13 | $30

Huntington Station | 179 Walt Whitman Rd. (bet. Sprucetree Ln. & Weston St.) | 631-385-0800 | www.best-buffet.com

"Eat, enjoy and diet the rest of the week" sum up sojourners to this Chinese-Eclectic buffet in Huntington Station that's a "fabulous deal if you like to stuff yourself"; there's an "astounding variety" of dishes – from "can't-be-beat" crab legs to "well-prepared" Peking duck – just "get there early to avoid the gluttonous crowds" and "don't look too closely at the decor."

Bevanda   *Italian*   22 | 18 | 24 | $44

Great Neck | 570 Middle Neck Rd. (bet. Breuer Ave. & Brokaw Ln.) | 516-482-1510 | www.bevandarestaurant.com

"Everyone feels like a VIP" at this "gracious" Northern Italian in Great Neck dishing up "generous" plates of "consistently good", "comforting" cuisine; so even though a few tut that it's "time for some new decor", the "reasonable prices" and "complimentary biscotti" at meal's end seal the deal for "happy" regulars.

Big Daddy's   *BBQ/Cajun*   24 | 18 | 21 | $33

Massapequa | 1 Park Ln. (Front St.) | 516-799-8877 | www.bigdaddysny.com

"Cajun is ragin'" at this "little bit of N'Awlins" in Massapequa that's "still spicy and going strong" with a "daily-changing menu" of "sauced-up" Louisiana specialties plus "smoky BBQ" and "wild cocktails"; the staff gives "trustworthy recommendations" and the "jazzy" digs often play host to "rocking live music", though the "looong waits" and "hot" grub are "not for the faint of heart"; P.S. look out for "great deals during the week."

Bigelow's ⌷ *New England/Seafood*   24 | 9 | 20 | $23

Rockville Centre | 79 N. Long Beach Rd. (bet. Ongley St. & Sunrise Hwy.) | 516-678-3878 | www.bigelows-rvc.com

"Step back in time" at this "lovable" Cape Cod–style seafood "shack", a Rockville Centre "institution" (built in 1939) where fried-fish fans "belly up" to the original counter for battered, breaded bounty – including "some of the best Ipswich clams" around – along with "showstopper" chowders; the limited seating can get tight, but the "standing-room-only" crowd just cares about the "fresh" catch; P.S. cash only.

Bin 56 ●⊠ *Spanish* ▽ 24 | 21 | 22 | $37

Huntington | 56 Stewart Ave. (bet. Main St. & New York Ave.) | 631-812-0060 | www.bin56.com

With "terrific" Spanish tapas – from artisanal cheeses to bacon-wrapped dates – and an "accommodating", "knowledgeable" staff, this Huntington cousin to Bistros Cassis and Citron provides a "comfy", "place to hang, sip wine and have a bite or two"; the "relaxed", low-lit setting, furnished with a communal table and couches, is "perfect for late night", plus Tuesday tarot readings add some midweek magic.

Birchwood Tap Room *American/Polish* ▽ 20 | 13 | 21 | $30

Riverhead | 512 Pulaski St. (Hamilton Ave.) | 631-727-4449 | www.birchwoodtap.com

This "local" tavern in the heart of Riverhead's Polishtown district has been serving up "homestyle" Polish dishes (like "melt-in-your-mouth" pierogi) and American "classic pub" fare for a "good price" since 1929; while it's "kitschy", "dark and cluttered" to some, memorabilia mavens admire the tin ceiling, stained glass and "pictures of film and sports celebrities of a bygone day"; P.S. weeknight deals make it extra-affordable.

⚡ Bistro Cassis *French* 24 | 20 | 21 | $44

Huntington | 55B Wall St. (bet. Central & Gerard Sts.) | 631-421-4122 | www.bistrocassis.com

"Even the most discriminating Francophile approves" of this "popular" Huntington bistro (sister to Bistro Citron) offering "magnificent mussels", "divine duck" and a "delicious" Sunday brunch, all served with "great crusty bread"; a "well-trained" staff and tabs that "won't break the bank" help make up for the "cramped" setting with tables so "close together" it's "tough not to listen to other people's conversations."

Bistro Citron *French* 21 | 20 | 20 | $43

Roslyn | 1362 Old Northern Blvd. (bet. E. B'way & Main St.) | 516-403-4400 | www.bistrocitron.com

A spin-off of Bistro Cassis, this "adorable little bistro" in Roslyn is "always a favorite" for "terrific daily specials", "reliable" French "standards" and "the best burger within 50 miles"; the "lovely", "non-stuffy" setting features tables "overlooking the duck pond" and live music twice weekly, but nitpickers note "inconsistent" service, "tight seating" and slightly "pricey" fare that's "not as inventive" as it could be.

NEW Bistro Etcetera *American* - | - | - | E

Port Washington | 43 Main St. (bet. Bayles & Maryland Aves.) | 516-472-7780 | www.bistroetcetera.com

Chef Karen Melanie LaRocco (of the defunct Melanie's a Bistro) is behind this upscale Port Washington newcomer situated in the former Bistro Toulouse space, offering a New American menu that branches out a bit with dishes such as vegetable shepherd's pie; a wall of mirrors visually expands the narrow room, which also features dark oak floors and wainscoting.

Bistro 44 *American*

23 | 21 | 21 | $42

Northport | 44 Main St. (bet. School St. & Woodbine Ave.) | 631-262-9744 | www.bistro44.net

Fans of this "sophisticated" yet "unpretentious" Northport New American "love the food" served in a "handsome" setting designed with original 1850s woodwork and a "beautiful" heated patio; the village location works for dining "before or after a show" or taking a post-meal "stroll along the harbor", and though a few feel squeezed by the "too-small" room and moderately expensive menu, many are "impressed" by the "update" under a new owner and chef.

Bistro 72 *American*

- | - | - | E

Riverhead | Hotel Indigo | 1830 W. Main St. (Kroemer Ave.) | 631-369-3325 | www.indigoeastend.com

Woven-back chairs and a granite bar make for a chic setting at this American in Riverhead's renovated Hotel Indigo that offers a farm-to-table menu from chef Ralph DeLustro; outdoor poolside and fire-side dining, plus live music some nights, adds to the allure.

Bistro 25 *Eclectic*

- | - | - | M

Sayville | 45 Foster Ave. (bet. Middle Rd. & N. Main St.) | 631-589-7775 | www.bistro25li.com

Twenty-five $25 bottles of wine on the list inspired the name of this Eclectic Sayville bistro where monkfish medallions, braised short ribs and other entrees are all priced under $20; the dining area is decorated with white tablecloths, votive candles and paintings for sale from a local gallery, and there's a separate section with high tables.

B.K. Sweeney's
Parkside Tavern *American*

18 | 17 | 19 | $31

Bethpage | 356 Broadway (Powell Ave.) | 516-935-9597
B.K. Sweeney's Uptown Grille *American*
Garden City | 636 Franklin Ave. (bet. 6th & 7th Sts.) | 516-746-3075
www.bksweeneys.com

Locals gather to "eat, drink and be merry" at this pub pair in Garden City and Bethpage ("near the golf courses") turning out "hearty" burgers, steaks and other "well-priced" American eats along with "good tap beers"; service is generally "pleasant", even when the crowd gets a little "raucous" on "game days" and "after work."

Black & Blue *Seafood/Steak*

22 | 21 | 23 | $48

Huntington | 65 Wall St. (bet. Central & Gerard Sts.) | 631-385-9255 | www.blackandbluehuntington.com

"Super-friendly" servers who "go that extra mile" elevate this "lively" surf 'n turfer in Huntington, providing "innovative", "thoughtfully presented" dishes in a supper-club setting with "big booths" and a "beautiful" saltwater fish tank; the "classy" atmosphere gets a boost from "live music some nights", though critics caution about the "limited" menu, adding "watch your wallet, it'll take a hit."

Blackbirds' Grille *Cajun/Southern*   20 | 15 | 21 | $32

Sayville | 553 Old Montauk Hwy. (B'way Ave.) | 631-563-4144 | www.blackbirdsgrille.com

"Tasty" Cajun-Southern eats (including "the best fried pickles") are delivered by a "warm" staff at this simple, "homey" Sayville "road-house" decorated with a "coastal" motif; the "busy" room gets "loud" when there's "live music on weekends", and dishes can be "inconsistent" ("stick to basic grill fare"), but most agree it's "not bad for a decent, casual meal."

☒ Blackstone Steakhouse *Steak*   24 | 24 | 23 | $66

Melville | 10 Pinelawn Rd. (Broad Hollow Rd.) | 631-271-7780 | www.blackstonesteakhouse.com

They're "always on the top of their game" at this "see-and-be-seen" steakhouse on Melville's 110 corridor that not only "pleases the pickiest carnivore" with "excellent" cuts of meat, but offers "outra-geous sushi rolls" as well; the "contemporary" lodgelike setting with "gorgeous lighting" and "professional" service attracts a "power-house lunch" crowd as well as a "happening bar scene", but unfor-tunately "the noise level is almost as high as the prices."

Blackwells Ⓜ *Steak*   23 | 25 | 24 | $51

Wading River | Great Rock Golf Club | 141 Fairway Dr. (Sound Ave.) | 631-929-1800 | www.blackwellsrestaurant.com

There's a "private country-club atmosphere" at this "elegantly decorated" steakhouse overlooking the greens of the Great Rock Golf Club in Wading River, where "you can taste the freshness" of the local ingredients in the "fine" dishes crafted by chef Chris Gerdes; an "extensive wine list" highlighting LI vintages comple-ments the cuisine, as does the "professional, courteous" service; P.S. the prix fixe dinners are an "excellent value" and the early-bird is a "steal."

Bliss Ⓜ *American*   22 | 19 | 21 | $46

East Setauket | 766 Rte. 25A (Nicolls Rd.) | 631-941-0430 | www.blissli.com

Customers commend the "high-quality" cooking at this "upscale" East Setauket New American, which also delivers "one of the best" happy hours around; a new bar area should appeal to critics who called the layout "crammed", and though some find the dining expe-rience "pricier than it should be", most report "attentive" service and a "pleasant" meal.

Blond *American*   21 | 20 | 22 | $46

Miller Place | Aliano Shopping Ctr. | 691 Rte. 25A (Oakland Ave.) | 631-821-5969 | www.blondrestaurant.com

"Hidden in a strip mall" in Miller Place, this "swanky" "little" New American surprises with its "fresh, exciting menu" and "Manhattan" ambiance; the staff "accommodates special requests", and though a few maintain it's "middle-of-the-road" and "expensive for the area", at least the "fried Oreo shots" ("best dessert ever") make a memorable finish.

	FOOD	DECOR	SERVICE	COST

Blue 🗷 *American* | 22 | 23 | 22 | $47 |

Blue Point | 7 Montauk Hwy. (Nicolls Rd.) | 631-363-6666 | www.restaurantblue.com

With a clubby scene, a "South Beach"–style outdoor lounge, nightly bands and DJs, and a "tasty", "interesting" New American menu (including sushi), this "modern" Blue Pointer draws a "lively" crowd; a few guests gripe about "questionable food combinations", but most are won over by the "friendly" bar and "Lobsterfest in the summer."

Blue Fish *Japanese* | - | - | - | E |

Hicksville | Days Inn | 828 S. Oyster Bay Rd. (bet. Aerospace Blvd. & Meadow Ln.) | 516-605-0655 | www.bluefishli.com

Bright blue lights undulate over the onyx bar and red lights illuminate the booths at this sleek, upscale Japanese restaurant and lounge in Hicksville; the menu goes beyond sushi and sashimi, also offering hot fare such as shrimp and vegetable tempura.

Blue Moon *Italian/Pizza* | 20 | 16 | 19 | $28 |

Rockville Centre | 26 N. Park Ave. (bet. Merrick Rd. & Sunrise Hwy.) | 516-763-4900 | www.bluemoonpizzeria.com

"Pizza, pasta and panini" are the main draws of this "reasonable" Rockville Centre Italian whose "terrific" coal-fired pies and "basic" "red-sauce" plates work for a "quick bite" "pre- or post-movie"; the exposed-brick walls and checkered tablecloths lend a "comfortable" feel that's "nice for families", though some argue the decor and "limited" menu "need a little zip."

Blue Parrot Bar & Grill *Tex-Mex* | 15 | 15 | 15 | $37 |

East Hampton | 33 Main St. (Newtown Ln.) | 631-329-2583 | www.blueparroteasthampton.com

This "funky" Tex-Mex "cantina" in East Hampton was revived by "new celebrity owners" and given a "face-lift" in 2009 after a three-year hiatus, but "disappointing" food, "snooty" service and "schizophrenic" Western decor mar the comeback; regardless, it's a "good place to hang in the late afternoon" "slurping" a margarita, and the nightly "crowds" are "glad to have it back."

Blue Point Bistro & Grille 🅼 *American* | - | - | - | M |

Blue Point | 154 Montauk Hwy. (Homan Ave.) | 631-419-6850 | www.bluepointbarandgrillli.com

Situated in a little house with a front porch, this Blue Point American offers a moderately priced roundup of comfort food that includes burgers and entrees such as marinated skirt steak with tempura onion rings and chicken stuffed with goat cheese; the simple room is wrapped in wood wainscoting and is decorated with seasonal touches.

Boathouse, The *Seafood* | 19 | 22 | 17 | $51 |

East Hampton | Harbor Marina | 39 Gann Rd. (off Three Mile Harbor Rd.) | 631-329-3663 | www.easthamptonboathouse.com

In the former home of Bostwick's on the Harbor, this East Hampton seafooder is a "pleasure" with its "open-air deck", "priceless sunset views" and "newly decorated" digs resembling a vintage yacht; the expensive fin fare doesn't quite "live up to the atmosphere" ("simple entrees are the best") and service can be "amateurish", but "the young flock to it" nevertheless, keeping the "noise level at top decibel."

BobbiQue *BBQ*

21 | 15 | 18 | $26

Patchogue | 70 W. Main St. (Havens Ave.) | 631-447-7744 | www.bobbique.com

"Pull up your sleeves, loosen your belt" and get ready to "smack your lips" at this "true BBQ, blues and bourbon haven" in Patchogue offering a "fantastic" beer selection to boot; the "relaxed" atmosphere is livened up with "awesome" live music, so even if some say the "large", industrial setting has "no warmth", the "young, agile and thirsty" add heat.

Bobby's Burger Palace *Burgers*

21 | 15 | 18 | $17

NEW Garden City | Roosevelt Field Mall | 630 Old Country Rd. (bet. Clinton Rd. & Meadowbrook State Pkwy.) | 516-877-7777
Lake Grove | Smith Haven Mall | 355 Smith Haven Mall (bet. Middle Country Rd. & Nesconset Hwy.) | 631-382-9590
www.bobbysburgerpalace.com

Celeb chef Bobby Flay's "juicy, flavorful" burgers "cooked to order with a wide variety of toppings", plus "crisp", "house-made fries" and "amazing shakes" "feed your addiction" at this "upscale" Lake Grove fast-fooder; the mall location and orange-and-lime "McDonald's über-chic" atmosphere aren't for everyone, but the "quick", semi-self-serve" format ("place your order" at the counter, "then sit") helps keep the line moving; P.S. there's a new Garden City branch.

Bobby Van's Steakhouse *Steak*

22 | 19 | 20 | $60

Bridgehampton | 2393 Main St. (bet. Ocean Rd. & School St.) | 631-537-0590 | www.bobbyvans.com

This "bustling" "Bridgehampton watering hole" and meatery is "just 'Hamptons' enough" with its "chic" yet "not intimidating" digs, ideal for indulging in "excellent" steaks, "famous" burgers and "generous" drinks; service is a "cut above", catering to a "social scene spanning multiple generations", but doubters disapprove of the "big tabs, long waits" and "deafening" din in the "slightly dated" space; P.S. lunches and "midweek early dinner deals" make it more affordable.

Bob's Restaurant Ⓜ *American*

21 | 21 | 20 | $42

Floral Park | 230 Jericho Tpke. (bet. Flower Ave. & Park Pl.) | 516-354-8185 | www.bobsplacerestaurant.com

"A piece of Manhattan" in Floral Park, this "unexpected" locale captures "city quality" with its "modern yet classic styling", "creative" cocktails and "inventive", "enjoyable" New American menu touched by Asia and the Mediterranean; service can be "spotty" and the tabs "a bit expensive", but the Tuesday–Thursday prix fixe is a "bargain."

Boccaccio Ⓜ *Italian*

21 | 16 | 22 | $45

Hicksville | 275 W. Old Country Rd. (Newbridge Rd.) | 516-433-6262 | www.boccacciony.com

Regulars rely on this "comfortable" Northern Italian "family place" in Hicksville for "wonderful", "accommodating" service, "very good", if "not outstanding", fare and "reasonable prices" ("sign up for birthday-dinner discounts"); the interior may be caught in a bit of a "time warp", but that doesn't keep it from being a neighborhood "standby."

Bonbori Tiki *Japanese/Thai* ▽ 20 | 20 | 20 | $33

Huntington | 14 Elm St. (bet. Nassau Rd. & New York Ave.) | 631-673-0400

A "mainstay" "just off the main drag in Huntington", this "interesting" Thai-Japanese hybrid is a "delight in nice weather" when those in-the-know flock to the "secret garden"; the "relaxing" bi-level space, "attentive" staff and a menu that's "less expensive" than nearby eateries add up to an "enjoyable experience" for most.

Bonsai *Japanese* 22 | 16 | 20 | $31

Port Washington | 92 Main St. (bet. Evergreen & Haven Aves.) | 516-883-0103

"Always fresh", "well-presented" sushi and "excellent-value bento boxes" mean there's "usually a wait" at this "small", "popular" Port Washington Japanese; regulars recommend the "reasonable lunch specials" and appreciate the "family-friendly" service and "relaxing" vibe, "even if the decor is somewhat bland."

Bostwick's Chowder House *Seafood* 20 | 12 | 18 | $37

East Hampton | 277 Pantigo Rd. (Cross Hwy.) | 631-324-1111 | www.bostwickschowderhouse.com

A "busy" locale for real "Bonacker bites", this "casual" East Hampton roadside seafood shack (owned by the same team as Indian Wells Tavern) turns out "simple", "fresh" lobster rolls and "excellent clams and chowders" served by a "young staff that's full of energy"; it's "a little pricey" considering the "throw-away" plates, but "perfect after a day at the beach", especially if you can "snag one of the outdoor tables"; P.S. closed in the off-season.

Boulder Creek *Steak* - | - | - | M

Hicksville | Broadway Mall | 200 N. Broadway (Newbridge Rd.) | 516-942-7800 | www.bouldercreeksteakhouses.net

A Rocky Mountain theme plays out at this family-friendly Broadway Mall steakhouse with log poles, stone fireplaces and twig-style furniture as a rustic backdrop for a variety of cuts of beef, burgers and other midpriced fare; a popular way to kick off the meal is with the Boulder Blossom – a huge, battered and deep-fried onion, served with a spicy dipping sauce.

Bozena Polish-European Restaurant Ⓜ *Polish* ▽ 23 | 14 | 21 | $27

Lindenhurst | 485 W. Montauk Hwy. (bet. 7th & 8th Sts.) | 631-226-3001 | www.polishdinner.com

"Hooked" customers heed the hankering for "comfort food, old-country style" at this "big" Polish diner in Lindenhurst delivering "incredibly good", low-priced fare (including a "winning" sampler platter); if you can look past the "catering-hall tacky" decor and "weekend parties" with "loud DJs spinning disco and polka", you'll have yourself an "amazing" meal.

Brasserie Cassis *French*

23 | 20 | 21 | $43

Plainview | Plainview Ctr. | 387 S. Oyster Bay Rd. (Woodbury Rd.) | 516-653-0090 | www.brasseriecassis.com

Diners adore this "charming" "Parisian bistro" in Plainview, where the French "comfort food" is *"très bon"*, particularly the "terrific" mussels and frites (a real deal on Moules Mondays); despite the view of the surrounding "strip mall", a smattering of outdoor tables allows for "people-watching" when the weather warms, a plus considering how "noisy" it can get inside.

Brasserie Persil *French*

25 | 19 | 23 | $40

Oceanside | 2825 Long Beach Rd. (bet. Merle Ave. & Poole St.) | 516-992-1742 | www.persilrestaurant.com

You feel like you're "sitting on the Seine" at this "delightful" Oceanside brasserie (sister to Sage Bistro and Aperitif) that's deemed a "must-go" thanks to its "fabulous" French food and "great value"; the "close" bistro-style quarters tend to get "noisy", but a "helpful" staff deftly tends to the "crowds"; P.S. reservations accepted for parties of six or more.

Brasserie 214 *European*

20 | 22 | 21 | $44

New Hyde Park | Inn at New Hyde Park | 214 Jericho Tpke. (bet. 2nd & 3rd Sts.) | 516-354-7797 | www.innatnhp.com

Sporting a fresh name to reflect its bistro "makeover", this "stunning" European at the Inn at New Hyde Park "has come a long way" from its "dowdy" past to become a "feast for the eyes and stomach"; service is generally "very good" and the menu maintains some of the old German "standards" while incorporating hints of Belgium, France and the Mediterranean, though skeptics say the eats remain "nothing special" despite the "impressive" redo.

Brass Rail *American*

25 | 20 | 22 | $48

Locust Valley | 107 Forest Ave. (bet. Birch Hill Rd. & Weir Ln.) | 516-723-9103 | www.thebrassraillocustvalley.com

"Extraordinarily creative" chef-owner Kent Monkan delivers a "home-run" menu of "scrumptious", "market-driven" American dishes ranging from bar bites to small plates to full dinners, allowing diners to order according to their appetite and budget at this Locust Valley "gem"; the service is "on track" and the "beautiful bar" enhances the "casual", "old-time tavern" feel – no wonder "reservations fill up fast."

Bravo! Nader *Italian/Seafood*

24 | 13 | 22 | $52

Huntington | 9 Union Pl. (bet. New York Ave. & Wall St.) | 631-351-1200 | www.bravonader.com

Nader's Fish on the Run *Italian/Seafood*

Huntington | 217 New York Ave. (Mill Ln.) | 631-423-6300 | www.nadersfishontherun.com

Chef-owner and "devoted fisherman" Nader Gebrin has earned a "loyal following" for his "amazing" crab cakes, "superb" pastas and "fantastic" specials presented by a "personable" staff at this Huntington Southern Italian; the tabs can be "high" and the room so "tight" that you "get claustrophobic just thinking about it", but you'll probably "walk out with two friends from the next table"; P.S. Nader's Fish on the Run focuses on take-out tacos and sandwiches.

Bridgehampton Candy Kitchen ⇗ Diner | 15 | 12 | 17 | $20 |

Bridgehampton | Main St. (School St.) | 631-537-9885

It's a slice of "nostalgia" at this cash-only, "old-fashioned soda shop" circa 1926 in Bridgehampton where the "best" housemade ice cream, "thickest shakes" and "fast service" with a "vast tolerance" for tykes win fans; even if the "homespun ambiance" is "better" than the rest of the American eats, there's a chance to spot "celebs galore" at the "see-and-be-seen breakfasts", plus the prices leave "enough in your wallet to take the Jitney home."

Brio Ristorante Italiano Italian | 21 | 19 | 21 | $42 |

Port Washington | 45 Shore Rd. (bet. Mill Pond & Old Shore Rds.) | 516-767-0077 | www.brioportwashington.com

The "delicious", "well-presented" fare and an owner who "makes you feel like a guest in his home" are the highlights of this Northern Italian in Port Washington with an adjacent wine bar offering a "fantastic" list; the "pretty" room is suitable for "quiet dinners", while the "excellent" specials keep it a "staple on the restaurant roster" of many; P.S. Wednesday is Ladies Night, so groups of four or more women get 25 percent off their food bill.

Brooks & Porter Steak | 22 | 22 | 21 | $60 |

Merrick | 16 Merrick Ave. (Sunrise Hwy.) | 516-379-9400 | www.brooksandporter.com

This Merrick steakhouse with a slick "city feel" – and the prices to match – serves up "serious", "high-quality" beef, raw-bar delicacies and an after-work "scene"; the service is generally "up to par", though some doubters "don't know what the hype is about" and knock that "nothing can make up for the noise level", especially on the weekends.

☑ Bryant & Cooper Steakhouse Steak | 26 | 21 | 23 | $69 |

Roslyn | 2 Middle Neck Rd. (Northern Blvd.) | 516-627-7270 | www.bryantandcooper.com

Serving "phenomenal" cuts of meat "aged on-site" along with "ample sides" and a "stellar wine list", this "carnivore's delight" in Roslyn "rivals Manhattan's finest" with some of the "most expertly prepared steaks in the area" (you "can't go wrong" with the seafood either); "well-trained" servers who "know their job" help justify the "pricey" tabs, though some find the pace "rushed" and the whole package "too much of a scene"; P.S. "lunch is a lot more affordable", and the adjoining butcher shop is "superb."

B. Smith's Cajun/Southern | 18 | 22 | 18 | $52 |

Sag Harbor | Long Wharf Promenade (Bay St.) | 631-725-5858 | www.bsmith.com

"The view is the shining star" at style guru Barbara Smith's "sleek", seasonal Sag Harbor waterfront eatery, where you can sit "outside on the deck" and ogle the "magnificent yachts and sailboats" moored in the marina while sipping a fresh watermelon margarita; even though the "expensive" Cajun-Southern food veers between "creative" and "so-so", and the service can be "snippy", the "priceless" locale ensures big summertime crowds.

Buckram Stables Cafe *American* | 19 | 18 | 19 | $36 |

Locust Valley | 31 Forest Ave. (bet. Birch Hill Rd. & Weir Ln.) | 516-671-3080 | www.buckramstables.com

"Bigger on food than booze", this "clubby" Locust Valley pub "for the horsey set" provides "famous" burgers and other "reliable" American eats in a "friendly", "cozy" setting that "looks like a stable"; galloping gourmets say "don't expect haute cuisine", but be ready for a "busy", "noisy atmosphere" and know you'll "definitely need reservations."

Bulldog Grille, The ● *American/Continental* | – | – | – | I |

Amityville | 292 Merrick Rd. (bet. Bayview & Ocean Aves.) | 631-691-1947 | www.thebulldoggrille.com

The large bar establishes a laid-back vibe at this Amityville tavern (sibling of Babylon's Post Office Cafe) where the glass-enclosed dining area is elevated and the American-Continental menu aims to please all with options such as burgers, wings, steak and pasta; live bands entertain Saturday nights.

Buoy One *Seafood* | 23 | 9 | 18 | $30 |

Riverhead | 1175 W. Main St. (Mill Rd.) | 631-208-9737
Westhampton | 62 Montauk Hwy. (Sea Breeze Ave.) | 631-998-3808
www.buoyone.com

"Succulent", "simply prepared" seafood is the draw at this "quick", "reasonable", "no-frills" joint inside a Riverhead fish market; it's "not glamorous" and a few would "only go when you can eat outside", but "someone cooking behind the counter really knows what they're doing", so it's a real "find"; P.S. a more upscale Westhampton spin-off opened post-Survey.

Burger Spot *Burgers* | – | – | I |

Garden City | 150 Seventh St. (bet. Franklin & Hilton Aves.) | 516-746-6100 | www.theburgerspotonline.com

Veggie, chicken and even crab options join beef burgers at this popular little patty place in the heart of the Garden City shopping area that shuns antibiotics, hormones, fillers and preservatives in its ingredients; salads and shakes are also on the affordable menu, and although it's mostly takeout, the casual, green-walled setting has a few tables.

Burton & Doyle Steakhouse *Steak* | 24 | 23 | 23 | $69 |

Great Neck | 661 Northern Blvd. (Summer St.) | 516-487-9200 | www.burtonanddoyle.com

"Superb", "perfectly seared" steaks and "excellent" "flexitarian" choices like sushi call for a "splurge" at this Great Neck "standout" where a "gracious" staff "pulls out all the stops to please" the "elite"

North Shore set; "dark, woodsy" and "inviting", it's an "attractive date place" and frequently a "singles scene" at the bar.

☒ Butera's *Italian*   21 | 18 | 20 | $36

Seaford | 3930 Sunrise Hwy. (bet. Jackson & Washington Aves.) | 516-795-1929
Woodbury | Woodbury Village Shopping Ctr. | 7903 Jericho Tpke. (S. Woods Rd.) | 516-496-3633
Sayville | 100 S. Main St. (Collins Ave.) | 631-563-0805
Smithtown | 65 E. Main St. (Landing Ave.) | 631-979-9113
www.buteras.com

"Loyal" fans flock to this "consistent", "modern" quartet for its "extra-large portions" of "above-average Italian" like "garlicky chicken meatballs" plus "reasonable" wines; "long waits" and "hectic" surroundings are downsides, but the "accommodating" service and "solid value" make it a natural for "families" and "large groups."

Butterfields ☒ *American*   20 | 18 | 20 | $40

Hauppauge | 661 Old Willets Path (Engineers Rd.) | 631-851-1507 | www.butterfieldsrestaurant.biz

You're "always greeted with a pleasant smile" at this "after-work hangout" in an "industrial park" in Hauppauge, offering a "diverse" New American menu ranging from "wonderful burgers" to more ambitious items, plus "fabulous" weekday prix fixe dinners; since the live music, Saturday DJs and a "good-looking" 40-ft. mahogany bar make for a "loud" scene, don't expect to easily "carry on a conversation."

☒ Cafe Baci *Italian*   22 | 17 | 20 | $34

Westbury | 1636 Old Country Rd. (Merrick Ave.) | 516-832-8888 | www.cafebacirestaurant.com

Skip a meal and clear your schedule before visiting this Westbury stalwart where the dishes of "hearty, tasty", "super-fresh" Italian fare are so "gigantic" you "can swim in the bowl"; "there's always a wait" and the decor's a bit "tired", but a "vibrant" bar scene, "enthusiastic" service and major "bang for the buck" reward the "test of patience" for most; P.S. no reservations, except for parties of eight or more on weekdays.

Café Buenos Aires *Argentinean*   24 | 21 | 22 | $44

Huntington | 23 Wall St. (bet. Gerard & Main Sts.) | 631-603-3600 | www.cafebuenosaires.net

Guests "go crazy" ordering "awesome" tapas at this "festive", slightly "expensive" Huntington Argentinean (with a Spanish touch), which also dishes up "marvelous" steaks and pastas to go with "winning" wines; co-owner Hugo García, the "ultimate host", "makes you feel right at home" in a "warm" setting enhanced by a "fantastic bar", "fashionable" sidewalk dining and "entertaining tango dancers" (Friday nights and Sunday brunch), so the "only drawback" is the "long wait" for a table; P.S. reservations accepted for six or more.

	FOOD	DECOR	SERVICE	COST

Café Capriccio *Italian*

24 | - | 25 | $48

Port Washington | 14 Haven Ave. (bet. Franklin Ave. & Main St.) | 516-938-0220 | www.capricciorestaurant.net

This Northern Italian from chef/co-owner Elio Sobrero moved from Hicksille to Port Washington post-Survey, but you can still expect the likes of the "best duck with cherry sauce anywhere", served by a staff overseen by Sobrero's "watchful eye"; P.S. its new location, across from the train station, should make it an easy dinner option for commuters.

Café Formaggio *Italian*

20 | 17 | 20 | $37

Carle Place | 307 Old Country Rd. (bet. E. Gate & Lindberg Blvds.) | 516-333-1718 | www.cafeformaggio.com

Located near Roosevelt Field, this "congenial" Carle Place trattoria gives shoppers a place to rest their feet and dig into "hot" bread baskets before sampling an "extensive" Italian menu offering "good value for the money" (and a roster of "gluten-free delights"); weekends get "crowded" (dinnertime "valet parking is a plus"), so go midweek for a more "pleasant" repast with "great wine specials."

Cafe Havana Ⓜ *Cuban*

18 | 19 | 18 | $40

Smithtown | 944 W. Jericho Tpke. (bet. Ledgewood Dr. & Old Willets Path) | 631-670-6277 | www.cafehavanali.com

"Live music sets the mood" at this "hopping", "party"-ready Smithtown Cuban with a covered patio, stone fireplace, palm trees and pictures of Havana on the walls; "excellent" drinks are another plus, though many feel it's "too expensive" for food and service that are just "ok", adding it's a "great idea but not the greatest execution."

Cafe Joelle on Main St. *American/Eclectic*

22 | 17 | 20 | $35

Sayville | 25 Main St. (Railroad Ave.) | 631-589-4600 | www.cafejoelle.net

"Always reliable", this "petite" New American–Eclectic attracts gents and "ladies strolling through Sayville" with its "varied", "reasonably priced" menu, from "creative salads and sandwiches" to "well-prepared" pastas to "German-inspired" eats; the recently renovated, bistro-style setting is "pleasing" too, but since "no reservations" are taken, be prepared for a crowd of "BFFs" waiting for a table; P.S. the owners also run Pasta Pasta.

Cafe La Strada *Italian*

23 | 16 | 22 | $44

Hauppauge | 352 Wheeler Rd. (Central Ave.) | 631-234-5550 | www.cafelastradarestaurant.com

You "would never expect to find" this "exceptional" Italian in a "modest" strip-mall location in Hauppauge, but "someone is paying attention and making all the right moves", providing an "extensive" menu of "outstanding", "old-world" dishes, a "spectacular" wine list (there's a 20,000-bottle cellar) and "polite", formal service; it can get "pricey" (particularly if you order the specials) and the decor is "lacking", but fans say "that's ok" since everything else is "absolutely wonderful."

	FOOD	DECOR	SERVICE	COST

Cafe Max   *American/Eclectic*
| 23 | 15 | 22 | $44 |

East Hampton | 85 Montauk Hwy. (Cove Hollow Rd.) | 631-324-2004 | www.unhampton.com

Chef-owner Max Weintraub dishes up "seasonal, locally farmed (or fished)" American-Eclectic food that's "simply prepared" and served by an "enthusiastic", "professional" staff at this "relaxed" East Hamptoner; while there's "not much decor" (apart from "knotty" cedar), the owner really "cares about his customers" and "keeps the prices fair", so no wonder locals want to keep it "their little secret"; P.S. closed Tuesdays.

Cafe Rustica   *Italian/Mediterranean*
| 22 | 19 | 21 | $43 |

Great Neck | 200 Middle Neck Rd. (bet. Allenwood Rd. & Embassy Ct.) | 516-829-6464 | www.caferusticarestaurant.com

"Loyal repeat diners" frequent this Italian-Med in Great Neck for the "delicious", "hearty" dishes (including "great gluten-free" options), "comfortable" setting and "old-time, attentive" service; it's "a little on the expensive side", but the early-bird dinner is a "bargain."

NEW Café Taka Ⓜ *Mediterranean/Turkish*
| – | – | – | M |

Bay Shore | 164 E. Main St. (Gibson St.) | 631-647-4809 | www.cafetaka.net

Chef/co-owner Mike Sarac has created a mini mecca for Turkish-Mediterranean fare at this little red storefront on Main Street in Bay Shore, where he offers some unusual appetizers (e.g. pan-fried breaded veal-liver cubes) plus a midpriced lineup of kebabs, gyros and entrees such as whole grilled branzini; the simple yet cheerful setting has bright yellow walls, tie-back curtains over tall windows and paper placemats on wood tables.

Cafe Testarossa Ⓜ *Continental*
| 22 | 20 | 21 | $46 |

Syosset | 499 Jericho Tpke. (bet. Jackson Ave. & Seaford Oyster Bay Expwy.) | 516-364-8877 | www.cafetestarossa.com

As newer models roll onto the scene, this "classic" Continental still purrs with "modern twists" on "well-prepared" fare, served in an "elegant atmosphere" that keeps Syosset locals "revving their engines"; "trendy" with an "active bar scene", it's high on decibels and dollar signs, but in terms of value, "the sunset menu can't be beat."

Cafe Toscano   *Italian*
| 21 | 17 | 19 | $38 |

Massapequa | 746 North Broadway (bet. N. Manhattan & N. Richmond Aves.) | 516-798-4500 | www.cafetoscanofusion.com

"Delicious" "homemade" fare, "reasonable prices" and "wonderful service" that includes a "gracious host" make this Massapequa Italian a "reliable" "neighborhood" choice; there are "no surprises" given the "basic" menu and decor, and parking can be "a bit of a problem", but it's a "comfortable" choice that many "recommend."

Caffe Laguna   *Italian*
| 19 | 18 | 19 | $40 |

Long Beach | 960 W. Beech St. (bet. New Hampshire St. & Tennessee Ave.) | 516-432-2717 | www.caffelaguna.com

Just a block from the ocean, this "romantic" Long Beach "hideaway" does "date night" right with "inviting", if slightly "expensive" Italian eats (including "standout" brick-oven pizzas) balanced by a "reasonable wine list" and NYC flair; summer brings "alfresco" seating – and the area's typically "horrendous" street parking.

California Pizza Kitchen *Pizza*

| 17 | 14 | 16 | $24 |

Westbury | Costco Plaza | 1256 Old Country Rd. (Bert Ave.) | 516-683-3338
Huntington Station | Walt Whitman Mall | 159 Walt Whitman Rd. (Weston St.) | 631-423-7565
Lake Grove | Smith Haven Mall | 618 Smith Haven Mall (bet. Middle Country Rd. & Nesconset Hwy.) | 631-382-9610
www.cpk.com

"Clever", "unusual" pizzas (such as "BBQ chicken and Thai") and "creative" salads are the "stars" at this "gourmet" pie chain providing "something for everyone's taste"; it's "inexpensive", "prompt" and "consistent", though some complain the "wannabe eclectic offerings" have grown "tired" and the "overlit" surroundings just "don't have any charm."

Canterbury Ales
Oyster Bar & Grill *American/Seafood*

| 19 | 18 | 19 | $34 |

Oyster Bay | 46 Audrey Ave. (bet. South & Spring Sts.) | 516-922-3614 | www.canterburyalesrestaurant.com

You can "learn about Oyster Bay history" in the "vibrant", "pubby" surroundings of this rustic American with "walls covered in artifacts" and "photos of Teddy Roosevelt" (who "lived up the road at Sagamore Hill"); the "classic tavern fare" satisfies with "fresh local seafood" and "fantastic" beers, and despite sometimes "uneven" table service, the staff is full of "warmth"; P.S. it's a "bargain" Monday–Tuesday when all bottles of wine are half-price with dinner.

Caracalla Ristorante ☒ *Italian*

| 23 | 17 | 24 | $59 |

Syosset | 102 Jericho Tpke. (bet. Michael & Oak Drs.) | 516-496-3838

Customers tout the "top-of-the-line" cuisine at this Syosset Italian, a Roman-decorated palace of pasta bolstered by a 400-bottle wine list; it's a bit "stuffy" and certainly "not cheap", but some savor the "nostalgia" as well as the "elegant service", advising it's "well worth a visit."

NEW Caracara Mexican Grill *Mexican*

| - | - | - | M |

Farmingdale | 354 Main St. (bet. Conklin & Prospect Sts.) | 516-777-2272 | www.caracaramex.com

Colorful Warhol-like portraits of Mexican artist Frida Kahlo, flickering lights in wall niches, and a tin ceiling make for a romantic setting at this Farmingdale newcomer, where an upscale Mexican menu includes the likes of short ribs slow-cooked in Dos Equis beer; an extensive tequila selection adds to the vibe, as does live music some nights.

Carnival ● *Italian*

| 22 | 16 | 19 | $33 |

Port Jefferson Station | 4900 Nesconset Hwy. (Terryville Rd.) | 631-473-9772 | www.carnivalrestaurant.net

"Don't be fooled by the strip-mall location" because this "informal", family-owned Southern Italian in Port Jefferson Station proffers an "enormous" menu of "fabulous pastas", "mouthwatering" specials and "excellent" pizza (from the front counter) in portions so "humongous" "no one leaves without leftovers"; it's "hard to get in on the weekends" and the "acoustics need improvement", but "fair prices" help soften the edges.

Carrabba's Italian Grill Italian   19 | 19 | 21 | $30

Central Islip | 20 N. Research Pl. (Carleton Ave.) | 631-232-1070
Smithtown | 730 Smithtown Bypass (bet. Southern Blvd. & Terry Rd.) | 631-265-1304
www.carrabbas.com

"Outback goes to Rome" at this "energetic" sister-chain that "satisfies a craving for Italian", providing "solid", "generous" dishes amid "busy", sometimes "raucous" Central Islip and Smithtown settings tended by an "accommodating" staff; while detractors maintain it's "run-of-the-mill" and "hardly authentic", if you "keep your expectations reasonable", it's a "good-value" option.

Caruso's Italian   ▽ 23 | 15 | 20 | $33

Rocky Point | 41 Broadway (Rte. 25A) | 631-744-1117 | www.carusosrestaurant.com

Whether you "stop in for a quick slice" or have a "delicious" dinner in the "great outdoor area" warmed by a fire pit, this "local" Rocky Point Italian by chef/co-owner Wayne Wadington (La Plage) is a "pleasant surprise"; the interior's "a little dull", but "affordable" tabs and a "steady" staff that "couldn't be nicer" win over most diners.

Casa Luis Ⓜ Spanish   22 | 13 | 21 | $38

Smithtown | 1033 Jericho Tpke. (Cornell Dr.) | 631-543-4656 | www.casaluis.us

Take a "mini-trip to Spain" at this "convivial", "family-owned" eatery in Smithtown, where "long waits for a table" attest to the "wonderful paellas", "best-around" green sauce dishes and "great sangria"; more than a few take jabs at the tightly packed, "tired" surroundings that look like they "haven't changed" in 20 years, but more praise owners who "outdo themselves making everyone feel welcome."

Casa Rustica Italian   25 | 21 | 25 | $52

Smithtown | 175 W. Main St. (bet. Edgewood Ave. & Elliot Pl.) | 631-265-9265 | www.casarustica.net

Its reputation as "one of Suffolk's best" is "well-deserved" declare devotees of this Smithtown "favorite" serving "amazing" Italian "the way it should be" (the seasonal lobster in cognac butter sauce will "rock your world"); renovations "added charm" to the "old-fashioned", villa-style interior, and the "formal" service is "professional and caring", so even though it's a "tad expensive", many visit "as frequently as their budget allows."

Catfish Max American/Seafood   21 | 14 | 20 | $41

Seaford | 3681 Naomi St. (Ocean Ave.) | 516-679-2020 | www.catfishmax.com

A "sweet little treasure on a hot summer night", this "funky", "hard-to-find" New American seafooder is "best when you can sit by the water" "watching the boats dock" at Seaford Harbor; despite its "dumpy" looks, patrons praise the "hip", "imaginative specials" that "go a step beyond the usual" and a bar that "feels like it's served many old salts over the years."

Cattlemen's Steakhouse & Saloon *Steak* 19 | 17 | 18 | $35

Lindenhurst | 127 Montauk Hwy. (S. Wellwood Ave.) | 631-991-3542
Port Jefferson Station | 650 Patchogue Rd. (bet. Oakland & Wykoff Aves.) | 631-509-5130
www.cattlemenssteak.com

"You're back in the old West" at this "casual" Lindenhurst chophouse (with a Port Jefferson sidekick), a "family-friendly" beef barn where "congenial", "cowboy"-attired staffers serve "big slabs" of steak at a "low cost"; alas, more ornery types brand it "quantity over quality."

Cedar Creek American Bar & Grill *American* - | - | - | M

Glen Cove | 75 Cedar Swamp Rd. (bet. 2nd & 4th Sts.) | 516-656-5656 | www.cedarcreekli.com

Small and large plates are on the midpriced menu at this Glen Cove American bistro from the owners of Bayville's Mill Creek Tavern, where dishes run the gamut from warm homemade chips with blue-cheese fondue to crispy bluefin tuna; the warm setting in walnut wood and cream tones offers booth and table seating, and there's also a bar and a large brick patio.

☑ Chachama Grill *American* 27 | 21 | 27 | $52

East Patchogue | Swan Nursery Commons | 655 Montauk Hwy. (S. Country Rd.) | 631-758-7640 | www.chachamagrill.com

"Star" chef Elmer Rubio crafts "marvelous" New American meals at this "exciting", "Manhattan-type restaurant in a most unlikely location" (an otherwise "dreary" strip mall) in East Patchogue; once inside, you'll "enter another world where one dish is better than the next" and they're all "beautifully served" by a "considerate" staff that "makes you feel every day is a celebration", so it's always a "winner"; P.S. the $26 prix fixe is one of the "biggest bargains on LI."

Chadwicks at the Station *American/Continental* 22 | 21 | 23 | $41

Rockville Centre | 49 Front St. (bet. Clinton & N. Park Aves.) | 516-766-7800 | www.chadwicksli.com

There's "lots of competition in Rockville Centre for this style" of up-scale American-Continental cuisine, but this "underrated" stop "right across from the train station" is a "quiet", "comfortable" alternative to the bustling strip; there's "something for everyone", from signature rack of lamb to "fabulous" salads, the staff "makes you feel at home" and to seal the deal, "you can always get a table."

Chalet Restaurant & Lounge ◕ *American/Eclectic* ▽ 18 | 20 | 18 | $36

Roslyn | 1 Railroad Ave. (bet. Roslyn Rd. & Warner Ave.) | 516-621-7975 | www.roslynchalet.com

A "favorite with the railroad crowd after work" and the place "to be if it's after 11 PM and you're under 40", this loungey American-

Eclectic in Roslyn is known for its "upbeat" vibe and "late-night drinks"; still, the food is "surprisingly decent", especially the "great burger", and the white-toned decor has a refreshingly "un–Long Island" feel, particularly in summer when the upper deck is "the main attraction."

Chat Noir French/Tea Room
21	21	19	$28

Rockville Centre | 230 Merrick Rd. (bet. S. Park & Village Aves.) | 516-208-8521 | www.chatnoirtea.com

A "nice quiet retreat" decked in "French country" decor, this "unique" addition to the Rockville Centre scene does "decadent afternoon tea" – featuring "exquisite table settings" and "the best scones I've ever tasted" – then transforms into a "quaint" bistro for dinner; though a few feel it's "overpriced" and the service "needs help", it's often the perfect brew for "girlie" groups and the "carriage crowd"; P.S. closes at 5 PM Monday–Tuesday, 9 PM Sunday.

☑ Cheesecake Factory American
20	19	18	$30

Westbury | Mall at the Source | 1504 Old Country Rd. (Merchants Concourse) | 516-222-5500 ●

Huntington Station | Walt Whitman Mall | 160 Walt Whitman Rd. (Weston St.) | 631-271-8200

Lake Grove | Smith Haven Mall | 610 Smith Haven Mall (bet. Middle Country Rd. & Nesconset Hwy.) | 631-361-6600 www.thecheesecakefactory.com

"Humongous portions and humongous lines" characterize this American chain where the "textbook"-size menu offers "lots of choices" and a "broad price spectrum" to keep families "stuffed and happy"; the "herd 'em in, herd 'em out" feel isn't for everyone and critics knock "mass-produced" fare and "overdone" decor, but overall it's a "crowd-pleaser", especially when it comes to the "amazing" namesake dessert – even if you need to "take it home for much later."

Chefs of New York Italian/Pizza
19	12	19	$23

East Northport | 508 Larkfield Rd. (Clay Pitts Rd.) | 631-368-3156 | www.chefsny.com

"When you don't feel like cooking", this "little" East Northport Italian hits the spot with "consistently good" dishes and a "variety" of "delectable" pies, including a spinach pizza so memorable it was featured on the Food Network; "huge portions" at "low prices" and a "personable" staff help make up for the "typical back-of-a-pizzeria" set-up.

Chequit Inn American/Eclectic
19	18	19	$42

Shelter Island Heights | Chequit Inn | 23 Grand Ave. (Waverly Pl.) | 631-749-0018 | www.shelterislandinns.com

The "tasty", "not outstanding" but "more than ok" American-Eclectic fare at this "historic" Shelter Island Heights inn is most enjoyable when lunching on the "flower-surrounded" patio or having dinner on the porch, where you can "watch the sun go down over the harbor"; service is "not particularly polished" but "pleasant" enough as diners take in the sights on this "beautiful little island."

Chez Kama ◪ *Continental/Japanese* ▽ 25 | 18 | 22 | $45

Great Neck | 77 Middle Neck Rd. (bet. Cedar Dr. & Grace Ave.) |
516-482-8360

An "unusual mix" of dishes sets apart this "small" Japanese-Continental in Great Neck, offering "superb sushi", "delicious" LI duck and other "impeccable" items; "warm, inviting" service lends a "homey" feel to the "no-frills" room, but since it often gets "packed", be sure to "make reservations."

❷ Chez Noëlle ◪ *French* 27 | 19 | 25 | $55

Port Washington | 34 Willowdale Ave. (S. Bayles Ave.) |
516-883-3191 | www.cheznoellerestaurant.com

"Aging gracefully", this "old-fashioned French" in Port Washington is a "rare find" that "sticks to the basics and succeeds", attracting "well-dressed" guests who "appreciate" the "classic", "melt-in-your-mouth" cuisine, "gracious" greetings and the "owner's droll humor"; the "greatly improved", renovated setting boasts tables spaced out enough to "enjoy conversations", and though prices are "steep" (unless you go for the "bargain prix fixe"), it's worthy of a "special night."

Chi ◪ *Chinese/Eclectic* ▽ 25 | 23 | 24 | $47

Westbury | 103 Post Ave. (bet. Lexington & Madison Aves.) |
516-385-3795 | www.chidininglounge.com

"Amped-up" Chinese-Eclectic dishes go well with the signature martinis, energetic DJ sets and "sleek" decor awash in oranges and golds at this Westbury lounge that's "surprisingly" "excellent all around"; apart from the off-hours when it feels a bit "empty", it's a "great place to chill" or "meet up with a chick", if you can handle the spendy scene.

Chicken Coop *Colombian* - | - | - | I

Valley Stream | 159 Rockaway Ave. (W. Valley Stream Blvd.) |
516-568-2667

Peckish patrons have lots to choose from at this affordable Columbian cafe in Valley Stream where specialty *pollo a la brasa* (rotisserie chicken) just scratches the surface of a menu offering regional classics including seafood casserole and daily specials such as meatball soup; the casual setting is decked out in ceramics and giant cutlery, and a full bar adds to the cheerful vibe.

Chicken Kebab *Greek/Turkish* 21 | 10 | 17 | $25

Roslyn Heights | 92 Mineola Ave. (Elm St.) | 516-621-6828 |
www.chickenkebab.com

"Fast, tasty and cheap" Greek-Turkish eats (like a "delicious" chicken gyro) draw "lines out the door" of this Roslyn Heights "neighborhood" grill; there's "not much atmosphere", "terrible parking" and "too many kids", but "you know what you're getting" and it's a "solid value for your dining dollar."

Chipotle *Mexican* 20 | 12 | 16 | $13

Carle Place | 135 Old Country Rd. (Meadowbrook State Pkwy.) |
516-877-7720
Farmingdale | 901 Broad Hollow Rd. (Rte. 109) | 631-845-4598

(continued)

Chipotle

Great Neck | 44 Great Neck Rd. (S. Middle Neck Rd.) | 516-467-0505
Hempstead | 1166 Hempstead Tpke. (Glenn Curtiss Blvd.) | 516-483-1026
Hicksville | 215 N. Broadway (bet. Bethpage Rd. & John St.) | 516-822-4074
Mineola | 530 Jericho Tpke. (Herricks Rd.) | 516-294-0709
Deer Park | Tanger Outlets at The Arches | 1090 The Arches Circle (Long Island Ave.) | 631-586-0301
Hauppauge | 694 Motor Pkwy. (Long Island Expwy.) | 631-355-7073
Huntington Station | 435 Walt Whitman Rd. (Schwab Rd.) | 631-423-0127
www.chipotle.com

"Tasty", "gut-busting" burritos "custom-made for you" are the draw at this Farmingdale link in the "fresh-Mex" chain, which earns extra "respect" for its "commitment to organic ingredients" and "well-sourced" meats; the "line moves quickly" and prices are "fair", so even if the "sparse" setting is "not too comfortable", it works for "lunch or takeout."

Chop Shop *American*   24 | 24 | 23 | $43

Smithtown | 47 E. Main St. (bet. Bank & Landing Aves.) | 631-360-3383 | www.chopshopbarandgrill.com

"Well-prepared" "quality" steaks, seafood and a "mean dirty martini" are a "pleasant surprise" at this "nice" American addition to Smithtown, a sibling to Massapequa's Hudson's Mill; the "noisy", "NYC-chic" setting features low lighting and leather booths, while the "lovely" service is capped off by a chef who visits tables "during later hours"; P.S. "go early" to save money on "half-price drinks and bar food."

Cho-Sen Island *Asian/Kosher*   19 | 14 | 18 | $34

Lawrence | 367 Central Ave. (Frost Ln.) | 516-374-1199 | www.chosengarden.com

Cho-Sen Village *Asian/Kosher*

Great Neck | 505 Middle Neck Rd. (Baker Hill Rd.) | 516-504-1199 | www.cho-senvillage.com

It's "hard to believe" the "very good" Chinese food and "requisite" sushi rolls are kosher at this "family-friendly", slightly "expensive but worth it" Asian pair in Great Neck and Lawrence, where the staff helps "accommodate" special requests; even though it could use some "new decor" and "more exotic dishes", regulars who "stay with the standards" are satisfied; P.S. closed Friday–sundown Saturday.

Churrasqueira Bairrada Ⓜ *Portuguese*   25 | 15 | 22 | $34

Mineola | 144 Jericho Tpke. (Willis Ave.) | 516-739-3856 | www.churrasqueira.com

"Carnivores rejoice!" – this Mineola mecca for "meat lovers" delivers a procession of "incredible", "sizzling skewers" for a Portuguese "feast" that doesn't end "until you surrender"; the "world-class" chicken dinners also "wow", so if you don't mind the "madhouse" frenzy and "long waits", "you'll get more than you paid for" and "smooth" service to boot.

	FOOD	DECOR	SERVICE	COST

Ciao Baby *Italian* | 20 | 18 | 19 | $37 |

Massapequa Park | 50-74 Sunrise Hwy. (Block Blvd.) | 516-799-5200
Commack | Mayfair Shopping Ctr. | 204 Jericho Tpke. (Harned Rd.) |
631-543-1400
www.ciaobabyrestaurant.com
You'll have to "wear elastic pants" or bring an "entire football team"
to share the "monstrous plates" at this "loud", "family-style" Italian
duo in Commack and Massapequa Park that's "affordable" and fairly
"decent" but draws mixed reviews; the "Sinatra-era" theme is either
"cheesy" or just plain "fun" depending on the diner, and while some
find the service "too chummy", it's all part of the "schtick."

Cielo Ristorante Italiano Ⓜ *Italian* | 20 | 19 | 22 | $43 |

Rockville Centre | 208 Sunrise Hwy. (bet. N. Park & N. Village Aves.) |
516-678-1996 | www.cieloristorante.com
Admirers of this "enjoyable" Rockville Centre Italian tout the "traditional", "beautifully presented" offerings from the old country, "professional" service and "comforting" Tuscan-inspired decor with
columns and warm sunset tones; though a few feel it's "a little
stuffy" and "needs more variety", it's a primo place for a "quiet dinner" by the fireplace, and early-bird and midweek specials help tem-
per sometimes "pricey" tabs.

Cinelli's Pizzeria & Grill *Italian* | 18 | 14 | 19 | $26 |

Oceanside | 156 Davison Ave. (Oceanside Rd.) | 516-678-9494 |
www.cinellisoceanside.com
Cinelli's Pizzeria & Restaurant *Italian*
Franklin Square | 1195 Hempstead Tpke. (Doris Ave.) | 516-352-2204 |
www.cinellis.com
The original Franklin Square branch of this pizzeria pair turns out
"consistently good" pies, pastas and panini, while the separately
owned Oceanside offshoot adds rarely seen *piada* flatbreads to the
"basic Italian menu"; there's "nothing fancy" to be found at either, so
many opt to get the goods "hot on delivery."

Cipollini *Italian* | 21 | 21 | 20 | $49 |

Manhasset | The Americana | 2110C Northern Blvd. (Searingtown Rd.) |
516-627-7172 | www.cipollinirestaurant.com
"Manhasset's glitterati disembark from their Maseratis" for
"fabulous outdoor dining" (indoors too) at this "elegant" "see-and-
be-scenester" in The Americana, where the "terrific" Italian food,
including "brick-oven thin-crust pizza", often plays second fiddle to
the "latest nose jobs" among "dressed-to-the-nines" "ladies who
lunch"; the "wonderful bar" becomes a "major hook-up spot"
come evening (Thursdays are a "must-see"), and even though
service is mixed, the staff generally "takes care of singles" and
other "blingy" "regulars."

Circa Ristorante Enoteca *Italian* | 22 | 22 | 20 | $42 |

Mineola | Birchwood Plaza | 348 E. Jericho Tpke. (Jay Ct.) | 516-280-2234
This "beautiful" Mineola Italian with "NYC-style" sophistication
shines inside its otherwise bland "strip-mall locale", attracting a "vi-

brant" crowd with its "tasty", sometimes "ambitious" cuisine; when "tables are tight" on busy weekends, head to the "great" granite bar to enjoy the "daily specials" and nearly 300 wines from around the globe; P.S. the prix fixe lunch offers the "best value."

Cirella's Continental/Italian
21 | 16 | 19 | $37

Melville | 14 Broadhollow Rd. (Arlington St.) | 631-385-7380

Cirella's at Saks Fifth Avenue American/Eclectic

Huntington Station | Saks Fifth Avenue, Walt Whitman Mall | 230 Walt Whitman Rd. (Weston St.) | 631-350-1229
www.cirellarestaurant.com

"Everyone's treated like a regular" at this "long-standing" Melville "favorite", where "ample" servings of "consistently" *fabuloso* Northern Italian and Continental "comfort food" (and sushi too) keep the room "crowded" and "noisy"; mall-walkers maintain the maki and other "tasty" American-Eclectic eats at its Saks spin-off are "the only bargains" in the store.

Ciro's Italian Restaurant Italian
22 | 18 | 22 | $32

NEW **Hauppauge** | 470 Wheeler Rd. (Rabro Dr.) | 631-761-6378

Kings Park | 74 Main St. (bet. Church St. & Pulaski Rd.) | 631-269-2600
www.cirosrestaurants.com

"Accommodating" owners keep this Kings Park "neighborhood gem" full of "repeat customers" chowing down on "generous portions" of "consistent", "grandma-style" Italian food; regulars say the setting is "much improved since they moved" "up the road" to "delightful", "larger quarters", and the midweek specials are "a great buy"; P.S. a Hauppauge branch opened post-Survey.

Cittanuova Italian
20 | 18 | 18 | $44

East Hampton | 29 Newtown Ln. (bet. Main St. & Park Pl.) | 631-324-6300 | www.cittanuova.com

The "burgers are applause-worthy" and the rest is "quite good" at this "cool", "Euro-style" Italian "in the heart of East Hampton" that's ideal for "people-watching" from "summer sidewalk tables", catching a "game at the bar" or stopping for gelato "after a movie"; even though service can be "spotty" and the "scene" is too much for some, it's a "fairly priced" "crowd-pleaser" where you just might sit next to a celebrity.

City Cellar
Wine Bar & Grill American
21 | 23 | 20 | $41

Westbury | 1080 Corporate Dr. (bet. Ellison Ave. & Zeckendorf Blvd.) | 516-693-5400 | www.citycellarny.com

"Attractive" and "modern", this Westbury New American is dominated by a glass-enclosed wine cellar with 500 labels "stacked high in the sky" over the "vibrant" bar and "cavernous" dining room; the "diverse", "something for everyone" menu ranges from "crispy" brick-oven pizzas to steaks and seafood, and even if the "charming" service can be "inconsistent", that doesn't deter fans who "love" the lunch and vino specials.

	FOOD	DECOR	SERVICE	COST

Clam Bar at Napeague ⊘ *Seafood*   21 | 12 | 16 | $32

Amagansett | 2025 Montauk Hwy. (on Napeague Stretch) |
631-267-6348 | www.clambaronline.com

"There's something about" this "laid-back" Amagansett seasonal
seafood shack on the "side of the road" that "brings you back year
after year"; maybe it's the "darn wonderful lobster rolls", "fab chowders" and "fresh clams" served on "paper plates", or perhaps it's the
"lively", "good-looking crowd" (with the "occasional big celeb");
whatever it is, even those who "hate the road view" say "summer
wouldn't be complete without several trips" here.

Claudio's   *American/Continental*   16 | 16 | 17 | $40

Greenport | 111 Main St. (bet. Front St. & Greenport Harbor) |
631-477-0627 | www.claudios.com

A Greenport "legend" (since 1870), this seasonal American-
Continental "seafood shanty" offers multiple dining options, from
white-tablecloth rooms to an "antique" bar to "hot" waterfront tables with "beautiful views" and "live bands" providing a "party, party
on the weekends"; the food is "underwhelming" and "overpriced",
and the service "so-so", but it's a "treat" to "bask in the sun" and
soak in the "fun drinking atmosphere with a dock."

Cliff's Elbow Room   *Steak*   22 | 11 | 19 | $38

Jamesport | 1549 Main Rd. (S. Jamesport Ave.) | 631-722-3292
Cliff's Elbow Too Ⓜ *Steak*
Laurel | 1085 Franklinville Rd. (off Main Rd.) | 631-298-3262
Cliff's Rendezvous   *Steak*
Riverhead | 313 E. Main St. (Maple Ave.) | 631-727-6880
www.elbowroomli.com

This "aptly named, iconic" chophouse trio offers "delish" "marinated steaks" that "cut like butta", presented with a "smile" by longtime waitresses "who know their stuff"; sure, the "closet-sized"
rooms could use a "facelift", but since they're one of the "best values" around, look out for "inevitable waits on summer Saturday
nights"; P.S. reservations accepted only in Jamesport.

Clubhouse, The   *Steak*   21 | 17 | 22 | $55

Huntington | 320 W. Jericho Tpke. (Hills Rd.) | 631-423-1155 |
www.clubhousesteaks.com

A "diamond in the rough", this Huntington steakhouse is a "well-
kept secret" for "fine" cuts of beef, including an "excellent porterhouse for two", served by an "unpretentious", "hospitable" staff; a
few critics contend it offers "more sizzle than steak" and the "too-
dark" interior "needs refurbishment", but the "terrific specials" and
"late-night bar scene" help keep it "popular."

Coach Grill & Tavern   *American*   22 | 13 | 21 | $42

Oyster Bay | 22 Pine Hollow Rd. (bet. High St. & Lexington Ave.) |
516-624-0900 | www.coachgrillandtavern.com

A "perfect example of a great neighborhood pub" that's also a "family
place", this Oyster Bay New American "consistently" turns out
"good chow" with some "superb" standouts ("terrific duck"); it has

a "simple", "bar-and-grill atmosphere" tended by a staff that's "always willing to make diners happy", along with a "friendly host" who shares "fascinating stories."

Coast Grill *American/Seafood*

22 | 16 | 20 | $51

Southampton | 1109 Noyac Rd. (Turtle Pond Rd.) | 631-283-2277 | www.thecoastgrill.com

New owners Brian and Stacy Cheewing have "spruced up" this Southampton American on the harbor, highlighting "wonderfully prepared" seafood in a redone "contemporary" setting that "feels more like a proper eatery and less like a fish camp"; with "welcoming" service to boot, no wonder it wins votes for "best comeback" of the year; P.S. hours are seasonal, so call ahead.

NEW Cody's BBQ & Grill *BBQ*

- | - | - | M

Riverhead | 65 E. Main St. (Peconic Ave.) | 631-284-9520 | www.codysbbq.com

It's like the movie set of an old Western at this Main Street, Riverhead BBQ where wagon wheels, cow horns and a wall-sized mural of Buffalo Bill Cody riding a bull are the backdrop for a midpriced roundup of everything from a sandwich of grilled mac 'n' cheese with pulled pork to steak; roomy indoor and outdoor bars spur on the laid-back vibe, and there's Saturday night line-dancing to boot.

Colbeh *Persian*

21 | 17 | 19 | $42

Great Neck | Andrew Hotel | 75 N. Station Plaza (Barstow Rd.) | 516-466-8181
Roslyn Estates | 1 The Intervale (Warner Ave.) | 516-621-2200
www.colbeh.com

Experience an "adventure for the palate" at this kosher Persian pair (with two NYC branches) where the "amazing selection" of dishes provides a "taste of the Middle East" in "lovely, muted" surroundings (with a "more intimate", "romantic" feel in Roslyn Estates than Great Neck); it's "a little pricey" but "reasonable" considering the "plentiful" plates and "delicious freebies brought to the table" by an "amiable" staff; P.S. closes after sundown Friday and reopens Saturday night.

Comtesse Thérèse Bistro Ⓜ *French*

- | - | - | E

Aquebogue | 739 Main Rd. (Church Ln.) | 631-779-2800 | www.comtessetherese.com

Both the tasting room for Comtesse Thérèse vineyard and a French bistro spotlighting local ingredients (some from an on-site garden) are situated in this 1830s Aquebogue house; chef Arie Pavlou turns out classics such as escargots and lamb-shank confit with Madeira sauce, and it's all served in a cozy setting complete with needlepoint rugs, a tin ceiling and local art on the walls.

Cookroom, The *American*

- | - | - | I

Middle Island | 25 Middle Country Rd. (bet. Wellington & Westfield Rds.) | 631-696-4260 | www.thecookroomrestaurant.com

This old-fashioned Middle Island diner evokes a Norman Rockwell painting with its long counter, round stools and booths covered in

Naugahyde, making an unassuming setting for wallet-friendly daytime meals; breakfast specialties include oat pancakes with apples and walnuts, and double dipped, stuffed French toast with caramelized bananas, while lunch brings sandwiches and burgers, as well as homemade soups; P.S. open 7 AM to 2:30 PM, closed Tuesdays.

⊠ Coolfish *Seafood*   24 | 22 | 22 | $50

Syosset | North Shore Atrium | 6800 Jericho Tpke. (Michael Dr.) | 516-921-3250 | www.tomschaudel.com

Fin fans flip for the "sublime seafood" at this "casual-chic" Syosset fish house, a "slam dunk" by chef-owner Tom Schaudel, who brings "a little glamour", "solid" service and a variety of "fabulous", "innovative" creations (including "surprising" desserts) to a "tasteful" space buried within an office park; though it can get "costly", you "can't beat the prix fixe", plus a lighter menu is available at the bar.

Cooperage Inn *American/Continental*   22 | 23 | 22 | $43

Baiting Hollow | 2218 Sound Ave. (bet. Edwards & National Blvds.) | 631-727-8994 | www.cooperageinn.com

Guests of this "quaint" year-rounder in Baiting Hollow "applaud" its American-Continental cuisine that "takes advantage of the bounty of the surrounding farms and vineyards"; a few critics feel it's merely "ok" for the price, but most agree the "pretty" dining rooms with an "old-world" atmosphere and "polite" service create an "inviting setting for the brunch buffet or a romantic dinner", "especially around the holidays"; P.S. reservations recommended.

Copa Wine Bar & Tapas ● *Spanish*   ▽ 20 | 18 | 19 | $50

Bridgehampton | 95 School St. (Montauk Hwy.) | 631-613-6469 | www.copawineandtapas.com

Offering "tasty", high-end tapas and entrees complemented by a "large" selection of vino (and served late), this Spanish wine bar in Bridgehampton is a "nice addition to the scene"; the "cool, relaxed atmosphere", with a zinc-topped bar, skylights and "friendly" service, makes it all the more "fun to go with a group and share a bunch of dishes" – just know that "when it's busy, it's an acoustic nightmare."

⊠ Country House, The *American*   23 | 26 | 24 | $57

Stony Brook | 1175 Rte. 25A (Main St.) | 631-751-3332 | www.countryhouserestaurant.com

The "elegant" decor at this "quaint country house" (circa 1710) in Stony Brook "changes with the seasons" – they "really outdo themselves over the holidays" – and its status as a "romantic destination" is enhanced by a "charming", "professional" staff; while opinions on the "beautifully presented" New American food range from "excellent" to merely "decent" (and "expensive for what you get"), overall most are satisfied given the "relaxing", "special-occasion" atmosphere.

Cozymel's *Mexican*   17 | 17 | 17 | $27

Westbury | 1177 Corporate Dr. (Merchants Concourse) | 516-222-7010 | www.cozymels.com

Behind the Source Mall in Westbury, this chain "cantina" offers "ample" Mexican plates, "huge frozen drinks" and "tons of chips and salsa"; even if there are few surprises on the "off-the-rack" menu, the "fiesta environment" attracts the young and boisterous, while the "fast", "cheap" meals work for families and get everyone to the movies next door with time and dollars to spare.

Crabtree's
Restaurant *Continental/Mediterranean*
(aka Crabtree's)

21 | 20 | 22 | $38

Floral Park | 226 Jericho Tpke. (bet. Emerson & Hinsdale Aves.) | 516-326-7769 | www.crabtreesrestaurant.com

Gather the gang at this Floral Park Continental-Med, a "find" "if you dig great seafood", bountiful brunch and "pleasant" garden dining; in keeping with the nostalgic setting that pays homage to the *Little Rascals*, the "cordial" owner and servers are "as sweet as Darla", and "you won't be stymied by the price."

Crave 11025 *American/Vegetarian*

▽ 18 | 24 | 16 | $27

Great Neck | 68 Middle Neck Rd. (bet. Elm & Gussack Plaza) | 516-482-4800

A glossy "modern" interior with a black-and-white boutique look lends this Great Neck American-vegetarian the cachet of "hip surroundings", while the meat-free menu features a "simple" but "interesting" roster of omelets, salads, sandwiches and 'cravings' (which include pastas and fish); however, to some the service seems "a little overwhelmed."

Crew Kitchen & Bar Ⓜ *American*

24 | 22 | 24 | $51

Huntington | 134 New York Ave. (Ketewomoke Dr.) | 631-549-3338 | www.crewli.com

Fans of this reconceived, "first-class" Huntingtonian (formerly Aix en-Provence, still run by the same team) return "multiple times" for the "interesting selection" of "superb" New American dishes and bar bites; further kudos are tossed to the "good-mood" staff that "never lets a water glass go empty" as well as to an "attractive" redo of the "convivial" space; P.S. the owners also run Barney's in Locust Valley.

Crossroads Cafe *American*

22 | 14 | 20 | $39

East Northport | 26 Laurel Rd. (bet. Bellerose Ave. & LIRR) | 631-754-2000 | www.thecrossroadscafe.com

Don't judge this "local" East Northport haunt by its "gruff exterior" – it will "warm your heart" and sate your hunger with "fresh, tasteful" New American fare including "osso buco to die for"; the "cozy" confines are humble, but the "bargain" prix fixe and "lobster night" specials keep complaints in check.

Crow's Nest Ⓜ *Seafood*

▽ 19 | 17 | 17 | $44

Montauk | 4 Old West Lake Dr. (Montauk Point State Pkwy.) | 631-668-2077 | www.crowsnestmtk.com

Thanks to the "new ownership" of Manhattan hotel-bar czar Sean MacPherson, this once "dated" seasonal seafooder quartered in a Montauk inn recently "turned around" with "improved" fare served by a "helpful" staff; the "relaxing, rustic atmosphere" is now juxtaposed with "pretty people to watch", so even city slickers may find it "worth the stop."

Cull House *Seafood*

20 | 12 | 18 | $32

Sayville | 75 Terry St. (River Rd.) | 631-563-1546 | www.cullhouse.com
Sought out for "delightful" "summer seafood", including "excellent lobster specials", this year-round mainstay with a "bare-bones" but "beachy atmosphere" "near the Sayville Fire Island ferries" is the kind of "comfortable" "hangout" that's "perfect as is", even with "paper plates" and "plastic utensils"; true, a few find it "uninspired", but afishionados call it the "best bang for your buck" in town.

Curry Club *Indian*

20 | 16 | 20 | $30

NEW **Hicksville** | 96 N. Broadway (Thorman Ave.) | 516-719-2888
East Setauket | 10 Woods Corner Rd. (Nicolls Rd.) | 631-751-4845
www.curryclubli.com
Find a "true touch of India" at this "dependable" East Setauket eatery with a "terrific" $9.99 all-you-can-eat lunch buffet that's one of the "best deals" around; the "great vegetarian choices" and "courteous" service are a plus, but those who dis the "outdated decor" can just drop in for takeout; P.S. there's a new Hicksville branch.

Cuvée Bistro & Bar *French*

∇ 22 | 17 | 18 | $50

Greenport | Greenporter Hotel | 326 Front St. (4th Ave.) |
631-477-0066 | www.thegreenporter.com
"Don't overlook this Greenport bistro because of its unassuming exterior", since the "tasty" upscale French dishes made from "fresh local finds" often "impress"; with "lovely" outside dining in the summer, you can "soak up" the atmosphere over vintages from the varied by-the-glass list, and perhaps forget about the "Hamptons"-style service.

Cyril's Fish House ⊠ *Seafood*

18 | 13 | 16 | $35

Amagansett | 2167 Montauk Hwy. (on Napeague Stretch) | 631-267-7993
It's a "party on the East End" at this "casual", seasonal "local spot with character" in Amagansett that gets "packed in the evenings" with a "trendy" crowd downing "killer" "drinks in plastic" cups; owner Cyril is "a hoot" and the seafood's "fresh", but most go just to "sit outside, chill" and enjoy the "real beach feel, sans sand."

❷ Dario's ⊠ *Italian*

26 | 17 | 26 | $59

Rockville Centre | 13 N. Village Ave. (bet. Merrick Rd. & Sunrise Hwy.) |
516-255-0535
The "outstanding" Northern Italian food is "as good as it gets" at this Rockville Centre "old-schooler", leading guests to vow that if it's "served in heaven, I'll become a better person"; while it's "on the expensive side", and decor's a bit "stodgy", "gracious" "tuxedoed waiters" who "see to every request" offer an "elegant" diversion.

Dark Horse *American/Eclectic*

- | - | - | M

Riverhead | 1 E. Main St. (Peconic Ave.) | 631-208-0072 |
www.darkhorserestaurant.com
Situated on a prominent corner in the heart of Riverhead, this brasserie offers a diverse American-Eclectic menu from chef Jeffrey

Trujillo, with dishes such as lentil and potato stew and duck two ways; the high-ceilinged art deco setting features walls of windows facing Main Street, black leather banquettes and stainless-steel chairs.

Daruma of Tokyo *Japanese* — 23 | 14 | 18 | $38

Great Neck | 95 Middle Neck Rd. (Maple Dr.) | 516-466-4180
"A 25-year-old Great Neck institution", this "consistent" Japanese presents "excellent" sushi standards as well as "off-the-beaten-path choices" for moderate prices; though the "'80s" decor (including "lots of Mets paraphernalia") "needs updating" and the uneven service could use work too, it still manages to draw a "scene" – and being next to the movie theater is an "added plus."

☑ Dave's Grill *Continental/Seafood* — 27 | 18 | 23 | $61

Montauk | 468 W. Lake Dr. (bet. Flamingo Ave. & Soundview Dr.) | 631-668-9190 | www.davesgrill.com
This "cozy", "pricey" Continental "right on the docks" in Montauk "rocks the East End" with its "extensive menu" of "impeccably prepared", "tremendous seafood"; while chef Dave's "gracious" wife, Julie, is the "best hostess anywhere", the "same-day reservation policy" is a "pain" for many who insist "the odds" of getting a seat "are about the same as winning the lottery"; P.S. closed in the off-season.

Declan Quinn's *American* — ∇ 19 | 18 | 21 | $29

Bay Shore | 227 Fourth Ave. (bet. Cherry & E. Garfield Sts.) | 631-206-2006
It "can get a bit rowdy at times" at this "comfortable" pub-style American in Bay Shore, where the beach "volleyball court in back" and cover bands on the weekends keep the crowd hopping, and the 1938 setting lends a little "old-time charm"; just don't expect anything beyond "well-priced" "basic" bar fare and you won't be disappointed; P.S. it gets "packed" on Thursday 'steak and brew' nights.

Deco 1600 *American/Italian* — - | - | - | E

Plainview | Race Palace | 1600 Round Swamp Rd. (S. Service Rd.) | 516-586-6454 | www.deco1600.com
"Cool" art deco digs, "family-style" Italian dishes and an on-site OTB form a rare trifecta, but this spot at the Race Palace in Plainview makes it work with "very good" eats that range from traditional takes on veal, fish and pasta to casual American pub standards; the scene "leaves a little to be desired", but it's a safe bet for "large parties."

Dee Angelo's Pleasant Ave. Café *Italian* — ∇ 19 | 16 | 18 | $49

Westhampton Beach | 149 Main St. (Library Ave.) | 631-288-2009
"Sit outside and people-watch" at this "cute" Westhampton Beach Italian offering "comfort food" with "delicious sauces" served by a "friendly" staff; some feel it's "pricey, even for the Hamptons", though, reporting merely "ok" eats, service and atmosphere.

NEW Del Fuego *Tex-Mex* — - | - | - | M

St. James | 429 N. Country Rd. (Clinton Ave.) | 631-963-6900 | www.delfuegorestaurant.com
Situated in a little St. James strip mall, this funky, crowded Tex-Mex (a more casual sibling to Italian spots Ruvo and La Tavola) turns out

the expected tacos, burritos and other midpriced bites – but fills them with ingredients that are locally sourced; the setting includes a small bar with a tile roof plus a hodgepodge of wall art, while a selection of tequilas and housemade sangria fuel the scene.

Deli King *Deli*
19 | 10 | 16 | $24

New Hyde Park | Lake Success Shopping Ctr. | 1570 Union Tpke. (bet. Lakeville & New Hyde Park Rds.) | 516-437-8420 | www.deliking.us
"Big portions" of "old-school" kosher eats ensure that the "tasty" sandwiches aren't the only things "overstuffed" at this New Hyde Park pastrami purveyor that's reminiscent of a "true Brooklyn deli"; the "informal" digs and "appropriately grouchy" service appeal to some, but the rest report "takeout is best."

Desmond's *American*
▽ 20 | 19 | 21 | $43

Wading River | Inn at East Wind | 5720 Rte. 25A (¼ mile south of Sound Ave.) | 631-846-2335 | www.desmondsrestaurant.com
Though best known for its catered events, this dining room at the Inn at East Wind in Wading River serves a "wonderful" Sunday brunch buffet as well as other "reasonable" New American meals in a "really comfortable environment" enhanced by a pianist on weekends; lunch and dinner prix fixes are also a plus.

DiMaggio's Trattoria *Italian*
19 | 15 | 19 | $34

Port Washington | 706 Port Washington Blvd. (Davis Ave.) | 516-944-6363
Smithtown | 1012 W. Jericho Tpke. (Winston Dr.) | 631-543-6000
www.dimaggios.net
Fans of this "family favorite" for "home-run" pasta and pizza in Port Washington "love" the "charming" enclosed courtyard that's "doubled the space" and "eliminated long waits for a table"; "fair prices" and a "friendly staff" that "always greets you warmly" further explain why they "do a brisk business" here; P.S. the Smithtown branch was not surveyed.

Dish ☒ *American*
▽ 27 | 15 | 26 | $51

Water Mill | Water Mill Shoppes | 760 Montauk Hwy. (Station Rd.) | 631-726-0246
"Marvelous" and "quirky", this "tiny" BYO New American in Water Mill turns out "farm-fresh", "exciting" prix fixe menus that change "every weekend", prepared by the catering couple of Merrill Indoe and Peter Robertson; "personal service" is assured in the 12-seat space, which is "so-so" on looks but definitely one "unique experience for the Hamptons" that's "well-priced" to boot; P.S. hours vary and reservations are required (and "hard to get").

Diwan *Indian*
21 | 18 | 19 | $32

Hicksville | Patel Plaza | 415 S. Broadway (Ludy St.) | 516-513-1057
Port Washington | 37 Shore Rd. (Mill Pond Rd.) | 516-439-4200
Port Washington patrons "danced in the streets" when this branch reopened after a seven-year hiatus, joining its Hicksville cousin to offer "excellent" Indian fare delivered by a "friendly, professional" staff; the "fabulous" buffet lunch provides a "wide array of authentic

dishes" at an "economical" price, and the "view of Manhasset Bay" from the second floor at PW is a plus.

Dixie's Smokehouse *BBQ*

| - | - | - | I |

Kings Park | 12 Indian Head Rd. (bet. E. Main St. & Meadow Rd.) | 631-292-2520 | www.dixiessmokehouse.com

Budget-friendly fare includes sliders of beef, pork, chicken and crab at this Texas BBQ joint in Kings Park, where a brick wall, cowboy art and country-western soundtrack strike a casual chord; it might be somewhat hidden in a strip mall beside the railroad tracks, but a pretty patio helps make it worth seeking out.

Dock Bar & Grill, The ⊅ *Seafood*

| - | - | - | M |

Montauk | off West Lake Dr. (Montauk Docks) | 631-668-9778 | www.thedockmontauk.com

Funky and very local, this low-key saloon near the Montauk docks is both a perch for fishermen recounting the day's adventures and for locals looking for seafood fresh from the boat; dark wood lines the small rooms and regulars know the 'rules' – no checks, no credit cards, no cell phones, no screaming children – are strictly enforced.

Dockers Waterside Restaurant & Marina *Seafood/Steak*

| 20 | 24 | 18 | $49 |

East Quogue | 94 Dune Rd. (Dolphin Ln.) | 631-653-0653 | www.dockerswaterside.com

An "incomparable" view across Shinnecock Bay boasting "spectacular sunsets" is the draw at this "crowd-pleasing" East Quogue seasonal surf 'n' turfer whose "fresh", "unfussy" eats are served by "pleasant" (if "not always efficient") summer help; with frequent "live music" too, it's a "happening place" to "chill after a day at the beach" – and "if you arrive by yacht you won't mind the prices."

Dockside Bar & Grill *Seafood*

| 21 | 16 | 19 | $42 |

Sag Harbor | American Legion Bldg. | 26 Bay St. (Ryson St.) | 631-725-7100 | www.docksidesagharbor.com

"Surprisingly delicious" seafood comes with "cheery" service at this "unpretentious" Sag Harbor eatery "tucked away" in the unlikely setting of an American Legion hall; the "loud", "cramped" interior is "nothing special", but in warm weather you can "dine under umbrellas on the patio" and take in "pretty views" of boats docked in the marina.

Dodici *Italian*

| 24 | 21 | 22 | $43 |

Rockville Centre | 12 N. Park Ave. (bet. Merrick Rd. & Sunrise Hwy.) | 516-764-3000 | www.dodicirestaurant.com

This "fabulous" fixture on Rockville Centre's restaurant row "continues to hit the mark" with its "delicious" Italian dishes (including "guaranteed-to-please" wood-fired pizza), "awesome wine list" and "lovely" Tuscan atmosphere; when the weather warms, French doors swing open for sidewalk dining, a "nice touch" that lessens the "agita" from the "exceptional loudness" inside; P.S. it's easy to "spend a chunk of money" on vino, but there are affordable bottles too.

Domo Sushi *Japanese* | 21 | 21 | 22 | $33 |

East Setauket | Stop & Shop Shopping Ctr. | 180 Rte. 25A (bet. August St. & The Hills Dr.) | 631-751-2299 | www.domosushiny.com

"Terrific sushi", "imaginative rolls", "interesting appetizers" and a "nice selection of sake" at "decent prices" are enough to win "neighborhood" loyalty at this "above-average" Japanese in an East Setauket strip mall; the "wonderful staff" and modern setting are further pluses, and while a couple of critics call it "typical", most consider it a "treat."

NEW DoraNonnie 🏠Ⓜ *Asian/Italian* | - | - | - | M |

Glen Head | Bernard's Gourmet Mkt. | 716 Glen Cove Ave. (Chestnut Ave.) | 516-759-9100 | www.doranonnie.com

Bernard's Market in Glen Head has been home to various cafes, and its most ambitious eatery yet is this midpriced taparia offering up small and large plates of Italian/Asian-Fusion dishes – such as Sicilian-Asian braised short-rib sliders – prepared by chef Danny Gagnon (his grandmothers Dora and Nonnie inspired his cooking); screens separate the dining area from the store, and a tile floor, wood tables and culinary quotes along the walls create a casual ambiance.

Dosa Diner *Indian/Vegetarian* | 23 | 11 | 17 | $20 |

Hicksville | 128 Broadway (bet. Cherry & Nicholai Sts.) | 516-681-5151 | www.dosadiner.us

Even "omnivores" "love" this vegetarian South Indian in Hicksville, whose "fantastic", "inexpensive" buffet lunches, full Thali dinners and 20 varieties of "crispy", "crave"-able dosas make it an "incredible value"; as the room is "weather-beaten" at best, "forget the ambiance" and just focus on the "rewarding" fare that keeps you "full for hours"; P.S. BYO only with no corkage fee.

Downtown Burger
at Five Points Café *American/Burgers* | - | - | - | I |

Sayville | 1 Main St. (Railroad Ave.) | 631-567-5655 | www.fivepointscafe.com

Located on a five-point corner in the heart of Sayville, this burger specialist flips a variety of patties while offering inexpensive American eats including salads and sandwiches to boot; the small, casual digs feature warm rust-and-brown colors and a patio separated from the sidewalk by a low brick wall.

Duke Falcon's
Global Grill *American/Eclectic* | 22 | 18 | 21 | $39 |

Long Beach | 36 W. Park Ave. (bet. Edwards & National Blvds.) | 516-897-7000 | www.dukefalcons.com

Like a "jewel" unearthed by its namesake world-traveler, this "engaging" Eclectic–New American in Long Beach enchants fans with a "huge range" of "inventive", "alluring" creations and "quality service", all for a "modest" price; sure it's "kitschy", but "unusual" decorations from fictional journeys up the "fun" factor, while a recent expansion "adds much needed space."

	FOOD	DECOR	SERVICE	COST

Duryea's Lobster Deck ⊄ *Seafood* | 22 | 15 | 12 | $37 |

Montauk | 65 Tuthill Rd. (bet. Flamingo Ave. & Fleming Rd.) |
631-668-2410 | www.duryealobsters.com

With "one of the best waterside views on the East End", this "cash-only" "seafood shack" in Montauk is "always crowded", as much for the "beautiful sunsets" as for the "sensational" lobster and "affordable" bill (courtesy of the BYO-only policy); you'll "stand on line" to order, then nab a "picnic table" on a deck that "could use a spruce-up", but "never mind the minimalist digs", just enjoy the "briny breeze" and get cracking; P.S. closed mid-October to mid-April.

Dynasty of Port Washington *Chinese* | 20 | 15 | 20 | $28 |

Port Washington | 405 Main St. (2nd Ave.) | 516-883-4100

Standing out "in a town filled with Chinese restaurants", this Port Washington Cantonese comes through with "tasty", "classic" fare, "pleasant" service (the owner "makes the rounds") and a "lovely location" close enough to the water to "take a walk on the wharf at sunset"; there's "nothing trendy" about the "dull" decor, but the house is "always full" nonetheless, and lunch is a particularly "good deal."

East by Northeast *American/Asian* | 21 | 23 | 21 | $51 |

Montauk | Stone Lion Inn | 51 S. Edgemere St. (bet. Elwell St. & Erie Ave.) | 631-668-2872 | www.harvest2000.com

"Perfect when you're ready to leave the flip-flops behind", this "attractive", "trendy" sib to Harvest proffers "exciting" New American-Pan Asian fare (the "duck tacos are a perennial favorite") accompanied by "killer" views of Montauk's Fort Pond; even if it's "pricey", the majority "never tires" of it – just "get there early" to catch the "unbelievable sunset"; P.S. hours are seasonal.

NEW East Hampton Grill *American* | - | - | - | E |

East Hampton | 99 N. Main St. (Cedar St.) | 631-329-6666 |
www.easthamptongrill.com

Opened in the former Della Femina space by the team behind national chain Houston's, this white-tablecloth East Hampton American serves classic apps and mains, some 'locally inspired'; its fresh and airy dining room features an open kitchen, and a separate bar area with tables provides a more casual atmosphere; P.S. a terrace offers summer cocktails.

Z East Hampton Point *American* | 19 | 26 | 18 | $61 |

East Hampton | 295 Three Mile Harbor-Hog Creek Rd.
(4 mi. north of Hook Windmill) | 631-329-2800 |
www.easthamptonpoint.com

"You go for" the "drop-dead gorgeous views" of Three Mile Harbor at this "lively" East Hamptoner whose "simply prepared" New American dishes are for the most part "not special", but "decent" and "enjoyable" nonetheless; so despite "expensive" tabs and sometimes "slow" service, cares wash away with the "breathtaking" sunset, and "prices are more palatable" out on the deck; P.S. closed mid-September to April.

E. B. Elliot's ❷ *American*
18 | 18 | 18 | $38

Freeport | 23 Woodcleft Ave. (Front St.) | 516-378-8776 | www.ebelliots.com

This bi-level "Nautical Mile mainstay" in Freeport draws diners for "scenic eats" overlooking the bay or "for drinks" and "live music on the weekends"; opinions of the New American grub range from "delicious" to "pedestrian" for the price, and "service could be swifter", but regulars "go all the time" and focus on the "burgers, beers" and "views"; there's also a late-night menu served till 4 AM.

Eddie's Pizza ❷⊄ *Pizza*
21 | 7 | 17 | $21

New Hyde Park | 2048 Hillside Ave. (Marcus Ave.) | 516-354-9780 | www.eddiespizzany.com

The "renowned thin crusts" at this old-time New Hyde Park "pizza dive" will "rock your world" affirm admirers who dub the "addictive" signature pies the "best around"; you'll get "no apologies" for the "retro decor", so you can call it "a dump, but that's part of the allure."

Edgewater *Italian*
22 | 20 | 23 | $40

Hampton Bays | 295 E. Montauk Hwy. (bet. Ocean View & Valley Rds.) | 631-723-2323 | www.edgewaterrestaurant.com

Loyalists love the "huge", "luscious" plates of "creative" Italian at this "steady" seasonal Hampton Bays option where the "seafood is done to order" and the oysters are "fresh" for the "slurping"; the "lovely" interior and deck, offering "nice views" of Shinnecock Bay, "gets packed during the summer", but the staff "works hard" to run a tight ship, plus the midweek summertime early-bird is a "great value."

NEW 18 Bay *Italian*
- | - | - | E

Shelter Island | 23 N. Ferry Rd. (Duvall Rd.) | 631-749-0053 | www.18bayrestaurant.com

After shuttering in Bayville, this pricey dinner-only Italian has resurfaced on Shelter Island, offering a single prix fixe menu based on daily market finds such as locally sourced fish and produce; huge windows and a whitewashed, open dining room create an airy feel in the old Victorian house setting featuring ceiling fans; P.S. closed all of January, otherwise on Tuesdays and Wednesdays.

Elaine's Asian Bistro & Grill *Asian*
22 | 23 | 21 | $38

Great Neck | 8 Bond St. (bet. Grace Ave. & N. Station Plaza) | 516-829-8883 | www.elainesbistro.com

"Distinctive", "delectable" Pan-Asian dishes, including "fantastic sushi", stand out at this "beautiful" Great Neck "'in' place" where "charming hostess" Elaine oversees the "quality" service in a "tastefully ornate, dramatic" setting; the "Manhattan" vibe suits an "intimate dinner or meeting a group of friends", while the "reasonable" prices keep it the local "default" for many.

Elbow East *Steak*
19 | 12 | 19 | $38

Southold | 50 N. Sea Dr. (Kenney's Rd.) | 631-765-1203

"It's a little off the beaten path" and "just steps" from the beach in Southold, but the reason for bending the elbow here is the "scrump-

"tious" steaks made with their secret marinade and paired with "local wines"; there's a "summer feeling" year-round, especially in warm weather when you can drink on the deck, and tabs are moderate, so "this is where the locals eat."

El Parral *Italian/Spanish*

| 21 | 8 | 20 | $34 |

Syosset | 8 Berry Hill Rd. (Muttontown Eastwoods Rd.) | 516-921-2844 | www.elparral.com

"If you want paella" and a pitcher of the "best" sangria – or fettuccine and a carafe of Chianti – Syosset locals say this "longtime" Spanish-Italian combo is the "place to go" for "fresh", affordable fare that "doesn't disappoint"; meanwhile, the "hospitable" staff "makes every meal comfortable", even if the "outdated" decor "does the exact opposite."

El Pio *Peruvian*

| - | - | - | M |

Glen Cove | 63 Glen St. (bet. Cove & School Sts.) | 631-801-4807 | www.elpioperuvianrestaurant.com

Nestled in a little Glen Cove storefront, this moderately priced Peruvian cafe serves the expected whole rotisserie chicken while also offering more unusual choices such as Peruvian-Chinese dishes and a combination plate of regional fare; the simple decor includes paintings of South American village scenes, wall sconces and tablecloths topped with butcher paper.

Emilio's *Pizza*

| 23 | 16 | 18 | $28 |

Commack | Harrow's Shopping Ctr. | 2201 Jericho Tpke. (Ruth Blvd.) | 631-462-6267

It's "always busy for a reason" at this Commack "family destination" where there's "perfect", "crispy" pizza from the counter and a "huge variety" of "well-done" Italian dishes with "garlic, garlic and more garlic" in the back dining room; a few paesani take potshots at the "long lines", "noisy" setting and "iffy" service, but most are "prepared to wait" for the "affordable", "quality" eats.

Ernesto's East Ⓜ *Italian*

| 22 | 16 | 23 | $48 |

Glen Head | 10 Railroad Ave. (bet. Glen Head Rd. & School St.) | 516-671-7828

The "out-to-please" owners and "efficient" staff "make you feel really at home" at this Glen Head "gem" near the train station serving "old-fashioned", "authentic" (and somewhat "pricey") Italian food; the "cozy" room, with tin ceilings and an oak bar, "fills up fast", however, so "make reservations."

NEW España Tapas & Wine Bar *Spanish*

| - | - | - | M |

St. James | 655 Middle Country Rd. (Lake Ave.) | 631-656-1564 | www.espanatapasli.com

Co-owner Julio Caro (who hails from Madrid) strives for authenticity in the Spanish fare at this midpriced St. James entry, where tapas include the likes of chorizo frito (pork sausage sautéed in sherry) and the house specialty paella is made to order; a long bar dominates the front, while a large dining room beyond is adorned with white tablecloths topped with colorful placemats.

Estia's Little Kitchen *American*
23 | 13 | 20 | $40

Sag Harbor | 1615 Bridgehampton-Sag Harbor Tpke. (bet. Carroll St. & Clay Pit Rd.) | 631-725-1045 | www.estiaslittlekitchen.com

The "portions are huge" (though "not cheap") at this "peanut-sized" Sag Harbor American where "phenomenal", "garden"-fresh dishes with an "offbeat" flair (including "amazing" breakfasts) are delivered by an "attentive" crew; locals plead "don't tell anyone", but the "waits" testify the word is out; P.S. dinner served weekends only.

Ethos *Greek*
21 | 20 | 18 | $45

Great Neck | 25 Middle Neck Rd. (bet. Grace Ave. & N. Station Plaza) | 516-305-4958 | www.ethosrestaurants.com

This Great Neck Greek (with two Manhattan siblings) is noted for its "superb grilled whole fish" and "lots" of "delicious" appetizers – all offered in a "pleasant atmosphere"; so while some cite "slow" service and "NY prices", the weekday early-bird is a deal.

Fado *Portuguese*
∇ 21 | 19 | 21 | $34

Huntington | 10 New St. (Main St.) | 631-351-1010

Early word on this "small" Portuguese "tucked away on a side street" in Huntington commends an "interesting" menu featuring the "freshest calamari", *bacalhau a bras* (shredded cod) and other "winners"; lined with photos of the old country, the "attractive" space can be "quite filled", especially since most declare they'll "definitely be back."

Famous Dave's *BBQ*
19 | 16 | 18 | $27

Westbury | 1060 Corporate Dr. (bet. Ellison Ave. & Zeckendorf Blvd.) | 516-832-7300

Smithtown | 716 Smithtown Bypass (Terry Rd.) | 631-360-6490

www.famousdaves.com

The "mouthwatering" brisket and other "smoky" specialties are a "joy" at these "above-average" BBQ chain links in Smithtown and Westbury, so "don't let the fact that some of the food is served on trash-can lids turn you off"; though naysayers call them "nothing special" and knock their "kitschy" looks ("like a movie set of a Texas" joint), the "chipper" service and "fair" prices keep them a "favorite."

Fanatico *Italian*
20 | 18 | 19 | $29

Jericho | Waldbaum's Shopping Ctr. | 336 N. Broadway (bet. Burke & Scott Aves.) | 516-932-5080 | www.fanatico-restaurant.com

"Freshly made" pastas, "super-thin pizza" and other "consistently good" Italian fare at "moderate" prices make for a "crowded" scene full of "families" at this Jericho strip-mall eatery (a sibling of Emilio's, Passione Della Cucina and Pasta-eria); there's a "bright, comfortable" setting and "friendly" service, but a handful isn't sure it's worth the "long" weekend waits.

Farm Country Kitchen *American*
23 | 14 | 20 | $29

Riverhead | 513 W. Main St. (bet. Marcy & Sweezy Aves.) | 631-369-6311 | www.farmcountrykitchen.net

"Overlooking the beautiful Peconic River with paddlers" floating by, this "little old house" in Riverhead offers a "peaceful" setting for enjoying "splendid" New American dishes served by an engaging, sometimes "kooky" staff that "makes you laugh"; it's "hard to find", "parking is terrible" and the "decor needs help", but the prices are "bargain-basement", and you "feel as though you're cruising down the river"; P.S. it's BYO only.

Fatfish Wine Bar & Bistro ⊠ *Mediterranean/Seafood*

| 21 | 20 | 19 | $43 |

Bay Shore | 28 Cottage Ave. (Clinton Ave.) | 631-666-2899 | www.fatfish.info

It's "all about the water views" from the patio of this Bay Shore seafooder that's "perfect on a beautiful summer night" when the two bars are "packed" and acoustic rock is playing; the "enjoyable" fin fare pleases many, but those annoyed by "long waits" and a "fat bill" feel the "run-of-the-mill" menu "doesn't do justice" to the "sparkling" Great South Bay location; P.S. no reservations; closed in the winter.

Fatty Fish *Japanese*

| 22 | 15 | 18 | $38 |

Glen Cove | 2 Glen St. (Bridge St.) | 516-676-1823

Customers commend this Glen Cove Japanese for its "creative", "high-quality" sushi, "aromatic" dishes and "bargain bento boxes", all served with an "upscale presentation"; a few frown on the "narrow" space that's "not much to look at", but most are won over by the "exciting" food, "hip" feel and sidewalk dining in the summer.

F.H. Riley's *American*

| 23 | 18 | 22 | $32 |

Huntington | 400 New York Ave. (bet. Carver & Fairview Sts.) | 631-271-7600 | www.fhrileys.com

Benefitting from "good word-of-mouth", this usually "crowded" Huntington "local hangout" serves "ridiculously large" portions of "excellent" "pub fare" (the "best" meatloaf and fish 'n' chips) as well as refined American bistro bites including "wonderful salads" and "fantastic" gumbo; there are "no complaints" about the "pleasant" service", solid "bar scene" or pricing that works "for families", either, so patrons predict "you'll become a regular"; P.S. the $14 all-you-can-eat Sunday pasta special is a "nice treat."

Fifth Season, The *American*

| 26 | 23 | 23 | $48 |

Port Jefferson | 34 E. Broadway (bet. Main St. & Mariners Way) | 631-477-8500 | www.thefifth-season.com

"Top-notch all around", this Port Jefferson standout presents "artful", "locavore" New American cuisine served by a "caring" staff; the "warm" dining room has "beautiful" harbor views, so "sit by the windows" or "on the veranda" in summer, and offset the "high prices" with a BYO bottle – there's "no corkage fee" if it's from Long Island; P.S. closed on Mondays in winter.

56th Fighter Group *American*

| 16 | 20 | 17 | $36 |

Farmingdale | 7160 Republic Airport (Rte. 110) | 631-694-8280 | www.56thfgrestaurant.com

"Nostalgics" have a soft spot for this "World War II–themed" American eatery at Farmingdale's Republic Airport, where they can "watch the planes take off", listen to "old-time radio broadcasts" and peruse lots of "flight memorabilia"; while "families" love the "something-for-everyone" Sunday brunch buffet ("make reservations early"), modernists dis the "mediocre" "airline fare" and "spotty" service, declaring it a "kitschy", "trip back to the '40s" that's "had its day – and it's just not today."

Fishbar on the Lake *Seafood* ▽ | 18 | 13 | 16 | $45

Montauk | Gone Fishing Marina | 467 E. Lake Dr. (opp. Montauk Airport) | 631-668-6600 | www.freshlocalfish.com

"Fresh seafood shines" at this seasonal Montauker, largely a "rustic" covered deck with tables "overlooking the water"; an "anything-to-please" attitude, "fair prices" and "breathtaking views" ensure it's "crowded on weekends", though a few diners are "disappointed" with the meal; P.S. reservations taken for groups of eight or more only.

Fisherman's Catch *Seafood* 20 | 18 | 20 | $41

Point Lookout | 111 Bayside Dr. (Hewlett Ave.) | 516-670-9717 | www.fishermanscatchrestaurant.com

"Watch the boats" bring home the day's catch at this "upbeat" Point Lookout seafooder overlooking Reynolds Channel and dishing a "tasty" (though "not special") variety of marine treats; prices are modest considering the "gorgeous" waterside view, though some wish the "blah" interior would rise from its "cafeteria"-like depths.

Fishery, The *Seafood* 19 | 15 | 19 | $35

East Rockaway | 1 Main St. (Atlantic Ave.) | 516-256-7117 | www.thefishery.kpsearch.com

NEW Fishery Grill *Seafood*

Glen Head | 41 Glen Head Rd. (Oaklawn Ave.) | 516-759-0100 | www.thefisherygh.com

Just as popular for "meeting friends" as it is for cracking shells, this East Rockaway joint hooks "locals" with "great chowders" and other "decent seafood" at "favorable prices"; while some say it's "hit or miss", few take issue with the "outdoor scene", a "delight" in the summer when the "lovely" canalside patio "rocks" with live music and a "hopping" bar; P.S. the Glen Head branch opened post-Survey.

Fish Store, The Ⓜ *Seafood* - | - | - | I

Bayport | 836 Montauk Hwy. (Bayport Ave.) | 631-472-3018 | www.thefishstoreonline.com

Open since 1978, this Bayport fish store has added two small blue-and-white dining rooms complete with table service and decorated with coastal photos as a bright-and-airy setting for digging into an inexpensive lineup of fresh-from-the-counter seafood (fried, broiled or grilled) plus specialties like Blue Claw crab cakes and tortilla-crusted tilapia; outdoor seating is planned.

Ⓩ Five Guys *Burgers* 21 | 9 | 15 | $12

Hicksville | 265 N. Broadway (bet. Nevada & Princess Sts.) | 516-822-8022
Levittown | 3497 Hempstead Tpke. (bet. Jerusalem & Wantagh Aves.) | 516-796-1237

(continued)

Five Guys

Long Beach | 2 W. Park Ave. (Edwards Blvd.) | 516-431-1999
Merrick | 2099 Merrick Rd. (Hewlett Ave.) | 516-208-8601
Amityville | Bay Village Plaza | 35 Merrick Rd. (Ketcham Ave.) |
631-691-6800
🆕 **Commack** | 6546 Jericho Tpke. (Commack Rd.) | 631-858-0003
Deer Park | 1942 Deer Park Ave. (bet. Long Island Ave. & Nicolls Rd.) |
631-243-4447
Hauppauge | 601 Veterans Hwy. (Wheeler Rd.) | 631-265-0335
Huntington Station | 350 Rte. 110 (bet. Norwich St. & Schwab Rd.) |
631-271-4144
🆕 **Port Jefferson Station** | Nesconsett Shopping Ctr. | 5120
Nesconsett Hwy. (bet. Jayne Blvd. & Terryville Rd.) | 631-331-0400
www.fiveguys.com

What fans call "the best burgers on the planet" are the "big, fat, juicy" specimens "with all the trimmings" at Long Island's No. 1 Bang for the Buck, an Obama favorite also praised for fries that are "potato perfection" and free "peanuts while waiting" for your order; so even if doubters pooh-pooh "all the fuss", devotees of this "no-frills" but "fast and friendly" franchise "don't know why anyone would go to another chain."

🆕 516 American
Kitchen & Bar *American*

–	–	–	E

Syosset | 4 Berry Hill Rd. (Cold Spring Harbor Rd.) | 516-364-0516
Small and large plates of American fare are on the menu at this Syosset newcomer that replaced Moules et Frites, both from the Reststar Group (Bistro Cassis, Bistro Citron and other Long Island and NYC go-tos); a setting of creamy walls, beamed ceilings and marble-topped tables with iron pedestals gains a sense of place from vintage photos of Nassau County (area code 516) on the walls.

Foody's *BBQ/Pizza*

▽ 21	9	18	$30

Water Mill | Water Mill Shoppes | 760 Montauk Hwy. (Station Rd.) |
631-726-3663
The wood-burning grill lends a distinctive bit of "smoke" to "comfort food", including "great pizza" and BBQ selections at this Water Mill eatery by chef/co-owner Bryan Futerman (ex Nick & Toni's); "it is what it is" say some, noting an "unappealing, poorly lit" space with outdoor seating that's "almost in the parking lot", but on the plus side it's a low-cost, easy place for "families with young children."

Fork & Vine *American*

23	19	23	$51

Glen Head | 32 Railroad Ave. (bet. Prospect & School Sts.) |
516-656-3266 | www.forkandvineny.com
"Creative" "small-plate tastings" paired with "extensive wine offerings" "impress" at this "reinvented" American (fka On 3) near the Glen Head train station, geared toward a kid-free crowd; though it can get "cramped" and "loud", it's "attractive enough" with changing local artwork, Wednesday night jazz and "professional" service, plus there's a "romantic backyard garden when the weather is warm."

	FOOD	DECOR	SERVICE	COST

Fortune Wheel *Chinese*

| 22 | 10 | 15 | $26 |

Levittown | Nassau Mall | 3601 Hempstead Tpke. (Wantaugh Ave.) | 516-579-4700

If you want "authentic dim sum" that makes you feel like "you're halfway across the globe", this "hard-to-find" Levittown Chinese in the Nassau Mall is a "must-visit", though if you don't "go with someone who speaks Cantonese", "be prepared to point"; there's "absolutely no atmosphere", the service can be downright "surly" and the "always-crowded" weekends mean "long lines", but regulars insist it "rivals Chinatown" for "very respectable" eats.

Four Food
Studio Ⓢ *American*

| 21 | 24 | 19 | $50 |

Melville | 515 Broadhollow Rd. (Baylis Rd.) | 631-577-4444 | www.fourfoodstudio.com

"Modern", "eye-catching" digs, boasting four "unique" rooms representing "each season" plus a "slick", "jaw-dropping bar scene", define this "NYC-chic" Melville "hangout" for "happening" "young professionals"; the "seasonally changing" New American menu puts a "different twist on some standard fare" (plus the "cotton candy with the check" is a "perfect ending"), but the "cheeky" staff and "deafening roar" from revelers prompt some patrons to wonder if they "want to be a club or a restaurant."

490 West Ⓜ *American*

| - | - | - | E |

Carle Place | 490 Westbury Ave. (bet. Cherry Ln. & Rushmore Ave.) | 516-338-0848 | www.490west.com

Situated in the Carle Place space that was long home to Camille's, this New American is turning out fare with an eye toward local products (e.g. Long Island duck breast); the white-tablecloth setting has gold-colored walls, and a three-course early-bird is available Tuesday–Thursday and all day Sunday.

𝗡𝗘𝗪 420 North *American*

| - | - | - | VE |

Great Neck | 420 Northern Blvd. (bet. Lakeville & Merrivale Rds.) | 516-504-9690 | www.the420north.com

Artisan pizzas from a wood-burning oven are just some of the highlights on the American menu at this decidedly upscale yet casual Great Neck newcomer where steaks are aged in house; beamed ceilings, mahogany wood and an open kitchen lend character to the setting, which also features a granite bar.

Franina
Ristorante Ⓜ *Italian*

| 26 | 22 | 24 | $60 |

Syosset | 58 W. Jericho Tpke. (bet. Haskett & Oak Drs.) | 516-496-9770 | www.franina.com

"Exquisite" Italian fare sets apart this Syosset "winner" serving "classic" dishes, "intriguing specials" and "exotic" game for more adventurous types in an "inviting" Tuscan setting ("you're no longer in a little strip mall" once you step inside); as the staff is "committed to excellence and personal attention", indulging in such a "superior" experience is worth the "splurge."

Frankly Thai ⓜ *Thai*
| - | - | - | M |

Franklin Square | 959 Hempstead Tpke. (Court House Rd.) |
516-616-4393 | www.franklythai.com

An owner named Frank and a Franklin Square address are behind the
name of this Thai spot, where the unique, moderately priced menu
offers the likes of a curry potato puff with cucumber sauce and fried
chive pancakes with a sweet dip; the crimson and cinnamon-colored
walls of the little storefront setting are hung with colorful tapestries,
as well as historic Thai storytelling paintings by a local artist.

Frank's Steaks *Steak*
| 21 | 18 | 21 | $51 |

Jericho | Jericho Shopping Plaza | 4 Jericho Tpke. (Aintree Rd.) |
516-338-4595

Rockville Centre | 54 Lincoln Ave. (S. Village Ave.) | 516-536-1500
www.frankssteaks.com

Known for its "melt-in-your-mouth" Romanian skirt steak, this "refreshingly unpretentious" duo is proof "you don't need to go to the
bigger-name steakhouses" for a "good" cut of beef; the "old-school"
Rockville Centre outpost is "much less noisy" than the "busy", recently renovated Jericho branch, but both offer the same "courteous" service, "crayons on the tables for closet artists" and "upscale"
yet "reasonable" tabs.

Frederick's ⓩ *Continental*
| 23 | 17 | 23 | $48 |

Melville | 1117 Walt Whitman Rd. (bet. Arlington St. & Old Country Rd.) |
631-673-8550 | www.fredericksofli.com

The "congenial", "aim-to-please" staff "welcomes regulars and first-
timers" like they're "old friends" at this Melville Continental that
offers plenty of "cozy" comfort for "power lunches" (i.e. "expense
account dining in your grandparents' house"); most find the "classic",
"consistent" menu (beef Wellington, stuffed fillet of sole) "fantastic", even if it "hasn't changed in 25 years", but customers "bored"
by the "same old" eats and "blah" decor feel a "refurbish" is in order.

Fresco Crêperie & Café ⌿ *French*
| 23 | 14 | 20 | $18 |

Long Beach | 150 E. Park Ave. (bet. Long Beach & Riverside Blvds.) |
516-897-8097

Williston Park | 72 Hillside Ave. (bet. Broad & Cross Sts.) | 516-280-6630
www.frescocreperie.com

Turning out "marvelous" French crêpes for "any craving", this "cute
little" Long Beach cafe is perfect for a "light bite" near the board-
walk, whether it's a "sweet" dessert or more "savory" stuffing you
seek; factor in "wonderful salads", some of the "best soups in town"
and a full coffee bar, and it's a good thing the "charming respite"
takes cash only, otherwise fans fear they'd "max out" their credit
cards; P.S. a Williston Park offshoot opened post-Survey.

Fresno *American*
| 22 | 19 | 22 | $56 |

East Hampton | 8 Fresno Pl. (bet. Gingerbread Ln. & Railroad Ave.) |
631-324-8700 | www.fresnorestaurant.com

"As homey as it gets" in East Hampton, this "perennial favorite" (related to Beacon and red bar) offers "excellent" New American cui-

sine (particularly when it comes to "local fish"), "snappy" service and a "warm, clubby atmosphere" enlivened by a "hopping" bar and a "beautiful" garden with a fountain and fire pit; "fair prices" and prix fixe options are another plus, making it a "class act" all around; P.S. closed Monday–Tuesday in the off-season.

Frisky Oyster *Eclectic*

25 | 20 | 23 | $57

Greenport | 27 Front St. (bet. 1st & Main Sts.) | 631-477-4265 | www.thefriskyoyster.com

New owner Robert Beaver (chef here since 2008) crafts an "inspired" Eclectic menu that changes daily at this Greenport "hipster joint", incorporating "local ingredients" into "bright", "exceptional" dishes, while holding service to a "high standard"; so though a few diners dis the "noise" and "expensive" tabs, most praise the "chic" room with a "dynamite" atmosphere, affirming that the whole package will "wow you"; P.S. no children under the age of six permitted; closed Monday–Wednesday in the off-season.

Fulton & Prime Fish and Steakhouse *Seafood/Steak*

23 | 20 | 22 | $56

Syosset | 352 Jericho Tpke. (bet. Bruce St. & Seaford-Oyster Bay Rd.) | 516-921-1690

One of the more "understated" North Shore steakhouses, this "secret" Syosset chop shop camouflaged by a strip mall "excels" at both the surf and the turf – especially the signature porterhouse for two – setting a "relaxing" vibe that's ideal for "couples" or "the whole family"; the service is "accommodating" too, and while it's not cheap, most feel the "generous" "prime" cuts are "priced right."

NEW Fusion 84 *American*

- | - | - | VE

Sayville | 298 West Main St. (bet. Benson Ave. & Sunset Dr.) | 631-569-5104 | www.fusion84sayville.com

Both small and large plates are served at this newcomer to the Sayville scene offering upscale American bites including mini fried chicken and waffles and Thai chicken lollipops plus pricey entrees such as Chilean sea bass and panko-crusted veal; the classy, earthy-colored dining room has tablecloths, oak floors and a stone fireplace, while the casual bar area has sports TV and Wednesday night karaoke.

Galangal *Japanese/Thai*

23 | 23 | 22 | $31

Syosset | 140 Jericho Tpke. (Underhill Blvd.) | 516-682-0688 | www.galangal2.com

Surveyors are smitten with this "delightful" Syosset newcomer that boasts "superb", "artistic" Thai and Japanese dishes (including "excellent" sushi), all served with "smiles from the staff" at relatively "inexpensive" prices; the stylish dining room "dazzles" with an indoor waterfall and pool guarded over by a large Buddha statue, a perfectly "tranquil" reward for those maddened by the "hard-to-find" location behind a real-estate building.

	FOOD	DECOR	SERVICE	COST

Galleria Ristorante *Italian*   26 | 20 | 25 | $55
(fka Galleria Dominick)
Westbury | 238 Post Ave. (bet. Drexel & Winthrop Aves.) | 516-997-7373 | www.galleriaristorante.com

"Devoted patrons" can't get enough of the "wonderful" Northern Italian specialties at this "upscale" Westbury veteran, a "beautiful" escape into "old-world elegance" and a "perennial favorite" for "special occasions"; the "European feel" is enhanced by "first-class service", live piano on weekends and "personal attention" so "pleasant" that "Dominick should run a charm school."

Garden Grill *American*   21 | 23 | 22 | $40
Smithtown | 64 N. Country Rd. (bet. Judges Ln. & Main St.) | 631-265-8771 | www.thegardengrill.com

The "lovely ambiance" in a "delightful" old Victorian house with several "beautiful rooms", a fireplace and lots of "lace and candles" is the highlight of this "soothing" Smithtown American, though the "reliable", "welcoming" service runs a close second; even if the menu offers "no surprises", the dishes are "very good" and there are "fine choices" at the three-course early-bird dinners.

Gasho of Japan *Japanese/Steak*   20 | 17 | 19 | $35
Hauppauge | 356 Vanderbilt Motor Pkwy. (bet. Kennedy Dr. & Marcus Blvd.) | 631-231-3400 | www.gasho.com

"You go for the show" at this hibachi house in Hauppauge, where "the chefs try their best to make you laugh" as they "toss around pieces of shrimp" and "cook in front of you"; it's "great for family parties" and the "kids love it", but spoilsports snap that the Japanese steakhouse fare is "nothing special" and the "tired" room "needs a makeover."

George Martin *American*   22 | 19 | 21 | $43
Rockville Centre | 65 N. Park Ave. (bet. Front St. & Sunrise Hwy.) | 516-678-7272 | www.georgemartintheoriginal.com

The patriarch of the George Martin Group, this Rockville Centre "classic" ("the original and still the best") combines "creativity with quality" as it turns out "delicious" New American "comfort food" in a "convivial" setting; on weekends, expect "long waits" and a "noisy" bar scene, so visit during the week for a more "enjoyable ambiance" (and discounts on Wine Down Wednesdays).

George Martin's Grillfire *Burgers*   20 | 19 | 19 | $33
Long Beach | 152 W. Park Ave. (bet. Magnolia & National Blvds.) | 516-889-3366 | www.grillfirelongbeach.com
Merrick | 33 W. Sunrise Hwy. (Merrick Ave.) | 516-379-2222 | www.georgemartingroup.com
Rockville Centre | 13 N. Park Ave. (bet. Merrick Rd. & Sunrise Hwy.) | 516-678-1290 | www.georgemartingroup.com

There's "always something appealing on the menu" at this "friendly" trio grilling up a "great burger" and an assortment of "surefire" pub standards; kids of all ages "can't resist" the "pretzels with mustard to start" and "cotton candy at the end" (like eating "at the ballpark"), while adults delight in "moderate prices" and a "jumping" social scene.

	FOOD	DECOR	SERVICE	COST

George Martin's Strip Steak *Steak*
- | - | - | VE

Great River | 60 River Rd. (Woodhollow Rd.) | 631-650-6777 |
www.georgemartinsstripsteak.com

Situated on a country road in a shingled cottage complete with a front porch, this Great River addition to the George Martin family offers high-end steakhouse fare in a classy setting featuring leather upholstery, fireplaces and a large mural evocative of the 1920s; a large wine display at the entrance hints at house selections.

Georgica *American*
18 | 16 | 16 | $67

Wainscott | 108 Wainscott Stone Rd. (Montauk Hwy.) |
631-537-5603 | www.georgicarestaurant.com

Earning mixed reviews, this seasonal Wainscott New American, headed by "*Hell's Kitchen* graduates" Robert Hesse and Seth Levine, pleases some reviewers with its "quality" fare and "fabulous bargain" of a prix fixe (served till 7 PM on weekends), but disappoints others who find "rude" service, "outrageous" drink prices and "more of a lounge/disco than a restaurant", given the "trendy club" scene; the "exquisite" location overlooking Georgica Pond remains a powerful lure, but be warned: "it's not for mature types."

Giaccone's Pizzeria & Restaurant *Pizza*
- | - | - | I

Mineola | 124 Old Country Rd. (Willis Ave.) | 516-877-7790 |
www.giaccones.com

Popular with the lunch crowd from the nearby county courthouse, this Mineola pizzeria offers a huge selection of pies on a menu that branches out with sandwiches, burgers, pastas and such; the casual, smallish room is geared more to takeout than eating in and parking's limited, but prices are reasonable and lines are out the door.

Giulio Cesare Ristorante 🔳 *Italian*
25 | 17 | 24 | $56

Westbury | 18 Ellison Ave. (Old Country Rd.) | 516-334-2982

"Some things never change", and this "outstanding" "old favorite" in Westbury is one of them, which is fine with "regulars" who dub its "authentic" Northern Italian delicacies (including "delectable" seafood and osso buco) the "best around"; the staff ensures all are "happy and content", but beware tabs that "add up quickly" and decor as "dated" as the Roman Empire.

Golden Pear
Cafe, The *American/Coffeehouse*
18 | 11 | 14 | $21

Bridgehampton | 2426 Montauk Hwy.
(bet. Bridgehampton-Sag Harbor Tpke. & Corwith Ave.) | 631-537-1100
East Hampton | 34 Newtown Ln. (bet. Main St. & Osborne Ln.) |
631-329-1600
Sag Harbor | 111 Main St. (Spring St.) | 631-725-2270
Southampton | 99 Main St. (Nugent St.) | 631-283-8900
www.goldenpearcafe.com

This quad of East End American coffeehouses serves an "eclectic selection" of "attractive beverages and sandwiches", "decent" baked goods and soups that "hit the spot" (basically "yuppie equivalents of luncheonette" items); the spaces are "cramped" as the "subway", and the prices could leave you feeling "mugged in the Hamptons", but "superior people-watching" means "it's the scene that's golden here."

NEW Golden Temple *Chinese/Japanese*   - | - | - | M

Syosset | 417 Jericho Tpke. (bet. Cedar Swamp Rd. & Jackson Ave.) | 516-364-6476 | www.goldentempleny.com

Tucked away in a small Syosset mall, this Chinese-Japanese hybrid serves an extensive sushi menu plus specialties such as Beijing duck and a smattering of Malaysian and Thai dishes; moderate prices and colorful decor with bright jade, turquoise and purple walls add to the appeal.

Goldmine Mexican Grill *Mexican*   ▽ 21 | 10 | 15 | $14

Greenlawn | 99 Broadway (bet. Central St. & Pulaski Rd.) | 631-262-1775

Burrito fans make a beeline for "top-tier", "inexpensive" Mexican food at this Greenlawn counter-service joint with just "a few tables for eat-in"; a "bad attitude" puts off some customers, who shrug that it's squandering "so much potential", but many consider it the "best" nonetheless.

Gonzalo's American Café *American*   ▽ 21 | 13 | 19 | $26

Glen Cove | 5 School St. (Highland Rd.) | 516-656-0003

Loyalists "love" the "home-away-from-home comfort food" at this Glen Cove American "next to the movie theater" – from "always-made-fresh" soups to "kid"-friendly fare like "excellent" burgers and mac 'n' cheese; the "drab, crowded" interior "has seen better days", but the service is "friendly", it's a good "value" and there's "enough variety to make every member of the family happy."

Gosman's Dock *Seafood*   19 | 19 | 17 | $43

Montauk | 500 W. Lake Dr. (Soundview Dr.) | 631-668-5330 | www.gosmans.com

You "can see the fishing boats from your table" at this "huge" "Montauk landmark" that draws "both day-trippers and local families" for "abundant, tasty" seafood served in four dining areas, including an outdoor deck; sure, you're "paying for" the location and "it's always a wait" with no reservations and "amateur" service, but "one scrumptious bite" of those "steamed lobsters" while taking in "knockout views" and it's "worth it"; P.S. closed November–May.

Grand Lux Cafe *Eclectic*   19 | 21 | 18 | $32

Garden City | Roosevelt Field Mall | 630 Old Country Rd. (bet. Clinton Rd. & Meadowbrook Pkwy.) | 516-741-0096 | www.grandluxcafe.com

Offering "pages and pages of options" for Garden City guests, this "classier counterpart" to the Cheesecake Factory serves "nicely done" Eclectic dishes in a "loud", somewhat "over-the-top" "high-ceilinged" setting inspired by European grand cafes; portions are as "ridiculously large" as the original's (but a bit "more expensive"), so there's still "no room" for the "decadent" desserts.

| | FOOD | DECOR | SERVICE | COST |

Grasso's *American*
24 | 21 | 23 | $52

Cold Spring Harbor | 134 Main St. (bet. Elm & Poplar Pls.) |
631-367-6060 | www.grassosrestaurant.com

A "sophisticated crowd" coos over this Cold Spring Harbor "gem" for its "amazing", "creative" New American fare, "top-notch" staff and "romantic" setting with "terrace tables for hot nights"; more things to "love" include live jazz, a bar that's "easy to hang out in" and the "charming" location in a "seaside village" – just be ready for "expensive" tabs on par with the "affluent neighborhood."

Greek Village *Greek*
19 | 12 | 19 | $25

Commack | Macy's Plaza | 44 Veterans Memorial Hwy. (bet. Jericho Tpke. & Sunken Meadows Pkwy. S.) | 631-499-6590 |
www.greekvillagecommack.net

"Go for the regular standbys and you won't be disappointed" at this Greek staple that's been around "forever" (since 1980), dishing up "hearty" salads and spanakopita in a Commack shopping center; there's "no decor" in the "glorified-diner" setting, but "efficient" service and "good-value" pricing make that easy to ignore.

Green Cactus Grill *Mexican*
20 | 10 | 15 | $15

Garden City Park | 2441 Jericho Tpke. (bet. Herricks Rd. & Marcus Ave.) | 516-248-0090

Plainview | Plainview Ctr. | 397 S. Oyster Bay Rd. (Woodbury Rd.) | 516-937-3444

Rockville Centre | 288 Sunrise Hwy. (Park Ave.) | 516-536-0700

Roslyn Heights | 215 Mineola Ave. (bet. MacGregor Ave. & Powerhouse Rd.) | 516-626-3100

Wantagh | Cherrywood Shopping Ctr. | 1194 Wantagh Ave. (Jerusalem Ave.) | 516-781-4900

North Babylon | 1209 Deer Park Ave. (Woods Rd.) | 631-242-2008

Huntington | 1273 E. Jericho Tpke. (Manor Rd.) | 631-673-1010

Huntington | 318 Main St. (bet. Green & Prospect Sts.) | 631-271-8900

Oakdale | 1274 Montauk Hwy. (Oakdale-Bohemia Rd.) | 631-567-8226

Stony Brook | 1099 Rte. 25A (bet. Cedar St. & Hawkins Rd.) | 631-751-0700

www.greencactusgrill.com

Considering the "always-fresh" ingredients, "awesome fish tacos" and a fixin's free-for-all at the "self-serve" salsa bar, "what's not to like?" ask fans of this local Mexican chain; since the "brisk" counter service and "no-frills" atmosphere lack even a hint of spice, many say it's best to take your "cheap" eats "on the go."

Grey Horse Tavern Ⓜ *American*
23 | 23 | 25 | $40

Bayport | 291 Bayport Ave. (Railroad St.) | 631-472-1868 |
www.greyhorsetavern.com

"Put your money on this horse" cheer fans of this Bayport New American, a "locavore's delight" turning "organic ingredients" from LI farms into "inventive", "stylish" dishes in a 140-year-old bi-level space (a former stagecoach stop) with a "quaint bar" and "outstanding" live music on weekends; the service is "wonderful" too, so

FOOD | DECOR | SERVICE | COST

even if some dub it "pricey" for tavern fare, the rest maintains it's "completely worth every penny"; P.S. check out the family-style dinners on Sundays.

NEW Grill 454 *Steak*

- | - | - | VE

Commack | King Kullen Plaza | 88 Veterans Memorial Hwy./ Rte. 454 (Sunken Meadow Pkwy.) | 631-499-4454 | www.grill454.com

A sibling of Manhattan's A.J. Maxwell's Steakhouse, this new Commack meatery in the King Kullen Plaza offers the expected pricey roster of beef, fish and poultry, plus a lighter, less-expensive grill menu in the bar area; sepia-toned photos of Venetian canals and terraces decorate the three dining rooms.

Grill on Pantigo *American*

21 | 21 | 19 | $52

East Hampton | 203 Pantigo Rd. (bet. Maple Ln. & Patingo Pl.) | 631-329-2600 | www.thegrillonpantigo.com

Under the same owners as 1770 House, this "terrific addition to East Hampton" (in the former Wei Fun space) is open seasonally, offering an "attractive", "dependable" New American menu in a "crisp", "pretty" setting; so while the service varies (maybe it's still "shaking out the start-up kinks") and pricing's on the "fancy" side, there's universal appeal in the "bargain" prix fixe (offered every night but Saturday).

Grill Room ☒ *American*

21 | 19 | 21 | $41

Hauppauge | 160 Adams Ave. (bet. Arkay & Commerce Drs.) | 631-436-7330 | www.thegrillroomrestaurant.com

"Use your GPS" to find this "off-the-beaten path" New American in a Hauppauge office park, and you'll be treated to "surprisingly good" seasonal fare delivered by a "helpful" staff to a "business-casual" crowd; the "beautiful", "modern" setting sports an outdoor patio, "lively bar scene" and "music on the weekends" (it can get "loud"), but a few are "not overly impressed", remarking it "tries to be a city place" but only "gets as far as Queens."

Grimaldi's *Pizza*

23 | 15 | 19 | $23

Garden City | 980 Franklin Ave. (bet. 9th & 10th Sts.) | 516-294-6565 | www.grimaldisrestaurant.com

No need to stand on line in Brooklyn – the "outstanding" pies that put the famous original on the map might make you "weep" at this Garden City parlor, a bastion of brick-oven pizza fired to "pure perfection"; "red-checkered tablecloths" and a bridge-and-skyline mural color a dining room that's "nothing special" otherwise, while "lots of kids" and plenty of "big parties" keep it "bustling."

Gulf Coast Kitchen *Italian*

▽ 21 | 23 | 22 | $55

Montauk | Montauk Yacht Club Resort & Marina | 32 Star Island Rd. (W. Lake Dr.) | 631-668-3100 | www.montaukyachtclub.com

The jury's still out on this Italian at the Montauk Yacht Club: proponents praise the "fantastic" local seafood served in a "relaxing" space featuring frequent live jazz and a "great view" of the lake; a few are "disappointed" by the pricey cuisine, however, and feel it hasn't fulfilled its initial "promise"; P.S. closed December–March.

| | FOOD | DECOR | SERVICE | COST |

Haiku *Japanese*

| - | - | - | M |

Riverhead | 40 E. Main St. (bet. East & Roanoke Aves.) |
631-727-7778 | www.haikuriverhead.com

Fare from sushi to hot dishes is served in a snazzy surround featuring an arched beamed ceiling, black leather chairs and a large fish tank at this midpriced Riverhead Japanese where a wall of windows looks out on Main Street; no alcohol is served, but you're welcome to BYO.

Haiku Asian Bistro & Sushi Bar *Asian*

| 24 | 19 | 22 | $34 |

Woodbury | Woodbury Town Plaza | 8025 Jericho Tpke. (bet. S. Woods & Woodbury Rds.) | 516-584-6782 | www.haikuasianbistro.com

"They know what they're doing" at this "modern" Woodbury standout that's "worth hunting down" for its "amazing sushi" and "lots of different things to try" on a menu that veers from Japanese to Chinese to Malaysian and Thai; the "beautiful setting" (bamboo, waterfall, hanging lanterns), "helpful" service and "bargain" lunch special are further reasons its fans swing by "all the time."

Hampton Chutney Co. *Indian*

| 22 | 9 | 15 | $19 |

Amagansett | Amagansett Sq. | Main St. (Hedges Ln.) |
631-267-3131 | www.hamptonchutney.com

Dosa doyens descend on this "wholesome" counter-service "gem" in Amagansett for "tasty", "fast" Indian fare in "shabby-chic" digs (the outdoor picnic tables are a "nice touch"); "wildly popular with the yoga set", it's the type of "addictive" place "you obsess about" later.

Hampton Coffee Company *Coffeehouse*

| 19 | 13 | 18 | $19 |

Water Mill | 869 Montauk Hwy. (Davids Ln.) | 631-726-2633
Westhampton Beach | 194 Mill Rd. (Oak St.) | 631-288-4480
www.hamptoncoffeecompany.com

This East End duo proffers "high-quality" coffee ("roasted on premises") to go with "rustic" sandwiches, "delicious" scones and other sweets; the "tiny" Westhampton Beach location is the place to "catch up on village gossip", while the larger, full-service Water Mill branch is the "place to be seen on Saturday or Sunday mornings in the summer", when you can "eat in the lovely garden."

Harbor Bistro *American*

| 21 | 19 | 19 | $49 |

East Hampton | Maidstone Harbor Marina |
313 Three Mile Harbor-Hog Creek Rd. (4 mi. north of Hook Windmill) |
631-324-7300 | www.harborbistro.net

"Members of the clean-plate club" commend the "solid" New American cuisine (with some "unusual combinations") at this seasonal East Hamptoner offering "mesmerizing views" of the harbor, especially "at sunset from the terrace"; sealing the deal, the "early dinner specials" are an "incredible bargain"; P.S. Harbor Grill, a year-round, more casual branch is located down the street.

Harbor Crab *Seafood*

| 18 | 16 | 19 | $37 |

Patchogue | 116 Division St. (bet. River & West Aves.) |
631-687-2722 | www.harborcrab.com

Champions of this Patchogue seafooder "love" sitting on the "floating dock" enjoying "well-prepared" catches and "awesome drinks", especially during the "packed happy hour"; "reasonable" prices are another plus, though critical crabs complain the tiki-style decor "needs some help" and the fare is just "so-so", adding "you go for the outdoor deck, live entertainment" and "views"; P.S. "it's locally known for having the most flattering mirror in the world in the ladies' room."

Harbor Grill *American/Burgers* | - | - | - | M |

East Hampton | 367 Three Mile Harbor Rd. (Squaw Rd.) | 631-604-5290 | www.harborgrill.org

Unlike its big sister Harbor Bistro, this East Hampton cafe is open year-round, offering a midpriced menu of burgers and sandwiches, plus dinner entrees such as fish 'n' chips and gorgonzola-crusted flank steak; hardwood floors, hand-hewn ceiling beams and wainscoting make for a fittingly casual setting.

Harbor Mist *American* | ▽ 19 | 22 | 19 | $43 |

Cold Spring Harbor | 105 Harbor Rd. (off Lawrence Hill Rd.) | 631-659-3888 | www.harbormistrestaurant.com

"Breathtaking views of Cold Spring Harbor at sunset" draw diners to this two-floor New American where the "accommodating" kitchen turns out "good" fare and appealing "specials on Sundays and Mondays"; despite a hard-working staff, surveyors say the food and service sometimes "miss" and the restaurant is going through "growing pains" while the management tries to "get it together."

Harbor-Q ⊅ *BBQ* | 21 | 14 | 21 | $26 |

Port Washington | 84 Old Shore Rd. (Shore Rd.) | 516-883-4227 | www.harborq.com

Chef-owner "Keith [Dorman] is a welcome addition" to Port Washington say 'cue fans "craving the ribs", "melt-in-your-mouth" steaks and "phenomenal" housemade potato chips (plus "custom salads") at this "real-deal" BBQ "destination"; the "bare-bones", "college bar–like setting" in an old metal-shipping building is "questionable", but the "kid-friendly" service and "fast, efficient takeout" for "weekend football parties" is "right on the money."

☒ Harvest on Fort Pond ⓜ *Italian/Mediterranean* | 26 | 22 | 22 | $53 |

Montauk | 11 S. Emery St. (Euclid Ave.) | 631-668-5574 | www.harvest2000.com

Remember that "one entree feeds two", so be ready to "share" at this "sensational" Tuscan-Med serving "simply wonderful" dishes that some call "the best on the South Fork"; it's ideal for "alfresco dining on a summer evening", with a "gorgeous garden" for watching the sunset over Fort Pond, but "long waits" for a table "even with reservations" make some yearn for the "off-season"; P.S. half-portions are now available.

Heart of Portugal *Portuguese* | 20 | 16 | 20 | $39 |

Mineola | 241 Mineola Blvd. (bet. Jackson & Jefferson Aves.) | 516-742-9797 | www.heartofportugalrestaurant.com

So "authentic" it's "like eating in Lisbon", this "unpretentious" Mineola Portuguese turns out "perfect paella", "good sangria" and some excellent "wine values" to "satisfy" diners in the know; the "competent" staff is "accommodating", and while "a little change" would give the decor a lift, the "pleasant courtyard" and piano player on Saturdays "add a nice touch."

Hellenic Snack Bar & Restaurant Greek   20 | 11 | 17 | $31

East Marion | 5145 Main Rd. (bet. Maple & Shipyard Lns.) | 631-477-0138 | www.thehellenic.com

"Zorba would be proud" of this "go-to Greek" in East Marion where the "fabulous broiled fish", "divine lemonade" and other specialties are all "fresh and appetizing"; so despite the "dated" digs, the covered patio "can't be beat in the summer", and "generous" plates make it a "great value for the money"; P.S. reservations only taken for large groups; closed mid-November to mid-January.

Hemingway's American   19 | 19 | 19 | $35

Wantagh | 1885 Wantagh Ave. (bet. Brooktree Ln. & Park Ave.) | 516-781-2700 | www.hemingwaysgrill.com

Offering exactly what you'd expect from a "neighborhood pub", this "comfortable" Wantagh fixture provides a "solid" mix of New American fare so there's "something for everyone when you go with a group", complemented by "aim-to-please" service (though it's "usually a tad green") and "TVs at the bar" to "watch the game"; it's "not spectacular" by any means, but comes through with "reasonable prices" and a "great" Sunday brunch buffet.

Hideaway, The Eclectic   19 | 17 | 17 | $39

Ocean Beach | Housers Hotel, Fire Island | 785 Evergreen Walk (Bay Walk) | 631-583-8900 | www.housersfireisland.com

Sunsets seen from "outdoor tables" "overlooking the Great South Bay" are "breathtaking" at this seasonal spot in a "hidden" Ocean Beach hotel; its "upbeat" service and Eclectic lineup of "basic but fresh" seafood are "better than most" on Fire Island, but the "scenic view" remains the real bait.

Hildebrandt's Ⓜ American   19 | 13 | 19 | $21

Williston Park | 84 Hillside Ave. (bet. Roslyn Rd. & Willis Ave.) | 516-741-0608 | www.hildebrandtsrestaurant.com

Bringing back "fond memories", this seriously "old-school" soda shop in Williston Park harbors "no pretenses", just some of the "best" housemade ice cream, shakes and fountain drinks on the Island; there's "regular" American "luncheonette" grub as well, but do yourself a favor and order the "hot fudge sundae" with "real whipped cream" because "life's too short to waste on anything else."

Hinata Japanese   23 | 18 | 22 | $41

Great Neck | 6 Bond St. (Grace Ave.) | 516-829-3811

"Unique rolls" and other "excellent creations" are delivered by "efficient" servers in a "calm, quiet atmosphere" at this slightly expensive Great Neck sushi bar with an "Asian fusion" touch; add in a "hospitable owner" (offering up the occasional "sake bomb") and a decor face-lift, and it's clear why it's dubbed a "neighborhood favorite."

	FOOD	DECOR	SERVICE	COST

Homura Sushi *Japanese* ▽ 23 | 11 | 20 | $35

Williston Park | 636 Willis Ave. (bet. Fordham & Harvard Sts.) |
516-877-8128 | www.homurasushi.com

"Super-fresh, delicious" sushi – and "don't forget" the tuna pizza –
at "modest prices" makes this "friendly", "consistent" Williston
Park Japanese a "true find" for many; there's "never a long wait", but
the "semi-divey" setting means it's "best for takeout."

Honu Kitchen & Cocktails Ⓜ *American* 22 | 25 | 22 | $49

Huntington | 363 New York Ave. (bet. E. Carver & Elm Sts.) |
631-421-6900 | www.honukitchen.com

It "still has what it takes" report regulars of this "electric"
Huntington New American with "beautiful, Manhattan-style" looks
and a "fun bar" boasting "lots of pretty people" partaking in a "boisterous pick-up scene"; it's "hard to keep up" with the "constantly
changing menu", but the dishes are "tasty" (if "pricey") and the
drinks "amazing", all served by a "knowledgeable", "sexy" staff;
P.S. under new ownership post-Survey.

Horace & Sylvia's Publick House *American* 20 | 18 | 20 | $34

Babylon | 100 Deer Park Ave. (bet. Grove Pl. & Main St.) |
631-587-5081 | www.horaceandsylvia.com

"Regulars" see real improvement at this "homey" Babylon bistro
where "new owners have introduced a seasonal" New American
menu with "local ingredients" and are paying "attention to the
ambiance" in a "gastropub" kind of way; the "bar is pretty lively
on weekends", and despite some complaints of "inconsistent"
quality, most feel it's a "cut above" and appreciate the range of
"price levels" too.

Hotoke Sushi & Steakhouse *Japanese/Steak* 21 | 22 | 20 | $36

Smithtown | Village Ctr. | 41 Rte. 111 (E. Main St.) | 631-979-9222 |
www.hotokejapanese.com

A "citified" space is the backdrop for "beautiful" sushi, "distinctive" rolls and "bursts of flame from hibachis" at this "busy" midpriced Smithtown Japanese steakhouse where locals "bring the
kids and let them enjoy a free show", or else go later on for "date
night"; the "noisy" atmosphere and uneven service are sore
points for some, but others swear by the "awesome" martinis for a
"rocking" good time.

House of Dosas *Indian/Vegetarian* 25 | 9 | 20 | $19

Hicksville | 416 S. Broadway (Boehme St.) | 516-938-7517 |
www.houseofdosas.com

"Eat like a king and you'll never break the bank" at this Hicksville
South Indian offering "exceptional" dosas in sizes "you wouldn't believe", as well as other "spicy" vegetarian dishes "so rich and flavorful" you'll "forget there isn't any meat"; the "spartan interior limits
the appeal", but fortunately the "owner and staff go out of their way
to make you feel at home."

	FOOD	DECOR	SERVICE	COST

House of India Indian
21 | 15 | 20 | $30

Huntington | 256 Main St. (New York Ave.) | 631-271-0059 |
www.houseofindiarestaurant.com

"Flavorful", "filling" Indian food "prepared as hot or as mild as you want" wins over customers of this "family-run", "accommodating" subcontinental on Huntington's main drag; though the "old-fashioned" decor "lacks imagination", the "freshly made", moderately priced dishes "won't disappoint."

Houston's American
22 | 20 | 21 | $35

Garden City | Roosevelt Field Mall | 630 Old Country Rd. (bet. Clinton Rd. & Meadowbrook Pkwy.) | 516-873-1454 | www.hillstone.com

The "crème de la crème" of "grill chains", this "stylish, adult" place in Garden City delivers "properly done", midpriced American eats in a "fern bar" setting with a "happening" after-work scene; "well-informed, efficient" servers add to the "welcoming" vibe, but "long" weekend waits for a table are a drawback.

H.R. Singleton's American
18 | 18 | 19 | $33

Bethpage | 150 Hicksville Rd. (Hempstead Tpke.) | 516-731-7065 |
www.hrsingletonsrestaurant.com

Offering a "decent", "pub-style" American menu served by a "well-trained" staff, this "comfortable", "family-friendly" "neighborhood place" in Bethpage does the "basics" well, and can even be "fun on the weekends"; the meals are fairly "predictable", but the lunch prix fixe is a "great value."

H2O Seafood Grill Seafood
23 | 21 | 21 | $53

Smithtown | 215 W. Main St. (Edgewood Ave.) | 631-361-6464 |
www.h2oseafoodgrill.com

Veteran LI chef Michael Meehan offers both "classic" and "imaginative" dishes – from "stellar sushi" to "must-have" seafood crêpes – at this "charming, beachy" Smithtowner specializing in "carefully prepared" fish; there's "accommodating" service, patio seating (though "Jericho Turnpike is not very scenic") and "entertainment some nights in the bar", but some are put off by the Hamptons-level tabs.

Hudson & McCoy Seafood
18 | 19 | 16 | $43

Freeport | 340 Woodcleft Ave. (bet. Manhattan & Suffolk Sts.) |
516-868-3411 | www.hudsonmccoy.com

"With a young crowd more interested in drinking" than dining, this seasonal seafooder on Freeport's Nautical Mile gets "packed" on summer weekends when "overpowering" live bands play on the patio; upstairs, there's a "balcony view and quieter seating", but the "just ok" eats and "spotty" service strike some as "overpriced"; P.S. closed October–May.

Hudson's Mill American
22 | 22 | 21 | $43

Massapequa | 5599 Merrick Rd. (Carman Mill Rd.) | 516-799-5394 |
www.hudsonsmill.com

Massapequans high on this "inviting" New American commend its "Manhattan-quality" offerings, especially the "sensational steaks and wines" (hit the bar for "recommendations from the 'wine guy'"); its "relaxing", bistro-style interior benefits from "excellent" service and weekly live guitar, and while the prices are slightly upscale, regulars call it "reasonable" all around.

Hunan Taste *Chinese* | 22 | 16 | 19 | $35 |

Greenvale | 3 Northern Blvd. (Wellington Rd.) | 516-621-6616 | www.hunantasterestaurant.com

"Once you go, you'll definitely go back" to this "winning" Hunan "haunt" in Greenvale declare devotees of its "fairly priced" Chinese cuisine, including "terrific" Peking duck, "delicate" dumplings and "noteworthy" seafood; it's "noisy" and "crowded most of the time" and service can feel "rushed", but most affirm it's "worth the effort to get in" (especially if you "go early").

NEW Huntington Social M *American* | - | - | - | E |

Huntington | 330 New York Ave. (Main St.) | 631-923-2442 | www.huntingtonsocial.com

This quasi 1920s speakeasy – reached by climbing a set of stairs to the second-floor of a downtown Huntington building – further evokes the theme with oak floors, exposed-brick walls, a beamed ceiling and red-velvet booths, plus liquor lockers that can be leased; chef Christopher Lee (ex Aureole in NYC) serves a spendy American gastropub menu offering the likes of spice-crusted venison loin, with signature and classic cocktails to wash it all down.

Iavarone Cafe *Italian* | 21 | 14 | 19 | $33 |

New Hyde Park | Lake Success Shopping Ctr. | 1534 Union Tpke. (bet. Lakeville & New Hyde Park Rds.) | 516-488-4500 | www.iavaronecafe.com

"Home-cooked" Italian that's "always spot-on" is the attraction at this "family-run" New Hyde Park trattoria, a "definite winner" thanks to "nicely prepared" entrees and "crisp" pizza with "first-rate" toppings; situated in a "shopping center", the "busy", "diner"-esque room (behind the pizzeria) could use an "update", but service from a "cheery staff" is a plus, and so is the gourmet retail store next door.

Il Capuccino Ristorante *Italian* | 19 | 17 | 20 | $42 |

Sag Harbor | 30 Madison St. (bet. Main & Sage Sts.) | 631-725-2747 | www.ilcapuccino.com

"Trustworthy" Italian classics (complemented by "irresistible", "deadly" garlic knots) are served in a "casual" setting decorated with traditional "trappings" like "cute checkered tablecloths and Chianti bottles hanging from the ceiling" at this "old Sag Harbor fave"; even if the room "could be more pleasing", it's a "good family" place where the staff "remembers you" and prices are "decent" as well, so most guests leave "smiling."

Il Classico M *Italian* | 23 | 19 | 22 | $47 |

Massapequa Park | 4857 Merrick Rd. (bet. Cartwright & Park Blvds.) | 516-798-8496 | www.ilclassico.net

This "fabulous Northern Italian should be in NYC" praise Massapequa Park paesani who call it an "outstanding eatery masquerading as a simple neighborhood restaurant"; "personal service", "beautiful" surroundings and live music on Thursdays further elevate the up-scale experience, particularly for "special dinners and celebrations."

☒ Il Mulino New York *Italian*   27 | 23 | 25 | $77

Roslyn Estates | 1042 Northern Blvd. (bet. Cedar Path & Searingtown Rd.) | 516-621-1870 | www.ilmulino.com

"Exceptional", "abundant" Northern Italian cuisine "delivered with panache" by a "superb" staff creates an "exquisite" (if "over-the-top") experience at this "romantic" Roslyn branch of the Manhattan classic, geared toward the "LI elite"; while some patrons pout about "dim" lighting and "too much of everything" for "shockingly expensive" tabs, most don't mind splurging on the "amazing" "feast"; P.S. the Sunday prix fixe is a more "reasonable" option.

Il Villagio Trattoria *Italian*   ▽ 24 | 22 | 24 | $44

Malverne | 366 Hempstead Ave. (Arlington Ave.) | 516-792-6336

Shoehorned into a tiny "strip-mall" storefront, this "cozy" Italian ar-rival brings "delicious" food, "upscale ambiance" and "top-notch" service to Malverne; convenient to the train station, it's quickly be-come a "go-to place" for locals, though some "just wish the space were bigger."

Imperial Seoul *Japanese/Korean*   - | - | - | E

New Hyde Park | 3365 Hillside Ave. (bet. Herricks Rd. & Moore St.) | 516-741-2340

Waitresses dressed in traditional Korean billowy skirts and embroi-dered tops greet guests at this classy New Hyde Parker where the menu ranges from Japanese sushi and sashimi to Korean BBQ; the red-and-white tiled rooms are divided by bamboo stalks, with shoji screens creating small, private dining areas.

Indian Wells Tavern *American*   17 | 15 | 18 | $34

Amagansett | 177 Main St. (bet. Cozzins & Windmill Lns.) | 631-267-0400 | www.indianwellstavern.com

A "lively", "family-oriented" "locals' hangout" in Amagansett, this year-round East Ender offers "standard" but "satisfying" American tavern grub with service that's "more consistent" at lunch; even if it's a fairly "typical bar" (with "acoustics that could use some adjust-ing") the "unpretentious atmosphere" and "good prices" make it a "nice change from the chichi" competition; P.S. BYO welcome, with a $10 corkage fee.

Inlet Seafood *Seafood*   21 | 19 | 20 | $48

Montauk | 541 E. Lake Dr. (opp. Montauk Airport) | 631-668-4272 | www.inletseafood.com

"Right on the inlet", this "casual" (yet slightly "pricey") two-floor Montauk seafooder boasts "amazing" sunset views to accompany the "limited menu" of fin fare (including "great sushi") that's fresh "off the boats" of the "fishermen owners"; there's a "lovely wine list, especially from local vineyards", though "long waits" and no reser-vations are a drawback; P.S. closed January–March.

	FOOD	DECOR	SERVICE	COST

Inn Spot on the Bay ● *Eclectic/Seafood* | 19 | 21 | 19 | $53 |

Hampton Bays | 32 Lighthouse Rd. (Foster Ave.) | 631-728-1200 |
www.theinnspot.com

Bringing together "spectacular" views of the bay and "tasty" seafood-centric Eclectic fare, this "gorgeous" Hampton Bays charmer in a Victorian beach house is fit for a "romantic sunset dinner"; some critics complain of "inconsistent" food that's "not worth the price", but others are pleased with the "accommodating" kitchen and "enjoyable" setting; P.S. in winter, it's open for Thursday–Sunday dinner and weekend brunch.

NEW Insignia *Seafood/Steak* | - | - | - | VE |

Smithtown | 610 Nesconset Hwy. (Mt. Pleasant Rd.) |
631-656-8100 | www.insigniasteakhouse.com

Swaggering into Smithtown, this high-end sibling of Blackstone Steakhouse (Melville) and Rare 650 (Syosset) offers steakhouse fare plus a sushi menu in a striking space boasting 20-foot ceilings and formal dining rooms decked out in an array of wall coverings, from faux reptile and pony to an ivory-toned bas-relief of a beach scene; a horseshoe bar area leads to an outdoor patio with a fireplace, while on the second floor, the 700-bottle wine collection is on display in glassed-in rooms.

Intermezzo *Italian* | 23 | 18 | 21 | $34 |

Fort Salonga | Village Plaza | 10-12 Fort Salonga Rd. (Bread & Cheese Hollow Rd.) | 631-261-4840 | www.intermezzorestaurantny.com

It's "not just pizza" (though that is "thin-crusted" and "delicious") but "fine Italian dishes" at this "little gem tucked away in a shopping center" in the "restaurant desert of Fort Salonga"; "affordable prices" and service that "makes you feel so welcome" help offset the "small", "somewhat noisy" surroundings.

International | 18 | 9 | 17 | $20 |
Delight Cafe ⊘ *American/Diner*

Bellmore | 322 Bedford Ave. (Wilson Ave.) | 516-409-5772
Rockville Centre | 241 Sunrise Hwy. (bet. N. Park & N. Village Aves.) |
516-766-7557 ●

"Leave room for dessert" advise sweet-toothed surveyors who frequent these Bellmore and Rockville Centre diners for good old American "comfort food" and "heavenly" gelato (enough flavors to "make your head spin") scooped high on "terrific" Belgian waffles; without the sundae they're just plain vanilla in menu and atmosphere, but still do the trick for a "quick, cheap" bite; P.S. cash-only; open late on the weekends.

Irish Coffee Pub *Continental/Irish* | 23 | 22 | 23 | $41 |

East Islip | 131 Carleton Ave. (bet. Stewart & Wall Sts.) |
631-277-0007 | www.irishcoffeepub.com

"Calling it a pub is a misnomer" report regulars of this "huge" East Islip "icon" with several "warm, comfortable" dining rooms providing the "best potato soup in NY" as well as other "excellent" Continental and Irish dishes; a "well-dressed", "congenial" crowd and frequent live Irish folk music create a "party atmosphere", while "top-shelf service" ("usually with a brogue") completes the "night out in the old country"; P.S. it's a popular venue for "catered events."

Iron Skillet M⌿ *American* | - | - | - | M |

Mattituck | 730 Love Ln. (bet. Middle Rd. & Pike St.) | 631-298-1235 | www.ironskilletmattituck.com

Bob Hartz and Mary Ann Price are the passionate cooks behind this quaint 1860s Victorian farmhouse in Mattituck, where a small front room is the cozy setting for moderately priced American comfort food such as meatloaf and other housemade specialties including Sunday breakfast waffles and New York–style cheesecake; P.S. dinner is served Friday–Sunday only, and it's BYO with no credit cards accepted – plus there's an antiques sale on the lawn on some Saturdays.

Island Mermaid *American/Seafood* | 20 | 20 | 19 | $48 |

Ocean Beach | Fire Island | 780 Bay Walk (Evergreen Walk) | 631-583-8088 | www.islandmermaid.com

A "real summer tradition" for "breathtaking" sunset drinks and "creative" New American fare enjoyed on a "wonderful deck", this Ocean Beach seafooder next to the ferry basin is still a "great place to gather" after 20 years; the "friendly" "island feel" is just right for a "daycation", though a couple of patrons pooh-pooh the food as merely "ok"; P.S. there's a $39 prix fixe "Taste of Fire Island" special that includes a ferry ticket and parking.

Itgen's *Ice Cream* | - | - | - | I |

Valley Stream | 211 Rockaway Ave. (bet. E. Hawthorne & E. Jamaica Aves.) | 516-791-7444

This old-fashioned Valley Stream soda parlor and all-day luncheonette has changed little since it opened in 1967, sporting a counter with swivel stools along one wall, booths along the other and a sweet shop area up front laden with penny candy and boxes of housemade chocolates; sundaes built with homemade ice cream, syrups and toppings are the big draw, while there are breakfast items, burgers, sandwiches and platters too – all at old-timey low prices.

Ivy Cottage *American* | 23 | 19 | 21 | $46 |

Williston Park | 38 Hillside Ave. (Nassau Blvd.) | 516-877-2343 | www.ivycottagerestaurant.com

"Succulent", high-end American dishes are served in "hearty" portions at this "delightful little place" "nestled in the quaint village" of Williston Park; service is "above average" and the "snug" setting is "lovely for small gatherings", though not ideal for "accommodating large ones"; P.S. "make a reservation about a month in advance."

Izumi M *Asian* | ▽ 23 | 23 | 24 | $35 |

Bethpage | Bethpage Mktpl. | 440 N. Wantagh Ave. (Carson St.) | 516-933-7225 | www.izumifood.com

Customers give "kudos" to this Asian eatery in a Bethpage strip mall that "doesn't look like much from the outside" but puts forth

	FOOD	DECOR	SERVICE	COST

"impressively presented", "outstanding sushi" and "unique appetizers" among an array of Thai, Chinese and Japanese dishes; a "hip", "city" feel and "warm, efficient" service also help "separate it" from the competition.

Jack Halyards
American Bar & Grill *American/Seafood*

| 23 | 17 | 22 | $40 |

Oyster Bay | 62 South St. (Hamilton Ave.) | 516-922-2999 | www.jackhalyards.com

"A refreshing change" from "its previous life as Fiddleheads", this American in Oyster Bay serves "inventive", "seafood-oriented" fare in a "fixed-up" space with a nautical theme and a "welcoming" "neighborhood feel"; add an "attentive staff", "affordable" tabs and live music some nights, and most "can't wait to go back."

Jackson Hall
American Bar & Grille *American*

| - | - | - | M |

East Islip | 335 E. Main St. (Overlook Dr.) | 631-277-7100 | www.jacksonhallbarandgrille.com

Airy and handsomely designed with mahogany woods, white tablecloths and a stacked stone wall, this East Islip New American offers an extensive menu, from salads, pastas and seafood to stone-cooked pizza, as well as gluten-free items; live music on Fridays and a snazzy lineup of martinis (there's even a creamsicle rendition) tempt tipplers to stay at the inviting bar, sip and nibble on classic apps.

NEW Jack's Shack *American/Burgers*

| - | - | - | I |

Glen Head | 671 Glen Cove Ave. (Glenwood Rd.) | 516-676-7001 | www.jacksshack.com

William Jack Degel (of Uncle Jack's Steakhouses in NYC) goes casual at this Glen Head fast-fooder featuring all-natural ingredients in its affordable American menu of burgers, tacos, hot dogs and salads that can be individualized with a variety of seasonings and sauces; the save-the-environment theme includes decor touches such as wood and corrugated metal salvaged from old barns, and frying oil that gets recycled into biodiesel fuel.

NEW Jake's Steakhouse *Steak*

| - | - | - | VE |

East Meadow | 2172 Hempstead Tpke. (bet. 1st & 2nd Sts.) | 516-222-8400 | www.jakessteakhouse.com

An offshoot of the Bronx original, this pricey East Meadow newcomer serves a traditional steakhouse menu complete with raw-bar fare in its white-tablecloth setting of wainscoted walls, tin ceiling and bucolic paintings; the separate, more casual Grille Room offers the likes of sandwiches and salads, and in summer, a large covered outdoor patio will become a beer garden.

Jamesport Country Kitchen *American*

| 23 | 17 | 22 | $38 |

Jamesport | 1601 Main Rd. (Manor Ln.) | 631-722-3537 | www.northfork.com

"Relying on local produce and seafood", chef-owner Matthew Kar prepares "inspired", "sophisticated" New American dishes paired with a "wonderful selection of Long Island wines" at this "quaint" "farmhouse setting" in Jamesport; add in "pleasant" service and "reasonable" prices, and you have a "true country kitchen experience" with a bit of "big-city" expertise.

⧫ Jamesport Manor Inn Ⓜ *American*
23 | 25 | 22 | $56

Jamesport | 370 Manor Ln. (bet. Main Rd. & Sound Ave.) | 631-722-0500 | www.jamesportmanorinn.com

Inside a "beautifully reconstructed old" Jamesport manor, this "first-rate" New American by owner Matthew Kar (Jamesport Country Kitchen) provides "high-end" dishes with "unexpected" touches and a "good choice of local wines" served by a generally "courteous, competent" staff; though it's a bit "out-of-the-way", most agree it's "worth loading the GPS for", plus the "second-floor art gallery makes for an interesting diversion after your meal"; P.S. closed Tuesdays.

J&C 68 *Asian*
- | - | - | M

Farmingville | 654 Horseblock Rd. (Pommer Ave.) | 631-736-6688

Handling a hat trick of cuisines – Japanese, Chinese and Thai – this casual Farmingville Pan-Asian plies a midpriced menu running the gamut from spicy basil beef to Hunan lamb, with the owner turning out impressive rolls at a two-seater sushi bar; the unfussy setting sports compact booths and a koi-filled fish tank.

Jean Marie Patisserie & Bistro *American*
∇ 22 | 12 | 20 | $20

Great Neck | 66 Middle Neck Rd. (bet. Elm St. & Gussack Plaza) | 516-304-5439 | www.jmpb66.com

After a recent move to roomier digs in the heart of Great Neck, this "casual" bakery/cafe now underpins its "superb" pastries and "inventive sandwiches" with American bistro fare to furnish "well-prepared" "light" bites for lunch or dinner; "friendly" servers and "reasonable" prices round out a "delightful surprise", even if it's "far from real French"; P.S. the Decor score does not reflect the relocation.

NEW Jewel *American*
- | - | - | VE

Melville | Rubie Corporate Plaza | 400 Broadhollow Rd. (S. Service Rd. LIE) | 631-755-5777 | www.jewelrestaurantli.com

Chef/co-owner Tom Schaudel (A Mano, Coolfish, A Lure Chowder House) has done it again with this splashy New American ensconced in Melville's new Rubie Corporate Plaza, where the multi-room setting includes a lofty dining area with colorful glass-ball chandeliers, a waterfall-backed curvy bar, a lounge with a glass floor accented by flashing lights, and a formal white-tablecloth dining room; the pricey menu skews local and the extensive wine list is strong on Long Island bottles, plus there's a cigar and cognac room complete with a patio for those so inclined.

Jimmy Hays *Steak*
25 | 21 | 23 | $62

Island Park | 4310 Austin Blvd. (Kingston Blvd.) | 516-432-5155 | www.jimmyhayssteakhouse.com

"Don't waste gas to go to a North Shore steakhouse" when this handsome "carnivore's delight" near the beach in Island Park "delivers on all fronts", with a "professional" team serving "top-grade", "properly cooked" beef and lobster, along with "kick-ass" cocktails; a "premium price" comes with the "buzzing" "NYC ambiance", but filet fanatics don't mind forking it over for a "superb" meal.

NEW J. Michaels
Tuscan Steakhouse *Steak*

| - | - | - | VE |

Northport | 688 Ft. Salonga Rd. (Ray Pl.) | 631-651-9411 | www.jmichaelstuscansteakhouse.com

Located in a restored 19th-century house, this Northport newcomer lists a nightly roundup of steaks and chops on the blackboard, while also offering a pricey Italian menu of dishes ranging from spaghetti and meatballs to cast-iron-seared tuna *papa carlo*; warm decor touches include wood floors and umber-colored walls, and the main level features a cozy fireplace and a communal table.

NEW Joe's Crab Shack ● *Seafood*

| - | - | - | E |

Oceanside | 3555 Long Beach Rd. (Daly Blvd.) | 516-255-3705 | www.joescrabshack.com

Dropping anchor in Oceanside, this national chain link offers an array of seafood platters and steam pots, buckets of crab, plus sandwiches and such, with an eye toward local ingredients; the spacious quarters have a very casual vibe with bare wood tables set with rolls of paper towels; P.S. no reservations are accepted, and waits can be long.

John Harvard's Brew House ● *Pub Food*

| 16 | 15 | 17 | $29 |

Lake Grove | Smith Haven Mall | 2093 Smith Haven Mall (Moriches Rd.) | 631-979-2739 | www.johnharvards.com

"Terrific beer" is all you need to know about this "casual" brewpub branch in Lake Grove dispensing a "wide selection" of "craft-brewed" suds to wash down "ok" American "comfort food"; though it can "feel like a frat house" ("expect a drinking crowd"), it's perfectly "adequate" as an "after-work hangout" with "reasonable prices."

Jolly Fisherman &
Steak House Ⓜ *Seafood/Steak*

| 21 | 16 | 20 | $48 |

Roslyn | 25 Main St. (bet. E. B'way & Old Northern Blvd.) | 516-621-0055 | www.jollyfishermanrestaurant.com

Longtime loyalists of this "family-oriented" Roslyn "landmark" laud its "rock-solid seafood", "reliable" steaks and "specialty breads", saying it's "still great after all these years" with "helpful" service and a "bargain" lunch deal; though some patrons ponder "what's older, the menu or the crowd?" and deride "downer" decor, the gist is "nothing ever changes, and you either love that or hate it."

Jonathan's *American*

| 20 | 20 | 21 | $39 |

Garden City Park | 3000 Jericho Tpke. (Herricks Rd.) | 516-742-7300 | www.jonathansrestaurant.net

"Always dependable", this Garden City Park standby comes through with a "moderately priced", "extensive" New American menu offering "something to please everyone's palate"; the spacious, "attractive" dining rooms and "hospitable" service are a hit with "families and large parties", while the bar is a "better experience" for intimate meals, though the whole package is a little "boring" for some.

	FOOD	DECOR	SERVICE	COST

Jonathan's Ristorante *Italian* | 24 | 22 | 23 | $50 |

Huntington | 15 Wall St. (bet. Gerard & Main Sts.) | 631-549-0055 | www.jonathansristorante.com

"Refined" Italian dishes, "lovely specials" and an "impressive" wine list draw diners to this "high-end" standout in the "crowded food hamlet of Huntington village"; the staff "makes you feel like you're the only table in the place" while the "charming atmosphere" is enhanced by a "cute little patio", so forget the "upscale price tags" and "enjoy."

JT's Corner Cafe *American* | 23 | 14 | 18 | $25 |

Nesconset | 204 Smithtown Blvd. (bet. Joseph Pl. & Lake Ave. S.) | 631-265-5267 | www.jtscornercafe.com

It's "like News 12 – local as local gets" remark regulars of this "little diner-style" American "storefront" in Nesconset turning out "top-quality", "eclectic" breakfast and lunch items all day (including "all different types of pancakes and French toast"); service can be "spotty" and it may "not be worth a special trip", but it's a "satisfying" choice for most; P.S. closes at 8 PM (3 PM Sundays).

Kabul Afghani Cuisine *Afghan* | 23 | 16 | 21 | $31 |

Huntington | 1153 E. Jericho Tpke. (bet. Dix Hills Rd. & Park Ave.) | 631-549-5506 | www.kabulny.com

"Tender" kebabs and "terrific vegetarian" eats "awaken new taste buds" at this Huntington Afghan "mainstay in a strip mall" that's been "consistently" "wonderful" "for many years"; though it's "time to change the decor", the "affordable" fare, "excellent" service and "entertaining belly dancing on Fridays" make dining here a "treat."

King Umberto *Italian* | 23 | 15 | 22 | $38 |

Elmont | 1343 Hempstead Tpke. (Meacham Ave.) | 516-352-3232 | www.kingumberto.com

The distinctive "aroma of garlic" and red sauce wafts through the air at this "popular", "slightly upscale" Elmont "throwback" where the "masses" assemble for "standout" pizza, Italian dishes "done right" and a "value-filled wine list"; "cheerful banter with the staff" is another plus, and "you'll be pleasantly surprised at the results" if you "ask for suggestions"; P.S. "reservations are a must."

Kinha Sushi *Japanese* | - | - | - | M |

Garden City | 988 Franklin Ave. (bet. 9th & 10th Sts.) | 516-877-0888 | www.kinhasushi.com

Some 30 sakes are on hand at this midpriced Japanese in Garden City where a fusion influence can be found in dishes such as lobster mango ceviche and Peking duck crêpe with pickled plum and mentaiko butter sauce; chairs and banquettes are covered in black leather and red fabric in a setting illuminated by seductive lighting.

Kiraku *Japanese* | ∇ 26 | 20 | 22 | $37 |

Glen Head | 127 Glen Head Rd. (bet. Benjamin & Wall Sts.) | 516-676-3686 | www.kirakurestaurant.com

The "innovative sushi" at this "gracious" Glen Head Japanese looks "too pretty to eat", but once you do "you're in heaven" sigh loyalists who laud a menu with "so many different rolls, it's hard to decide"; though often "busy", the setting is "romantic" enough for "date night", while "nice" tatami booths, an array of cocktails and "reasonable" prices pull in larger groups.

Kiran Palace *Indian*
24 | 14 | 23 | $26

Hicksville | Delco Plaza | 67-75 E. Old Country Rd. (B'way) | 516-932-5191 | www.kiranpalacehicksville.net
Levittown | Dunkin Donuts Plaza | 2934 Hempstead Tpke. (bet. Center Ln. & Division Ave.) | 516-796-2600 | www.kiranpalacelevittown.com
Commack | Commack Corners | 6092 Jericho Tpke. (Commack Rd.) | 631-462-0003 | www.kiranpalace.net

The "fabulous, authentic" Indian fare, including a "bargain lunch buffet" with plenty of "interesting choices" and "subtly spicy" dishes, makes diners "happy" at this subcontinental trio with "helpful" service; though calling it a palace may be a stretch given the "hole-in-the-wall" surroundings, it's "popular" nonetheless – and there's always takeout.

Kiss'o *Japanese*
21 | 16 | 19 | $36

New Hyde Park | Lake Success Shopping Ctr. | 1532 Union Tpke. (bet. Lakeville & New Hyde Park Rds.) | 516-355-0587 | www.kisso-sushi.com

Make a day of sushi, sake and shopping at this New Hyde Park strip-mall "oasis" where the "special rolls are delicious" and the bento-box "lunch deals are not to be missed"; "for those not into raw fish, there's plenty" to enjoy, all at a "decent price" and served "without attitude."

⏩ Kitchen A Bistro ⊘ *French*
27 | 19 | 23 | $51

St. James | 404 N. Country Rd. (Edgewood Ave.) | 631-862-0151 | www.kitchenabistro.com

It "doesn't get any better" declare devotees of this "super-relaxed" "rare find" in St. James, where "outstanding" chef-owner Eric Lomando crafts "awesome" French bistro dishes (including "unique" seafood specials) with "novel twists and turns"; it's a touch "less crowded" now that it's in "the old Mirabelle space", and the staff provides "helpful" service, plus it's a "bargain with BYO and no corkage charge"; P.S. cash-only and "reservations are a must", so "plan in advance."

⏩ Kitchen A Trattoria ⊠ Ⓜ ⊘ *Italian*
28 | 16 | 25 | $42

St. James | 532 N. Country Rd. (Lake Ave.) | 631-584-3518 | www.kitchenatrattoria.com

It's even "better than Kitchen A Bistro" marvel guests of this "exciting" St. James spin-off from chef-owner Eric Lomando, a "foodies' haven" proffering "inspired seasonal Italian dishes" you "dream about", served by a "terrific" staff; the "shockingly small" space is "still a bit rough" and it "takes a while to get a reservation" (required on weekends), but it's "worth adjusting your schedule to eat here"; P.S. the BYO policy and prix fixe specials "make it a steal."

Koenig's *Continental/German*

19 | 14 | 19 | $36

Floral Park | 86 S. Tyson Ave. (Mayflower Pl.) | 516-354-2300 | www.koenigsrestaurant.com

"Still going strong", this moderately priced Floral Park "institution" "hits the spot" when only "roast beef on that fabulous rye" or "sauerbraten you can eat without a knife" will quiet a German-Continental craving; it's a "sentimental favorite" for "older" customers who take comfort in the familiarity and "amicable" service and don't mind being "transported back to 1950" to enjoy it.

☑ Kotobuki Ⓜ *Japanese*

27 | 18 | 20 | $41

Roslyn | Harborview Shoppes | 1530 Old Northern Blvd. (bet. Northern Blvd. & Skillman St.) | 516-621-5312
Babylon | 86 Deer Park Ave. (Main St.) | 631-321-8387
Hauppauge | 377 Nesconset Hwy. (bet. Brooksite Dr. & Hauppauge Rd.) | 631-360-3969
www.kotobukinewyork.com

"Best. sushi. ever." declare diners in awe of this "phenomenal" Japanese trio, "Long Island's answer to Nobu" serving fish so "sumptuous" it's worth getting in line and "waiting for the doors to open"; the "highly skilled chefs" create other "inventive" dishes as well, and the value's "amazing", but remember that variable service and "cramped" settings (apart from the Roslyn patio) are part of the deal; P.S. no reservations.

NEW K·Pacho Cocina & Tequila Ⓜ *Mexican*

– | – | – | E

New Hyde Park | 1270 Union Tpke. (bet. Lakeville & New Hyde Park Rds.) | 516-358-2222 | www.kpacho.com

The Four Food Studio team has transformed their New Hyde Park space (formerly Two Steak & Sushi Den) into this upscale cantina by way of barn-wood walls, an expanded bar, communal tables and a Day of the Dead theme; guacamole prepared tableside and small and large Mexican plates are joined by an enormous tequila selection, plus margaritas in giant glasses; P.S. yes, their signature cotton candy still comes with the bill.

Kumo Sushi *Japanese*

25 | 18 | 19 | $37

Plainview | Manetto Hill Mall | 18 Manetto Hill Rd. (bet. Old Country Rd. & Washington Ave.) | 516-681-8881 | www.kumosushi.net

Reviewers "rave" about the "delectable" sushi creations, e.g. a "unique" spicy-tuna "pizza sandwich", at this Japanese "hidden treasure" "in a Plainview strip mall"; though service varies and the "packed" crowd can be "ear-numbing", most agree it's a "top-notch" place to "spend an evening with friends" when you "don't want to spend a fortune."

Kura Barn Ⓜ *Japanese*

24 | 17 | 21 | $37

Huntington | 479 New York Ave. (bet. High & Hillcrest Sts.) | 631-673-0060 | www.kurabarn.com

Serving "fresh, inventive sushi", this "charming" Japanese that's "been in Huntington forever" (since 1978) is a "popular" choice with moderate prices; the "peaceful interior" and "efficient service" are further draws, attracting regulars who say it "feels like home"; P.S. reservations taken for groups of five or more.

Kurofune ⌧ *Japanese* | 23 | 16 | 22 | $34 |

Commack | 77 Commack Rd. (Jericho Tpke.) | 631-499-1075 | www.kurofunerestaurant.com

"Excellent" sushi and other "authentic" Japanese eats served by a "marvelous staff" are the calling cards of this Commack veteran that's been a "neighborhood" staple "for many years"; "there are more attractive" settings than the "modest" space here, but given the "unpretentious", "comfortable" vibe and "consistently fresh" offerings, most believe it "should be busier than it is."

Kyle's ⌐ *American* | - | - | - | E |

Shelter Island | 27 N. Ferry Rd. (bet. Duvall Rd. & School St.) | 631-749-0579 | www.kylescooking.com

Funky and unique, this Shelter Island American mines a vintage look with its display of tempting pastries at the entrance, sofa and stained-glass window in the dining room, and billowy white curtains on the wraparound porch; the menu offered by the eponymous Kyle changes weekly depending upon what's freshest at the market, featuring the likes of chicken breast stuffed with mushrooms and Parmesan; P.S. dinner hours are limited in winter.

La Bottega *Italian* | 21 | 15 | 18 | $22 |

Floral Park | 49 Covert Ave. (Drew Ave.) | 516-216-5177
NEW **Franklin Square** | 700 Franklin Ave. (bet. Midway Ct. & Park Ln.) | 516-837-3060
Garden City | 147 Nassau Blvd. (bet. Newmarket Rd. & Stratford Ave.) | 516-486-0935
Garden City | Roosevelt Field Mall | 630 Old Country Rd. (bet. Clinton Rd. & Meadowbrook Pkwy.) | 516-248-4529
Oceanside | 3216 Long Beach Rd. (Montgomery Ave.) | 516-543-4540
Plainview | Plainview Ctr. | 397 S. Oyster Bay Rd. (Woodbury Rd.) | 516-605-1280
Rockville Centre | 234 Merrick Rd. (Village Ave.) | 516-593-4930
Roslyn | 1424 Old Northern Blvd. (Remsen Ave.) | 516-621-2685
www.labottegagourmet.com

Caffe Barocco *Italian*

Garden City | 143 Nassau Blvd. S. (7th St.) | 516-292-0144 | www.caffebarocco.com

La Bottega Wine Bar ⌧ *Italian*
(aka La Bottega Carle Place)

Carle Place | 465 Westbury Ave. (bet. Cherry Ln. & Rushmore Ave.) | 516-408-3190 | www.labottegacarleplace.com

"Panini paradise" can be found at this boldly "expanding" Italian chain that's "taken LI by storm" with its "dizzying" selection of "flavor-packed" sandwiches and "fresh", "inventive" salads; detractors denounce "slow service", "cramped quarters" and "largely absent" decor, but takeout is always an option for "one of the best bargains" around; P.S. Caffe Barocco features a "creative" tapas-style menu and 400-bottle wine list.

	FOOD	DECOR	SERVICE	COST

La Bussola *Italian* | 23 | 18 | 22 | $54 |

Glen Cove | 40 School St. (bet. Glen St. & Highland Rd.) |
516-671-2100 | www.labussolaristorante.com

It's "been there forever" for a reason say fans of this "real keeper" (the parent of Piccola Bussola) that dishes out "hefty" portions of "robust", upscale Italian in Glen Cove; the "on-point" staff is always "willing to please" ("if something is not on the menu, they'll make it"), so even if the "dark", "old-fashioned" interior seems a bit "dated" to some, the majority maintains "you won't be disappointed."

NEW La Casa Latina *Pan-Latin* | – | – | – | M |

Westbury | 611 Old Country Rd. (bet. Longfellow & Tennyson Aves.) |
516-280-7795 | www.lacasalatinany.com

The fare of Latin America – and especially El Salvador – stars at this midpriced Westbury newcomer from chef-owner Roberto Herrera (Bryant & Cooper in Roslyn) where the roster of dishes also includes Salvadoran, Honduran and Colombian platters featuring typical meats and vegetables; the setting is simple but colorful, with a row of tiles topped by a wall-spanning mirror, plus a tile floor and tablecloths topped with butcher paper.

La Cocina de Marcia *American/Spanish* | – | – | – | I |

Freeport | 77B W. Merrick Rd. (bet. Church St. & Guy Lombardo Ave.) |
516-442-2463 | www.lacocinademarcia.com

Located in a storefront in Freeport, this Spanish-American serves affordable fare such as Dominican chicken soup and mofongo (mashed plantains), chopped roast pork and barbecued chicken in warmly colored quarters hung with brightly colored paintings; it's named for one of the owners, whose mom is also in the kitchen.

La Coquille *French* | 24 | 22 | 24 | $61 |

Manhasset | 1669 Northern Blvd. (Manhasset Woods Rd.) |
516-365-8422 | www.la-coquille-manhasset.com

The "quintessential go-to place for any special occasion", this "upper-class" Manhasset "tradition" has "stood the test of time", with its "meticulously prepared", *magnifique* French dinners enhanced by "white-glove" service, "fine wines" and a "delightful rolling table of desserts"; the setting is full of "old-world charm" "reminiscent of Paris", though a few just "wish it were open for lunch"; P.S. the "prix fixe during the week is a plus."

La Famiglia Ⓜ *Italian* | 22 | 16 | 21 | $35 |

Plainview | 641 Old Country Rd. (bet. Barnum & Belmont Aves.) |
516-938-2050

NEW Babylon | 90 W. Main St. (Deer Park Ave.) | 631-661-0101

Smithtown | 250 W. Main St. (Brookside Dr.) | 631-382-9454
www.lafamiglia-ny.com

As the name suggests, "family-style" dining rules at these "nice-value" Plainview and Smithtown Italians (now with a Babylon branch) that are "better with lots of friends" since you "never leave without leftovers"; they're "not fancy" and are sometimes "crowded", but they're made more "comfortable" by a "thoughtful" staff and "homey" food that's "worth returning for"; P.S. reservations accepted for parties of six or more.

La Ginestra Italian
25 | 18 | 23 | $56

Glen Cove | 50 Forest Ave. (bet. Elliott Pl. & Walnut Rd.) | 516-674-2244 | www.laginestrarestaurant.com

"Innovative specials", "unforgettable" homemade pastas, "out-of-this-world" seafood and "excellent desserts" all shine at this "outstanding" Sicilian in Glen Cove staffed by a "personable", "professional" crew; though it's "expensive" and a handful says the "homey" room could use some "updating", "you always feel welcome" and know you'll be treated to "traditional Italian at its best."

La Gioconda ☑ Continental/Italian
21 | 17 | 24 | $40

Great Neck | 21 N. Station Plaza (bet. Bond & Park Sts.) | 516-466-2004 | www.lagiocondarestaurant.com

"Exceptional" hospitality marks this "small", "family-owned" trattoria near the Great Neck train station, where an "attentive" team serves "hearty" portions of "classic" Continental-Southern Italian cooking "done right"; it's "a bit old-fashioned", but the "consistent" quality and appealing "price point" (especially for the Tuesday-Thursday and Sunday prix fixe) ensures "many repeat" customers – and they "remember you when you return."

Laguna Grille Nuevo Latino
20 | 17 | 19 | $30

Woodbury | Woodbury Village Shopping Ctr. | 7927 Jericho Tpke. (S. Woods Rd.) | 516-682-8000 | www.lagunagrille.com

Loyalists "love to take the family" to this "vibrant" Nuevo Latino in a Woodbury shopping center where "kids eat free" (up to two per party, age 10 and under) and the "huge menu", including "delicious fried plantains" and "tasty, filling salads" with "Caribbean flair", has "something for everyone"; the servers are "friendly", so even when it's "busy" and "noisy", fans don't mind soaking up the "amazing energy" and "sipping a margarita."

☑ Lake House ☑ American
28 | 24 | 26 | $60

Bay Shore | 240 W. Main St. (bet. Garner Ln. & Lawrence Ave.) | 631-666-0995 | www.thelakehouserest.com

"Spectacular meals" deliver "pure bliss in every aspect" at this Bay Shore "beauty" where co-owners Eileen and Matthew (a "true artist" chef) Connors provide "exquisite" New American dining accompanied by "gorgeous views" of the lake; the outdoor fire pit is "perfect for a romantic occasion" and the "exceptional" staff pulls it all together, so it's "well worth the cost" and the "drive" to experience "one of the best restaurants on Long Island."

NEW La Maison Blanche French
- | - | - | E

Shelter Island Heights | La Maison Blanche Hotel | 11 Stearns Point Rd. (bet. Behringer Ln. & Shore Rd.) | 631-749-1633 | www.maisonblanchehotel.com

Located on a quiet country road near Crescent Beach in Shelter Island Heights, this French brasserie in a quaint white house with renovated guestrooms (the former Olde Country Inn) features several intimate dining rooms plus tables on an expansive outside deck and in a gazebo; the menu offers Gallic favorites such as escargots and steak frites; P.S. closed Tuesday–Wednesday in the off-season.

La Marmite *French/Italian*

24 | 21 | 24 | $56

Williston Park | 234 Hillside Ave. (bet. Campbell Ave. & Mineola Blvd.) | 516-746-1243 | www.lamarmiterestaurant.com

"Fantastic" French–Northern Italian dishes are served by a longtime "first-class" staff ("they watched my kids grow up") at this "taste-ful" Williston Park veteran, an "elegant" choice for "celebrating major events"; the room is "traditional" and a bit "sedate", but most can't get enough of its "old-world atmosphere."

La Nonna Bella Ristorante Ⓜ *Italian*

▽ 21 | 20 | 22 | $41

Garden City | 660 Franklin Ave. (7th St.) | 516-248-0366 | www.lanonnabella.com

"Classic" homestyle cooking and meatballs "to die for" are served at this "well-run" Italian on the Garden City scene that's "getting more popular" as new ownership under chef Lino De Vivo (who has always cooked there) takes a somewhat more refined turn; "bring the family" and settle into plush banquettes while the "efficient" staff sees to your needs, or get "comfortable" at the large bar.

La Novella Ristorante Ⓜ *Italian*

▽ 19 | 12 | 22 | $41

East Meadow | 364 E. Meadow Ave. (Prospect Ave.) | 516-794-6248 | www.lanovella.com

A "home away from home" for East Meadow neighbors, this "charming family place" earns props for its "well-prepared" Northern Italian specialties, "warm" greetings from the owner and live guitar during the week; the lunch prix fixe is a further draw, though some call it just "ok" with "outdated" digs.

La Pace with Chef Michael Ⓜ *Italian*

25 | 22 | 25 | $60

Glen Cove | 51 Cedar Swamp Rd. (3rd St.) | 516-671-2970 | www.lapaceglencove.com

Glen Covers commend this "top" Tuscan that's been an "excellent choice for years" with its "superb", high-end menu, "interesting spe-cials" and "fine service" (chef Michael Mossallam himself "likes to walk around and meet patrons"); there are "lovely private areas for parties or romance" as well as a "vibrant" bar, but the whole pack-age feels too "antiquated" and "exclusive" to some.

La Panchita *Mexican/Spanish*

▽ 22 | 16 | 22 | $27

Smithtown | 67 W. Main St. (bet. Karl & Maple Aves.) | 631-360-0627

It's "always festive" at this Smithtowner serving "well-done" Spanish and Mexican dishes and "pitchers of homemade sangria" for "reasonable prices"; though the interior doesn't dazzle, the "wonderful" staff and "sweet serenades" from occasional mariachi bands make it a "favorite" for many.

☑ La Parma *Italian*

23 | 15 | 20 | $42

Oceanside | 410 Merrick Rd. (Saratoga St.) | 516-763-1815
Port Washington | 415 Main St. (2nd Ave.) | 516-439-4960

(continued)

La Parma

Williston Park | 707 Willis Ave. (Henry St.) | 516-294-6610 Ⓜ
Huntington | 452 Jericho Tpke. (bet. Chickory & Sheppard Lns.) |
631-367-6360 Ⓜ
www.laparma.com

"Expect to wait" or "go on a weekday to avoid the crowds" at this
Italian quartet that's best for "large groups" given the "abundant"
plates of "tasty", "family-style" fare with "garlic, garlic, garlic"; critics complain that service is "rushed", prices are "a little steep for the
style" and the decor "leaves a lot to be desired", but others shrug it's
"no frills – just a great meal."

La Parmigiana Ⓜ *Italian* 22 | 10 | 17 | $32

Southampton | 48 Hampton Rd. (bet. Main & Pine Sts.) | 631-283-8030

"Still going strong" after 38 years and counting, this *"famiglia"*-run
Southampton joint slings "delicious" "red-gravy" Italian in "humongous portions" ("you need two doggy bags") served "family-style"
by folks "who make you feel right at home"; the "great value" keeps
the "casual" quarters "packed and noisy" with "lots of kids", so
touchy types tend to "prefer the takeout."

La Piazza *Pizza* 21 | 14 | 17 | $27

Merrick | 2191 Merrick Rd. (bet. Frankel & Lincoln Blvds.) |
516-546-2500
Plainview | Crossroads Shopping Ctr. | 1137 Old Country Rd.
(Manetto Hill Rd.) | 516-938-0800
Melville | 512 Walt Whitman Rd. (Holland St.) | 631-425-0500
www.lapiazzaonline.com

Pie partisans brave lines "out the door" and "loud" crowds to dig into
"delicious" brick-oven pizza and "flavorful" pasta at this affordable,
"family-oriented" trio; "decor and service are secondary" and "all
the commotion could be a turnoff" to some, but most agree that
these joints "get it right."

Z La Piccola Liguria Ⓜ *Italian* 27 | 21 | 27 | $59

Port Washington | 47 Shore Rd. (bet. Mill Pond & Old Shore Rds.) |
516-767-6490

A "loyal cadre of regulars" "loves to hear" the "highly experienced" waiters recite a "mind-boggling" list of specials in "succulent detail" at this "outstanding" Port Washington Italian
where the "brilliantly executed" dishes are among "the best on
the Island"; the "minimally decorated", "sweet setting" fills up
fast, so it's "hard to get a reservation" (and "not cheap"), but once
inside you're treated "like royalty."

La Pizzetta Ⓜ *Italian* 21 | 14 | 20 | $34

East Norwich | 1008 Oyster Bay Rd. (bet. Hawthorne Rd. &
Northern Blvd.) | 516-624-7800 | www.lapizzettaeastnorwich.com

Marinara mavens get their Italian "comfort-food" fix at this East
Norwich "neighborhood joint", the "perfect venue for an easy meal",
whether it's "great pasta and pizza" or other "well-prepared" dishes;
though some say there's "no ambiance" to speak of, others call it

"upscale casual", adding the "everyone-knows-everyone" vibe goes well with the "steady" "home cooking."

⚡ La Plage *Eclectic*

27 | 19 | 24 | $59

Wading River | 131 Creek Rd. (Sound Rd.) | 631-744-9200 | www.laplagerestaurant.net

Though it's an "unlikely location" for "truly inventive" cuisine, this "beachy" "oasis" in Wading River is a "special" "find" for "exuberant cooking" from chef-owner Wayne Wadington, whose "elegantly prepared", "beautifully presented" Eclectic dishes are matched with "knowledgeable" service; the "small" "cottage" setting may seem at odds with the "steep" tabs, but most maintain it's "totally charming" and "so worth the trip"; P.S. "reservations are a must" on weekends.

La P'tite Framboise *French*

22 | 19 | 20 | $40

Port Washington | 294 Main St. (bet. Bank & Jackson Sts.) | 516-767-7164 | www.laptiteframboise.com

Fans of this "romantic little bistro hiding in Port Washington" (sister to Bistros Cassis and Citron) find it a "pleasant" choice for "solid" French fare served in a simple setting with a "nice buzz"; the service and value are "good", so though there's "room for improvement", most say it's "worth" tolerating the "lousy parking" situation.

Lareira *Portuguese*

∇ 20 | 14 | 19 | $40

Mineola | 66 E. Jericho Tpke. (Columbus Pkwy.) | 516-248-2004 | www.lareirarestaurant.com

It's "Portugal without a passport" at this Mineola mainstay, "a must for fish lovers" and anyone who relishes "authentic" Iberian eats in a "quiet", congenial setting; "marvelous sangria" is a sweet complement to the food, but due to a "stale" interior that "needs serious dusting off", some critics say it only rates as a "back-up place."

La Rotonda *Pizza*

∇ 19 | 15 | 19 | $29

Great Neck | 8 Bond St. (bet. Grace Ave. & N. Station Plaza) | 516-466-9596 | www.larotondarestaurant.com

"It's all about the pizza" at this "brick-oven" pie palace in Great Neck, which also turns out "decent" "homestyle" pastas and such in "very casual" but "friendly" surroundings; it's viewed as a "local staple" that's "satisfying" "if you're in the nabe", but "not a destination."

La Spada *Italian*

21 | 17 | 23 | $48

Huntington Station | 315 Walt Whitman Rd. (bet. Old Walt Whitman & Schwab Rds.) | 631-549-3033 | www.laspadarestaurant.com

"You can always count on" this Southern Italian in Huntington Station for a "warm greeting" and "superb pasta" in the company of "lots of regulars"; what the simple, burgundy-toned space "lacks in decor", it "makes up for" with "top-notch" service and "quality", upscale fare.

La Strada *Italian*

20 | 20 | 21 | $36

Merrick | 2100 Merrick Ave. (bet. Miller Pl. & Smith St.) | 516-867-5488 | www.lastradaofmerrick.com

"Satisfied" customers chow down on "tasty" Italian cuisine at this moderately priced Merrick trattoria that some report has "much im-

	FOOD	DECOR	SERVICE	COST

proved since it opened" a few years ago, serving wood-fired pizzas and other "solid" fare in "accommodating" style; though a few feel the meals are "nothing special", the "beautiful", brick-floored setting, reminiscent of a courtyard in Italy, is a draw in itself.

NEW Las Viñas *Peruvian*

| - | - | - | E |

Manhasset | 118 Plandome Rd. (George St.) | 516-365-1324 | www.lasvinasny.com

A big selection of hot and cold Peruvian tapas and entrees – including ceviche, empanadas and paella with seafood and chorizo – is offered at this stylish Manhasset newcomer; a black-and-white tile floor in the bar, brick walls and a dark tin ceiling provide a fitting backdrop.

La Tavola *Italian*

| 22 | 21 | 21 | $42 |

Sayville | 183 W. Main St. (bet. Greeley & Greene Aves.) | 631-750-6900 | www.latavolasayville.com

"Not your usual spaghetti-and-meatballs Italian", this "happening", "new-wave" Sayville trattoria (from the brothers behind Ruvo) offers "wonderfully different", slightly "expensive" seasonal dishes in "rustic" environs furnished with hand-built wood tables; since you "can't beat the happy hour", the bar's popular for "refreshing cocktails" after work, while the "outside patio is great" for hanging out on "summer evenings."

La Terrazza ☑ *Italian*

| ▽ 22 | 17 | 21 | $50 |

Cedarhurst | 142 Spruce St. (bet. Chestnut St. & Willow Ave.) | 516-374-4949

Just steps from the Cedarhurst train station, this "intimate" Italian pleases with its "varied", "well-prepared" cuisine (including specials worth "paying attention" to) and "professional" service; it's often "noisy" and a bit "pricey", but that doesn't deter diners who appreciate the "welcoming" atmosphere.

La Viola *Italian*

| 20 | 15 | 21 | $40 |

Cedarhurst | 499 Chestnut St. (bet. Cedarhurst Ave. & Spruce St.) | 516-569-6020 | www.laviolarestaurant.com

"Family-style dining excels" at this Cedarhurst "fixture" that delivers "traditional red-sauce" Italian and sends diners home happy "with a doggy bag in hand"; though the room is "starting to look frayed", it's "relaxed" and "friendly" "whether you're a regular or a first-timer", and gets a boost from live "opera songs" or Broadway tunes on the first Friday of the month.

La Volpe Ristorante ☑ *Italian*

| 23 | 22 | 23 | $43 |

Center Moriches | 611 Montauk Hwy. (Brookfield Ave.) | 631-874-3819 | www.lavolperestaurant.net

"Impressed" eaters praise the brick-oven pizza, "delicious" dishes and "creative" specials at this slightly "upscale" Center Moriches Italian run by a "hands-on" family that "clearly loves its business" and "knows what good food is"; the "attractive" setting with a Tuscan "farmhouse look" benefits from "expert" service, live weekly music and patio seating, and the three-course lunch deal enhances the "value."

NEW Lawson Pub *American*
- | - | - | M

Oceanside | 3112 Lawson Blvd. (W. Windsor Pkwy.) | 516-307-8753 | www.lawsonpub.com

Chef-owner Joe Bonacore (ex Solé) has renovated this historic pub situated at the Oceanside train station, outfitting it with stained glass and wood tables; the moderately priced Contemporary American menu is similarly familiar yet updated, featuring some of the original's favorites – such as thumb-bits (sliced filet mignon on garlic bread topped with mozzarella) – plus new additions like lobster sliders and pan-seared branzino with multi-grain risotto.

Le Chef *Continental/French*
22 | 17 | 21 | $49

Southampton | 75 Jobs Ln. (bet. Main St. & Windmill Ln.) | 631-283-8581 | www.lechefbistro.com

"A longtimer in Southampton" (since 1980), this "pretty little" French-Continental bistro reliably provides "nicely prepared" "old-line" dishes and "personal" service in a "cozy" setting that "feels like the French countryside"; despite "nothing new to offer", it draws "steady patrons" who promise you get your "money's worth", especially when opting for the all-night prix fixe.

NEW Left Coast Kitchen *American*
- | - | - | M

Merrick | 1810 Merrick Rd. (bet. Beach Dr. & Montauk Ave.) | 516-868-5338 | www.lckny.com

New American gastropub fare with regionally inspired dishes is the draw at this affordable Merrick newcomer from California native Chris Randell (ex City Cellar); a large bar area with wooden booths opens into the dining room, giving it a casual feel, and there's live music Friday and Saturday; P.S. lunch is served Wednesday–Sunday, with breakfast weekends.

NEW Legacy Asian Fusion *Asian*
- | - | - | E

Huntington | 92 E. Main St. (Woodhull Rd.) | 631-425-7788 | www.legacyhuntington.com

Settling into the former Dao space (and keeping its striking decor), the new owners of this Huntington spot have introduced an Asian fusion menu, offering a pricey array of sushi and sashimi, hibachi dinners and Thai, Mongolian and Vietnamese entrees; the setting features a shiny gold-colored ceiling, a large fish tank and a raised platform on which a pianist performs most nights.

Legal Sea Foods *Seafood*
20 | 18 | 19 | $41

Huntington Station | Walt Whitman Mall | 160 Walt Whitman Rd. (Weston St.) | 631-271-9777 | www.legalseafoods.com

Enjoy some of "Boston's best seafood in your backyard" via this "high-quality" chain link in Huntington Station that's "deservedly popular" for its "always fresh" offerings, including "legendary New England clam chowder"; though it's a bit "basic" for the "upscale" prices and the "modern" decor isn't for everyone, the servers are "accommodating" and the gluten-free menu earns it "huge props."

	FOOD	DECOR	SERVICE	COST

Legends Eclectic | 23 | 20 | 21 | $44 |

New Suffolk | 835 First St. (bet. King & Main Sts.) | 631-734-5123 |
www.legends-restaurant.com

"The best of both worlds" awaits at this "welcoming" "find" in "the quiet village of New Suffolk", where a "robust" "sports bar" adjoins a "sedate dining room" serving "generous" portions of "surprisingly creative" Eclectic fare prepared with "flair and finesse" and conveyed by a "caring" staff; also offering "200-plus bottled beers", it's a legendary "local" favorite that's "well worth seeking out" despite tabs inclined to be "a little steep."

Lemonleaf Grill Ⓜ Thai | 22 | 12 | 19 | $24 |

Hicksville | Compare Food Shopping Ctr. | 536 S. Broadway (bet. Farm Ln. & Lewis St.) | 516-939-2288
Port Jefferson Station | 208 Rte. 112 (bet. Cherub Dr. & Dayton Ave.) | 631-928-8880
www.lemonleafgrill.com

"Terrific", "gently seasoned" Thai food "pleases the entire family" at these "reliable" Hicksville and Port Jefferson eateries that "aren't fancy" but offer "good value"; even those who call the "quiet" settings a "step above a take-out kitchen" and service merely "adequate" are "never disappointed in the food", but heat-seekers be warned that "nothing will set your mouth on fire" here.

Lemon Leaf Thai Restaurant Thai | 20 | 11 | 17 | $25 |

Carle Place | 227 Old Country Rd. (bet. Glen Cove Rd. & Meadowbrook Pkwy.) | 516-739-3666
Mineola | 197 Mineola Blvd. (Grant Ave.) | 516-877-1899
www.lemonleafthairestaurant.com

The cooks deliver "flavorful" standards – and "they don't stumble with the drunken noodles, either" – at this Thai twosome catering to the "not-too-spicy" set; the newer Mineola branch is more "charming" than the rather "run-down" original in Carle Place, but both come through with "real bang for the buck."

ⓩ Le Soir Ⓜ French | 27 | 21 | 25 | $52 |

Bayport | 825 Montauk Hwy. (Bayport Ave.) | 631-472-9090 |
www.lesoirbayport.com

It's "getting better with age" report regulars who've gone "for years" to this "outstanding" French destination in Bayport serving "exquisitely prepared" dinners by chef/co-owner Michael Kaziewicz; the service is "amazing" too, so even if the "slightly fussy" room "could use a spruce-up", it's still a "nice place for date night" and a "favorite" for the "bargain" prix fixe Tuesday–Thursday and Sunday.

Library Cafe ◗ American | 18 | 21 | 19 | $29 |

Farmingdale | 274 Main St. (Conklin St.) | 516-752-7678 |
www.thelibrarycafe.com

"Ironically, it's one of the loudest places you can go" remark guests of this "adorable", "neighborhood pub" set in a former Farmingdale library (sibling to Babylon's Post Office Cafe), where "scrumptious" burgers and other "comforting" New American grub bolster "one of the best happy hours around"; the staff "makes you feel welcome" and the martinis "actually have a kick", so it's "enjoyable" if you're into the "scene."

☑ Limani *Mediterranean/Seafood*   26 | 27 | 24 | $71

Roslyn | 1043 Northern Blvd. (bet. Middle Neck Rd. & Port Washington Blvd.) | 516-869-8989 | www.limaniny.com

Bestowing a "beautiful atmosphere for beautiful people", this "gorgeous" Roslyn Mediterranean with teak floors, mosaic tiles and a "bar scene that's a bit of a show" also "wows" in the kitchen, providing "incredible" fare ("fabulous" seafood "cooked to perfection") matched by a "formidable" wine list; "extremely accommodating" service is another plus, but just be ready for a "noise level that's off-the-charts" and tabs so "expensive" it might be "cheaper to go to Greece."

Little Mexico *Mexican*   - | - | - | I

Westbury | 280 Post Ave. (bet. Belmont & Lewis Aves.) | 516-333-2038 | www.littlemex.com

Though mostly for takeout, this tiny, budget-friendly Mexican cafe in the heart of Westbury village is equipped with some tables for digging into the likes of fajitas, chimichangas and beef-tongue tacos on the premises; wine, beer and sangria are also available, and so-papillas (pastries) for dessert provide a sweet finish.

NEW Little Red Ⓜ *American*   - | - | - | E

Southampton | 76 Jobs Ln. (bet. Pond Ln. & S. Main St.) | 631-283-3309 | www.littleredsouthampton.com

Tucked away in a parking lot beside Southampton's Agawam Park, this suave sibling of Red Bar in Southampton welcomes with a truly red bar at the entrance plus French cafe chairs in the dining room, an outdoor lounge and a spacious covered summer patio; the Gallic-inspired American menu focuses on local ingredients, offering the likes of monkfish with escargot butter.

NEW L.I.V.E. ◑ *Vegetarian*   - | - | - | I

Seaford | 3601 Merrick Rd. (bet. Kenora Pl. & Seaford Ave.) | 516-785-5483 | www.longislandvegetarianeatery.com

Filling a long-neglected local niche, this Seaford newcomer offers its wallet-friendly vegan and vegetarian eats beyond daytime, staying open until midnight weeknights and till 3 AM on weekends; though the cafe is mostly takeout, at the Leaky Lifeboat bar under the same ownership next door, you can sip suds and dig into spaghetti and (soy-based) meatballs or other fare delivered to your perch.

Living Room, The *American*   25 | 25 | 22 | $68

East Hampton | c/o The Maidstone | 207 Main St. (Mill Hill Ln.) | 631-324-5006 | www.themaidstone.com

"We should all have a living room like this" gush "impressed" patrons at this "high-end" East Hamptonite in the c/o The Maidstone hotel, where chef James Carpenter (ex Della Femina) does a "terrific take on Slow Food", showcasing "local" ingredients via "sophisticated", "Scandinavian-inspired" New American dishes; bright, "elegant decor" and "superb" service add to the "amazing" experience, and though such "quality doesn't come cheap", epicures "with deep pockets and refined taste buds" shrug "we only live once."

LL Dent ⓜ *Southern* 23 | 13 | 20 | $31

Carle Place | 221 Old Country Rd. (bet. Glen Cove Rd. & Meadowbrook Pkwy.) | 516-742-0940 | www.lldent.com

From the "chicken and catfish to die for" to the "mouthwatering desserts", the "good ol' Southern cuisine" at this Carle Place "gem" is the "real thing" (and not for "calorie-counters"); "sweetheart" owners put their "personal touch" on the affordable meal – daughter Leisa Dent works the kitchen while mother Lillian provides "great hospitality" up front – though the small, "simple" space lacks the "flair" of the fare.

Lobster Roll *Seafood* 19 | 12 | 17 | $33

Amagansett | 1980 Montauk Hwy. (on Napeague Stretch) | 631-267-3740 | www.lobsterroll.com

"Once you've been here, you're hooked" claim fin fans about this seasonal Amagansett "shack" (nicknamed 'Lunch' for its sign) that's been a lure since the '60s for its "delicious lobster rolls", "fried puffers" and the like; "it's the antithesis of elegant" and some call it "overpriced", but the "beachy atmosphere" and homemade desserts by the owner enhance the appeal for a "local, lively crowd."

Lobster Roll Northside ⓜ *Seafood* 20 | 16 | 18 | $35

Baiting Hollow | 3225 Sound Ave. (Roanoke Ave.) | 631-369-3039 | www.lobsterroll.com

Fans "love the lobster rolls" and "awesome puffers" at this seasonal Baiting Hollow "favorite" (which originated as an offshoot of the Amagansett locale); with "weekend music in the summer" and a "pretty", kid-friendly setting in a plaza with "interesting shops", it's a "traveling staple" for many, despite the "pricey platters."

Lola ⓜ *Eclectic* 24 | 23 | 23 | $54

Great Neck | 113 Middle Neck Rd. (Maple Dr.) | 516-466-5666 | www.restaurantlola.com

"Truly gifted" chef-owner Michael Ginor (Tel Aviv) "is beyond an artist" at this "top-flight" Great Neck "destination", where the "thrilling" lineup of "remarkably" "imaginative" Eclectic "delights" – many enhanced with "decadent foie gras" from his own farm – includes an "extensive small plate" selection ("go hungry and try lots"); "attentive" servers oversee a "vibrant and sexy" setting with a "marvelous" "glowing red bar", and while you can "expect quality rather than quantity", the 'wow' factor" is "well worth the money."

Lola's Kitchen & Wine Bar *American* 20 | 21 | 21 | $36

Long Beach | 180 W. Park Ave. (Magnolia Blvd.) | 516-442-1090

A "cool" "Key West" vibe "enlivens" this "relaxing" Long Beach "crowd-pleaser", where merrymakers escape the daily grind with "enticing" New American fare and an "excellent" vino lineup; inside it "can get a bit loud", but a "cute outdoor area" furthers the "vacation" feel and "nightly specials" mean it's both "happening" and "affordable" ("a recipe for success").

Lombardi's on the Bay *Seafood/Steak*   23 | 24 | 21 | $48

Patchogue | 600 S. Ocean Ave. (Masket Dock) | 631-654-8970 |
www.lombardisonthebay.com

"A view to relish" from a "multilevel deck with lots of tables" is part of the package at this Patchogue special-occasion place (related to Lombardi's on the Sound and Mamma Lombardi's) serving "abundant" portions of "quality" surf 'n' turf, with a few Italian accents; the interior is "gracious" too, though some critics contend it's all a bit "too much" – "a catering hall should not try to be a restaurant also."

Lombardi's on the Sound *Italian*   21 | 23 | 20 | $45

Port Jefferson | Port Jefferson Country Club at Harbor Hills |
44 Fairway Dr. (Village Beach Rd.) | 631-473-1440 |
www.lombardisonthesound.com

"Unbeatable views" of Long Island Sound along with "enormous portions" of "sumptuous" Italian food make this Lombardi's family player "enjoyable for special events", in addition to big catered affairs and a "Sunday brunch buffet like no other"; so while a few consider it "overpriced" with variable service, most agree that lunch offers a more "affordable" option for soaking in the "beautiful" scenery.

Long River *Asian*   ▽ 21 | 15 | 20 | $23

Kings Park | 4 Main St. (Indian Head Rd.) | 631-544-4666

"Solid" selections of "well-done" Chinese and Indonesian dishes (including "wonderful" fried dumplings) are served by a "fast, friendly" staff that "works hard" at this veteran Pan-Asian near the train station in Kings Park; given the so-so setting, though, some say it's "best for takeout" – especially since it's always "ready on time and right, no matter how much you order."

Los Compadres *Mexican*   ▽ 23 | 6 | 19 | $18

Huntington Station | 243 Old Walt Whitman Rd. (bet. Chichester Rd. & Livingston St.) | 631-351-8384

"Everything is homemade and fresh, right down to the corn chips" and "dreamy chimichangas" at this "authentic" Huntington Station Mex where "you can tell" the owner "takes pride in his food"; since it's a "terrific value", no one's complaining about "paper plates and plastic utensils" or the "bare-bones", "hole-in-the-wall" setting; P.S. no alcohol served.

Lotus East *Chinese*   21 | 14 | 19 | $27

Mount Sinai | 331 Rte. 25A (Rte. 347) | 631-331-6688
St. James | 416 N. Country Rd. (Edgewood Ave.) | 631-862-6030

There's a "wide variety" of Chinese at these "mainstays" in Mt. Sinai and St. James, turning out "consistently excellent", "classic" dishes for a "reasonable" price; still, a portion finds the fare "pedestrian" and the "bland", "musty" settings in need of an "extreme makeover."

	FOOD	DECOR	SERVICE	COST

Louie's Oyster Bar & Grille *Seafood*
`17` `20` `18` `$46`

Port Washington | 395 Main St. (Prospect St.) | 516-883-4242 |
www.louiesoysterbarandgrille.com

"Spectacular" sunset views are the draw of this "landmark" (circa 1905) Port Washington seafooder with an "extensive" outdoor deck to "watch the boats go by" and an "attractive" nautical-themed interior; the lobster's "delicious", but for the most part the food and service rate as just "average" with "above-average prices", so some just go for "drinks and apps"; P.S. look out for "Frank Sinatra nights" on Mondays with a live band.

Love Lane Kitchen *American*
`23` `15` `19` `$34`

Mattituck | 240 Love Ln. (bet. Main Rd. & Pike St.) | 631-298-8989 |
www.lovelanekitchen.com

"Upscale", locally sourced "comfort food" from an "ambitious", "ever-evolving" New American menu is "well-executed" and served in "unpretentious style" at this "super-casual" Mattituck "gem", which is also beloved for its "wonderful" "house-roasted coffee"; the pace "can be slow" when it's "busy", but "reasonable" prices and a staff "so sweet you could swear they've been spun from sugar" make it "easy to stroll in" for breakfast, lunch or dinner.

LT Burger ☒ *Burgers*
`16` `15` `13` `$30`

Sag Harbor | 62 Main St. (bet. Garden & Spring Sts.) | 631-899-4646 |
www.ltburger.com

Co-owned by celeb chef Laurent Tourondel, this "very casual" "addition to the Sag Harbor eating scene" serves up "all kinds of burgers" (classic, Tex-Mex, turkey, veggie, et al.) in a "white-tiled" retro-industrial space; critics beef about "just ok" food, "clueless" service and "lots of hype", but "it's kid friendly" and "won't break the bank", so be ready for "massive lines in summer."

Lucé ☒ *Italian*
`22` `21` `23` `$60`

East Norwich | 1053 Oyster Bay Rd. (bet. Johnson Ct. & Northern Blvd.) |
516-624-8330 | www.luce-ristorante.com

"Elegant in every way" from the white tablecloths to the colorful mosaics, this "upscale" East Norwich Italian "makes you feel special" indulging in the "delicious" likes of potato-wrapped halibut and grilled veal paillard set down by an "attentive" staff; but while "they really take pride in the food", they also attach a "hefty price tag", leading some to prefer "lunch when it's quiet" – and lighter on the wallet.

☒ Luce & Hawkins *American*
`25` `27` `26` `$65`

Jamesport | Jedediah Hawkins Inn | 400 S. Jamesport Ave. (bet. Main Rd. & Peconic Bay Blvd.) | 631-722-2900 | www.jedediahhawkinsinn.com

If you "like to be surprised and challenged", "run, don't walk" to this New American in the "gorgeous restored" Victorian home that's now Jamesport's "magnificent" Jedediah Hawkins Inn, where chef/co-owner Keith Luce "loves to tantalize" by "coaxing wonderful flavors" out of the "farm-to-table" "local ingredients" (many from his own "garden in the back") showcased in his "inspired" dishes; with a "terrific" team staffing an "elegant" yet "comfortable" venue, it's a "gourmet" experience to "savor."

Lucy's Café & Bistro ⊠Ⓜ *American*   ▽ 25 | 18 | 23 | $39

Babylon | 135 Deer Park Ave. (James St.) | 631-669-1640 | www.lucysbistro.com

The "talented" new chef-owner pays "attention to detail" at this "fabulous" "little" Babylon Village "gem", where the "up-to-date" New American menu is prepared "to perfection" with "top-of-the-line ingredients" and served by an "attentive" staff; the "charmingly casual" (if "tight") quarters are secreted down a "brick-lined alley-way", but it's "well worth finding" and tolerating the occasional "wait."

Ludlow Bistro Ⓜ *American*   24 | 19 | 23 | $47

Deer Park | 1945 Deer Park Ave. (Schwartz Pl.) | 631-667-9595 | www.ludlowbistro.com

Once you "get past the fluorescent orange exterior", this Deer Park New American is liable to "surprise" with "innovative" "twists" on a "fantastic" seasonal menu and service from a "first-rate" crew; the "convivial atmosphere" fostered by a "very present" owner and "funky" interior sporting "cool artwork" further prompt patrons to observe you can "never judge a book by its cover."

Luigi Q ⊠ *Italian*   23 | 18 | 20 | $56

Hicksville | 400B S. Oyster Bay Rd. (Woodbury Rd.) | 516-932-7450

Admirers of chef-owner Luigi Quarta's "charming" "old-school Italian" in Hicksville attest the "excellent" "traditional" cuisine and "warm, personable service" are "a perfect delight" "for that special occasion or just because"; those low on lire object it's "overpriced", but "when it's on, it's on."

Luso Ⓜ *Portuguese*   22 | 17 | 22 | $33

Smithtown | 101 E. Main St. (bet. Bellemeade & Landing Aves.) | 631-406-6820 | www.lusorestaurant.com

Indulge the "carnivore in you" with "never-ending meats" "smoking-hot from the grill" at this Portuguese BBQ joint in Smithtown, where "efficient" servers bring on the "wonderful" rodizio specialty in a "flavorful" "parade" that "stops only when you say so"; prices are "reasonable" and the "small space" expands with a "bonus" patio in summer, but "plan on skipping breakfast the day after."

Mac's Steakhouse *Steak*   23 | 23 | 22 | $60

Huntington | 12 Gerard St. (bet. New York & Stewart Aves.) | 631-549-5300 | www.macssteakhouse.com

"An emphatic wow", this Huntington meatery "powerhouse" presents "excellent" prime cuts, "delicious sides" and a "terrific", 350-vintage vino list ferried by "gracious" staffers who "bend over backward for you"; the "impressive digs" brandish "beautiful" "dark wood" and a glassed-in private wine cellar, and though the "high prices" are "not for every day", "if you're up for a special meal" and have "deep pockets" it's "solid" to the max; P.S. it hosts live music on Fridays.

RESTAURANTS

	FOOD	DECOR	SERVICE	COST

Madras Woodlands *Indian/Vegetarian*
▽ 22 | 14 | 24 | $23

New Hyde Park | 1627 Hillside Ave. (New Hyde Park Rd.) |
516-326-8900 | www.madraswoodlands.com

Dosas are "made to perfection" and "authentic South Indian" spices "dance in your mouth" at this New Hyde Park subcontinental stand-out, where the "top-notch" kosher Vegetarian cooking brings out "flavors so complex" that even card-carrying carnivores "never miss the meat"; the prices are as "light" and "satisfying" as the food, and the "excellent" staffers will gladly "give advice" to neophytes.

Maguire's *American*
19 | 19 | 19 | $45

Ocean Beach | Fire Island | 1 Bay Walk (Ocean Rd.) | 631-583-8800 |
www.maguiresbayfrontrestaurant.com

"Beautiful sunset views" from a "delightful" deck "right on the bay" are a "popular" draw at this seasonal New American in Ocean Beach, an "old-time Fire Island" stalwart with a "simple" menu of "tried-and-true favorites" ("Thursday night lobsterpalooza" is "the best value"); though it offers "no surprises" foodwise, the "alfresco" scenery alone is "worth the price of the meal"; P.S. the $45 'Taste of Fire Island' includes parking, a three-course dinner and round-trip ferry service from Bay Shore.

Main St.
Bakery & Cafe Ⓜ *Bakery/Sandwiches*
- | - | - | I

Port Washington | 170 Main St. (bet. Madison & Monroe Sts.) |
516-304-5214 | www.mainstreetbakerycafe.com

Breakfast, brunch and lunch are offered at this bakery/sandwich shop in Port Washington where savory items include a turkey and avocado baguette and eggs Benedict with fingerling-potato hash; among the numerous treats in a huge glass pastry case is the decadent house specialty – a multi-layered candy bar meant to be eaten either sliced or with a knife and fork.

Majors Steak House *Steak*
19 | 16 | 20 | $39

East Meadow | 284 E. Meadow Ave. (Fairhaven Rd.) |
516-794-6600
Woodbury | 8289 Jericho Tpke. (bet. Juneau Blvd. & Woodbury Rd.) |
516-367-7300
www.majorssteakhouse.com

"When funds are tight", these "busy" East Meadow and Woodbury beef barns cater to the "budget-minded" "masses" with "fantastic" burgers and "basic but passable" steaks for a price you "can't beat"; they're "nothing elegant", but supporters say "enough has rubbed off" from parent Bryant & Cooper "to make it worthwhile" when you want to "bring the family" and leave "full."

Mama's *Italian*
21 | 14 | 20 | $32

Centereach | Centereach Mall | 605 Middle Country Rd. (Holbrook Rd.) |
631-585-1498
Holbrook | 1057 Main St. (bet. Furrows Rd. & Railroad Ave.) |
631-981-6262

(continued)

(continued)

Mama's

Oakdale | LaSalle Commons | 587 Montauk Hwy. (Dale Dr.) | 631-589-9640
www.theoriginalmamas.com

This "red sauce" threesome wins support from "local" families seeking "reliable" Italian "standards" (think pastas and pizza) in "big portions" "for the buck"; though the food and generic decor are "not particularly memorable", they're "trustworthy" enough to attract "long lines at peak times"; P.S. the Centereach and Oakdale outlets' $13.95 Wednesday prix fixe is "a very good deal."

Mamma Lombardi's *Italian*

23 | 19 | 21 | $41

Holbrook | 400 Furrows Rd. (Patchogue-Holbrook Rd.) | 631-737-0774 | www.mammalombardis.com

Beloved "through the years" for "humongous portions" of "mouth-watering" Southern Italian "like you wish your mama could make", this Holbrook vet is a "wonderful family-style" "mainstay"; though the "old-fashioned" setting "could use a makeover" and "there's always a wait" owing to the "no-reservations policy", "spot-on" service and a "doggy bag" that "can last for days" render "every visit" "satisfying"; P.S. the owners also run a nearby gourmet market, Lombardi's on the Sound and Lombardi's on the Bay.

Manucci's *Italian/Pizza*

∇ 19 | 15 | 17 | $37

Montauk | Kenny's Tipperary Inn | 432 W. Lake Dr. (Flamingo Ave.) | 631-668-4455 | www.manuccis.com

Now settled in new quarters at Kenny's Tipperary Inn, this Montauk Italian's "old-school" staples and brick-oven pizzas "can be quite tasty", and the Sunday buffet breakfast and Monday pasta night add "family value"; less satisfied sojourners say it's "inconsistent" but "ok" "in a pinch" if you "stick to the basics"; P.S. hours vary by season.

NEW Mara's Homemade *BBQ/Cajun*

- | - | - | M

Syosset | Muttontown Plaza | 236 W. Jericho Tpke. (bet. Michael & Oak Drs.) | 516-682-9200 | www.marashomemade.com

No need to fly to the Big Easy for a BBQ-Cajun fix since the arrival of this little strip-mall Syosset transplant from NYC's East Village offering a midpriced menu with the likes of Louisiana crawfish boil (flown in when in season), fried green tomatoes and smoked meats and ribs; the down-home setting has mini green lights outlining a picture window, and walls hung with photos of Mardi Gras and jazz greats.

Marco Polo's *Asian/Italian*

- | - | - | M

Westbury | Viana Hotel & Spa | 3998 Brush Hollow Rd. (Montrose Rd.) | 516-333-2230 | www.marcopolos.weebly.com

East meets West at Westbury's Viana Hotel and Spa, where the midpriced Asian and Italian menu offers not only the likes of truffle ravioli and grilled salmon with sweet Chinese mustard, but also a fusion-style chicken française egg roll; the feng shui-inspired, eco-friendly decor features a dramatic entryway with a fireplace and a compass floor design, black granite dining tables and a red underlit bar.

RESTAURANTS

	FOOD	DECOR	SERVICE	COST

Mario *Italian*
| 25 | 21 | 25 | $44 |

Hauppauge | 644 Vanderbilt Motor Pkwy. (bet. Marcus Blvd. & Washington Ave.) | 631-273-9407 | www.restaurantmario.com

"Still going strong" after more than 30 years, this "old-style" Hauppauge Northern Italian remains a "fave" for "terrific" cuisine set down by "pleasant and professional" staffers who'll "change anything you wish" to suit your palate; even if spoilers suggest the "deep red" "flashback decor" could use some "updating", for a "consistently excellent" meal that "won't break the bank", "you can't miss."

NEW Market Bistro *American*
| - | - | - | E |

Jericho | Birchwood Plaza | 519 N. Broadway (bet. I-495 & Jericho Tpke.) | 516-513-1487 | www.marketbistroli.com

Chef-owner Bill Holden (West End Cafe in Carle Place) recruited his chef-son Christopher to man the stoves at this upscale-casual New American in Jericho's Birchwood Plaza; the handsome room features exposed brick with beer barrels forming a divider alongside the open, glassed-in kitchen, and a wall of windows in front will open to the sidewalk come summer.

☑ Maroni Cuisine 🅂🅼⌦ *Eclectic/Italian*
| 28 | 18 | 26 | $109 |

Northport | 18 Woodbine Ave. (bet. Main St. & Scudder Ave.) | 631-757-4500 | www.maronicuisine.com

"Inventive is an understatement" for chef-owner and "genial genius" Michael Maroni's "phenomenal" Eclectic-Italian tasting menu, which makes dining at his cash-only Northport standout an "exciting" "event" as "personable" servers convey course after course of "perfectly executed" "delicacies" (like those "famous" "tender" meatballs in "lush red sauce") till you "need help getting up"; it's "always worth" the "splurge" to be "wowed" by a "dream meal" "you'll never forget", but "reservations are a must" for a spot in the "shoebox" space; P.S. there's also a fair-weather courtyard and a party room.

NEW Martini Grill *Mediterranean*
| - | - | - | E |

Speonk | 190 Montauk Hwy. (bet. Mill Rd. & N. Phillips Ave.) | 631-325-2200

Chef-owner Ali Fathalla and his wife Adriana have operated several Westhampton Beach eateries (including the defunct Le Bistro), and their latest is this Mediterranean bistro situated in a historic Speonk roadhouse with decor featuring the titular drink in paintings and tabletop votive candles in martini glasses; a separate bar includes a pool table.

Massa's 🅼 *Pizza*
| 23 | 10 | 17 | $20 |

Huntington Station | 146 W. Jericho Tpke. (bet. Collins Pl. & Pine Tree Rd.) | 631-935-0200 | www.massaspizzeria.com

"For those who know the true virtues of coal-oven pies", this Huntington Station parlor's "amazing" pizza – featuring a "crisp", "paper-thin crust", "fresh mozzarella" and just the "right amount" of "delicious" sauce – is "one of the best" "ever"; sure, the "decor is slim to nonexistent" and service isn't stellar, but with pies like these, "who cares?"

	FOOD	DECOR	SERVICE	COST

Matsulin *Asian*
22 | 18 | 20 | $39

Hampton Bays | 131 W. Montauk Hwy. (Springville Rd.) |
631-728-8838 | www.matsulin.com

An "extensive" menu of "surprisingly high quality" – whether Thai, Chinese, Malaysian, Vietnamese or "fresh sushi" – makes this Hampton Bays Pan-Asian "a real find" "in an unexpected place" (i.e. "a former bank"); regulars rely on the "reasonable prices" and "efficient service" to outweigh any lack of "luster."

Matsuya *Asian*
21 | 19 | 20 | $36

Great Neck | Gardens Mall | 6 Great Neck Rd. (bet. Brompton & Middle Neck Rds.) | 516-773-4411 | www.matsuyasushi.com

With a "stepped-up menu" providing "more Pan-Asian choices" and cooked dishes to complement the "top-notch" sushi "creations" from a "chef who works magic", this "unpretentious" Great Neck "go-to" "keeps getting better with age"; "gracious and accommodating" service and a "colorful", wall-length "tank of tropical fish" ("like going to a real aquarium") also ensure it "stands out" in the area.

⊠ Matteo's *Italian*
23 | 16 | 20 | $44

Bellmore | 416 Bedford Ave. (Wilson Ave.) | 516-409-1779
Roslyn Heights | 88 Mineola Ave. (bet. Elm & Willow Sts.) | 516-484-0555
Huntington Station | 300 W. Jericho Tpke. (West Hills Rd.) |
631-421-6001
www.matteosristorante.com

"Those who love lots of garlic" can "count on" this "family-style" Italian quartet, where "helpful" staffers deliver "oversized" platters of "well-prepared" "comfort" fare; dissenters are distracted by the "loud", "tacky" settings, but they're "busy, busy" with "a happy crowd" that's willing to "wait on line", so "they must be doing something right."

Matthew's *Seafood*
▽ 22 | 19 | 21 | $43

Ocean Beach | Fire Island | 935 Bay Walk (bet. Evergreen & Surfview Walks) | 631-583-8016

This seasonal Ocean Beach vet "packs" in Fire Island fin fans lured by "tasty" seafood – there's a featured catch of the day – and "beautiful water views" from the deck and "private dock" overlooking the Great South Bay; though the food is "fine", the open-air "atmosphere is why you pay the price"; P.S. shoppers can also net fresh fish from the adjacent market.

Maureen & Daughters'
25 | 20 | 22 | $20
Kitchen ⌷ *American*

Smithtown | 108 Terry Rd. (Larsen Ave.) | 631-360-9227

"Holy cow!", this "bustling", "cash-only" morning "nirvana" in Smithtown "takes care of you for the day" with "bountiful" "homemade" breakfasts built on "phenomenal pancakes", "fabulous French toast" and "too-good-to-be-true" baked oatmeal (the lunchtime "sandwiches are interesting and tasty too"); the bovine-themed interior is "adorable" and the "lightning-fast" service is the "sweetest around", but before you "indulge yourself", "be prepared" to "brave the lines."

	FOOD	DECOR	SERVICE	COST

Maxwell's ◐ *American*
| - | - | - | M |

Islip | 501 Main St. (bet. Grant & Locust Aves.) | 631-210-0011 |
www.lessings.com

Conviviality reigns at this Islip saloon (sibling of Post Office Cafe)
where a huge wood bar and raised dining area with booths and tables beckon locals for drinks and moderately priced American grub
such as burgers and babyback ribs; prancing carousel horses divide
the eating and drinking areas, and a tin ceiling gleams in the stylishly
casual setting; P.S. weeknights bring happy hours.

Mediterranean
| ∇ 21 | 12 | 20 | $27 |

Grill-Kebab *Mediterranean*

Hewlett | 10-12 Franklin Ave. (bet. B'way & W. B'way) |
516-374-4203 | www.mygrillkebab.com

"Value" seekers cite "large portions" and "unbelievably cheap"
tabs at this Mediterranean "local" near the Hewlett train station,
where a "friendly" if "laid-back" crew serves up "very good" kebabs, gyros, Greek salad and the like; naysayers skewer a
"dreary" space in need of "a little sprucing up" but concede it's "ok
to run in" for takeout.

Mediterranean
| 22 | 8 | 18 | $27 |

Snack Bar ⊞ *Greek/Mediterranean*

Huntington | 360 New York Ave. (bet. E. Carver & Elm Sts.) |
631-423-8982 | www.medsnackbar.com

"Excellent since the day it opened" in 1975, this "popular"
Huntington Village "fixture" serves "super-delicious" Med staples
including "fantastic Greek salads", "quality gyros", "moussaka like
Mom's" and owner Steve Soulellis' "fresh-caught seafood"; it's a
"great value", but you'll have to ignore the "tight", "no-frills" setting
or opt for "takeout"; P.S "beware: no credit cards."

Meeting House, The *American/Mediterranean*
| 20 | 18 | 18 | $44 |

Amagansett | Amagansett Sq. | 4 Amagansett Square Dr. (Montauk Hwy.) |
631-267-2764 | www.meetinghouseamagansett.com

Reopened with spiffed-up decor and a New American–Mediterranean
menu that's strong on small plates, this Amagansett Square
standby appeals to "neighborhood" types seeking "well-
prepared", "sensibly priced" bites; everything's "amicably
served" in a "lively" space with an "active bar" and a predictably
vigorous "noise level"; P.S. the Food and Decor scores do not reflect
a renovation and menu change.

Melting Pot *Fondue*
| 18 | 20 | 20 | $45 |

Farmingdale | 2377 Broadhollow Rd. (Smith St.) | 631-752-4242 |
www.meltingpot.com

"It's all about sharing" and "cooking your own food" at this
Farmingdale chain link serving "every kind of fondue", including
"delicious" chocolate pots; while it's a "romantic" "treat" for
"younger couples" and "fun to do with a group", critics contend it's
"overpriced" and "pretentious", and would prefer a "more casual"
setup; P.S. go with a large party if you want "two burners."

	FOOD	DECOR	SERVICE	COST

Mercato Kitchen & Cocktails *American/Italian*

20 | 20 | 21 | $32

Massapequa Park | Southgate Shopping Ctr. | 4958 Merrick Rd. (Whitewood Dr.) | 516-308-3582 | www.mercatokitchen.com
Fast becoming a "favorite" in Massapequa Park, this "inviting" American-Italian is "better than your average" "neighborhood joint" for "unpretentious" bites like its "delicious" specialty flatbreads ("think pizza without the guilt") at a "reasonable" cost; the "gregarious", "welcoming" staff is "trying hard", and the "lively bar" is a "popular" draw "just for drinks and appetizers."

NEW Meridian Kitchen 🅢 *Asian/Continental*

– | – | – | E

Locust Valley | 23 Birch Hill Rd. (bet. Elm St. & Forest Ave.) | 516-676-2620 | www.meridiankitchen.com
Chef-owner Gary Lanza expanded the dining area of his former Bin 23 to create this Locust Valley newcomer, where a casually elegant Colonial West Indies feel comes via faux-candle chandeliers and plush velvet booths; the Asian-Continental fusion menu offers extensive sushi selections, plus entrees that range from roast duckling with Grand Marnier glaze to pan-seared tofu teriyaki; P.S. Meridian Kitchen to Go is a few doors away.

Meson Iberia *Continental/Spanish*

22 | 14 | 22 | $34

Island Park | 4335 Austin Blvd. (bet. Kingston Blvd. & Sagamore Rd.) | 516-897-4911 | www.mesoniberia.com
The paella "loaded with seafood" and "homemade sangria" "are *muy bueno*" at this "warm", "family-owned" Island Parker, a fallback for fans of its "authentic", "flavorful" Spanish-Continental "standards" presented with a personal touch; maybe the "dated" room's "in need of a makeover", but it's "not too expensive" and "you always feel at home."

Metropolitan Bistro *American*

∇ 22 | 22 | 19 | $39

Sea Cliff | 39 Roslyn Ave. (10th Ave.) | 516-801-4500 | www.themetropolitanbistro.com
Locals applaud this "wonderful" "addition to Sea Cliff" (in the former Tupelo Honey space) for its concise menu of midrange New American fare – notably the "smoky, juicy burger" and "outstanding" Chatham cod – delivered by "unobtrusive" staffers in a "relaxed" setting sporting French doors and a patio; a hedger or two hints they're "still finding their way", but it's coming to be a "neighborhood" "favorite."

Michael Anthony's Food Bar *Eclectic*

24 | 16 | 21 | $48

Wading River | 2925 N. Wading River Rd. (bet. Hulse Ave. & Hulse Landing Rd.) | 631-929-8800 | www.michaelanthonysfoodbar.com
An "inventive menu" of "awesome" Eclectic dishes in "picturesque" presentations marks this Wading River "hideaway", where the "talented" eponymous chef is "likely to arrive at your table at any moment to see how you're enjoying his masterpieces"; "top-notch" servers tend the "comfortable", "recently redecorated" space, so while "it's not easy to find", it's "worth the effort" and "the price of admission"; P.S. closed Tuesdays.

	FOOD	DECOR	SERVICE	COST

Michaels' at Maidstone Beach *American*   18 | 15 | 21 | $45

East Hampton | 28 Maidstone Park Rd. (off Three Mile Harbor Rd.) | 631-324-0725 | www.michaelsofmaidstone.com

"Hidden away" "off the beaten track" in East Hampton, this "old-timer" is "known by the locals" for its "good, honest" American fare (crab cakes, Long Island duck) and "very un-Hamptons" atmosphere; true, a few feel the well-worn digs "need a makeover", but regulars who prize it as a "best-kept secret" still plead "don't tell anyone!"

Milk & Sugar Café *American*   21 | 24 | 19 | $30

Bay Shore | 49 W. Main St. (Park Ave.) | 631-969-3655 | www.milkandsugarcafe.com

"Meet the girls for a catch-up lunch" at this "cute" Bay Shore "rendezvous", a "quaint and offbeat" setup akin to "a friend's house" with "cozy couches" to "just melt into" while enjoying "comforting" American eats and "delectable desserts" served day and night "at affordable prices"; it's a "sweet" spot to "relax and chat", but go with "time to linger" since the staff sometimes shows "the attentiveness of a bad ex."

Mill Creek Tavern Ⓜ *Seafood/Steak*   21 | 20 | 21 | $39

Bayville | 275 Bayville Ave. (Pine Park Ave.) | 516-628-2000 | www.millcreekny.com

Everyone from "grandma to grandchild will be happy" with the "huge menu" at this Bayville "sister restaurant of Mim's", which "lures you back like a magnet" with "reliable" surf 'n' turf (including "huge buckets of mussels") and "warm" atmospherics kindled by a "very personable" owner who "hops tables" to "get the party going"; it's "popular" for "everyday casual dining", and the "consistency shows why."

Milleridge Inn *American*   16 | 22 | 19 | $40

Jericho | 585 N. Broadway (bet. Jericho Tpke. & Market St.) | 516-931-2201 | www.milleridge.com

"History surrounds you" at this Jericho "standby" for "family celebrations" set in a "grand" Colonial home with 14 fireplaces and a neighboring "village" of "cute" "little shoppes", which is at its best "during the holidays when everything's decorated" and "carolers in 1700s costume" roam the rooms; for many, the prix fixe-only menu's "traditional American" fare is "mediocre" and the service merely "satisfactory", but it stays "busy" with stalwart supporters who come "for old time's sake"; P.S. a separate cottage and carriage house are available for private events.

Mill Pond House *Seafood/Steak*   25 | 23 | 23 | $54

Centerport | 437 E. Main St. (bet. Centershore & Little Neck Rds.) | 631-261-7663 | www.millpondrestaurant.com

"Amazing views" of the eponymous pond, especially from "the terrace in summer", combine with "top-notch steaks and seafood" ("surprisingly" "excellent" sushi included) and "unbeatable service" to make this "lovely" Centerport "cousin to Piccolo" "a special-occasion magnet"; warm weather also brings on a "jumping" "tiki bar scene", and though dinner's admittedly "pricey", the prix fixe lunch "is an incredible value."

Mim's *American*

20 | 17 | 19 | $36

Roslyn Heights | 235 Roslyn Rd. (bet. Jane & Thelma Sts.) | 516-625-7305
Syosset | 33 Berry Hill Rd. (bet. Church St. & Muttontown Eastwoods Rd.) | 516-364-2144
www.mimsny.com

Mum's certainly not the word on these "always-busy" "standbys" in Roslyn Heights and Syosset, where the "mind-boggling" variety of "well-prepared", "substantially portioned" New American faves sends patrons home hauling "big doggy bags"; they can "get a little hectic" and "deafening", but with "accommodating" service and a "terrific" early-bird deal, they're "convenient" for "comfort-type" dining "without having to take out a loan."

Minado *Japanese*

21 | 13 | 16 | $34

Carle Place | 219 Glen Cove Rd. (bet. Old Country Rd. & Westbury Ave.) | 516-294-9541 | www.minado.com

"Fresh and plentiful" sushi is only the highlight among "endless choices" at this "mother of all buffets" in Carle Place, a "cavernous all-you-can-eat" "wonderland" for Japanophiles "gorging on" "tasty" seafood, salads and teppanyaki till they "roll out of the place"; despite the "mass-produced" feel, it's "a fun indulgence" and "family favorite" "for the price of admission" ("they charge kids by height").

Minami *Japanese*

∇ 26 | 18 | 22 | $34

Massapequa | 12 Central Ave. (bet. Grand Ave. & Veterans Blvd.) | 516-799-4799 | www.minamijapaneserestaurant.com

Afishionados favor this "Japanese gem" in Massapequa for "consistently" "delectable" sushi that's "not the same old, same old", served "fresh" "from the ocean right to your plate" and "reasonably priced" to boot; a "caring staff" that "greets repeat customers" helps explain why its "loyal clientele" is "willing to bypass" the competition.

NEW Mint *Asian*

- | - | - | E

Garden City | Roosevelt Field Mall | 1 Ring Road W. (Ring Rd.) | 516-307-8677 | www.mintny.com

Situated in a stand-alone building beside Garden City's Roosevelt Field, this flashy new Indo-Asian fusion hot spot features a waterfall at the entrance and a spacious dining room decked out in vibrant hues of persimmon, tangerine and lime; an upstairs roof garden is the fair-weather destination, offering multiple bars and sexy semi-private lounge areas set off with billowy white curtains, plus its own menu of specialty cocktails, apps and entrees.

Mirabelle, Restaurant Ⓜ *French*

25 | 23 | 24 | $67

Stony Brook | Three Village Inn | 150 Main St. (Shore Rd.) | 631-751-0555 | www.lessings.com

"Another winner" for "top chef" Guy Reuge, his "extraordinary" French flagship (relocated from St. James) now occupies a "refined", fireplace-equipped space in Stony Brook's "venerable" Three Village Inn, where "superior" cuisine is prepared with "inventive" "subtlety" and matched with "marvelous" service; a few nostalgists "miss the old" locale, but most declare they'll "follow this Guy wherever he goes"; P.S. for those put off by "high prices", the more affordable Mirabelle Tavern awaits under the same roof.

Mirabelle Tavern *American* 21 | 22 | 21 | $47

Stony Brook | Three Village Inn | 150 Main St. (Shore Rd.) | 631-751-0555 | www.lessings.com

For a "more relaxed" taste of "culinary impresario" Guy Reuge's "creative" cooking, try this "inviting" sidekick in a "delightful" tavern space "mere feet away" from Stony Brook's Restaurant Mirabelle; applying the same "meticulous preparation" to a more affordable, "small plates"-centric New American menu, it "raises the bar for casual dining", though some say the "noise" and "occasional slow service" "can dampen enthusiasm"; P.S. the $27 prix fixe lunch is a "great deal."

Miraj Healthy Grill *Mediterranean/Persian* - | - | - | M

Williston Park | 171 Hillside Ave. (bet. Park & Willis Aves.) | 516-747-3181 | www.mirajhealthygrill.com

Focusing on healthy fare, this midpriced Med-Persian cafe in Williston Park offers salads and grilled vegetables and meats (e.g. charbroiled Cornish hen), plus more complex dishes such as a chicken stew with walnuts in a pomegranate sauce; the simple setting features wood paneling and burgundy tablecloths.

NEW Miraku *Japanese* - | - | - | M

Great Neck | 31 S. Middle Neck Rd. (bet. Schenk Ave. & Station Plaza) | 516-466-6369 | www.mirakuny.com

Located just a stone's throw from the Great Neck train station, this midpriced modern izakaya serves a frequently changing menu focusing on seasonal Japanese small plates and hard-to-obtain fish (think tuna-tofu sliders or fried blowfish); the setting features a sushi bar and kotatsu tables, with a separate drinks bar specializing in sake and sochu that also offers a full cocktail list and food, should you wish.

⊠ Mirko's Ⓜ *Eclectic* 26 | 22 | 24 | $79

Water Mill | Water Mill Sq. | 670 Montauk Hwy. (bet. Cobb & Old Mill Rds.) | 631-726-4444 | www.mirkosrestaurant.com

"Absolutely exquisite" Eclectic fare via a chef who "really knows how to cook" and "clubby" service led by his co-owner/hostess wife lure a "loyal" clientele to this Water Mill class act set in a "lovely", country-style space with a fireplace and seasonal patio; even with "high prices" it's "often tough to get in", though a few opine "it helps to be known here"; P.S. open seasonally.

NEW Mitch & Toni's American Bistro ⊠ *American* - | - | - | M

Albertson | 875 Willis Ave. (Meldon Ave.) | 516-741-7940 | www.mitchandtonis.com

Owners Mitchell SuDock (the chef) and Toni Contino (the manager) of recently closed Bistro M are behind this midpriced Albertson

American serving a seasonally inspired menu of small and large plates; its casual dining area features an open floor plan and separate bar.

Mitsui *Japanese*   ▽ 24 | 19 | 22 | $38

Bay Shore | 1 W. Main St. (4th Ave.) | 631-630-9890 | www.mitsuisushi.com

Jonesing sushiphiles can get their mitts on "fantastic", "super-fresh" fish – including "creatively presented" rolls that "send your palate soaring" – at this "true hidden gem in Bay Shore"; with "pleasant" service, "competitive prices" and a venue where "you can actually have a conversation", it's a local "go-to" for Japanese.

MoCa Asian Bistro *Asian*   18 | 22 | 19 | $40

Hewlett | 1300 Peninsula Blvd. (bet. Gibson Blvd. & Mill Rd.) | 516-295-8888 | www.mocaus.com

Bringing "sexy", "swanky" style to "an unlikely strip-mall location", this neon-lit Hewlett Pan-Asian lures Five Towners seeking "Manhattan"-style scenery to "meet friends" over "creatively presented" fusion fare and cocktails; but the buzz doesn't sway skeptics, who charge it's "overpriced" given the "small portions", "noise level" and focus on the "chic interior" "rather than the food."

Modern Snack Bar Ⓜ *American*   18 | 11 | 19 | $28

Aquebogue | 628 Main Rd. (bet. Church Ln. & Edgar Ave.) | 631-722-3655 | www.modernsnackbar.com

"Torn from the 1950s", this "popular" Aquebogue "fixture" has "been around since forever", earning a "well-deserved" rep for "reliable" American "home cookin'" à la "delicious mashed turnips" and "insanely good" "slabs of pie" ("save room") served by "friendly" waitresses in retro "uniforms"; while "nothing fancy", it's a "bargain" and "you won't go hungry", so there may be a "line at the door"; P.S. closed December–April.

⦿NEW Monsoon *Asian*   – | – | – | E

Babylon | 48 Deer Park Ave. (bet. Grove Pl. & Main St.) | 631-587-4400 | www.monsoonny.com

Housed in an impressive former bank building in Babylon with 35-foot ceilings, this upscale Pan-Asian newcomer under the aegis of the Bohlsen Group (Tellers in Islip, Prime in Huntington) melds Vietnamese, Chinese and Thai cuisines with American tastes, and serves the dishes family-style in a hip, bi-level setting that features glowing red walls, a huge movie screen showing nature photos, and a long onyx bar; P.S. there's a DJ some nights.

⦿ Morton's The Steakhouse *Steak*   25 | 23 | 24 | $70

Great Neck | 777 Northern Blvd. (Susquehanna Ave.) | 516-498-2950 | www.mortons.com

A steakhouse "standard-bearer", this "big-ticket" chain offers "excellently prepared" cuts of beef and "grand sides" "served professionally" amid an "ambiance of wealth and class" in Great Neck; some find it a bit "staid" and wish they'd "lose the raw-meat presentation" and "high" wine pricing, but the many who love its "traditional" ways consider it "one of the best."

❷ Mosaic ⊠Ⓜ *American* | 28 | 21 | 27 | $64

St. James | 418 N. Country Rd. (Edgewood Ave.) | 631-584-2058 | www.eatmosaic.com

The "spectacular" "ever-changing, five-course tasting menu" via "geniuses in the kitchen" Tate Morris and Jonathan Contes "never fails to please" at this diminutive St. James "gem", where "adventurous diners" are awestruck by the "flavors and textures" of "inspired" New American dishes "paired with exquisite wines"; add in "cheerful" servers who "never miss a beat" and a "cozy", "quiet" space, and it's an "unexpected treat for the palate" – "bravo!"

Mother Kelly's *American/Italian* | 21 | 12 | 18 | $30

Cedarhurst | 490 Chestnut St. (bet. Cedarhurst Ave. & Spruce St.) | 516-295-5421

Syosset | Long Island Industrial | 575 Underhill Blvd. (Jericho Tpke.) | 516-802-0333

www.motherkellysli.com

"Dress down" and "don't be on a diet" at this "boisterous" Cedarhurst "staple", where the "ginormous" portions ("mamma mia!") of "awesome" Italian-American "comfort food" and pizza will bust your belt but not your budget; the "casual" quarters "resemble a mess hall", but a "loyal following" "for so many years" attests it's "tough to go wrong" here; P.S. the Syosset spin-off offers takeout only.

🆕 MP Taverna *Greek* | - | - | - | M

Roslyn | 1363 Old Northern Blvd. (bet. E. B'way & Main St.) | 516-686-6486 | www.mptaverna.com

Michael Psilakis (NYC's Kefi, Fish Tag) has opened this chic yet casual Greek in Roslyn featuring a reasonably priced menu (most entrees are under $20) that ranges from grilled seafood to a lamb burger; the bi-level setting has an open, welcoming feel, with a central horseshoe bar, pine floor and oversized mirrors on the walls.

Mumon *Japanese* | ∇ 22 | 25 | 21 | $48

Garden City | 1300 Franklin Ave. (bet. 13th & 14th Sts.) | 516-747-3388 | www.mumonrestaurant.com

"All-around classy", this Garden City stunner (the moniker is Japanese for 'dream') is a fantasy come to life for sushi savants savoring "lovely presentations" of the "best quality" fish – along with "excellent" cooked dishes – in an "upscale", "modern Asian" milieu with "wonderful" "Zen" decor and "top-notch" service; it aims to impress "much like a Manhattan hot spot", leaving a few to yen for "more affordable" prices.

Muse in the Harbor *American* | 23 | - | 22 | $54

Sag Harbor | 16 Main St. (bet. Nassau & Water Sts.) | 631-899-4810 | www.museintheharbor.com

"Enthusiastic" East End chef Matthew Guiffrida closed his Water Mill Aquatic Lounge to snag this larger, more visible Main Street, Sag Harbor space where service is "excellent" as ever and patrons can still "watch the aquatic life" in the beautiful fish tank (it's just no longer imbedded in the bar); the "creatively delicious" New

American menu has been broadened, while continuing to feature tongue-in-cheek names for dishes such as Not Ya Mama's Meatballs, with decadent desserts also figuring prominently.

☒ Nagahama *Japanese*

| 28 | 15 | 22 | $37 |

Long Beach | 169 E. Park Ave. (bet. Long Beach & Riverside Blvds.) | 516-432-6446 | www.nagahamasushi.com

For "real quality", "you just can't beat" "inventive" chef-owner Hide Yamamoto's "pristine sushi" at this "reliable" Japanese, where the "incredibly fresh" fish and "warm" service have the natives feeling "lucky to live in Long Beach"; the renovated space is still "as small as a bento box" and "packed" to the gills, so dragon-roll disciples either get their "fix during the week" or "have them on speed-dial" for delivery.

Nagashima ☒ *Japanese*

| 24 | 13 | 19 | $35 |

Jericho | Jericho Office & Shopping Plaza | 12A-1 Jericho Tpke. (Brush Hollow Rd.) | 516-338-0022 | www.nagashimali.com

"It doesn't look like much", but this Japanese "hole-in-the-wall" in a Jericho "strip mall" is a "proven" "treasure" for sushi seekers known for its "terrific variety" of "consistently fresh" fish, notably the "innovative" "specialty rolls"; touchy types nag that the "service is not the nicest", but it's "quick" enough that "your cup of green tea never goes low."

Nanking *Chinese/Thai*

| ▽ 19 | 20 | 16 | $34 |

New Hyde Park | 2056 Hillside Ave. (bet. Aster Dr. & Marcus Ave.) | 516-352-0009 | www.nankingrestaurantgroup.com

Representing the "diversity of Asian cuisine", this New Hyde Park branch of a regional chainlet is a "reasonably consistent" source of midpriced Chinese-Thai fare in eye-pleasing environs equipped with plush banquettes, copper-top tables and a "huge Buddha"; it strives to be something "different", though doubters declare they're "trying for fusion" but producing "mostly confusion."

Nautilus Cafe *Seafood/Steak*

| 24 | 17 | 23 | $46 |

Freeport | 46 Woodcleft Ave. (bet. Adams & Front Sts.) | 516-379-2566 | www.nautiluscafe.com

"Whether it's surf or turf", this Freeport "fixture" is "a winner" among "ever so many" rivals "on the Nautical Mile" thanks to its "super seafood", "wonderful" steaks and "right-on" service from a "courteous staff"; the interior is "nothing fancy", but there are views "across the street to the waterside" and the early-bird deal is "one of the best" going.

Navy Beach *American*

| 19 | 20 | 17 | $49 |

Montauk | Port Royal | 16 Navy Rd. (off Industrial & 2nd House Rds.) | 631-668-6868 | www.navybeach.com

"Beautiful sunsets" snare shorebirds at this seasonal "'in' spot" on Montauk's Fort Pond Bay, where "picnic tables" on the sand and a "nautical" dining room set the "beachy" scene for a "limited" but "surprisingly tasty" American menu of seafood and burgers; snipers say the service is "amateurish" given the "expense", but that doesn't lower the "buzz" that draws "weekend crowds" despite the "hard-to-find location."

Nello Summertimes *Italian*   ∇ 16 | 21 | 13 | $116

Southampton | Nello Summertimes | 136 Main St. (bet. Hampton Rd. & Post Crossing) | 631-287-5500

If you're "just people-watching", this seasonal Southamptoner (via an Upper East Side original) is a "showstopper" with "gorgeous surroundings", a "lively bar" and an especially sceney "outdoor terrace"; but given merely "average" Northern Italian food and lacking service, it's "hard to justify" "absurdly expensive" tabs that are "enough to make even a longtime Hamptonite gasp" – "what's the point?"

New Chilli &   ∇ 26 | 15 | 24 | $27
Curry Restaurant Ⓜ *Indian*

Hicksville | 106 Woodbury Rd. (bet. Charles & Max Aves.) | 516-932-9180

"Hot means hot" at this "tiny" Hicksville hideaway, where "spectacular" Northern Indian dishes – along with "innovative" Chinese and Thai "fusion" fare – are prepared "as spicy as you can stand it", even if you need "a fire extinguisher at meal's end"; "incredibly friendly" staffers welcome all "like long-lost family", and the "cozy digs" are often "bustling" now that "the locals have discovered it"; P.S. "you can't beat" the $7.95 lunch buffet.

New Paradise Cafe *American/Eclectic*   22 | 17 | 21 | $56

Sag Harbor | 126 Main St. (bet. Nassau & Spring Sts.) | 631-725-6080 | www.newparadisecafe.net

"It's a keeper" confirm "the locals" at this "solid" Sag Harbor "favorite" (under the same ownership as Robert's in Water Mill), "one of the better" area options for "tasty and innovative" New American-Eclectic eats and "welcoming" service with "no attitude"; the "neighborhood vibe" extends to the "attractive bar" and summertime deck, and the "dependable" performance brings the faithful "back on a regular basis."

Nicholas James Bistro Ⓜ *American*   22 | 17 | 21 | $37

Merrick | 2057 Merrick Rd. (bet. Hewlett & Merrick Aves.) | 516-546-4805 | www.njbistro.com

Regulars relish the "creative menu" at this "shining star in Merrick", a "neighborhood eatery" where the New American fare and "accommodating service" are "consistently" "a cut above"; penny-pinchers protest it's "on the pricey side", but the "understated" yet "appealing" space is "almost always crowded."

Nichol's *American*   17 | 12 | 19 | $38

East Hampton | 100 Montauk Hwy. (Daniels Hole Rd.) | 631-324-3939

Like "the Cheers of East Hampton", this "unpretentious", "very local" "hangout" is an "easy" option for "decent" burgers and other "simple" American grub served in "friendly, pub-type" surroundings; "bargain" prices boost its "popularity", and come summer "you can sit outdoors" if you don't mind "cars whizzing by."

	FOOD	DECOR	SERVICE	COST

☒ Nick & Toni's *Italian/Mediterranean* — 24 | 22 | 22 | $69

East Hampton | 136 N. Main St. (bet. Cedar St. & Miller Terr.) | 631-324-3550 | www.nickandtonis.com

"Classy and consistent", this "legendary" East Hampton "standout" is still "bustling" with "the 'in' crowd" drawn to its "first-rate" Italian-Med plates (some via a "wood-burning oven"), "spot-on" service and "celebrity aura"; though "wallet pain" may set in, it "hasn't lost its touch" for "memorable" dining – assuming "you can get a reservation."

Nick's *Pizza* — 23 | 16 | 21 | $26

Rockville Centre | 272 Sunrise Hwy. (bet. Morris & N. Park Aves.) | 516-763-3278 | www.nicksrvc.com

Pizzaphiles hail this "family-friendly" Rockville Centre Italian (with siblings in Manhattan and Forest Hills) as a "step above the rest" for its "superb thin-crust" pies ("they don't sell slices"), but "bring an appetite" for the "plentiful" portions of *delicioso* pastas, salads and calzones too; add "fair prices", "great service" and "Sinatra singing to you in the background", and "what more do you want?"

Nick's Tuscan Grill ⓜ *Italian* — 21 | 21 | 21 | $39

Long Beach | 40 E. Park Ave (bet. Edwards & Riverside Blvds.) | 516-432-2690 | www.nickstuscangrill.com

After a "transformation" from the seafood-centric Coastal Grill, this "feel-good" Long Beach eatery is now the George Martin chain's link to Northern Italy, upholding the same "even-keeled" "standards" with its "hearty", "quite tasty" "traditional" menu and "smooth" service; lodged in a "warm setting" with Tuscany brick and earth tones, it "knows how to please", even if have-nots nix it as "too highly priced."

Nisen ⓜ *Japanese* — 25 | 24 | 20 | $49

Woodbury | Woodbury Village Shopping Ctr. | 7967 Jericho Tpke. (S. Woods Rd.) | 516-496-7000 | www.nisenwoodbury.com

Nisen Sushi *Japanese*

Commack | 5032 Jericho Tpke. (Larkfield Rd.) | 631-462-1000 | www.nisensushi.com

"Awesome sushi" "the way it should be", as well as "perfect" Japanese dishes presented like "art on a plate" in "beautiful" "modern" settings catapult this "pricey" Commack and Woodbury duo to "winner" status among its "good-looking", "lively" crowd; a handful gripes about staff with "attitude", but most like the "trendy" "Manhattan feel"; P.S. there's a DJ in Woodbury Thursday and Friday nights.

☒ Noah's *American* — 26 | 18 | 21 | $50

Greenport | 136 Front St. (bet. 1st & 3rd Sts.) | 631-477-6720 | www.chefnoahschwartz.com

"Adventuresome" chef/co-owner Noah Schwartz (formerly of Southold's now-defunct Seafood Barge) lends his "highly imaginative" flair to this "welcome addition to Greenport", where the New American menu showcases "inspired", seafood-centric small plates alongside full entrees and a raw bar; the "professional" staff is "helpful with choices", and despite a "stark", "too-noisy" setting that's "more SoHo than NoFo", the "fabulous" "grazing" ensures it's "always hoppin'."

NEW Nobu at Capri Ⓜ Japanese

| - | - | - | VE |

Southampton | Capri | 281 County Rd. 39A (N. Main St.) | 631-488-4248 | www.caprisouthampton.com

This celeb-friendly hot spot in Southampton's Capri resort (newly redecorated by Cynthia Rowley) serves Nobu Matsuhisa's famed Peruvian-tinged Japanese menu, plus several dishes created just for the Hamptons; very cool and breezy-chic, the indoor/outdoor dining room is awash in white, from the walls and tables to the drum chandeliers; P.S. open summer only.

Nonnina Ⓜ Italian

| 25 | 24 | 23 | $53 |

West Islip | 999 Montauk Hwy. (bet. Gladstone Ave. & Oak Neck Rd.) | 631-321-8717 | www.nonninarestaurant.com

Count on "terrific" "interpretations of the classics" at this "upscale" West Islip Italian, where the "fabulous food", "stellar service" and "beautiful" but "comfortable" surroundings are "perfect for a romantic" "special occasion" or a "wonderful" "night out with friends"; devotees who "are never disappointed" deem it "so worth" "the trip and the price."

NEW North Fork Oyster Co. Seafood

| - | - | - | E |

Greenport | Stirling Sq. | 300 Main St. (Bay Ave.) | 631-477-6840 | www.northforkoystercompany.com

Nestled in the back of Greenport's Stirling Square in a refurbished 19th-century horse barn, this white-tablecloth seafooder proffers local fish, oysters and more, all served alongside cocktails and a wine list featuring many local vinos; patrons can relax in the comfortable dining room done up in off-white tones or sit in the patio area or the bar up front.

Ⓩ North Fork Table & Inn American

| 29 | 25 | 27 | $77 |

Southold | North Fork Table & Inn | 57225 Main Rd./Rte. 25 (bet. Boisseau & Laurel Aves.) | 631-765-0177 | www.northforktableandinn.com

Chef Gerry Hayden (ex Aureole) "has reached new heights" at this "stellar" Southold "destination", which secures the No. 1 rating for Food in this Survey with "a constantly evolving, brilliantly realized" New American menu crafted from "the freshest local ingredients" and matched with "gold-standard" desserts from Claudia Fleming (ex Gramercy Tavern); "impeccable, gracious" service that's also rated No. 1 on Long Island and a "civilized" "rural setting" round out an experience as "unforgettable" "as anything in NYC, period"; P.S. the Lunch Truck is planted out back, dispensing midday lobster rolls, artisan hot dogs and such at gentle prices.

Novitá Wine Bar & Trattoria Italian

| 23 | 22 | 22 | $41 |

Garden City | 860 Franklin Ave. (bet. 9th St. & Stewart Ave.) | 516-739-7660 | www.novita-ny.com

"Inventive", "trendy" and a "wine lover's dream", this stylishly "modern" Garden City spot pairs its "wonderful" Italian bites with

100 "fantastic" vinos by the glass dispensed from a state-of-the-art system by an "educated" staff; while "totally worth" "every penny", it's "definitely a scene" "for singles looking to mingle", so "eat early or bring earplugs" if you're "over the age of 35."

Oak Chalet Ⓜ *Continental/German*　19 | 19 | 20 | $37

Bellmore | 1940 Bellmore Ave. (bet. Beltagh Ave. & Natta Blvd.) | 516-826-1700 | www.oakchalet.net

Home to Continental-German dishes "done right", this "old standby" in Bellmore proffers a "meat-and-potatoes" menu and a "wide variety" of *bier* in "homey", "inviting" quarters tended by "friendly people"; detractors who discern "nothing spaetzle" contend it "needs updating", but fans of the "change of scenery" and "homemade taste" counter "who really cares?"

Oakland's *American/Seafood*　18 | 21 | 18 | $49

Hampton Bays | 365 Dune Rd. (Rd. H, at Shinnecock Inlet) | 631-728-6900

Sundays on the Bay *American/Seafood*

Hampton Bays | 369 Dune Rd. (Rd. H, at Shinnecock Inlet) | 631-728-2611 www.oaklandsrestaurant.com

"Go just before sunset" for "unbeatable views" from the "waterfront" deck "on Shinnecock Inlet" (a "boat-watcher's dream") that draw "crowds galore" to this seasonal Hampton Bays American (with a year-round sibling, Sundays on the Bay); those who find the seafood-leaning menu and "undertrained" service merely "adequate" for the price prefer it for the "ocean breeze", "live music" and "enjoyable" open-air bar.

Oar Steak & Seafood Grill *Seafood/Steak*　21 | 19 | 20 | $38

Patchogue | Sun Dek Marina | 264 West Ave. (Mulford St.) | 631-654-8266 | www.theoar.com

As it's "accessible by boat", seafarers and landlubbers alike can enjoy "alfresco" "dockside dining" on "solid" fish and steaks at this "funky" "warm-weather" "favorite" in Patchogue's Sun Dek Marina; the "casual" interior's walls are aptly "covered in paddles", and "live bands" on summer weekends ensure there's a "good time to be had by all."

Oaxaca Mexican Food Treasure *Mexican*　23 | 10 | 22 | $24

Huntington | 385 New York Ave. (bet. Main & W. Carver Sts.) | 631-547-1232 | www.oaxacamenu.com

"Don't tell anyone" plead "in-the-know" compadres "blown away" by this Huntington "joint", whose "amazing", "super-cheap" "peasant food" delivers "homemade" "Mexican authenticity at its best"; the "lovely" staff "makes you feel like a regular", and "don't be fooled by" the "divey" digs – it's an "unpolished gem" that "really is a treasure"; P.S. serves beer and wine only.

Ocean Grill Ⓜ *American/Seafood*　▽ 23 | 18 | 22 | $50

Freeport | Ocean Marina | 499 S. Main St. (Laurel Rd.) | 516-208-9604 | www.oceangrillfreeport.com

Fans find "fresh" seafood, "modestly priced burgers" and other American and Italian eats at this family-oriented Freeporter; there's patio seating in the summer, and a simple, red-accented, white-tableclothed interior.

NEW Oceans 5 M *Seafood* — | — | — | E

Shoreham | Shoreham Plaza | 99 Rte. 25A (bet. Miller Ave. & Tesla St.) | 631-849-6414 | www.oceans5seafood.com

Part market, part white-tablecloth restaurant, this Shoreham new-comer features a long glass display case filled with fresh seafood leading to the dining area, where the menu focuses on organically raised fish and shellfish; the setting includes huge photos of fishing villages and boats, and there's a small bar in the back accented with bright blue lights.

Off the Hook Seafood Market & Grill *Seafood* ▽ 20 | 9 | 17 | $30
(fka Jeff's Seafood & Galley)

East Northport | Elwood Plaza | 1965 Jericho Tpke. (Elwood Rd.) | 631-858-2393 | www.offthehookseafoodmarket.com

Expect nothing less than "fresh seafood" at this "takeout"-geared East Northport eatery that's simply a "fish store with a few tables on the side", dressed up with murals and an ocean of teal and sea blue; kids get a kick out of kitschy maritime effects like barrels and net-ting, and for adults, "BYO is always fun", even if a few feel it's "a little pricey" for the portions.

Old Fields *American/Steak* — | — | — | M

Greenlawn | 81 Broadway (Railroad St.) | 631-754-9868 | www.oldfieldsgreenlawn.com

Owners David Tunney and his wife, Christine, renovated this vintage Greenlawn American steakhouse while keeping period details in-cluding a fireplace, wooden booths, tin ceiling and knotty-pine panel-ing; a moderately priced menu offers both the house strip steak – marinated according to a 55-year-old recipe – and newer items like a beef patty nestled between two grilled cheddar-cheese sandwiches.

Old Mill Inn *American/Seafood* 20 | 20 | 20 | $44

Mattituck | 5775 W. Mill Rd. (Naugles Rd.) | 631-298-8080 | www.theoldmillinn.net

Although "really off the beaten path", this "waterfront" New American in a restored mill with a "pretty view" of Mattituck Inlet is a "charming" "surprise" where "friendly" staffers serve a "well-prepared" menu focused on local seafood; with an interior sporting "polished wood" that "evokes an old yacht" and an "excellent" "deck" for summer, it's worth using "a GPS to find"; P.S. closed November–April.

Olive Oils *Italian* 20 | 16 | 18 | $29

Point Lookout | 28 Lido Blvd. (Bellmore Ave.) | 516-432-0000 | www.oliveoilsrestaurant.com

For a "decent" fix of pizza, panini or "something parmigiana", Point Lookout denizens turn to this "little" "local Italian" at the foot of the Loop Parkway; though "very ordinary", its "casual" bites and

Monday prix fixe pasta nights are "surprisingly good" for the price, and there's seating "outside in the summer."

O'Mally's ◐ *Pub Food*
| 18 | 15 | 20 | $31 |

Southold | 44780 North Rd. (bet. Horton Ln. & Youngs Ave.) | 631-765-2111 | www.omallysisopen.com

"You'd be amazed how many ways" they can prepare a burger (30 or so are on the menu) at this Southold "standby" for "solid" American pub fare delivered by "cheerful" staffers in "comfortable", "kid-friendly" digs; "fair prices" and service "until midnight" keep "locals and weekenders" alike "coming back" for more.

1 North Steakhouse Ⓜ *Steak*
| 22 | 18 | 21 | $48 |

Hampton Bays | 1 North Rd. (bet. Montauk & Sunrise Hwys.) | 631-594-3419 | www.1northsteakhouse.com

Most diners are "proud to bring friends" to this upscale Hampton Bays "tavern" boasting a porterhouse that's "soft as silk", "excellent" sides and "creative" options like a lobster mac 'n' cheese; service is generally "pleasant" and there's live music Friday nights, but despite a double-sided fireplace, few warm up to the "bland" decor with a bit of a "shopping-mall" feel.

Onsen Sushi *Japanese*
| - | - | - | M |

Oakdale | 597 Montauk Hwy. (bet. Dale Dr. & La Salle Pl.) | 631-567-1688

Chef/co-owner Jason Chen (ex Nisen in Commack) is luring sushi enthusiasts to this tiny, moderately priced Japanese in Oakdale for creations such as the Kenny Special roll – seared tuna wrapped with chopped shrimp; hot dishes from chef-partner Eric Wu include an eggplant sandwich stuffed with seafood and wasabi, and add further incentive to look past the simple storefront setting.

Onzon Thai House Ⓜ *Thai*
| 24 | 12 | 21 | $27 |

Bellmore | 2618 Merrick Rd. (bet. Centre & St. Marks Aves.) | 516-409-6113

"First-rate" Thai dishes with "authentic", "delicate" spicing "always satisfy" at this Bellmore "neighborhood" "benchmark"; the "welcoming" staff and "reasonable prices" (with a BYO policy that "adds to the value") lead its "loyal following" to forgive the "small", "bland" space.

Orchid *Chinese*
| 23 | 20 | 22 | $35 |

Garden City | 730 Franklin Ave. (bet. 7th St. & Stewart Ave.) | 516-742-1116

"Below street level" but way "above standard" Chinese, this Garden City "institution" is "always jumping" with longtime loyalists relishing the "subtle flavors" of "upscale Cantonese" specialties ("Peking duck is a must") "prepared to perfection" and "artfully served" by a "cheerful" staff; decor featuring a mirrored ceiling is "a real blast from the past" that lends '80s-era "class" to the "basement location."

☒ Orient, The *Chinese*
| 27 | 9 | 19 | $27 |

Bethpage | 623 Hicksville Rd. (bet. Courtney & Fiddler Lns.) | 516-822-1010

As "authentic as going to Chinatown", this Bethpage Chinese is "the real thing" for "phenomenal", "richly flavored" Cantonese and "wonderful dim sum" that "can't be beat for quality and value"; "welcoming" owner Tommy Tan leads a team of "skilled waiters" who can "suggest terrific off-menu specials", and though it "gets completely packed" (on weekends particularly) "it's definitely worth the lines"; P.S. the Decor score doesn't reflect an extensive post-Survey renovation.

NEW Orto Ⓜ⌗ Italian
- | - | - | E

Miller Place | 90 N. Country Rd. (Landing Rd.) | 631-473-0014 | www.restaurantorto.com

In a quaint little Miller Place cottage that has housed numerous restaurants, Eric Lomando (Kitchen A Bistro and Kitchen A Trattoria) has opened this Italian hideaway, serving hearty dishes such as lasagna Bolognese and baked lamb and potato stew; a beamed ceiling, wide-plank pine floors and non-working fireplaces add rustic character, while a deck offers summertime tables; P.S. credit cards are not accepted.

Osaka ☒ Japanese
∇ 24 | 16 | 22 | $31

Huntington | 328 W. Main St. (bet. Green & Prospect Sts.) | 631-673-7271

"Amazing" sushi and "excellent" cooked dishes qualify this fairly priced Huntington Japanese as an unsung "favorite" in the nabe; staffed by a chef-owner and his "friendly" crew, the small, spare setup tends to be "quiet" – and the regulars say "let's keep it that way"; P.S. serves beer and wine only.

O's Food & Wine Bar ❶ French
22 | 21 | 21 | $44

St. James | 552 N. Country Rd. (bet. Acron Rd. & Lake Ave.) | 631-584-4600 | www.osfoodandwinebar.com

A "terrific" "way to explore different dishes", this "creative" St. James French from chef-owner Philippe Corbet (ex Bouley) specializes in an "exciting" "tapas menu" that "highlights foods from a different country each month"; it's "fun for a light or full dinner" with "eager" service in "comfy beach house" environs enhanced by two fireplaces, live music Wednesday–Friday and a "hopping" "bar scene."

Osteria da Nino Italian
24 | 19 | 23 | $46

Huntington | 292 Main St. (bet. Green & New Sts.) | 631-425-0820 | www.osteriadanino.com

"Compliments to the chef" cheer champions of this "homey" Huntington Italian (sibling to nearby Red), which "never misses" with "authentic pastas" and other "fabulous" "rustic" dishes "made with love and care" "at a reasonable price"; "professional service" and a "warm", "comfortable setting" further explain why it's a former "secret" "that's becoming more and more popular."

Ozumo Japanese Restaurant Japanese
23 | 17 | 20 | $34

Bethpage | 164 Hicksville Rd. (Hempstead Tpke.) | 516-731-8989 | www.ozumojapaneserestaruant.com

This Bethpage Japanese remains a fish fancier's "favorite" thanks to "superb sushi" professionally served in either a dining area bedecked with photos of sumo wrestlers (Ozumo being the sport's Super Bowl) or a tatami room; but while "the quality hasn't waned" foodwise, foes wrestling with the "run-down feel" suggest "they need to update."

Pace's Steak House *Steak*

| 22 | 20 | 22 | $59 |

Hauppauge | 325 Nesconset Hwy. (bet. Brooksite Dr. & Hauppauge Rd.) | 631-979-7676
Port Jefferson | 318 Wynn Ln. (Main St.) | 631-331-9200
www.pacessteakhouse.com

Reminiscent of "NYC without the drive", this fast-paced Hauppage and Port Jefferson pair plies "humongous" cuts of meat "cooked to perfection" (plus "fresh and delicious seafood") and matched with "fine service" amid "classy" "traditional" atmospherics; they're "busy" and "loud" and it's easy to "run up your tab", but carnivores who call them a "first local choice" "still come back for more."

Paddy McGees *Seafood*

| 18 | 18 | 18 | $40 |

Island Park | 6 Waterview Rd. (Pettit Pl.) | 516-431-8700 | www.paddymcgeesfishhouse.com

Diners from land and sea ("ample boat parking" is available) wash up at this "rustic" Island Park stalwart, where the deck's "water views" of Reynolds Channel give a "Jimmy Buffett-like" boost to the "average" fish and very "relaxed" service; there's also a "mean" Sunday brunch "spread", and on weekends a "massive" "summertime bar crowd" "takes over" for "loud", "rowdy" revelry; P.S. seasonal hours.

🆕 Page at 63 Main *Eclectic*

| - | - | - | E |

Sag Harbor | 63 Main St. (bet. Bay & Washington Sts.) | 631-725-1810

Sag Harbor restaurateur Jerry Wawryk has replaced Blue Sky with this white-tablecloth Eclectic (named for a 19th-century whaling captain), serving a locally inspired menu of small and large plates by Jessie Flores (ex Della Femina); tan-and-white wainscoting gives the upscale dining area an airy feel and there's a quick-service cafe in the back offering organic breakfast and lunch fare plus juices and smoothies.

Page One *American/Eclectic*

| 22 | 18 | 22 | $41 |

Glen Cove | 90 School St. (bet. Highland Rd. & North Ln.) | 516-676-2800 | www.pageonerestaurant.com

Glen Cove converts are "totally seduced" by "talented", "personable" chef/co-owner Jeanine Dimenna's "creative cooking" at this "welcoming" American-Eclectic "treasure", where the "fabulous" fare is "presented artistically" and served "with a smile" by an "excellent" staff; "reasonable" prices (including a "budget-friendly" prix fixe) make it one "amazing treat", so "don't miss out."

Painters' Ⓜ *Eclectic*

| 20 | 20 | 19 | $36 |

Brookhaven Hamlet | 416 S. Country Rd. (Montauk Hwy.) | 631-286-6264 | www.paintersrestaurant.com

About the "coolest place" in Brookhaven Hamlet (and beyond), this "offbeat" Eclectic is a "relaxed" "change of pace" with "spot-on

	FOOD	DECOR	SERVICE	COST

food, tables you can draw on" and "changing artwork displayed" wall-to-wall; as a "casual" "hangout" it lures legions of "locals" who come to "mingle" above "the din" and catch live bands on weekends.

☒ Palm, The *Seafood/Steak*

26 | 20 | 23 | $71

East Hampton | Huntting Inn | 94 Main St. (Huntting Ln.) | 631-324-0411 | www.thepalm.com

"Perfect" lobster, "superb" steaks and "hefty" cocktails are the signatures of this "bustling", "special-occasion" chophouse chain link in The Huntting Inn, with a "dark men's-club" look and "wonderful atmosphere" enhanced by "caricatures of celebs" (and "locals") covering the walls; "impeccable", "old-school" service seals the deal, so while it's "not cheap", most conclude it's "worth it."

☒ Palm Court
at the Carltun Ⓜ *American/Continental*

24 | 28 | 25 | $61

East Meadow | The Carltun | Eisenhower Park (Merrick Ave.) | 516-542-0700 | www.thecarltun.com

"Get pampered" like "a member of an upscale club" at this "lovely" Continental-New American set in a mansion in East Meadow's Eisenhower Park, which oozes "class all the way" with "beautiful surroundings" rated Long Island's No. 1 for Decor (look for paintings of flying monkeys overhead) and "spectacular" presentations of "inventive" cuisine complemented by "extraordinary" wines and "gracious" service; "they charge you accordingly", but "it all works" "if you want to make an impression" or "feel special" – and lunch is "truly a bargain."

Palmer's American Grille *Continental*

21 | 19 | 21 | $41

Farmingdale | 123 Fulton St. (Hempstead Tpke.) | 516-420-0609 | www.palmersamericangrille.com

A "nice surprise" in Farmingdale, this onetime pub now "looks great all around" with a tastefully "comfortable" dining room lined with historic photos, an "inviting" "bar area" with live music on the weekends and a sizable terrace; "accommodating" staffers serve an "excellent" Continental menu, and most sum it up as "a winner."

Pancho's Cantina *Tex-Mex*

19 | 15 | 19 | $28

Island Park | 4245 Austin Blvd. (Audubon Blvd.) | 516-897-8300 | www.panchostexmex.com

"When a fajita fix is needed", this "busy" Tex-Mex in Island Park "caters to families" with "tasty" staples served in "easygoing" environs with "crayons on the tables"; it's "loud", but "plentiful" portions, "obliging" service and "decent prices" are reason enough to "¡ándale!"

Panini Café at Diane's *Sandwiches*

▽ 23 | 15 | 16 | $22

Roslyn | 23 Bryant Ave. (bet. Roosevelt Ave. & Skillman St.) | 516-621-2522 | www.trattoriadiane.com

"Pick up a quick lunch or delicious dessert" "on the cheap" at this "casual cafe" annexed to Diane's Bakery in Roslyn, where "very appetizing" panini, salads and "hot dishes" are prepared "fresh daily" along with the expected "out-of-this-world" baked goods; the "cozy, homey" locale with second-floor seating and a terrace is a midday "favorite."

	FOOD	DECOR	SERVICE	COST

Papa Razzi *Italian*

| 18 | 18 | 19 | $35 |

Westbury | 1500 Jericho Tpke. (Glen Cove Rd.) | 516-877-7744 | www.paparazzitrattoria.com

For "hearty Italian" in a "casual", "kid-friendly" setting that's "spacious" enough for a "large group", this Westbury "staple" from a regional chain is a "decent" choice; "quick service", an "engaging atmosphere" and "reasonable prices" help make it a "popular place."

Park Place *American/Seafood*

| - | - | - | M |

Floral Park | 41 Covert Ave. (bet. Beverly & Marshall Aves.) | 516-775-9004 | www.parkplacefp.com

Earthy colors and a grandly arched, stained-glass window are the backdrop for seafood-centric American small plates such as a lobster BLT at this midpriced Floral Park gastropub; live bands perform Friday and Saturday nights.

NEW Passione Della Cucina *Italian*

| - | - | - | M |

Carle Place | 231 Old Country Rd. (bet. Glen Cove Rd. & Meadowbrook Pkwy.) | 516-741-4800 | www.passione-restaurant.com

Emilio Branchinelli (of Emilio's, Fanatico and Pasta-eria) expands his empire with this new pizzeria/trattoria in Carle Place near Roosevelt Field offering a large selection of moderately priced pies, pastas and Italian mains such as lobster arrabiata and veal milanese; seating includes an informal front area and a dining room with chandeliers, upholstered booths, tables and a wall-size mural of Venice; P.S. a side patio features tall stone walls.

Pasta-eria *Italian*

| 23 | 13 | 17 | $27 |

Hicksville | Woodbury Shopping Ctr. | 440 S. Oyster Bay Rd. (Woodbury Rd.) | 516-938-1555

It's a "very casual" setup at the rear of a strip center pizzeria, but this Hicksville Italian is a "local favorite" offering "all kinds" of "tasty" pastas and pies "on the cheap"; but since it's a "busy" go-to with "slow" service and "tables on top of each other", some suggest it's "way better for takeout."

Pasta Pasta *Italian*

| 25 | 20 | 23 | $41 |

Port Jefferson | 234 E. Main St. (Prospect St.) | 631-331-5335 | www.pastapasta.net

Paesani proclaim this "charming" Port Jefferson Italian (sister to Sayville's Cafe Joelle) "one of the best" for "top-of-the-line" renderings of its namesake and other "excellent" dishes ("it ain't just pasta"), all served by a "wonderful" staff at an "affordable" price; housed in the "cutest little" space, its only downside is "a huge following", so "be sure to make a reservation" on weekends.

Pastrami King Ⓜ *Deli/Sandwiches*

| 20 | 11 | 16 | $24 |

Merrick | 196 Merrick Rd. (bet. Central Pkwy. & Babylon Tpke.) | 516-377-4300 | www.pastramiking.com

"If pastrami's your thing", you "can't do much better" hereabouts than this Merrick deli "standby", where "overstuffed sandwiches" lead an "enjoyable" lineup of Jewish ("but not kosher") staples and Eclectic eats; the "decor is somewhat tacky" and service can be "sluggish", but it's a "cheap" "fix" "when you're in the mood."

NEW Patio, The Ⓜ *American/Seafood* — | — | — | M

Freeport | Freeport Inn & Marina | 445 S. Main St. (President St.) | 516-623-2980 | www.patiofreeport.com

Boaters cruise in to this waterside American overlooking a marina on Freeport Creek to enjoy an affordable seafood-centric menu served in a dining room featuring its original 1960s decor and a sleek black-topped bar; floor-to-ceiling windows open to create seamless indoor-outdoor dining, and the outside patio has multiple fire pits, a huge wide-screen TV and a waterfall; P.S. there's a DJ-driven dance party Friday nights.

Patio at 54 Main, The *American* 19 | 16 | 20 | $52

Westhampton Beach | 54 Main St. (bet. Potunk & Sunset Lns.) | 631-288-0100 | www.thepatiowhb.com

The "reliable" roster of meat and fish renders this Westhampton Beach New American a "solid" "local" pick for "upscale comfort food" served by "attentive" types in a space featuring a glass-encased patio; while "nothing novel", it's an "enjoyable" fallback with live music on weekends and a $25 prix fixe to temper tabs that may seem "pricey for what you get."

Pearl East *Chinese* 23 | 20 | 19 | $37

Manhasset | 1191 Northern Blvd. (bet. Maple St. & Norgate Rd.) | 516-365-9898 | www.pearleastny.com

"Not your run-of-the-mill Chinese", this Manhasset "bastion of quality" boasts an "imaginative and fresh" "gourmet" menu that its "steady customers" "can depend on" (and sushi is an "added plus"); with a "gracious owner" who's "always on hand" to "oversee" the "lovely", antiques-filled setting, it's something "really special", though it "does tend to crowd up."

Pentimento *Italian* 22 | 20 | 22 | $48

Stony Brook | Stony Brook Village Ctr. | 93 Main St. (bet. Christian Ave. & Rte. 25A) | 631-689-7755 | www.pentimentorestaurant.net

A "dedicated clientele" touts this "charming" "little" Stony Brook Italian as "a great find" for "sophisticated" seasonal fare from an "upbeat" staff that "doesn't rush you out the door"; installed in "cozy", "comfortable" digs with "delightful" "garden seating in the back", it's a "reliably" "memorable experience" albeit one priced at the "high end for the area."

Pepe Rosso 24 *Italian* — | — | — | M

Port Washington | 24 Manorhaven Blvd. (bet. Ashwood & Boxwood Rds.) | 516-944-9477 | www.peperosso24.com

Pizza comes in round, square, ultra-thin and stuffed variations at this midpriced Port Washington Italian that also serves pastas, panini and entrees; painted murals on the walls add a fanciful touch to the casual setting with a take-out section on one side and a dining room with a tile floor and wood tables on the other; P.S. a pianist performs Wednesday nights.

Peppercorns Continental

19 | 16 | 19 | $35

Hicksville | 25 E. Marie St. (B'way) | 516-931-4002 | www.peppercornsny.com

"Tucked away in Hicksville", this "long-term" "local" "staple" is "inviting" enough for "ample" helpings of "consistently good" steaks and Continental fare served by a "friendly and competent" crew; it's "convenient" for "a quick bite", and though nitpickers may knock the "bar atmosphere", at least the "price is right."

PeraBell Food Bar American/Eclectic

26 | – | 23 | $40

Patchogue | 69 E. Main St. (bet. Maple & Ocean Aves.) | 631-447-7766 | www.perabellfoodbar.com

Now relocated "down the street" next to the Patchogue Theatre, this "delightful" "neighborhood find" still "shines" thanks to the "scrumptious", "artfully prepared" dishes on "terrific chef" John Peragine's "oh-so-comforting" American-Eclectic menu; add an "attentive" staff and "larger digs" that "should help with crowd control", and its admirers "can't rave enough"; P.S. it moved post Survey.

Perfecto Mundo Latin Fusion Bistro ⓜ Pan-Latin

▽ 24 | 21 | 26 | $34

Commack | Northgate Shopping Ctr. | 1141 Jericho Tpke. (Kings Park Rd.) | 631-864-2777 | www.perfectomundoli.com

"Forget about the location" in a strip mall and the modest decor, 'cause this "wonderful" Commack Pan-Latin shows "a lot of promise" when it comes to "amazing" fusion fare from chef Steven Del Lima (ex Black & Blue); with such "unique and delicious" dishes as chile-glazed salmon and hickory-spiced steak, "pleasantly surprised" early arrivers promise they'll "definitely be back."

Per Un Angelo Italian

22 | 17 | 22 | $43

Wantagh | Jones Beach Hotel | 3275 Byron St. (bet. Atlantic Blvd. & Willow St.) | 516-783-6484 | www.jonesbeachhotel.com

Sited "off the beaten path" in Wantagh's Jones Beach Hotel, this "old-world" Northern Italian is a haven for "consistent" cuisine from a "professional" staff led by "personable" owners who "greet visitors with open arms"; a keyboardist performs three nights a week, and though modernists insist the "dated" setting "needs a makeover", that doesn't deter backers who've "been going here for years."

🅩 Peter Luger ⊄ Steak

27 | 17 | 21 | $71

Great Neck | 255 Northern Blvd. (bet. Jayson Ave. & Tain Dr.) | 516-487-8800 | www.peterluger.com

"Xanadu for steak", this Great Neck offshoot of the "iconic" Williamsburg meatery extends its run as Long Island's Most Popular restaurant by regaling "ravenous carnivores" in "traditional" style with "succulent, buttery beef" set down by "brusque" but "professional" "old-school waiters"; even loyalists concede the tabs are "gargantuan" and "cash will go out of existence before they accept credit cards", but it's still "the platinum standard": "calling them a steakhouse is like calling a Ferrari a car."

P.F. Chang's China Bistro *Chinese*
20 | **21** | **18** | **$34**

Westbury | Mall at the Source | 1504 Old Country Rd. (Merchants Concourse) | 516-222-9200 | www.pfchangs.com

"Light, delicious", "Americanized" Chinese food keeps fans "coming back" – especially for the "standout" lettuce wraps – to this "trendy", "stylish" chain link in Westbury; though not everyone is convinced ("overpriced", "ordinary", "loud"), the "consistent" service is a plus, as is the "smart" menu "catering to people with allergies" and other needs.

PG Steakhouse *Steak*
22 | **13** | **21** | **$66**

Huntington | 1745 E. Jericho Tpke. (Ware Ave.) | 631-499-1005 | www.pgsteakhouse.com

It's "not elegant", but this durable Huntington meatery does a "pretty decent" job providing "very good" cuts of beef and "attentive" service; maybe the "worn", "old-style" room "needs upgrading", but if you can "forget the decor", it's "all a steakhouse needs to be."

Phao *Thai*
21 | **16** | **20** | **$45**

Sag Harbor | 29 Main St. (bet. Bay & Washington Sts.) | 631-725-0101 | www.phaorestaurant.com

"Thai done right" makes this latest next-door neighbor to "sister restaurant Sen" a "welcome" "surprise" in Sag Harbor for fans of its "beautifully spiced and aromatic" cooking, "great cocktails" and "cool" dishabille vibe; others opine the "price is a little high" and note after 11 PM on weekends it "turns into more of a club."

NEW Phoenix, The *American*
- | **-** | **-** | **M**

Seaford | 3915 Merrick Rd. (Jackson Ave.) | 516-809-9693 | www.thephoenixny.com

Small plates from earth (tempura carrots with sweet and spicy sauce), land (chicken-fried pork belly) and sea (oven-charred octopus) join a selection of cheeses, cured meats and pizzas on the midpriced American menu of this Seaford newcomer; the setting sets a sophisticated tone with white tablecloths and a U-shaped bar area.

Piccola Bussola *Italian*
23 | **17** | **22** | **$41**

Mineola | 159 Jericho Tpke. (bet. Mineola Blvd. & Willis Ave.) | 516-294-4620

Huntington | 970 W. Jericho Tpke. (bet. Round Swamp Rd. & Sheppard Ln.) | 631-692-6300

www.piccolabussolarestaurant.com

"Go hungry" and "mangia" on "superior family-style Italian" at this "popular" pair in Huntington and Mineola, where the "substantial servings" of "garlicky" "red-sauce" "standards" and "accommodating" service are "always satisfying"; a few feel the "homey" settings could use "a pick-me-up", but most don't mind as long as "the price is right" and they "go home with leftovers."

☑ Piccolo *American/Italian*

27 | 20 | 25 | $56

Huntington | Southdown Shopping Ctr. | 215 Wall St.
(bet. Mill Ln. & Southdown Rd.) | 631-424-5592 |
www.piccolorestaurant.net

A "faithful crowd" stays true to this "upscale" New American–Italian in Huntington, which "deserves its reputation" for "superb cuisine" spanning "delicious pastas" to "phenomenal meat and fish"; the "top-notch" service and "intimate" setting with a pianist Sunday–Thursday will "make any occasion special", but "close quarters" lead to "long waits on weekends", so reserve ahead.

Piccolo's Ⓜ *Italian*

24 | 18 | 22 | $39

Mineola | 150 E. Jericho Tpke. (Congress Ave.) | 516-248-8110 |
www.piccolosny.com

"Anyone who eats here knows" you "must try" the signature chicken zingarella and "wonderful" varieties of "homemade ravioli" to understand why this "nothing-fancy" Northern Italian is a long-running fixture in Mineola; given the "homey" backdrop, it's no surprise the "owner greets you" "like you're part of the family."

Pie, The *Pizza*

21 | 17 | 20 | $25

Port Jefferson | 216 Main St. (Arden Pl.) | 631-331-4646 |
www.thepieofportjeff.com

Serving "many varieties" of "fabulous" thin-crust, brick-oven pies with "unique toppings" plus "decent pasta dishes" in "casual" digs, this Port Jefferson pizzeria weighs in as an "inexpensive", "family-friendly" choice; a "personable" staff and "big booths" add to the attraction, but be prepared to "wait" because it's "often crowded."

Pier 95 Ⓜ *Mediterranean*

24 | 21 | 23 | $47

Freeport | 95 Hudson Ave. (bet. Norton & Overton Sts.) |
516-867-9632 | www.pier95.com

A somewhat "hidden pearl" "close to Freeport's Nautical Mile", this "first-class" Portuguese-leaning Med by the waterfront offers "marvelous" seafood and an "excellent wine list" brought by a "knowledgeable", "charming" staff; the "out-of-the-way" location means it's "quiet enough" to "hear your partner's conversation" and feels "less rushed" than others in town, plus the "beautiful views" and "lovely" live music on weekends make it suitable for "intimate" dinners.

Pierre's *French*

21 | 19 | 17 | $58

Bridgehampton | 2468 Main St. (bet. Bridgehampton-Sag Harbor Tpke. & Hull Ln.) | 631-537-5110 | www.pierresbridgehampton.com

Francophiles favor this Bridgehampton bistro for "outstanding" fare with an "emphasis on seafood" in a "cozy", "charming" setting with a patisserie up front that "feels like France"; chef-owner Pierre Weber is a "wonderful", "friendly host", and though a few sniff that "attitude is the name of the game" here, that doesn't stop the multitudes from "waiting"; P.S. there's live jazz Tuesday and Sunday nights.

	FOOD	DECOR	SERVICE	COST

Pine Island Grill *American* | 18 | 25 | 16 | $52 |

Bayville | Crescent Beach Club | 333 Bayville Ave. (bet. Ships Ln. & Sound Beach Ave.) | 516-628-3000 | www.thecrescentbeachclub.com

"It's all about" the "breathtaking view of Long Island Sound" that's "especially" "enchanting" "as the sun sets" at this New American "right on the water" in Bayville's Crescent Beach Club; if the "so-so" food is "overpriced" and the service "slow", it still "feels like a mini-vacation" if you "relax with cocktails" "on the deck" and enjoy the "heavenly real estate."

Pita House *Mediterranean/Turkish* | 22 | 16 | 20 | $30 |

East Setauket | Heritage Sq. | 100-27 S. Jersey Ave. (Rte. 25A) | 631-675-9051

Patchogue | 680 Rte. 112 (bet. E. Woodside & Old Medford Aves.) | 631-289-2262

www.pita-house.com

"Authentic", "well-prepared" Mediterranean-Turkish offerings – "amazing" red lentil soup, kebabs "to love" – make this "consistent" pita pair a "unique" choice; service is "friendly", and though the decor in Patchogue "needs a makeover" and the East Setauket spot is "buried behind a shopping center", "reasonable" prices more than make up for any shortcomings.

Pizza Place 🍴 *Pizza* | ▽ 24 | 10 | 19 | $16 |

Bridgehampton | 2123 Montauk Hwy. (Hildreth Ln.) | 631-537-7865

It's the "best pizza around" proclaim local fans of the "remarkable" thin-crust pies at this Bridgehampton joint where some 30 different toppings are offered (try the bacon cheeseburger); beer and wine plus cheap tabs compensate for a "charmless" setting, and day-trippers declare it's always the "first stop" on a trip out East or their perfect "snack before the ride home."

☒ Plaza Café *Seafood* | 26 | 22 | 24 | $70 |

Southampton | 61 Hill St. (bet. 1st Neck & Windmill Lns.) | 631-283-9323 | www.plazacafe.us

"They set the bar really high" at this "civilized" "Southampton gem", where chef/co-owner and "real pro" Douglas Gulija's "superb" seafood is prepared "with care" and "presented to perfection", paired with "unusual wines"; the "courteous staff" oversees a "cozy", "quiet" setting with "high ceilings and a fireplace", and while it's "a bit expensive", it's "worth seeking out" for "adult dining" "in a class by itself."

Poco Loco *Mexican* | 17 | 14 | 17 | $31 |

Roslyn | 1431 Old Northern Blvd. (bet. E. B'way & Skillman St.) | 516-621-5626 | www.pocolocorestaurant.net

"*Delicioso*" Mexican offerings – from "chips, salsa and guac" to "wonderful margaritas" – at prices that are "cheap enough" make this "old standby" in Roslyn a "popular place" for a "not-too-fancy" outing; the staff is "friendly and efficient", and though the decor's a little "worn", there's always the "outdoor patio" for a "warm summer evening."

Pollo Rico Latin Bistro *Pan-Latin*

| 20 | 16 | 19 | $30 |

Centereach | 2435 Middle Country Rd. (bet. Hammond Ln. & Oak St.) | 631-471-0585 | www.polloricolatinbistro.com

"Unique", "tasty" Pan-Latin dishes draw fans to this "lovely" "family-run" Centereach "bang for the buck", where the "arroz con pollo" is a must and the sangria is "wonderful"; service is "accommodating", and the "bistro" setting is sweetened with a trompe l'oeil mural of a garden courtyard – though it's not the place for "quiet conversation."

Pomodorino *Italian*

| 19 | 15 | 18 | $33 |

Huntington | 326 W. Jericho Tpke. (bet. Jones St. & Oakwood Rd.) | 631-425-1196 | www.pomodorino.com

Located in Huntington, this last remaining branch of a former quartet of "checkered-tablecloth" Italians is pretty "predictable", delivering "large portions" of "tasty" pasta and pizza at reasonable prices in "pleasant" quarters where carafes of "house wine" are on the table and you're "charged by the glass"; service is generally "reliable" and if the decor's a bit ho-hum, it's still a "solid choice."

NEW Pop's Seafood Shack & Grill *Seafood*

| - | - | - | E |

Island Park | 15 Railroad Pl. (off Austin Blvd.) | 516-432-7677 | www.popsseafoodshack.com

This Island Park seafooder offers a variety of options for eating and drinking including indoors overlooking the water, outdoors on the seaside deck with a retractable skylight, an open-air section with a sand floor and palm trees, and at the rows of fire pit tables on the beach beneath strings of lights; P.S. there's boat docking – with service on board also available (call ahead to reserve).

Porters on the Lane *Seafood/Steak*

| 20 | 21 | 20 | $46 |

Bellport | 19 Bellport Ln. (bet. Bell St. & S. Country Rd.) | 631-803-6067 | www.portersonthelane.com

Whether "on the porch in summer" or in the "cozy back room with a fireplace" in the winter, fans of this Bellport surf 'n' turfer enjoy "delicious" pastas, "fresh" fish and a "fantastic" wine list; pressed-tin ceilings and wood floors add character to the decor, but it can get "noisy", as there's an "active bar" scene and live music Fridays and Saturdays.

Porto Bello *Italian*

| ▽ 22 | 21 | 22 | $45 |

Greenport | Stirling Harbor Marina | 1410 Manhanset Ave. (bet. Beach Rd. & Champlain Pl.) | 631-477-1515 | www.portobellonorthfork.com

"Set right on the water" in the Stirling Harbor Marina, this Greenport seasonal Italian's bright surroundings and dockside "window views" provide a "lovely" backdrop for "big portions" of "well-done" "traditional" dishes; with "friendly" service led by an "owner who mixes with patrons", it's a "dependable" performer that typically draws a "lively crowd."

	FOOD	DECOR	SERVICE	COST

Porto Vivo ● *Italian*　　22 | 25 | 20 | $59

Huntington | 7 Gerard St. (Stewart Ave.) | 631-385-8486 | www.porto-vivo.com

"NYC style" comes to Huntington via this tri-level "hot spot" where an "intimate" dining room features a fireplace on the top floor and a "sexy bar" attracts "major crowds" of the "young and beautiful", adding to the "happening" scene; yes, it's "expensive", and reviews are mixed on "inconsistent" service ranging from "outstanding" to "inattentive", but the "inventive" Italian menu wins praise.

Post Office Cafe ● *American*　　19 | 20 | 19 | $31

Babylon | 130 W. Main St. (bet. Carll & Deer Park Aves.) | 631-669-9224 | www.thepostofficecafe.com

Set in a "cute" former post office with "eclectic" touches (carousel horses, a fake chicken hanging from the ceiling), this "upbeat", "friendly" Babylon "fixture" (sibling to Farmingdale's Library Cafe) draws fans for American "favorites" like "Buffalo wings" or "a burger and beer" while catching "the game" with the "young crowd"; "cool happy hours", "live music"and DJ nights amp up the "noise level."

Post Stop Cafe *American*　　17 | 16 | 17 | $35

Westhampton Beach | 144 Main St. (bet. Mill Rd. & Sunset Ave.) | 631-288-9777

If you're "lucky enough to get a table outside", this Westhampton Beacher is a "picturesque", "people-watching" spot serving "reliable" midpriced American fare ("burgers, salads, soups") that's "decent for lunch" if "a bit frumpy for dinner"; the vintage post office interior is "quaint", but some suggest the "slow" staff may be mailing it in.

Press 195 *Sandwiches*　　- | - | - | I

Rockville Centre | 22 N. Park Ave. (bet. Merrick Rd. & Sunrise Hwy.) | 516-536-1950 | www.press195.com

Hot off the presses are panini at this affordable Rockville Centre sandwich specialist (with siblings in Queens and Brooklyn) offering some 40 varieties plus accompaniments including crispy Belgian fries; a long black granite bar leads to a dining room with dramatic arches and colorful backlit glass tiles; P.S. there's live music Wednesday nights.

☑ Prime *American*　　23 | 27 | 22 | $67

Huntington | 117 New York Ave. (bet. Ketewomoke Dr. & Youngs Hill Rd.) | 631-385-1515 | www.restaurantprime.com

"Beautiful" "both inside and out", this "amazing" waterfront New American (from the owners of H2O and Tellers) with floor-to-ceiling windows is even more "prime" in summer when outdoor seating affords "amazing views" of Huntington Harbor and "fabulous people-watching"; "excellent" if "expensive" fare, including "first-rate steaks" and a "fantastic Sunday brunch", plus generally "gracious" service make this one a "special-occasion" standout; P.S. boat docking is available.

	FOOD	DECOR	SERVICE	COST

NEW Prime Burger *Burgers*
— | — | — | I

Albertson | 1008 Willis Ave. (Willow Pl.) | 516-621-2471 |
www.primeburgersonline.com

Rare in that it's not a chain, this affordable Albertson burger joint offers a choice of 15 patties – including one with hoisin sauce and crispy wontons – plus a variety of add-ons; its storefront setting features vibrant orange walls, a tile floor and a glass case displaying decadent desserts; sodas, shakes and beer are available too.

Prime Catch *Seafood*
— | — | — | E

Rockville Centre | 41 S. Park Ave. (Lenox Rd.) | 516-705-5340 |
www.primecatchseafoodgrill.com

Fin fanciers are hooked on this loungelike seafooder in Rockville Centre, where chef Axell Urrutia is turning out upscale creations such as crab-stuffed salmon with sambuca-laced Dijonaise sauce; the room is saturated in red – from the walls to a glittery divider screen – and floor-to-ceiling windows in the bar area open to the sidewalk, providing additional fair-weather seating; P.S. there's live entertainment on weekends.

NEW Primo Piatto *Italian*
— | — | — | M

Huntington | Bay Hills Plaza | 138 E. Main St. (Loma Pl.) |
631-935-1391 | www.primopiattorestaurant.com

Tucked away in a corner of Bay Hills Plaza on the outskirts of Huntington, this midpriced newcomer serves pastas, pizzas, panini and a long list of Italian entrees; the dual setting offers the option of eating either in a pizza bar/take-out area with a tin ceiling and sepia-toned photos, or in the cafe with a granite bar, tablecloths and colorful prints on the walls.

Public House 49 *American*
20 | 17 | 19 | $37

Patchogue | 49 E. Main St. (bet. Maple & Ocean Aves.) |
631-569-2767 | www.publichouse49.com

It's "worth adding to your rotation" report regulars of this moderately priced Patchogue New American where chef Craig Attwood offers a "creative take" on pub fare with the likes of pulled-pork nachos and chicken milanese Caesar salad; service is "good", and a large bar with a dance floor and weekend DJs keeps things "lively."

Puglia's of Garden City M *Italian*
— | — | — | E

Garden City | 987 Stewart Ave. (bet. Selfridge Ave. & South St.) |
516-222-1421 | www.pugliascitycafe.com

A supper club with upscale food and retro music acts on the menu, this sizable Italian in Garden City's former City Café space offers a lively alternative to quiet neighborhood establishments; the front evokes a village cafe in Puglia, with umbrella-topped sidewalk tables, while the crisp beige-and-brown interior features two carpeted dining rooms – one with a fireplace, one bi-level – plus a spacious bar and a small dance floor.

Pumpernickels *German*
21 **17** **21** **$38**

Northport | 640 Main St. (Fort Salonga Rd.) | 631-757-7959 | www.pumpernickelsofnorthport.com

"Loyal local" followers find "rib-sticking" "traditional" German dishes, including "tender" sauerbraten, at this midpriced Northport "old-timer" that "works hard to get it right"; decor that hasn't "changed in years" and "friendly" "waitresses who dress the part" assure a "vintage feel" for a "satisfying meal."

Quetzalcoatl *Mexican*
20 **17** **19** **$33**

Huntington | 296 Main St. (bet. Green & New Sts.) | 631-427-7834 | www.quetzalcoatlmexrest.com

Mole mavens maintain there's "better than average" Mexican fare served in "huge" portions at this bi-level Huntington sibling to nearby Oaxaca, where the "colorful", "quirky" decor includes a rainforest mural and Mayan sculptures; "hospitable" service and "pitchers of margaritas keep the festivities going", and the lunch prix fixe is an even better "deal."

Race Lane *American*
19 **19** **19** **$53**

East Hampton | 31 Race Ln. (bet. Gingerbread Ln. & Railroad Ave.) | 631-324-5022 | www.racelanerestaurant.com

Installed in digs once occupied by The Lodge and longtime favorite The Laundry, this "welcome addition" to East Hampton now "looks much spiffier" with its "freshened decor", freestanding fireplace and brick courtyard; there's "something for everyone" on the "surprisingly good" New American menu and service is "pleasant and helpful", so though it's "still learning", early admirers "will be back."

Rachel's Cafe *Italian*
22 **15** **21** **$38**

Syosset | 57 Berry Hill Rd. (bet. Church & East Sts.) | 516-921-0303 | www.rachelscafe.net

"Quaint", "cozy" and "full of warm smiles", this "sweet" Syosset "neighborhood standby" pleases with "inventive takes" on "homemade pastas" and other "classic Italian fare" followed by "amazing" desserts that "are worth saving room for"; however, the "tight quarters" tend to be "busy" "with the locals", "so be prepared to wait."

Rachel's Waterside Grill *American/Seafood*
20 **15** **18** **$37**

Freeport | 281 Woodcleft Ave. (bet. Manhattan & Suffolk Sts.) | 516-546-0050 | www.rachelswatersidegrill.com

Go "for the views" of the "boats passing by" say patrons who've "never had a bad meal" (but "never had a great" one) at this seafooder on Freeport's Nautical Mile; weekly live music and "lively" terrace dining add appeal, and while some call for a decor "revamp", the staff is "solicitous" and the specials "a pleasant surprise."

Ragazzi *Italian*
- **-** **-** **M**

Nesconset | 2950 Middle Country Rd. (bet. Alexander Ave. & Moriches Rd.) | 631-265-8200 | www.ragazzi-ny.com

This Nesconset Italian gains contemporary flair from its setting of multiple dining areas outfitted with wood tables, industrial ceiling

| | FOOD | DECOR | SERVICE | COST |

ducts and drum light fixtures, plus arched panes of multicolored glass; the moderately priced menu features a selection of panini, pastas and entrees, including chicken parmigiana and veal milanese, and panna cotta for dessert.

Ram's Head Inn *American/Eclectic*   20 | 24 | 20 | $62

Shelter Island | Ram's Head Inn | 108 Ram Island Dr. (N. Ram Island Dr.) | 631-749-0811 | www.shelterislandinns.com

A "quintessential summer spot", this seasonal "classic" in a circa-1929 Shelter Island "country inn" turns on the "romantic" "charm", especially when you head for the "beautiful terrace" to "watch the sun set" over Coecles Harbor; the American-Eclectic dishes are "well-prepared" and service is "accommodating", but it's a location "right out of *The Great Gatsby*" that merits the "ferry ride."

Rangmahal Ⓜ *Indian*   23 | 15 | 23 | $36

Hicksville | 355 S. Broadway (Lawnview Ave.) | 516-942-7256 | www.rangmahalcuisine.com

Run with "passion and energy" by a "charming husband-and-wife team", this Hicksville veteran is a "favorite" for its "adventurous", "modern interpretations of Indian cuisine"; an "attentive" staff ascertains your "tolerance for spice", and though there's not much decor, weekly live sitar music guarantees a "lively crowd."

Rare 650 *American/Steak*   24 | 24 | 22 | $68

Syosset | 650 Jericho Tpke. (Cedar St.) | 516-496-8000 | www.rare650.com

As a "hipper" "reinvention of the former Sagamore Steakhouse", this classed-up Syosset New American is "a rare find" with a "superb" menu focused on "thick" steaks and sushi and an "iPad" "wine list to make your head spin", all ferried by an "outstanding" staff; with a "beautiful" layout boasting an "outdoor dining option" and a "noisy" "singles scene" in the bar, it appeals to "designer" types who advise "don't forget your wallet."

Ravagh *Persian*   ∇ 22 | 13 | 21 | $36

Roslyn Heights | 210 Mineola Ave. (bet. High St. & Powerhouse Rd.) | 516-484-7100

Huntington | 335 Main St. (bet. Clinton Ave. & West Neck Rd.) | 631-923-2050

"Lots of interesting" "real Persian" dishes get a "thumbs-up" at this Roslyn Heights eatery (with a Huntington sibling) where "excellent" kebabs and "amazing" stews are delivered by a "pleasant" staff; it may not be much to look at, but that doesn't faze fans who "love" it for "tasty", "large portions" at "reasonable" prices.

Red *American*   25 | 22 | 25 | $49

Huntington | 417 New York Ave. (bet. High & W. Carver Sts.) | 631-673-0304 | www.redrestaurant.com

Café Red Ⓜ *American*

Kings Park | 107 Main St. (Pulaski Rd.) | 631-544-4500 | www.caferedli.com

You'll "taste heaven" sigh worshipers of the "creative" New American fare and "phenomenal wine list" at this "highly" recommended Huntington "prize"; a "gracious", "well-trained" staff works the "attractive", red-accented space that includes a zinc bar, velvet lounge chairs and an "amazing" "secret" "garden in summer"; P.S. the Kings Park cafe opened post-Survey.

Red Bar Brasserie Ⓜ *American/French* | 22 | 19 | 21 | $62 |

Southampton | 210 Hampton Rd. (bet. Lewis St. & Old Town Rd.) | 631-283-0704 | www.redbarbrasserie.com

With its "consistently superior" New American-French fare, "glowing ambiance" and "excellent service", this "sophisticated" "fave" earns "a thumbs-up" as "one of Southampton's better choices"; many maintain the "deafening" "noise level" makes it harder to "share the rapture with tablemates", but "once you've eaten here you'll understand" why it's a "popular" draw despite the price; P.S. Little Red, a more casual sib, is located nearby.

Red Fish Grille *American/Seafood* | 23 | 17 | 20 | $43 |

Plainview | Woodbuy Row Plainview Ctr. | 430 Woodbury Rd. (S. Oyster Bay Rd.) | 516-932-8460 | www.redfishgrille.com

A "dependable local" "favorite" most outsiders "don't know about", this Plainview New American "in an innocuous strip-mall setting" surprises with "an innovative menu" featuring "an excellent variety of fresh fish" served "with a smile" "for a decent price"; but it's apt to be "jumping" with regulars and so "noisy" you'll risk "returning home with laryngitis."

Red Rooster Bistro *American* | ▽ 16 | 20 | 17 | $37 |

Cutchogue | 4805 Depot Ln. (bet. Main & Middle Rds.) | 631-734-8267 | www.redroosterrestaurant.com

"Burgers, ribs" and "old-fashioned dinners" are the kinds of plates that make this midpriced American bistro a "homestyle heaven" for Cutchoque comfort-food seekers; sometimes "inattentive" service might be nothing to crow about, but chef-owner Nick Nikolov (of Pepi's in Southold) has decked the place out in "cute" "rooster-theme decor" that makes for a "lovely setting."

🆕 Red Tomato *Pizza* | - | - | - | I |

East Norwich | Messina Market Plaza | 6245 Northern Blvd. (bet. Mill River & Oyster Bay Rds.) | 516-802-2840 | www.redtomatopizza.com

The owners of nearby Messina Market caterers and the popular La Bonne Boulangerie have opened this sleek pizzeria in the same East Norwich strip mall, turning out an artisanal lineup of wood-fired pies that include kid-friendly options such as mac 'n' cheese; square marble-topped tables, steel chairs and a small counter with stools make for modern digs.

Rein *American* | 23 | 24 | 24 | $53 |

Garden City | Garden City Hotel | 45 Seventh St. (bet. Cathedral & Hilton Aves.) | 516-877-9385 | www.gardencityhotel.com

"If you just feel like spoiling yourself", this "posh" New American in the Garden City Hotel flaunts an "elegant" interior (think burnished wood, paintings and a fireplace) and "fabulous service" that add a "touch of class" whether for a "high-end" meal, afternoon tea or

Sunday brunch; sophistos say it's "like being in NYC", complete with the "big price."

NEW Relish ☒ American
`-` | `-` | `-` | `I`

Kings Park | 2 Pulaski Rd. (Main St.) | 631-292-2740 | www.relishkingspark.com

This casual Kings Park newcomer celebrates the classic neighborhood diner both with its appearance and its budget- and family-friendly American menu of salads, sandwiches, burgers and root-beer floats; the nostalgic setting includes wood tables, pear-green Naugahyde booths and a counter lined with swivel stools, while tiny lights illuminating the trees outside add a fanciful nighttime touch.

Rialto ☒ Italian
26 | 20 | 25 | $57

Carle Place | 588 Westbury Ave. (bet. Glen Cove Rd. & Post Ave.) | 516-997-5283 | www.rialtorestaurantli.com

"Top-notch" "each and every time", this "small" Carle Place Italian attracts adoring *amici* willing to go "out of the way" for "heavenly" "old-line" cuisine (including "wonderful whole fish") "served with style" by "warm hosts" who look after you like "their only customer"; it's "pretty pricey" and "worth every penny", but "they don't have room for a crowd", so "don't tell."

Ristorante Gemelli ☒ Italian
24 | 24 | 23 | $51

Babylon | 175 E. Main St. (bet. Cooper St. & Totten Pl.) | 631-321-6392 | www.gemellirestaurant.com

Paesani praise this Babylonian for its "top-shelf" Italian cuisine – "decadent lobster risotto", "phenomenal" osso buco – and "warm", "romantic" setting that's "like dining in a small village piazza"; a staff that goes "overboard" (including owners who always "visit your table") further justifies the "pricey" tabs; P.S. the family's fine-food market is down the street.

Ristorante Italiano Toscanini Italian
∇ 24 | 18 | 26 | $39

Port Washington | 179 Main St. (bet. Madison & Monroe Sts.) | 516-944-0755 | www.toscaninipw.com

"Friendly service" starts with a "warm and gracious" owner at this Port Washingtonian where the midpriced Italian fare includes "outstanding specials" and "amazing desserts"; the "attractive setting" features murals of the Tuscan countryside, adding to the "welcoming" vibe.

Ritz Cafe, The Continental
19 | 12 | 17 | $34

Northport | 42 Woodbine Ave. (bet. 5th & Scudder Aves.) | 631-754-6348 | www.ritzcafenorthport.com

Surveyors say this "unassuming little bar" near the Northport waterfront "packs a wallop" with "tasty" Continental fare at "sane prices"; it's "definitely not ritzy" – "loud and crowded" is more accurate – and the service is "so-so", but when you "gaze out at the bay" you "forget all your stress"; P.S. the $12 brunch prix fixe "can cure whatever ails you."

	FOOD	DECOR	SERVICE	COST

Z Riverbay Seafood Bar & Grill *Seafood* | 23 | 19 | 21 | $50 |

Williston Park | 700 Willis Ave. (bet. Charles & Henry Sts.) | 516-742-9191 | www.riverbayrestaurant.com

"Incredibly fresh seafood" – including a "vast" selection at the "fabulous raw bar" – plus a "knockout Sunday brunch" lures fans to this Williston Park "favorite" from the owner of the Central Park Boathouse; the "vibrant" scene in a nautically decorated former Masonic Hall can get "loud", but service is generally "accommodating" – just expect it to cost "an arm and a leg"; P.S. it's "always crowded", so "be prepared to wait, even with a reservation."

NEW Riverhead Project *American* | – | – | – | E |

Riverhead | 300 E. Main St. (Maple Ave.) | 631-284-9300 | www.theriverheadproject.com

Dennis McDermott, one of the founding partners behind Greenport's Frisky Oyster, has turned a former bank into this sleek and classy New American in namesake Riverhead; a large fireplace separates the lounge from the main room (where the lime-green and purple accents were inspired by a pair of McDermott's favorite pants), and there are also outdoor seats in a bar patio and covered dining area.

Riviera Grill *Italian* | ▽ 26 | 17 | 24 | $49 |

Glen Cove | 274 Glen St. (bet. Elm & Hendrick Aves.) | 516-674-9370 | www.rivieragrillrestaurant.com

"Terrific" Italian fare including "plentiful" specials and "homemade limoncello" at meal's end wins "repeat customers" for this Glen Cove "charmer"; even if the dining room, with paintings of the Italian Riviera, is "not extravagant", a "superb", "gracious host" and a staff that treats you "like one of the family" make the setting feel "perfect."

NEW Roast Sandwich House ⊠ *Sandwiches* | – | – | – | I |

Melville | 827 Walt Whitman Rd. (Fletcher Pl.) | 631-629-4869 | www.roastsandwichhouse.com

Roasting various meats in-house and tailoring artisanal breads to match, this affordable Melville shop puts a unique spin on its sandwiches; though parking is limited at the little stucco building off busy Rte. 110, the digs are snappy thanks to high-tech steel tables and chairs and photos of roasted veggies on lime-green walls.

Robata of Tokyo *Japanese* | ▽ 20 | 11 | 18 | $32 |

Plainview | 1163 Old Country Rd. (Manetto Hill Rd.) | 516-433-5333 | www.robatasushi.com

With a "dizzying array" of "fresh sushi" and "grilled Japanese" fare from the namesake robata, this Plainview spot aims to please everyone; the "outdated" "interior is nothing to look at", but given the "unpretentious service and decent prices", locals shrug "no matter."

Robert's *Italian* | 25 | 21 | 23 | $69 |

Water Mill | 755 Montauk Hwy. (bet. Nowedonah Ave. & Station Rd.) | 631-726-7171 | www.robertshamptons.com

"Outstanding", "beautifully presented" Italian cuisine that's as "imaginative" as it is "delicious" comes "highly" recommended at

Robert Durkin's Water Mill "respite" from the "happening Hamptons scene", set in a "lovely old farmhouse" with summer patio seating; service is "serious" and "professional", and if the tabs are a bit "pricey", that doesn't keep it from rising to "the head of the class"; P.S. hours vary by season.

Robinson's Tea Room Tearoom   23 | 22 | 22 | $23

Stony Brook | Stony Brook Village Ctr. | 97 Main St. (bet. Christian Ave. & Rte. 25A) | 631-751-1232

"Genuine high tea" is "beautifully served" – complete with "delicious" brews, "luscious scones", "homemade" cream, "fresh jams" and "finger sandwiches" – at this "cozy", lace-curtained and antiques-filled Stony Brook teahouse that's perfect for a "ladies' day out" or a treat with your "granddaughter"; given "wonderful quiches" and salads and a "pleasant" staff, you could "have lunch instead", just "reserve early."

Rockwell's Bar & Grill American   ▽ 22 | 18 | 21 | $30

Smithtown | 60 Terry Rd. (bet. Middle Country Rd. & Nesconset Hwy.) | 631-360-8900 | www.rockwellsbarandgrill.com

Sports fans and a "local après-work crowd" keep this Smithtown pub "humming", especially around the "huge bar" at Friday happy hour; for diners, there's a midpriced menu of "standard" American fare "with a twist" (e.g. baked clam casserole) and a "friendly" staff in a setting with lots of flat-screen TVs, plus outdoor seating; P.S. live bands play on Fridays and Saturdays.

Roe's Casa Dolce Bakery/Italian   ▽ 24 | 11 | 19 | $20

Rockville Centre | 486 Sunrise Hwy. (bet. Forest Ave. & Long Beach Rd.) | 516-536-2253

"Heaven on earth" for sweet tooths, this pint-sized Italian bakery-cafe in Rockville Centre is favored "mainly for" its pastries and other "sinfully delicious" desserts, though the lineup of breakfast and lunch fare is also "obviously prepared with care"; it's now under the ownership of its former head baker, "but the quality is still top-notch", and their "casa is your casa."

☑ Rothmann's Steakhouse Steak   25 | 22 | 23 | $66

East Norwich | 6319 Northern Blvd. (Oyster Bay Rd.) | 516-922-2500 | www.chasrothmanns.com

Meat eaters "dine like kings" at this "exceptional" East Norwich cow palace, which has the chops to "compete with any" of its "high-end" North Shore rivals and "all the bells and whistles you'd expect" of a "classy" "carnivore's lair"; the "fabulous" steaks, "professional service" and "attractive setting" are "well worth the expense", but beware of "noise" and "the real feeding frenzy" when "cruising cougars" hit the "hopping bar"; P.S. it's also known for its Sunday brunch.

Rowdy Hall Pub Food   20 | 16 | 19 | $36

East Hampton | Parrish Mews | 10 Main St. (bet. Fithian Ln. & The Circle) | 631-324-8555 | www.rowdyhall.com

Ever a "steady" "backup", this "convivial" member of "the Nick & Toni's family" "hidden" in an East Hampton village mews is "satisfying" for "basic", Gallic-accented pub fare ("can't beat those burgers") served by "spirited" sorts who "greet you with a smile"; the "reasonable prices" and "party atmosphere" make it "popular" with "rowdy" fans "of all ages", who agree it "feels like home."

Royal Bukhara Grill *Indian*   ▽ 22 | 18 | 21 | $31

Hicksville | 70 Broadway (bet. Herzog Pl. & W. Marie St.) | 516-822-2400 | www.royalbukharagrill.com

Fans of the "vibrant flavors" of Indian cuisine head for this Hicksville spin-off of Manhattan's Bukhara Grill (that's under different ownership) for the "outstanding breads", "excellent dal" and chicken tikka masala that "has a kick to it"; a simple, "dimly lit" setting and "warm", "efficient service" complete the experience.

RS Jones Ⓜ *Southwestern*   22 | 21 | 24 | $34

Merrick | 153 Merrick Ave. (bet. Miller Pl. & W. Loines Ave.) | 516-378-7177 | www.rsjones.com

For a "loud", "stompin' good time", Merrick wranglers recommend this "colorful local hangout" with the "friendliest" staff in town, where "kitschy", "Texas-rodeo decor" and "people-watching taken to a new level" create a "quirky" backdrop for "spicy", "imaginative" midpriced Southwestern fare including "delicious" chicken-fried steak and "so-o good cheese grits"; P.S. there's "live music" some nights.

Rumba *Caribbean*   - | - | - | E

Hampton Bays | 43 Canoe Place Rd. (bet. Argonne Rd. & Fanning Ave.) | 631-594-3544 | www.rumbarumbar.com

Nestled in a Hampton Bays residential area with gorgeous views of Shinnecock Bay, this seasonal Caribbean Islander delivers a laid-back vibe, aided in part by numerous rum concoctions; dishes such as salmon with coconut risotto, tacos with pineapple, and soy-marinated flank steak can get a bit pricey, but are in keeping with the tropical theme.

Runyon's *American*   18 | 16 | 19 | $31

Seaford | 3928 Merrick Rd. (bet. Jackson Ave. & Smith Ln.) | 516-221-2112 | www.runyons.com

A "busy local pub" with "standard" American fare, this Seaford "mainstay" offers "friendly" service and "inexpensive" eats including a "decent" "burger and beer"; dissenters dis "dated" decor that "needs work", but loyalists call it "comfortable."

🆕 Ruschmeyer's *American*   - | - | - | M

Montauk | Ruschmeyer's Resort | 161 Second House Rd. (bet. Industrial Rd. & S. Dewey Pl.) | 631-668-2877 | www.visitruschmeyers.com

As part of their remake of a longtime Montauk inn, the owners of hip Surf Lodge have transformed its seasonal eatery into a rustic, bucolic spot reminiscent of summer camp; the midpriced contemporary American menu highlights fresh seafood, and there's an open-air beer garden (complete with sand floor) plus a teepee and a hammock on the grounds.

	FOOD	DECOR	SERVICE	COST

Z Ruth's Chris Steak House *Steak* — 25 | 21 | 24 | $66

Garden City | 600 Old Country Rd. (Clinton Rd.) | 516-222-0220 |
www.ruthschris.com

Loyalists "love the sizzling platters" of "oh-so-good buttery steaks" at
this "top-quality" chophouse chain link in Garden City that comes
through with "winning" sides too; delivering "old-style service" in a
"traditional" setting, it's "expensive" (and "not for the dieter"), but "ut-
terly reliable", especially when "entertaining friends and clients."

Ruvo *Italian* — 22 | 20 | 21 | $42

Greenlawn | 63 Broadway (Smith St.) | 631-261-7700
Port Jefferson | 105 Wynn Ln. (Main St.) | 631-476-3800
www.ruvorestaurant.com

Red-sauce fans go for the "amazing pastas" and other "artfully prepared "rustic Italian standards" at this "homey" North Shore duo
where a "lovely" staff "goes out of its way to be nice"; both offer
"bargain prix fixe" options at lunch and dinner, and the Greenlawn
location has an attached butcher shop and market.

Sabai Thai Bistro *Thai* — ▽ 22 | 22 | 19 | $29

Miller Place | 825 Rte. 25A (bet. Harrison & Tyler Aves.) | 631-821-1780
The "lovely", "restful" setting – with granite-topped tables, gold
walls and gongs – rivals the "delicious" fare at this Miller Place Thai
where BYO with no corkage keeps tabs low; time-crunched critics
say "service is on the slow side" but admit that's just "more time to
enjoy" the "beautiful decor."

Sabor a Colombia *Colombian* — - | - | - | M

Levittown | 26 Division Ave. (bet. Hempstead Tpke. & Schoolhouse Rd.) |
516-513-1520

Tucked behind a Levittown gym, this midpriced Colombian serves
breakfast, lunch (including savory crêpes until 3 PM) and dinner entrees such as salmon with salsa and fried plantains; the decor makes
a colorful statement with yellow walls hung with parrot sculptures.

NEW Saffron **M** *American/Mediterranean* — - | - | - | E

Glen Head | 70 Glen Head Rd. (Railroad Ave.) | 516-609-9600 |
www.saffronli.com

Chef-owner John Forte has taken over this Glen Head train station
setting (formerly Bistro M), serving a pricey New American–Med
menu including the likes of Chicken Two Ways (a stuffed breast and
crispy thigh); saffron-yellow walls brighten the interior, while a covered patio expands seating options in warm weather.

Sage Bistro *French* — 24 | 20 | 22 | $43

Bellmore | 2620 Merrick Rd. (bet. Centre & St. Marks Aves.) |
516-679-8928 | www.bistrosage.com

Sage Bistro Moderne *French*

Woodbury | Woodbury Village Shopping Ctr. | 7955 Jericho Tpke.
(S. Woods Rd.) | 516-584-6804 | www.sagebistrogroup.com

"Fabulous" fare that "tickles your taste buds" – from "excellent mussels" to "steak tartare" and "wonderful boeuf bourguignon" – draws

Francophiles to this duo from the owner of Oceanside's Brasserie Persil; the newer Woodbury location has a "more formal feel" than the Bellmore original, but both get "crowded and noisy" on weekends and benefit from an "attentive" staff and an extensive martini list.

Sakaya *Japanese* | - | - | - | E |

Albertson | 1162 Willis Ave. (Netz Pl.) | 516-621-1887 | www.sakaya2.com
Blue LED lights and illuminated crystals add pizzazz to this upscale Japanese newcomer in the Albertson space that was formerly Hokkaido, while a soothing waterfall wall separates the main dining room from an area filled with hibachi tables; sushi fans have copious choices, with hot entrees on the menu too.

Salamander's General Store *Eclectic* | ▽ 24 | 15 | 17 | $26 |

Greenport | 414 First St. (bet. Center & South Sts.) | 631-477-3711
Akin to a mini "local version of Zabar's", this seasonal "gourmet" grocer in Greenport concocts an "amazingly good" array of Eclectic prepared dishes – notably the "legendary fried chicken" – to eat in at its two tables or on an "inviting" patio; "excellent salads", "zesty" "homemade soups" and plenty more also provide "terrific takeout" on "those lazy I-don't-want-to-cook days."

Salsa Salsa *Californian/Mexican* | 23 | 11 | 19 | $17 |

Bayport | 893 Montauk Hwy. (bet. Barrett & Sylvan Aves.) | 631-419-6464
Port Jefferson | 142 Main St. (bet. Mill Creek Rd. & Wynn Ln.) | 631-473-9700
Smithtown | Maple Commons Shopping Ctr. | 320 Maple Ave. (Rte. 111) | 631-360-8080
www.salsasalsa.net
Burrito-boosters bet on this "exceptional" Cal-Mex trio for "consistently" fresh, "reasonably priced" "quick" meals; there's a "friendly staff", but the "take-out" settings with "limited seating" are "a bit primitive" for eating in, so put it on "speed dial" and pick it up "to go."

NEW Salumi Tapas & Wine Bar ● *Italian/Spanish* | - | - | - | M |

Massapequa | 5600 Merrick Rd. (Carman Mill Rd.) | 516-620-0057 | www.salumibarli.com
A strip-mall storefront leads to the rustic wood-and-brick setting of this Massapequa Italian-Spanish newcomer where servers pour from an ever-changing wine list while preparing various tapas, salads and meat and cheese boards behind an antique timber bar; treats like marrow bone are foodie bait, while live guitar stokes the hip-casual vibe on some nights.

Salvatore's ⓂⒻ *Pizza* | 25 | 13 | 20 | $21 |

Port Washington | 124 Shore Rd. (bet. Manhasset Ave. & Soundview Dr.) | 516-883-8457
Pie at Salvatore's, The Ⓕ *Pizza*
Bay Shore | 120 E. Main St. (bet. 1st & 2nd Aves.) | 631-206-1060
www.salvatorescoalfiredpizza.com
"Just the right amount of sauce and cheese" grace the "awesome" brick-oven pies "made right in front of you", while the "ginormous"

calzones "are a treat" too, at this family-owned duo of pizza-and-pasta joints in Port Washington and Bay Shore that "stand above the rest"; the "delicious" fixin's are served in "always-crowded", "lively" "hole-in-the-wall" settings by a "friendly" staff, and though "take-out" is an option, the "crisp crusts" taste best when you "eat in"; P.S. remember it's "cash only."

Sam's *Italian/Pizza*   18 | 11 | 18 | $33

East Hampton | 36 Newtown Ln. (bet. Main St. & Osborne Ln.) | 631-324-5900 | www.samseasthampton.com

Known for "thin-crust pizza" that'll "satisfy any appetite", this enduring East Hampton "staple" also slings "not-bad" "basic Italian" in "plentiful" portions; maybe there's "no atmosphere" in the "old-fashioned" "bar-and-grill" digs, but those with "kids in tow" appreciate an "informal" option that's "as local as it gets."

Samurai Ⓜ *Japanese*   ▽ 24 | 21 | 20 | $45

Huntington | 46 Gerard St. (Wall St.) | 631-271-2588 | www.samuraihibachi.com

"Perfect for families" or "a group" looking for an "entertaining night out", this "always crowded" Huntington Japanese sibling to nearby Tomo is "just what you'd expect" from a "noisy" hibachi steakhouse; the "cute" "show is the same every time", and though it's a bit "pricey", the "kids love it" and the adults appreciate a "breathtaking Asian-inspired interior" and "surprisingly good sushi."

☑ San Marco *Italian*   26 | 21 | 26 | $46

Hauppauge | 658 Motor Pkwy. (bet. Kennedy Dr. & Marcus Blvd.) | 631-273-0088 | www.sanmarcoristorante.com

"Everyone is treated like a VIP" by a "top-notch", "black tie"–clad staff wheeling "carts with appetizers and desserts" at this "tried-and-true" Hauppauge "special-occasion" "favorite" serving "some of the best" Northern Italian on the Island; although some suggest the decor "needs a bit of updating", "you can't go wrong" here, even "after all these years" – and it "won't break the bank" either.

Sant Ambroeus *Italian*   24 | 20 | 22 | $70

Southampton | 30 Main St. (bet. Meetinghouse Ln. & Wall St.) | 631-283-1233 | www.santambroeus.com

The "beautifully prepared" Milanese cuisine and "caring service" are "a cut above" at this "civilized" seasonal Southamptonite with sibs in Manhattan and Milan, a "wonderful European" enclave that's also favored for its "terrific" espresso bar ("don't miss their cappuccino") and "fantastic" gelati and desserts; granted, it's so "insanely expensive" you may need "to take out another mortgage", but it's always "heavenly" "to sit on the patio" and scope the passing "parade."

Sapporo *Japanese*   23 | 19 | 23 | $35

Wantagh | 3266 Merrick Rd. (1 block east of Wantagh Pkwy.) | 516-785-3853

This longtime midpriced "staple for sushi" in Wantagh, offering "amazing hand rolls", "creative" Japanese dishes and a "nice assortment of sake" served by a "pleasant, prompt" staff, makes an "outstanding choice" for dining, with improved scores to prove it; the "quiet" setting – including a traditional "tatami" room where patrons "sit on the floor" – is "suitable for talking", leaving some saying now if they'd just "update" the decor, "it would be perfect."

Sapsuckers Hops & Grub *American*   `- | - | - | I`

Huntington | 287 Main St. (bet. Green & Wall Sts.) | 631-683-4945 | www.sapsuckersli.com

Artisanal and farm-raised ingredients are spotlighted on the affordable American menu at this slim-lined Huntington sibling of Café Red (Smithtown) and Osteria da Nino (Huntington); mirrors on the walls give the narrow quarters an illusion of space, and a copper ceiling and oak floor add warmth.

Sarabeth's *American*   `20 | 16 | 18 | $28`

Garden City | Lord & Taylor | 1200 Franklin Ave. (bet. 12th & 13th Sts.) | 516-742-7000
Manhasset | Lord & Taylor | 1440 Northern Blvd. (Shelter Rock Rd.) | 516-627-3000
www.sarabeth.com

"Serious shoppers" at the Garden City and Manhasset Lord & Taylor stores "recharge" their browsing batteries at these "convenient" branches of the Manhattan-based cafe chain, which "fit the bill" for "casual" lunching with a "surprisingly good" American menu of salads, sandwiches and desserts; they make a "pleasant" "respite", and though opening time isn't until at least 10 AM (depending on the day), breakfast bites are served all day.

Sarin Thai *Thai*   `24 | 18 | 22 | $33`

Greenvale | 43 Glen Cove Rd. (Wellington Rd.) | 516-484-5873
Kings Park | 25 Main St. (Henry St.) | 631-269-4130
www.sarinthaicuisine.com

You "can count on" this "longtime" Greenvale "favorite" for "amazing" Thai with a "sophisticated twist", from "wonderful" curry and "spicy duck" to "excellent pad Thai", accompanied by a "respectable wine list"; the staff "tries hard to please" in the "relaxed", "elegant" space, so admirers admit they'd "eat here more often" if not for the "parking problem"; P.S. an outpost in Kings Park opened post-Survey.

Savanna's *American*   `20 | 18 | 17 | $67`

Southampton | 268 Elm St. (Powell Ave.) | 631-283-0202 | www.savannassouthampton.com

"One of the 'in' places" in Southampton, this "glammy" seasonal hot spot appeals to "strivers" with "ambitious" New American fare and "great people-watching", "if you don't mind the prices"; critics complain of the "ear-throbbing" "noise factor", but there's a "peaceful" "garden in the rear" for those who "want to have a conversation."

Schooner *Seafood/Steak*   `17 | 17 | 18 | $43`

Freeport | 435 Woodcleft Ave. (Richmond St.) | 516-378-7575 | www.theschooner.com

"Lovely" "waterside views" in a "lively" setting with indoor and outdoor tables and an option to "come by boat and tie up" have kept this surf 'n' turfer on Freeport's Nautical Mile "around forever"; those who say the rest – from "so-so" fare to an interior that reminds you of "your grandparents' place" – "needs a makeover" will appreciate the recent redo of the patio and bar area, and as always, the "staff couldn't be nicer."

Scotto's *Italian/Pizza*   20 | 19 | 18 | $32

Westbury | Roosevelt Raceway Ctr. | 1195 Corporate Dr. (Merchants Concourse) | 516-222-1042

Pizzaphiles plug this "welcome addition" to Westbury from the Scotto Brothers hospitality team for the wood-fired, "ultra-thin-crust" pies leading an "enjoyable" "mix" that also includes pastas and other Italian staples; meanwhile critics claim the "cavernous", multiroom space "loses any intimacy" and the service "could use upgrading."

Scrimshaw *American*   23 | 20 | 19 | $56

Greenport | Preston's Wharf | 102 Main St. (bet. Front St. & Greenport Harbor) | 631-477-8882 | www.scrimshawrestaurant.com

Chef-owner Rosa Ross' "unpretentious" Greenport New American "never fails to satisfy" with "wonderful" dishes featuring "fresh local ingredients", a "focus on seafood" and a "melding of Asian" influences; outdoor seating "on the wharf" affords "beautiful waterfront views" of Greenport Harbor and Shelter Island that distract from the "high prices"; P.S. open Thursday–Sunday in the winter.

Sea Basin *Italian/Seafood*   19 | 18 | 22 | $34

Rocky Point | 642 Rte. 25A (bet. B'way & Polk St.) | 631-744-1643 | www.seabasin.com

A "local standby", this Italian seafooder in Rocky Point dishes up "reliable" "traditional" fare at "reasonable" prices, especially during "prix fixe lunches and dinners"; though "you won't get gourmet" here and the "tired decor" "hasn't been updated in many years", "excellent service" and "big portions" have regulars leaving "satisfied and happy."

Sea Grille *American/Italian*   ▽ 21 | 21 | 21 | $48

Montauk | Gurney's Inn | 290 Old Montauk Hwy. (bet. Fir Ln. & Maple St.) | 631-668-2345 | www.gurneysinn.com

The "view of the beach and ocean can't be beat" at this American-Italian in Gurney's Inn that serves up "excellent seafood" in a "relaxing" setting that works "even in winter" (Friday–Saturday DJs, and Thursday-night karaoke are year-round); though the service gets mixed marks and the tab can "add up quickly", fans dub it a Montauk "must."

Sea Levels ⊠Ⓜ *American/Seafood*   ▽ 22 | 19 | 21 | $43

Brightwaters | 391 N. Windsor Ave. (Orinoco Dr.) | 631-665-8300 | www.sealevelsrestaurant.com

"A great place to start out a Saturday night", this Brightwaters New American "pleases" with its "amazing" seafood and "cowboy steaks" by chef-owner John Peter Montgomery; though the "large" mahogany bar is a "raucous" "gathering place on weekends", when there's live acoustic music, the "separate", "quiet" dining room is buffered from the "noise"; P.S. there's a "terrific" prix fixe dinner special and monthly cooking and wine classes.

Seeda Thai *Thai*
| 23 | 17 | 21 | $31 |

Valley Stream | 28 N. Central Ave. (Merrick Rd.) | 516-561-2626 | www.seedathai.com

Valley Streamers "regularly" Thai one on at this "cozy", "relaxing" Siamese vet, a "reliable" fallback for "palatable" standards that also serves some "authentic" specialties (e.g. "more frogs' legs dishes than most"); even if the decor's "not so fancy", the "flavorful food" brings followers "back again and again" – especially once they seeda "reasonable prices."

⚡ Sempre Vivolo ⓩ *Italian*
| 27 | 24 | 27 | $56 |

Hauppauge | 696 Vanderbilt Motor Pkwy. (Old Willets Path) | 631-435-1737 | www.semprevivolo.com

"Always a pleasure", this "refined" Hauppauge Italian is a "long-standing" source of "delectable" cuisine presented by "impeccable", "tuxedo-clad" pros; with "jackets required on Saturday night", it's a "fabulous" chance to "slow down" and "carry on a conversation" in a pleasant "old-world" atmosphere.

Sen ⓩ *Japanese*
| 21 | 17 | 18 | $54 |

Sag Harbor | 23 Main St. (bet. Bay & Madison Sts.) | 631-725-1774 | www.senrestaurant.com

"Raw fish aplenty" and a "lively" atmosphere add up to "sushi à la Hamptons" at this Sag Harbor Japanese, a "rather excellent" source of "orthodox as well as nouvelle rolls" served by "polite" staffers; it's "clearly a hot spot" with "long waits on weekends", and wallet-watchers are sensitive to the "ridiculous prices", but "if you're recession-proof, go for it"; P.S. a larger Manhattan sibling is scheduled to open in summer 2012 with chef Wayne Nish at the helm.

Sensasian *Asian*
| - | - | - | M |

Levittown | 636 Wantagh Ave. (bet. Sprucewood Dr. & Stony Ln.) | 516-520-8811 | www.sensasianbistro.com

Offering a respite from its mall surroundings, this Levittown Asian serves Chinese and Japanese fare with a smattering of Thai dishes also in the mix; moody blue, red and orange neon lighting and dark walls create atmosphere, and moderate prices complete the package.

Serafina ● *Italian*
| 18 | 16 | 16 | $47 |

East Hampton | 104 N. Main St. (Cedar St.) | 631-267-3500 | www.serafinarestaurant.com

"Young, hip and single" sorts nosh on pizza, pasta and other Italian bites while "people-watching" "on the patio" at this "casual but chic" arrival, the East Hampton outpost of a Manhattan-based chain; some complain that you'll pay "city prices" for merely "adequate" food "served by amateurs", but it's already a "big scene", so "expect a wait."

NEW Serata ⑤Ⓜ *Italian*

- | - | - | E

Oyster Bay | 160 Mill River Rd. (bet. Glen Cove Rd. & Lexington Ave.) | 516-628-2800 | www.serata160.com

At 9 PM the lights are lowered, disco balls on the ceiling start spinning and dance music pulsates at this Oyster Bay Italian (its name means festive party) where revelers enjoy dishes inspired by family recipes from the old country; before 9, diners can watch old movies playing on any of the multiple TVs in a space accented by brick archways and crystal chandeliers.

❷ 1770 House
Restaurant & Inn *American*

25 | 25 | 24 | $66

East Hampton | 1770 House | 143 Main St. (Dayton Ln.) | 631-324-1770 | www.1770house.com

From the "thoughtfully prepared", "delectable" American fare to the "elegant, old colonial" setting with a "peaceful" patio and "blazing fireplaces", this "charming", "expensive" East Hampton eatery in an 18th-century inn is "first-rate" all around; the "ever-obliging service" extends to a "less formal" "downstairs tavern" offering a "reasonably priced" pub menu, so it's "cozy" and "civilized" even if you're not "East End–endowed."

Seventh Street Cafe *Italian*

20 | 19 | 20 | $39

Garden City | 126 Seventh St. (bet. Franklin & Hilton Aves.) | 516-747-7575 | www.seventhstreetcafe.com

"After shopping" "in the heart of Garden City", this "cute", "consistent Italian" "works" for "above-average" "standards" "at a reasonable price"; knockers caution the "ho-hum" menu "needs a little pick-me-up" and the "noise level might be off-putting", but in warm weather there's always "alfresco dining" on the tree-lined Seventh Street strip.

75 Main ● *Italian*

18 | 19 | 17 | $49

Southampton | 75 Main St. (bet. Jobs Ln. & Nugent St.) | 631-283-7575 | www.75main.com

New ownership "finally seems to be getting it right" at this Southampton Italian where the sidewalk tables offer "beautiful" "people-watching" and the redecorated interior sports a "cool, unpretentious ambiance"; opinions of the food range from "tasty" to "so-so", and service can be "choppy", but it's a "happening place with the under-30 crowd and those who wish they were", especially when the beat picks up with live music and DJs late night.

Shagwong *American/Seafood*

18 | 14 | 15 | $37

Montauk | 774 Main St. (bet. Edgemere & Essex Sts.) | 631-668-3050 | www.shagwong.com

"Salty character" defines this "old-school Montauk" "mainstay", which supplies "simple" seafood and other "decent" American eats in a "tavern" setting with "homegrown" regulars "hunched over the bar"; service is "spotty" and the "dingy" digs have "seen better days", but "natives" and "weekenders" keep it "thriving", "and they stay open all year."

	FOOD	DECOR	SERVICE	COST

Shiki *Japanese* ▽ 24 | 19 | 22 | $36

Babylon | 233 E. Main St. (Cooper St.) | 631-669-5404 |
www.shiki-longisland.com

"Repeat customers" are hooked on the "fantastic" fish at this "affordable" Japanese in Babylon, which specializes in "exquisite" presentations of "super-fresh" sushi bolstered by "delicious" "non-raw" items; it's "not a Nobu, but gaining", and the "low-key" milieu means "you won't be waiting for a table."

Shiki *Japanese* - | - | - | E

East Hampton | 47 Montauk Hwy. (bet. Baiting Hollow &
Cove Hollow Rds.) | 631-329-9821 | www.shikihamptons.com

This upscale Asian-Japanese addition to the East Hampton scene is in the space formerly occupied by Bamboo and sports a fresh coat of paint in the former shadowy, sexy colors; there's a new sushi bar for a variety of raw fish, and hot dishes include the likes of grilled Mongolian beef; P.S. a garden patio is a popular summer perch.

Shiro of Japan *Japanese* 22 | 20 | 22 | $38

Carle Place | 401 Old Country Rd. (Carle Rd.) | 516-997-4770 |
www.shiroofjapan.com

"This show never gets old" say fans of this "delightful" Carle Place Japanese, long known for "hibachi done right" with "plentiful" helpings of "yum-o" food and a "fiery" "performance" that's "a real treat" for "kids" and "groups"; the "amazingly fresh sushi" also wins favor, and though it's "a bit pricey", it's still "way better than Benihana."

Shogi M *Japanese* ▽ 25 | 9 | 28 | $33

Westbury | 584 Old Country Rd. (bet. Longfellow & Tennyson Aves.) |
516-338-8768

All are "well-treated and special" at this Westbury "neighborhood" Japanese, where the "terrific" hostess "makes the place come to life" and the chef crafts "wonderful", "exceptionally authentic" sushi (including "variations by request") from fish "so fresh" it's "practically flopping"; it's a humble setup, but it's "guaranteed to make you feel at home."

Show Win *Japanese* 20 | 15 | 19 | $35

Amagansett | 40 Montauk Hwy. (bet. Cross & Indian Wells Plain Hwys.) |
631-267-7600 | www.showwinsushi.com
Northport | 325 Fort Salonga Rd. (bet. Reservoir & Woodbine Aves.) |
631-261-6622 | www.sushishowwin.com

Admirers of this "dependable", "good-value" sushi duo say they "go into withdrawal when it's been too long" since they've had their "inventive" rolls and other Japanese fare; the Amagansett location's semi-private tatami room is a "big plus" for small groups, but Northport gets knocked for "needing an update big-time."

Z Siam Lotus Thai *Thai* 28 | 16 | 26 | $35

Bay Shore | 1664 Union Blvd. (bet. 4th & Park Aves.) |
631-968-8196 | www.siamlotus.us

A local "must" for a taste of "Bangkok at its best", this "exceptional" Bay Shore Thai brings you "all the classics" plus "delectable" daily specials, prepared "to a T" and "beautifully presented" courtesy of a kitchen that's "not afraid to use spice"; the "personal attention" is likewise "a cut above", so if the room's "nondescript", keep in mind "you don't go here for the decor."

Silver's Eclectic
23 | 16 | 16 | $46

Southampton | 15 Main St. (bet. Jobs Ln. & Nugent St.) | 631-283-6443 | www.silversrestaurant.com
They elevate "lunch to an art form" at this "sweet little" Southampton "favorite", where the Eclectic midday fare runs to "delicious" BLTs, lobster rolls, "homemade soups" and more served in a "sunny" space that's been in chef-owner Garrett Wellins' family since 1923; it'll cost you "some moola", but "everything they do, they do well"; P.S. dinner may now be offered on summer weekends.

Simply Fondue Fondue
17 | 19 | 18 | $44

Great Neck | The Gdns. | 24 Great Neck Rd. (bet. Brompton & Middle Neck Rds.) | 516-466-4900 | www.simplyfonduelongisland.com
Dip it yourself at this upstairs "find" in a Great Neck shopping center, where prix fixe fondue deals have "attentive" staffers bringing on "tasty tidbits" you cook "in the style of your choice" on tabletop burners, from "main-course meats and fish" to "dreamy" chocolate desserts; "it's not cheap" and can be a "slow meal", but after a few "signature martinis", it's "lots of fun", especially "for groups."

Simply Thai Thai
21 | 13 | 19 | $27

Rockville Centre | 274 Merrick Rd. (N. Park Ave.) | 516-255-9340
This "no-frills" Rockville Centre nook earns support with "solid Thai" favorites made all the more "tantalizing" by some of the "best value" around; the "small", "simple setting" is "not much to look at", but service is "quick" and you can always "take it to go."

Sip City Eclectic
- | - | - | E

Great Neck | 16 Middle Neck Rd. (Cutter Mill Rd.) | 516-482-1500 | www.sipcity.net
Equal parts dining room and lounge, this Eclectic bistro provides a glitzy alternative to more staid Great Neck spots with arty decor touches like red walls and cylindrical lights, plus tall windows that open to the street in warm weather; the menu scoots from the likes of Cajun chicken sliders to curried prawns, and live entertainment most nights plus dancing on Saturdays add to the scene.

🆕 Smashburger Burgers
- | - | - | I

Hicksville | 180 W. Old Country Rd. (Rte. 106) | 516-605-2235 | www.smashburger.com
Creating your own burgers (which really are smashed on the grill) and chicken sandwich combos is the thing to do at this Hicksville link in the national chain offering a variety of breads, sauces, toppings and cheeses to gild the meat; the sleek room has a lofty feel with high ceilings and an industrialized vibe, and it all comes cheap.

	FOOD	DECOR	SERVICE	COST

☑ Smokin' Al's Famous BBQ Joint *BBQ* | 23 | 17 | 19 | $31 |

Massapequa Park | 4847 Merrick Rd. (bet. Harbor Ln. & Park Blvd.) | 516-799-4900

Bay Shore | 19 W. Main St. (bet. 4th & 5th Aves.) | 631-206-3000

www.smokinals.com

"Wave goodbye to your diet" and "pig out" on "scrumptious" "Southern BBQ done right" at this "roll-up-your-sleeves" Bay Shore "mmmmeat" mecca and its Massapequa Park follow-up, "informal" outlets for "unbelievable" ribs, "tender brisket" and "awesome pulled pork" in "Flintstone-sized" portions "slathered" with "sloppy" sauce; the "raucous", "smoky" quarters are perpetually "mobbed" despite "insane" "waits" and "the trip to the dry cleaner" afterward.

Snapper Inn Ⓜ *Seafood* | 18 | 19 | 19 | $42 |

Oakdale | 500 Shore Dr. (½ mi. west of Vanderbilt Blvd.) | 631-589-0248 | www.thesnapperinn.com

Ever a "fixture" for "summertime dining" thanks to a "lovely location" overlooking the Connetquot River, this "old favorite" in Oakdale "takes you away" with its "relaxed atmosphere" and "really pretty" view; nonfans of the "so-so seafood" and "indifferent service" snap it's "living on its earlier legend", but loyal habitués say the "charm" "makes up for" everything.

☑ Snaps American Bistro Ⓜ *American* | 26 | 19 | 23 | $39 |

Wantagh | 2010 Wantagh Ave. (Sunrise Hwy.) | 516-221-0029 | www.snapsrestaurant.com

It's easy to "pass this diamond-in-the-rough" hidden in a Wantagh "strip of stores", but that would be a shame since "talented" chef/co-owner Scott Bradley creates an "ever-changing menu" of "extraordinary" New American dishes, including specials that "keep you coming back"; service is "excellent" and a recent "face-lift greatly improved" the "cool" space, plus the daily prix fixe and tasting menus make it such a "great value" you can't get in without "a reservation on weekends"; P.S. closed Monday–Tuesday.

Solé *Italian* | 26 | 15 | 21 | $40 |

Oceanside | 2752 Oceanside Rd. (Merle Ave.) | 516-764-3218 | www.soleny.com

"Despite its simple exterior", this "Italian gem" in Oceanside is a "terrific little spot" where a "marvelous" menu is served "with good humor" in a "bright", butter-hued space; the sole "drawback" is "large turnouts" that lead to "cramped and noisy" conditions and major "waits", but "top-notch" food at "moderate prices" easily outweighs "the negatives"; P.S. Fridays and Saturdays, reservations are accepted for parties of five or more only.

Southampton Publick House *Pub Food* | 18 | 17 | 19 | $38 |

Southampton | 40 Bowden Sq. (bet. N. Main St. & N. Sea Rd.) | 631-283-2800 | www.publick.com

"Fresh beer's always on tap" to wash down "standard American" pub grub at this roomy Southampton microbrewery, where the eating "meets expectations" even if the house-brand suds are "the big attraction"; it's a "friendly" enough "local hangout" "if you can handle" "the loud bar scene."

NEW Southampton Social Club *American*   – | – | – | E

Southampton | 256 Elm St. (bet. Powell Ave. & Pulaski St.) |
631-287-1400 | www.southamptonsocialclub.com

A young, vibrant crowd is drawn to the fire pit, covered patios and lounges on the lawn at this classy and trendy Southampton remake of Madame Tong's, now offering an American menu complete with a raw bar; inside features fireplaces and a librarylike nook with banquettes, and there's live music during the week and DJs on weekends; P.S. open seasonally.

South Edison *American*   ▽ 22 | 21 | 22 | $50

Montauk | 17 S. Edison St. (S. Etna Ave.) | 631-668-4200 |
www.southedison.com

Making waves in Montauk, this seasonal American in the heart of the village "hit the deck running" with chef-owner Todd Mitgang (of NYC's Cascabel Taqueria) highlighting his "creativity" via an "outstanding", seafood-leaning menu backed up by a "great raw bar"; sporting a casually "attractive" "beach feel", it's gathering followers who "can't wait" for summer.

NEW Southern Spice *Indian*   – | – | – | M

New Hyde Park | 1635 Hillside Ave. (bet. Kent & New Hyde Park Rds.) |
516-216-5448 | www.southernspice.net

Relocated from Flushing, NY, this New Hyde Park Indian specializing in the cuisine of the Chettinad region of Southern India dishes out a variety of hot and spicy curries, dosai and tandoori dishes – often served with a hard-boiled egg, as is the custom; while gold is featured in decor touches on the tabletops and chandeliers, tabs won't require a load of it.

Southfork Kitchen *Seafood*   – | – | – | VE

Bridgehampton | 203 Bridgehampton-Sag Harbor Tpke.
(bet. Montauk Hwy/.Rte 27 & Narrow Ln.) | 631-537-4700 |
www.southforkkitchen.com

An "outstanding" "gourmet addition" to Bridgehampton, this seasonal East Ender is "noteworthy" for its "inventive takes on seafood" as a "talented chef" "artfully draws" "subtle flavors" from "mostly local fish and produce" matched with wines from area vineyards; "attentive" servers oversee a rustic space with a "warm", "woodsy" vibe, so all in all diners with deep pockets "expect great things"; P.S. closed Tuesday and Wednesday.

Southside Fish & Clam *Seafood*   20 | 8 | 12 | $27

Lindenhurst | 395 W. Montauk Hwy. (bet. 4th & 5th Sts.) |
631-226-4700 | www.southsidefishandclam.com

In spite of the "plastic utensils", "self service" and "rudimentary decor", this '30s-era Lindenhurst seafooder remains a "mainstay" for "fresh fish" "on the cheap" including a "twin lobster deal" that "can't be beat"; still, those who expect "a bit more class" claim it's "much better" for retail fin fare at the on-site market.

	FOOD	DECOR	SERVICE	COST

Souvlaki Palace *Greek*   ∇ 24 | 8 | 18 | $22

Commack | 57 Commack Rd. (Jericho Tpke.) | 631-858-1482
A "hole-in-the-wall" "family operation", this "unpretentious" Commack Greek serves "huge" plates of "honest, well-prepared" standards, from the "best souvlaki" to "fresh whole fish", at "reasonable prices"; there's not much to the "modest" surroundings, but if your "priority is food" and "nothing else", it works.

Spare Rib, The *BBQ*   18 | 14 | 18 | $29

Commack | 2098 Jericho Tpke. (Indian Head Rd.) | 631-543-5050 | www.spareribonline.com
"For those who like a little body to their babybacks", this Commack joint is "the place to go for BBQ ribs, chicken" and other "satisfying", "economical" eats; but some have a bone to pick over "varying service", digs that "could use a makeover" and "interminable" weekend waits for what they dub "nothing-special" grub.

Spice Village Grill *Pakistani/Persian*   ∇ 20 | 13 | 19 | $28

Huntington | 281 Main St. (Wall St.) | 631-271-4800 | www.spicevillagegrill.com
When you're looking for something "a bit different", this Pakistani-Persian in Huntington is "surprisingly good considering its outer appearance"; the staff makes "helpful" recommendations while the BYO policy "keeps a night out within your budget", so the "simple", "cramped" space is easy to overlook.

Spicy's Barbecue *BBQ*   20 | 5 | 13 | $18

Bellport | 501 Station Rd. (bet. Atlantic & Patchogue Aves.) | 631-286-2755
Riverhead | 225 W. Main St. (bet. Griffing & Osborn Aves.) | 631-727-2781
Take a "quick trip to the Deep South" at these way "retro" BBQ joints in Bellport and Riverhead, where the "killer ribs" and "fabulous chicken wings" are a "delicious" "reward" at a "miniscule" price; just know that their "broken-down diner" settings make "takeout better than eating in."

NEW Spiro's *Steak*   - | - | - | VE

Rocky Point | 4 Patchogue Dr. (N. Country Rd.) | 631-744-4100 | www.spiroslounge.com
Chef-owner Spiro Karachopan (of nearby Sea Basin) branches out with this namesake lounge and steakhouse situated in a new Mediterranean-style stucco building on a prominent corner in Rocky Point; chops are joined by dishes such as stuffed lobster tail on the pricey menu served in a dining room hung with colorful paintings by local artist Barbara Bilotta, while a martini menu and twice-daily weekday happy hours keep things lively in the bar area.

NEW Spring Close *American*   - | - | - | M

East Hampton | 341 Pantigo Rd. (Spring Close Hwy.) | 631-324-3444
Located in a spacious East Hampton farmhouse, this affordable newcomer taking over for The Laundry delivers an American menu

emphasizing seafood and local ingredients; in addition to a main room with white tablecloths and rustic exposed beams, it also has a smaller, intimate 'library' framed with bookcases, a huge domed room with a gardenlike feel and a bar in the front with tables.

Squiretown American

▽ 20 | 19 | 20 | $45

Hampton Bays | 26 W. Montauk Hwy. (bet. Ponquogue Ave. & Springville Rd.) | 631-723-2626 | www.squiretown.com

"Yay for Hampton Bays!" cheer natives giddy over the arrival of this "delightful" American bistro, a "surprise" "hit" "in an unlikely location"; its "locally sourced" lineup of midpriced steaks and seafood complements an "airy", "serene setting" with a "modern" look defined by hardwood floors, earth tones and drum chandeliers.

Sripraphai Thai

25 | 16 | 18 | $29

Williston Park | 280 Hillside Ave. (Collins Ave.) | 516-280-3779 | www.sripraphairestaurant.com

The "best Thai food in Queens is now the best on LI" since this "vibrant" branch that's "just a tiny notch below" the Woodside original opened, bringing a "massive menu" of "amazing", "memorable", "hot and spicy" dishes to Williston Park; even if the "bright lime decor can be off-putting" to some and the "crowds on weekends" mean "long waits", it's a mighty "fine" purveyor of "authentic", "inexpensive" chow – and you don't need to "brave the LIE"; P.S. closed Wednesdays.

Sri Thai Thai

22 | 15 | 21 | $28

Huntington | 14 New St. (bet. Main & W. Carver Sts.) | 631-424-3422

Fans "can't wait to go back" to this "hidden" yet "popular" Huntington Thai where the "fantastic" dishes have a "subtlety of flavor not found in run-of-the-mill" recipes elsewhere; the staff is "pleasant", and while there's "limited seating" and "no ambiance", you "don't go for the setting" but for the "wonderful", "fairly priced" food.

Star Confectionery ⊄ American/Diner

▽ 22 | 19 | 22 | $17

Riverhead | 4 E. Main St. (Roanoke Ave.) | 631-727-9873

A family business dating to the 1920s, this "classic" "mom-and-pop" luncheonette in the heart of Riverhead is "perfect" for all-American breakfast and lunch fare in "suitable" vintage surroundings with wooden booths and a black-and-white checked floor; sweet tooths can count on "great ice cream" too, since they still make their own.

☒ Starr Boggs American/Seafood

26 | 23 | 22 | $62

Westhampton Beach | 6 Parlato Dr. (Library Ave.) | 631-288-3500 | www.starrboggsrestaurant.com

A perpetual Westhampton Beach "'in' spot", this "upbeat" New American shines bright with an "absolutely delicious" menu starring the eponymous chef-owner's "outstanding" seafood, served by a "terrific" team in "first-class" quarters flaunting original Warhols and a "gorgeous patio"; it provides "insanely sceney" "people-watching" on weekends, but if evading "pricey" tabs takes priority, there's a "wonderful" lobster bake deal on Mondays; P.S. open seasonally.

	FOOD	DECOR	SERVICE	COST

Stella Ristorante Ⓜ *Italian* — 24 | 18 | 22 | $41

Floral Park | 152 Jericho Tpke. (bet. Belmont & N. Tyson Aves.) |
516-775-2202 | www.stellaristorante.com

This circa-1960 "family favorite" in Floral Park "never gets old" as it
reliably indulges its followers with "magnificent" "old-fashioned
Italian fare" and "top-notch" hospitality headed up by the "namesake" "matriarch"; the "warm" if "dated" digs are "always busy", so
"reservations are a must on weekends" (and there still may be
"a long wait").

Steve's Piccola Bussola *Italian* — 24 | 16 | 22 | $42

Westbury | 649 Old Country Rd. (Tennyson Ave.) | 516-333-1335

Steve's Piccola Bussola II *Italian*

Syosset | 41 Jackson Ave. (Underhill Blvd.) | 516-364-8383
www.stevespiccolabussola.com

"Go with a group" and share "fabulous family-style" fare at these
"jovial" Westbury and Syosset "belly-busters", where there's "joy in
every bite" of Italian "classics" doused in "garlic-laden" "red gravy"
and "served promptly" at a "very reasonable" price; claustrophobes
may wish for "more elbow room" to "sop up the sauce", but these
places are "popular" "so be prepared to wait."

ⓩ Stone Creek Inn *French/Mediterranean* — 26 | 24 | 24 | $64

East Quogue | 405 Montauk Hwy. (bet. Carter Ln. & Wedgewood Rd.) |
631-653-6770 | www.stonecreekinn.com

There's "first-class" dining "nestled deep" in East Quogue at this
"culinary tour de force", where the "adventurous" seasonal menu of
"superior" French-Med cuisine shows off "fantastic variations and
flavors" in discreetly "sophisticated" environs overseen by a "gracious" staff; the "noise level is certainly robust" and you may need
to "negotiate a line of credit" to pay, but it's the stuff that "great
memories" are made of; P.S. closed January–March.

Stonewalls *American/French* — 23 | 21 | 23 | $52

Riverhead | Woods at Cherry Creek Golf Club | 967 Reeves Ave.
(bet. Doctors Path & Roanoke Ave.) | 631-506-0777 |
www.stonewalls-restaurant.com

"Fantastic chef" Guy Peuch "works wonders" with his "beautifully
prepared and presented" dishes at this New American-French "find",
which follows through with "outstanding" service and "lovely surroundings" overlooking Riverhead's Woods at Cherry Creek golf
course; surveyors applaud a "refreshingly consistent" performance
that "should be more widely appreciated"; P.S. open seasonally.

Stresa *Italian* — 25 | 21 | 23 | $61

Manhasset | 1524 Northern Blvd. (¼ mi. east of Shelter Rock Rd.) |
516-365-6956 | www.stresarestaurant.com

"Marvelous", "high-end" Italian food "prepared with finesse" continues to lure a "who's who of Nassau County" to this "longtime favorite"
where an "efficient, formal" staff enhances the "elegant" setting; still,
some Manhasset-ites maintain "it helps to be a regular on the weekend unless you have plenty of time to wait", "even with a reservation."

Sugar Dining Den & Social Club ☒Ⓜ *American/Asian*

FOOD	DECOR	SERVICE	COST
-	-	-	M

Carle Place | Staples Ctr. | 246 Voice Rd. (Glen Cove Rd.) | 516-248-7600 | www.sugarli.com

Glitzy and sexy, this lively restaurant and lounge located in a less-than-glam retail mall in Carle Place offers a spectacular setting – a vaulted ceiling glowing with lights, tree branches in glass cases lining the walls and whimsical murals – as a backdrop for midpriced Asian-American small plates designed for sharing; P.S. there's a DJ and dancing Thursdays, Fridays and Saturdays.

Sugo *American*

FOOD	DECOR	SERVICE	COST
23	20	20	$41

Long Beach | 62 W. Park Ave. (bet. Edwards & National Blvds.) | 516-431-7846 | www.sugocafe.com

"One of Long Beach's hidden treasures", this "cute, colorful" "local place" "stands out" with a "delightfully" "different" American lineup offering "inventive apps" and "excellent specials" alongside burgers and brick-oven pizza; the "arty interior" is staffed by "down-to-earth" types helmed by a "hands-on" owner who "makes you feel right at home"; P.S. the Food rating may not reflect a chef change.

Suki Zuki *Japanese*

FOOD	DECOR	SERVICE	COST
24	13	17	$41

Water Mill | 688 Montauk Hwy. (Old Mill Rd.) | 631-726-4600

"The size of the crowds" "testifies to the quality" at this Water Mill Japanese "favorite", "a real keeper" for "excellent sushi" ("try the 'tuna sandwich'") and "robata-grill" specialties "at moderate prices"; the "humble storefront setting" is apt to be "noisy and cramped" and the "no-reservations policy" means you'll "often have to wait", but it's "well worth it."

Sullivan's Quay *Pub Food*

FOOD	DECOR	SERVICE	COST
18	20	22	$32

Port Washington | 541 Port Washington Blvd. (Revere Rd.) | 516-883-3122 | www.sullivansquay.com

There'll be "no disappointments" if you "stick to the basics" – "burgers, chops, steaks" – at this "typical Irish pub" in Port Washington with a "nice staff" serving up traditional American fare and some "tasty" old-country specialties; it's a "comfortable" place to "watch the game" and a real "scene" Thursday nights for trivia and late-night karaoke.

Sundried Tomato Cafe *Italian/Pizza*

FOOD	DECOR	SERVICE	COST
21	13	20	$26

Nesconset | Nesconset Plaza | 127 Smithtown Blvd. (bet. Mayfair Rd. & Southern Blvd.) | 631-366-6310 | www.lisundriedtomato.com

"Huge portions" of "old-fashioned Italian" please patrons at this Nesconset "neighborhood" pizzeria/restaurant that's "worthy of a revisit" despite being "not much to look at"; a "friendly" staff and "bargain lunches" are further reasons there's "always a crowd."

Sunset Beach *Asian/French*

FOOD	DECOR	SERVICE	COST
18	24	16	$59

Shelter Island Heights | Sunset Beach Hotel | 35 Shore Rd. (Sunnyside Dr.) | 631-749-2001 | www.sunsetbeachli.com

It's like you've "landed in the South of France" at this seasonal beachfront "hangout" on Shelter Island, where the "bikinis, boats" and "people-sighting" are "a bit like a party" whether you "sit up-stairs" "watching the sunset" or surfside "with your toes in the sand"; meanwhile malcontents moan about "hit-or-miss" Pan-Asian and French bistro fare, service that caters to "the 'in' crowd" and "sky-high prices for what you get."

Surf Lodge *American*   ▽ 19 | 23 | 16 | $59

Montauk | Surf Lodge | 183 Edgemere St. (bet. Elwell St. & Industrial Rd.) | 631-238-5216 | www.thesurflodge.com

Once the sun sets over Montauk's Fort Pond, this "swingin'", beach-themed New American becomes a "trendy scene" fueled by cock-tails and "fresh seafood" from *Top Chef* vet Sam Talbot; it's "a blast" if you're willing to shell out "city prices", but the deluge of "hipsters" "dressing like surfers" makes it "hard to get in" and "score a table"; P.S. closed October–May.

Surf 'N Turf
Mediterranean Grill *Greek/Turkish*   ▽ 24 | 17 | 24 | $34

Merrick | 2205 Merrick Rd. (bet. Fox & Lincoln Blvds.) | 516-992-0918 | www.surfnturfgrill.com

It's a toss-up as to which is better at this Greek-Turkish Grill in Merrick – the "old-world-style" staff that treats you "like royalty" or the menu of "perfectly cooked" fish and other "simple, well-prepared" turf selections; tabs are moderate, so the "only draw-back" is that the "tight" space – decorated with an oak bar and pol-ished mahogany floors – easily gets "crowded" and "noisy."

Surfside Inn *Continental/Seafood*   ▽ 18 | 20 | 18 | $46

Montauk | Surfside Inn | 685 Old Montauk Hwy. (bet. School Ln. & Washington Dr.) | 631-668-5958 | www.surfsideinnmontauk.com

With its panorama of the "ocean surf", this longtime Continental sea-fooder is a "low-key" "summer pleasure" in Montauk that's extra "dreamy" if you snag a spot "on the deck"; the "well-prepared" food may be "a little pricey", but at least there are "no big surprises" to dis-tract from the "gorgeous view"; P.S. closed December to mid-March.

Surf's Out *Italian/Seafood*   ▽ 17 | 19 | 18 | $45

Kismet | Fire Island | 1 Bay Walk (E. Lighthouse Walk) | 631-583-7400 | www.surfsoutfireisland.com

"Everyone meets and greets" at this waterfront hub in Kismet, where Fire Islanders fraternize with Great South Bay and the sounds of live bands as the backdrop; meanwhile the "decent" Italian-and-seafood menu is "trying to be all things" but wipes out with critics who con-tend it's "expensive for what it is"; P.S. closed October to mid-April.

Sushi Palace *Japanese*   ▽ 24 | 16 | 21 | $30

Great Neck | 148 Middle Neck Rd. (Linden Blvd.) | 516-487-8460

The "all-you-can-eat offer" is "an all-out bargain" at this Great Neck Japanese, where for a fixed price patrons can "check off the quan-tity" desired from a "wide range" of "very good" "specialty rolls, su-shi and sashimi" as well as "hot food", all served "with a smile"; the "value" alone is "worth the visit", but it's also "lots of fun."

	FOOD	DECOR	SERVICE	COST

Sushi Ya *Japanese*

21 | 15 | 19 | $36

Garden City | 949 Franklin Ave. (bet. 9th & 10th Sts.) |
516-873-8818 | www.sushiyagc.com
New Hyde Park | 2311 Jericho Tpke. (Nassau Blvd.) |
516-741-2288

For "steady" sushi, regulars report ya can't go wrong at this mid-priced Japanese twosome in Garden City and New Hyde Park, which do double duty with "hibachi grills" joining their "consistently fresh" fish; they also put together "great bento boxes", though a few aesthetes train their sights on the "unimpressive decor."

Swallow 🖂 Ⓜ *American*

- | - | - | M

Huntington | 366 New York Ave. (bet. Carver & Elm Sts.) |
631-547-5388 | www.swallowrestaurant.com

Nested in a tiny space, this Huntington New American turns out midpriced small plates that update homey favorites, e.g. butternut squash cappuccino and mac 'n' cheese with orzo, bacon and peas; the decor stokes a comfort vibe with exposed brick, butcher-block tables illuminated by votive candles and – what else? – birdcages.

Sweet Mama's *Diner*

19 | 17 | 19 | $23

Northport | 9 Alsace Pl. (Fort Salonga Rd.) | 631-261-6262 |
www.sweetmamaskitchen.net

"Still one of the best breakfast places around", this "real treat" in Northport attracts a "brunch scene to rival anything in the city" and serves "solid, generous" American plates for lunch and dinner as well; the staff is "conscientious", but those not so sweet on the retro setting say it's "a little too plain" and "you can't hear yourself think" when it "gets overcrowded with families on weekends."

Sweet Tomato *Sandwiches*

- | - | - | I

Glen Cove | 170 Forest Ave. (St. James Pl.) | 516-671-4481 🖂
NEW Oyster Bay | 91 Audrey Ave. (bet. Maxwell Ave. & Spring St.) |
516-802-5353
www.mysweettomato.com

Health-minded fare is made to order by chef-owner Tina Mazzarella at this new cafe located opposite the Oyster Bay Town Hall in an old house with a red-and-white striped awning, where an affordable menu includes sandwiches, wraps, salads and breakfast items; it's a larger branch of a Glen Cove spot where there's limited seating at picnic tables, and while children's art decorates the original location, paintings are for sale at the offshoot.

Swingbelly's Beachside BBQ ◑ *BBQ*

23 | 15 | 19 | $29

Long Beach | 909 W. Beech St. (Wisconsin St.) | 516-431-3464 |
www.swingbellysbbq.com

"Chow down" on "dynamite" BBQ till your belly's "swinging low" at this ultra-"casual" Long Beach "joint", where "hefty" helpings of brisket and ribs chased with "a couple of brewskis" make for an "excellent" "pig out" at a "reasonable price"; it entails braving a "noisy bar crowd" with "sports blasting", but 'cue enthusiasts "don't go for the atmosphere."

	FOOD	DECOR	SERVICE	COST

Taiko ⓜ *Asian* | 24 | 17 | 23 | $37 |

Rockville Centre | 15 S. Village Ave. (bet. Lincoln Ave. & Merrick Rd.) | 516-678-6149 | www.taikorestaurant.com

"Reliable" "for decades", this "local" "find" in Rockville Centre "never fails to impress" with "heavenly", "swimmingly fresh" sushi and "outstanding" Asian fusion fare courtesy of a "terrific" staff led by the family owners; maybe the space is "not much to look at", but it's usually "humming" since the "price and quality" "cannot be beat."

Tai Show *Japanese* | 23 | 18 | 22 | $34 |

Levittown | 170 Gardiners Ave. (Hempstead Tpke.) | 516-731-1188
Massapequa | 4318 Merrick Rd. (Harrison Ave.) | 516-798-1119
Massapequa | 4320 Merrick Rd. (Harrison Ave.) | 516-798-3958
East Setauket | 316 Main St. (bet. Deering St. & Shore Rd.) | 631-751-2848
www.taishow.com

Tai Show East *Japanese*

Oakdale | 1543 Montauk Hwy. (Vanderbilt Ave.) | 631-218-0808 | www.taishoweast.com

"Superior sushi" and "Japanese steakhouse cooking" come with "fantastic" service at this "good-value" Long Island chainlet; there's a "rockin' hibachi grill" tended in "high-style at some locations, and though a few say the "small" spaces at other outposts are "semi-depressing", others recall the "sake bombs" are a blast.

Takara *Japanese* | ▽ 28 | 19 | 23 | $44 |

Islandia | Islandia Shopping Plaza | 1708 Veterans Memorial Hwy. (Blydenburg Rd.) | 631-348-9470 | www.takara-sushi.com

The "fresh-off-the-boat" fish gives all rivals "a run for their money" at this "excellent" Islandia Japanese, where skilled sushi chefs ("including the owner") slice a "super" "array of exotic rolls"; with a "sweetheart" hostess and "personal attention" from the servers to "make the experience even better", boosters urge "don't miss this one."

🆕 Tappo *Italian* | - | - | - | E |

Glen Cove | 284 Glen St. (bet. Elm & Hendrick Aves.) | 516-759-1913 | www.tappony.com

Tucked away in Glen Cove, this Italian newcomer serves lunch, dinner, antipasti and bar menus in warm-colored quarters featuring a brick wall and a display of corks (paying homage to the restaurant's name); there's live music some nights, and the Sunday Supper offers five-courses for $35 per couple.

Taste 99 *American* | ▽ 18 | 21 | 21 | $46 |

Farmingdale | Carlyle on the Green, Bethpage State Park | 99 Quaker Meeting House Rd. (Round Swamp Rd.) | 516-586-1355 | www.carlyleonthegreen.net

"You won't meet anyone you know" at this "quiet rendezvous spot" insist incognito eaters who savor both the "beautiful" room, decorated with mahogany tables and chandeliers, and outdoor patio with "views of the famed" Bethpage Black golf course; less impressive is the "ok" menu, which includes upscale American entrees as well as grilled pizzas and small-plate options, but some say the vista is "worth it."

Tate's ⊠☞ *American/Italian*   ▽ 26 | 15 | 21 | $32

Nesconset | 292 Smithtown Blvd. (Chestnut St.) | 631-676-3283 |
www.tatesrestaurant.com

Early fans of this "busy" family-run Nesconset arrival praise its
"amazing" New American–Italian eats, including housemade pastas
and "great cookies and baked goods", delivered by an "excellent"
staff in a cozy, white-tablecloth setting; the three-course prix fixe
dinner deal and "awesome" BYO-only policy (with no corkage fee)
help keep prices reasonable, but plastic's not accepted
so "bring cash."

NEW Tavern on the Plaza *American*   - | - | - | M

Locust Valley | Plaza Shoppes | 4 The Plaza (bet. Elm St. & Underhill Rd.) |
516-676-5793

Restoring the former name of this Locust Valley tavern, new
owners have brightened the interior, added plantation-style
blinds to the windows and installed a new kitchen to turn out a
midpriced American lineup of burgers, sandwiches and salads,
plus the likes of steaks and fish; multiple TVs in the bar are tuned
to the games, while the white-tablecloth dining room offers a quiet
respite for meals.

⊠ Tellers American Chophouse *Steak*   26 | 27 | 25 | $70

Islip | 605 Main St. (bet. Locust & Nassau Aves.) | 631-277-7070 |
www.tellerschophouse.com

Set in a "stately" "former bank building", this "high-class" Islip
chophouse is "a cut above the rest" according to South Shore carnivores savoring "signature rib-eyes" (like "something out of *The
Flintstones*") and other "superb" strips "done to perfection" and
matched with wines from an "impressive" cellar in the former vault;
you'll "drop a mortgage payment", but diners with "deep pockets"
are happy to be "treated royally."

NEW Ten Ten Bistro *Asian*   - | - | - | M

Mount Sinai | Northgate Plaza | 331 Rte. 25A (bet. School St. &
W. Gate Dr.) | 631-331-6888 | www.tentenbistro.com

Located in Mt. Sinai's Northgate Plaza, this new Pan-Asian storefront offers an enormous menu of moderately priced Japanese,
Chinese, Thai, Indian, Malaysian and Vietnamese dishes; red lights
illuminate the sushi bar that's a shoji screen away from a dining
room decked out in dark wood tables and chairs.

Tequila Jacks *Caribbean/Seafood*   ▽ 18 | 21 | 20 | $41

Port Jefferson | 201 Main St. (entrance on Arden Pl.) | 631-331-0960 |
www.tequilajacksportjeff.com

"Get lost in the Caribbean feel" at this "cheery" Downtown Port Jeff
seafooder – from the "knock-your-socks-off" mojitos to the somewhat upscale plates including "some favorites from Key West"; the
staff is "happy to talk you through the menu", but a few guests dub
the food "mediocre" and just go for the energetic bar scene and "live
bands on weekends"; P.S. "when the music starts" be prepared to
"read lips", since "no one will hear a word you're saying."

	FOOD	DECOR	SERVICE	COST

Tesoro Ristorante ☒ *Italian* | 23 | 17 | 22 | $47 |

Westbury | 967 Old Country Rd. (bet. New York Ave. & Sylvester St.) | 516-334-0022 | www.tesorosrestaurant.com

They "make you feel like family" at this Westbury "oldie but goodie", treasured by legions of "repeat customers" who "count on" its "*delizioso*" traditional Italian fare and "eager-to-please" service; maybe the "outdated" room "needs a makeover", but the "satisfying" comestibles and "moderate cost" more than compensate.

Thai Gourmet ☒➶ *Thai* | 26 | 14 | 19 | $24 |

Port Jefferson Station | Common Plaza | 4747-24 Nesconset Hwy. (bet. Terryville Rd. & Woodhull Ave.) | 631-474-0663

Boosters feel "blessed" by the "best Thai food this side of Bangkok" at this strip-mall "treasure" in Port Jefferson Station, where the "tempting" dishes "burst with flavor" and "prices are dirt cheap"; just "hit the cash machine" first and "bring your own bottle and patience", since "you may have to wait for a seat" in the "kitschy" digs; P.S. there's a "substantial takeout business" as well.

Thai Green Leaf *Thai* | 21 | 10 | 18 | $25 |

Copiague | 47 Merrick Rd. (bet. Baylawn & Jarvis Aves.) | 631-789-8866
East Northport | 1969 Jericho Tpke. (bet. Daly & Elwood Rds.) | 631-462-8666
www.thai.netau.net

Fit for both "Thai beginners" and vets who cry "bring on the hot sauce", the "tasty" dishes at these "everyday-type" Siamese "standbys" in Copiague and East Northport are "well executed", nicely spiced and "efficiently served"; the digs are "sparsely" appointed, but these spots "won't break your wallet" and diners "leave satisfied" so "who cares?"

Thai House *Thai* | 24 | 19 | 23 | $30 |

Smithtown | 53 W. Main St. (Maple Ave.) | 631-979-5242 | www.thaihousesmithtown.com

Admirers of this "surprising" Smithtowner say its "reputation is spreading" for "amazing, authentic" Thai, including "light, healthy" selections prepared "to your taste", from "mild to spicy"; the "personalized" service makes you feel "appreciated", and fans even "love" the "simple" look with warm tones and "decorations from Thailand", adding to an "enjoyable experience" for a "reasonable" price.

Thai Table *Thai* | 23 | 19 | 21 | $27 |

Rockville Centre | 88 N. Village Ave. (Sunrise Hwy.) | 516-678-0886

Lauded by "locals", this Rockville Centre "diamond in the rough" is ever "reliable" for "terrific Thai" with "plenty of spice" served by a "fast, attentive" staff "at giveaway prices"; the brick-lined digs are sparsely adorned but "relaxed" enough for "an enjoyable meal."

Thai USA *Thai* | 23 | 17 | 19 | $34 |

Huntington | 273 New York Ave. (bet. Gerard St. & Union Pl.) | 631-427-8464 | www.thaiusahuntington.com

"The food is always good and cooked to your liking" at this "consistent" Huntington Thai that draws a "regular following" for its "fresh, delicious", moderately priced fare; the redecorated space is "cool" and the staff "attentive", so it's both a "family favorite" and a "great date spot" that's "perfect before a movie."

34 New Street ☑ *Eclectic* 18 | 14 | 20 | $33

Huntington | 34 New St. (bet. Main & W. Carver Sts.) | 631-427-3434 | www.34newstreet.com

A "wide array" of "innovative" pies and other affordable Eclectic eats keeps this Huntington "standby" a "decent" choice "for the family"; though some say it's "not a star" given the "awkwardly constructed" space (pizza counter up front, bistro-style dining room in back) and a menu that "needs Ritalin to focus", it wins points for "value" and "warm greetings" at the door.

Thomas's Ham & Eggery Diner ⊄ *Diner* 22 | 10 | 19 | $17

Carle Place | 325 Old Country Rd. (bet. E. Gate Blvd. & Mitchell Ave.) | 516-333-3060

"Things in skillets really do taste better" attest early-risers who "leave smiling" from this "old-fashioned" Carle Place diner, a "distinctive" "breakfast stop" since 1946 specializing in "super omelets" served "in the frying pan", "pancakes light as clouds" and other "usual suspects"; the "brisk" pace doesn't prevent "lineups out the door on weekends", but for "plentiful" helpings "priced right", it's "worth any wait you have to endure."

Thom Thom *Seafood/Steak* 20 | 19 | 20 | $41

Wantagh | 3340 Park Ave. (bet. Beech St. & Wantagh Ave.) | 516-221-8022 | www.thomthomrestaurant.com

With a "unique" Asian-accented menu ranging from "steak to sushi and all sorts of eclectic plates", this "refined" yet "comfortable" Wantagh place attracts a "good crowd"; the service varies a bit, though, and a few knock that it's "expensive for the neighborhood" and "trying too hard to create a Manhattan feel."

388 Restaurant *American/Italian* 20 | 20 | 21 | $47

Roslyn Heights | 388 Willis Ave. (Cambridge St.) | 516-621-3888 | www.388restaurant.com

This "neat" American-Italian in Roslyn Heights (from ex-members of the "Matteo's gang") is attracting "a following" with the "flair and flavor" of its wide-ranging menu, served up in "plentiful" portions by a "friendly and attentive" staff; the atmosphere in the sizable, Tuscanesque space is "enjoyable" "all around", if sometimes "a little noisy."

Thyme Restaurant & Café Bar ☑ *American* 21 | 19 | 20 | $46

Roslyn | 8 Tower Pl. (bet. Main St. & Old Northern Blvd.) | 516-625-2566 | www.thymenewyork.com

"Refreshing, tasty" dishes and a "pretty ambiance" attract Roslynites to this "romantic" bi-level New American with a "beautiful" outdoor dining area "overlooking the pond"; the staff "always makes you feel welcome" and you can "sit at the bar" on weekends "listening to live music", but a few find it all just "a little basic" for the price; P.S. the prix fixe dinner is a "best buy" alternative.

	FOOD	DECOR	SERVICE	COST

Tide Runners *American*
▽ 16 | 18 | 16 | $36

Hampton Bays | 7 North Rd. (bet. Montauk & Sunrise Hwys.) | 631-728-7373 | www.tiderunners.com

Sit "on the deck" and "see the boats pass by" at this Hampton Bays joint "right on the Shinnecock Canal", where the "waterfront views", "fun atmosphere" and "live bands" are "the top draws"; the seafood-centric American menu is "run-of-the-mill" and slightly "pricey", but "location, location, location" keeps it "popular"; P.S. closed October–May.

Toast *Eclectic*
24 | 18 | 21 | $22

Port Jefferson | 242 E. Main St. (Thompson St.) | 631-331-6860 | www.toastcoffeehouse.com

"You're in for a treat" when you "come for breakfast" at this "quirky", "jumpin'" Port Jefferson Eclectic serving "creative" eats like "graham cracker French toast" ("a must"), along with "perfectly brewed" coffees and "fabulous" lunch items; it stays open for tapas and "late-night fondues" on Friday and Saturday nights, dished up by a "cute", "hipster" staff; P.S. expect a "long wait on the weekends."

Toast & Co. *American*
18 | 15 | 17 | $23

Huntington | 62 Stewart Ave. (bet. Main St. & New York Ave.) | 631-812-0056 | www.toasthuntington.com

There's a "good range of comfort-style options and caloric splurges" at this Huntington American specializing in "cut-above" omelets, pancakes and other breakfast items; a "hard-working staff" makes the "retro" space "buzz", though some critics crack that the service "needs improvement" and the rest is "nothing to get eggcited over."

☑ Toku *Asian*
25 | 26 | 23 | $60

Manhasset | The Americana | 2014 Northern Blvd. (Searingtown Rd.) | 516-627-8658 | www.tokumodernasian.com

"Lots of fancy cars parked out front" hint at the "swanky", "over-the-top" scene inside this "beautiful" Asian fusion player on Manhasset's Miracle Mile with a "spectacular ambiance" and service so adept that "everybody's treated as a somebody"; luckily, it's "worth going" for the "sensational" food and cocktails alone, so "take out a mortgage", "treat yourself" and have a "sublime" time - unless you're the easily "overwhelmed" type; P.S. the "singles crowd" comes out in full force on "Thursday nights."

Tokyo *Japanese/Korean*
▽ 24 | 14 | 24 | $33

East Northport | Laurelwood Ctr. | 192 Laurel Rd. (bet. Bellerose & Dickinson Aves.) | 631-754-8411 | www.tokyosushiny.com

"Although off the beaten path", this "tiny" East Northport fixture "saves the day" for natives craving the "freshest sushi", tempura and other "fantastic" Japanese fare augmented by Korean specialties; it "doesn't charge crazy prices" and the "sweet" staffers seem to "really care", which helps to explain why the "tight space" is often "jammed."

	FOOD	DECOR	SERVICE	COST

Tomo Hibachi *Japanese* | 20 | 18 | 20 | $39 |

Huntington | 286 Main St. (New St.) | 631-271-6666 | www.tomohibachi.com

"You get a show and a decent meal for a fairly reasonable price" at this Huntington hibachi house that's a "favorite among the kids" even if the performance "is the same every time"; it's "loud and smoky", but many enjoy the "communal" atmosphere as well as the "good" steak and sushi, and recommend it for "fun with the family."

Tony's Asian Fusion *Asian* | 19 | 14 | 17 | $33 |

East Quogue | 337 Montauk Hwy. (Seashore Ave.) | 631-728-8850 | www.tonysasianfusion.com

Tony's Fusion Express *Asian*

Hampton Bays | 1 W. Main St. (Squiretown Rd.) | 631-728-1799 | www.tonysasianfusion.com

NEW Tony's Fusion North *Asian*

Mattituck | 9650 Main Rd. (Rte. 25) | 631-298-2158 | www.tonysasianfusion.com

Tony's Fusion West *Asian*

Westhampton Beach | 23 Sunset Ave. (bet. Hanson Pl. & Main St.) | 631-288-8880 | www.tonysfusionwest.com

Tony's Sushi *Asian*

East Moriches | 466 E. Main St. (Atlantic Ave.) | 631-878-9575 | www.tonyssushi.net

There's a "wide array" "to choose from or mix" at these East End Asians, which proffer a "solid" selection of Chinese, Japanese and Thai with the addition of a "hibachi show" in East Quogue; the casual quarters are "not relaxing", but "your dollar goes a long way"; P.S. the Hampton Bays branch is a "grab-and-go" counter only.

Top of the Bay *American* | – | – | – | E |

Cherry Grove | Fire Island | 1 Dock Walk (Bayview Walk) | 631-597-6028

"The views are incredible" at this seasonal New American overlooking the Cherry Grove "ferry dock", a prime spot for summer sojourners to take in the "wonderful" sights of the Great South Bay, "especially at sunset"; offering dishes like crab cakes and rack of lamb in airy quarters sporting ceiling fans and banks of windows, it's top-of-the-line for Fire Island and priced accordingly.

Torcellos *Italian* | 21 | 15 | 20 | $27 |

East Northport | Elwood Shopping Ctr. | 1932 Jericho Tpke. (Elwood Rd.) | 631-499-8792 | www.torcellos.com

A "hometown" "favorite" since 1988, this "little Italian joint" in East Northport "always draws a crowd" with "traditional pizzas" and "generous" portions of "well-prepared" "staples"; "seating may be tight", but it's so "family-friendly" and "light on the wallet" that few mind.

Touch of Venice, A Ⓜ *Italian* | 21 | – | 20 | $46 |

Cutchogue | 28350 Main Rd. (bet. New Suffolk Rd. & Wickhams Dr.) | 631-298-5851 | www.touchofvenice.com

Surveyors who appreciated this longtime "favorite" for its "always authentic" Italian cuisine "with a twist", featuring "local seafood and produce" and delivered by "warm and friendly" servers, will be glad to know that it's completed its move from Mattituck to the center of Cutchogue; it no longer overlooks the water, but the pressed-copper ceiling and black-and-white tile floor in the entrance are welcome greetings.

Townline BBQ *BBQ*   19 | 15 | 15 | $27

Sagaponack | 3593 Montauk Hwy. (Townline Rd.) | 631-537-2271 | www.townlinebbq.com

The "smoky" aroma will "transport you to the South" at this Sagaponack "roadhouse" from the Nick & Toni's team, where the "Texas BBQ" is "up to par" for "cheap eats" if you "stick to the basics"; the rough-hewn, "counter-service" setup offers "a minimum of creature comforts", but it's "child-friendly" and "the bar scene is fun"; P.S. closed Tuesday and Wednesday.

Trata East ● *Greek/Seafood*   22 | 23 | 19 | $70

Water Mill | 1020 Montauk Hwy. (bet. Deerfield & Scuttle Hole Rds.) | 631-726-6200 | www.trata.com

"A well-heeled crowd" delights in "extraordinarily fresh" fish and other "outstanding" "upscale Greek" fare at this "classy" seafooder in Water Mill, whose "gorgeous" environs are "definitely the place to be seen"; it "lives up to" its "reputation for high quality", but be ready for "noise" and "attitude galore" and "bring your drachmas" to cover the "over-the-top" tabs; P.S. closed October–March.

Trattoria Diane Ⓜ *Italian*   25 | 21 | 23 | $56

Roslyn | 21 Bryant Ave. (bet. Roosevelt Ave. & Skillman St.) | 516-621-2591

A "relaxing" Roslyn respite for "delightful" Northern Italian fare and "scrumptious" desserts (it's affiliated with Diane's Bakery next door), this "elegant, unpretentious" spot is "lovely for a special occasion" or a "romantic" date; "artful presentations", "professional service" and an "unreal" Sunday-night deal ensure it's the "absolute favorite" of many.

Trattoria Di Meo *Italian*   21 | 15 | 20 | $48

Roslyn Heights | 183 Roslyn Rd. (Donald St.) | 516-621-4895 | www.trattoriadimeo.com

"Warm greetings" abound at this "neighborhood go-to" in Roslyn Heights that's celebrating 40-plus years serving "solid" Italian fare ("best red sauce east of the city") with a "personal touch"; despite the "high prices", it's "homey" enough to feel like "grandma's kitchen", and they "never rush you" through the meal.

Tricia's Café Ⓜ *American*   23 | 16 | 20 | $20

Babylon | 26 E. Main St. (Fire Island Ave.) | 631-422-7879 | www.triciascafe.com

"You could easily walk right past" this "small", "family-owned" "local joint" in Babylon, but you'd miss out on its "decently priced" lineup of "super" American fare, notably the "inventive burgers"; service can "take a while" when it's "busy", but that leaves more time to admire the walls full of '50s "memorabilia."

Trio *American*   ▽ 21 | 15 | 20 | $35

Holbrook | Holbrook Country Club | 700 Patchogue-Holbrook Rd. (Smith Ave.) | 631-585-4433 | www.triofinefood.com

Golfers gravitate to this "comfortable" New American that moved from its original Patchogue location to a "peaceful" setting with patio seating and views of the greens in the Holbrook Country Club; the interior is "nothing fancy", but there are "some excellent dishes" and early-bird specials; P.S. closed Tuesdays.

NEW **TR**   - | - | - | VE
Restaurant & Bar *Seafood*

Hampton Bays | Tully's Seafood Mkt. | 78 Foster Ave. (Lighthouse Rd.) | 631-728-8700

After serving as the executive chef at Southampton's Coast Grill for 10 years, Tom Rutyna opened this seasonal upscale seafooder of his own behind Tully's Seafood Market in Hampton Bays, serving an pricey ocean-centric menu sourced from local fishermen; the white-tablecloth dining room features picture windows offering distant marina views, while a huge silver-gilded marlin caught by Rutyna himself is mounted on one of the bright blue walls in the bar.

Z Trumpets   22 | 25 | 22 | $52
on the Bay *American/Continental*

Eastport | 58 S. Bay Ave. (south of Montauk Hwy.) | 631-325-2900 | www.trumpetsonthebay.com

"Pure romance" is in the air at this "lovely" American-Continental in Eastport, where the "breathtaking" views of Moriches Bay ("ask for a window seat") and "warm and attractive" setting manned by staffers who "can't do enough for you" will make "stress melt away"; though the "amazing" seascape is undeniably "their trump card", the "fine" cuisine is "always a safe bet" too.

Tula Kitchen *Eclectic*   24 | 25 | 25 | $33

Bay Shore | 41 E. Main St. (bet. 3rd & 4th Aves.) | 631-539-7183 | www.tulakitchen.com

Chef-owner Jackie Sharlup's "tip-top" Eclectic "gem" in Bay Shore is a "healthier" "alternative" that's "noteworthy" for "surprisingly" "delightful" "vegan- and vegetarian-friendly" choices, though "omnivores" "will be just as pleased" with the poultry and fish; with "red, velvety digs" and "lovely service", it's a "soothing" "bohemian" enclave that channels "a little bit of Manhattan" "without being pretentious."

Tulip Bar & Grill *Mediterranean/Turkish*   19 | 15 | 20 | $36

Great Neck | 4 Welwyn Rd. (Shoreward Dr.) | 516-487-1070 | www.tulipbarandgrill.com

Great Neckers turn to this "neighborhood" joint for a "consistently" "solid" Turkish-Med menu (now with "a selection of Indian as well") served by "friendly" types at a "reasonable price"; faultfinders feel the decor's "a little tired", but the experience gets a fez-tive boost with "fun, fun, fun belly dancing" on Saturday nights.

	FOOD	DECOR	SERVICE	COST

Turquoise *Seafood*   21 | 12 | 19 | $43

Great Neck | 33 N. Station Plaza (bet. Bond St. & Park Pl.) | 516-487-3737

"Plain" looks aside, this "local" seafooder near the Great Neck train station is "a real find" for "the freshest" "whole grilled fish" and "wonderful starters" like Israeli salad; "tight quarters" that can be "too close for comfort" are offset by a daily early-bird that's "always a good buy."

Tuscan House *Italian*   ▽ 22 | 18 | 22 | $52

Southampton | 10 Windmill Ln. (Jobs Ln.) | 631-287-8703 | www.tuscanhouse.us

"The real McCoy" for "fresh, homemade" Italian, this "lesser-known" Southamptonite features "huge portions" of "well-presented" specialties "timely delivered" in "warm", Tuscan-esque surroundings; caio-hounds who acknowledge it's "expensive but oh so good" pay compliments to "a worthwhile visit."

Tutto Il Giorno *Italian*   25 | 19 | 20 | $62

Sag Harbor | 6 Bay St. (Rector St.) | 631-725-7009 Ⓜ
NEW **Southampton** | 56 Nugent St. (bet. Main St. & Windmill Ln.) | 631-377-3611

Perfetto! cry partisans of the "absolutely amazing" cuisine and "warm service" that qualify this "creative" Italian as "a must-try" destination in Sag Harbor – and now in Southampton too, where a garden-equipped sibling arrived post-Survey; the "cozy quarters" and "wonderful" warm-weather terrace maintain an insidery vibe boosted by a "parade of celebrities" (Donna Karan's daughter Gabby is a partner in both branches), but be prepared for an "expensive" tab and a "queue to get in" (devotees "wish they would take reservations").

Tutto Pazzo *Italian*   20 | 21 | 21 | $42

Huntington | 84 New York Ave. (bet. Ketewomoke Dr. & Youngs Hill Rd.) | 631-271-2253 | www.tuttopazzo.com

Regulars relish the "reliable red-sauce" dishes at this "local" Huntington Italian that's "especially nice in warm weather when the windows are open to the harbor breeze" and the patio fills up; a "super-nice" staff helps makes it "great for groups" and "family celebrations", though grumpy gourmands "wish the food were equal to the service and location."

Tweeds Restaurant & Buffalo Bar *American*   21 | 21 | 21 | $44

Riverhead | J.J. Sullivan Hotel | 17 E. Main St. (bet. East & Roanoke Aves.) | 631-208-3151 | www.tweedsrestaurant.com

Bison steaks and burgers are "the house specialty" heading a "well-prepared" New American lineup at this "relaxed" Riverhead retreat in a "historic building", which adopts a "charming" "saloon look" down to the "buffalo head on the wall" over the "antique bar"; with "cozy" atmospherics and a "piano player" on weekends, it "really grows on you."

	FOOD	DECOR	SERVICE	COST

21 Main *Steak*
| 23 | 22 | 23 | $59 |

West Sayville | 21 Montauk Hwy. (Cherry Ave.) | 631-567-0900 | www.21main.com

It's "hard to beat" this "classy", "pricey" West Sayville chophouse delivering "huge", "tender" steaks along with "two-pound baked potatoes" and other "terrific sides"; the "on-point" staff and "cool", "convivial" surroundings, boasting several fireplaces and frequent live piano music, make it "awesome for date night"; P.S. "go for Wine Down Wednesdays", with half-priced bottles all night.

Umberto's *Italian/Pizza*
| 22 | 15 | 19 | $29 |

NEW Bellmore | 208 Bedford Ave. (Grand Ave.) | 516-409-1400 | www.originalumbertos.com

Garden City | 361 Nassau Blvd. S. (bet. Cambridge Ave. & Princeton Rd.) | 516-481-1279 | www.umbertoscg.com

New Hyde Park | 633 Jericho Tpke. (Lakeville Rd.) | 516-437-9424 | www.originalumbertos.com

Wantagh | Cherrywood Shopping Ctr. | 1180 Wantagh Ave. (Jerusalem Ave.) | 516-221-5696 | www.umbertosny.com

Angoletto Café *Italian/Pizza*
New Hyde Park | 1598 Hillside Ave. (New Hyde Park Rd.) | 516-358-2010

Village Pizzeria ⊄ *Italian/Pizza*
Floral Park | 169 Tulip Ave. (bet. Iris & Plainfield Aves.) | 516-775-0612

"Awesome" pizza "is the thing" at this family of parlors known for "sensational" slices (like the grandma and Sicilian) that are "worth traveling for", and sauce that "reminds you of Sundays at nonna's"; the otherwise "typical" sit-down menu and "long waits" don't faze fans; P.S. the original Umberto's (in New Hyde Park) is praised as a "step above the rest."

Uncle Bacala's *Italian/Seafood*
| 21 | 18 | 21 | $35 |

Garden City Park | 2370 Jericho Tpke. (bet. Herricks Rd. & Marcus Ave.) | 516-739-0505

NEW Smithtown | 368 Middle Country Rd. (Hillcrest Dr.) | 631-265-2300

www.unclebacala.com

"You'll never leave hungry" from this "family-style" Garden City Park "standby" where a "high-energy" staff delivers "decently priced", "generous portions" of Italian "staples" including seafood that keep the crowd "happy"; the "complimentary cotton candy" is even sweeter if you "go during the week", when the outing won't be soured by "deafening" decibels and "squished" seating; P.S. a Smithtown location opened post-Survey.

Uncle Dai's *Chinese*
| 18 | 11 | 18 | $26 |

Glen Cove | 26 School St. (bet. Glen St. & Highland Rd.) | 516-671-1144 | www.uncledais.com

"The menu doesn't change often" at this "inexpensive", "child-friendly" Glen Cove Chinese "but you don't want it to" given the "always dependable" Hunan selections accompanied by "free wine"; the staff is "fast and pleasant", but the "unappealing decor" leads many to opt for "takeout."

	FOOD	DECOR	SERVICE	COST

Varney's ⊠ *American/Seafood* | 23 | 9 | 19 | $29 |

Brookhaven | 2109 Montauk Hwy. (Westminster Ave.) |
631-286-9569 | www.varneysrestaurant.com

Known to "the local crowd" for 30 years, this "tiny" "shack" tucked
"out of the way" in Brookhaven is "an old reliable" for "palate-
pleasing" American "home cooking" focused on "fresh seafood"; it's
"not much to look at" and the pace is "leisurely" "when busy", but
the payoff is "satisfying grub" that "doesn't break the bank."

Venere Ristorante *Italian* | 20 | 14 | 20 | $33 |

Westbury | 841 Carman Ave. (bet. Lake & Land Lns.) |
516-333-2332 | www.ristorantevenere.com

"Mama would approve" of this Westbury "joint", "a longtime favorite" that plies the "locals" with "reliable" "homestyle Italian" till
their "pants won't fit"; holdouts huff the food's "nothing spectacular" and the decor's "seen better days", but with "friendly service"
and "reasonable prices", it remains a "neighborhood go-to."

⊠ Verace *Italian* | 26 | 26 | 25 | $47 |

Islip | 599 Main St. (bet. Locust & Willow Aves.) | 631-277-3800 |
www.veracerestaurant.com

"Another winner" from the owners of next-door neighbor Tellers,
this "sophisticated" Islip Italian takes an "inspired" approach to its
fare, showcasing "mouthwatering" "small-plate servings" (plus full
portions) presented by "professional" staffers tending the "stunning" interior and "cobblestone" patio; to sweeten the already "reasonable" cost, the "Monday wine dinner is a steal."

Vero *Italian* | - | - | - | M |

Amityville | 192 Broadway (bet. Greene Ave. & W. Oak St.) |
631-608-4340 | www.verorestaurant.biz

Chef Massimo Fedozzi (of the shuttered Palio) plans to soon reopen
this midpriced Amityville Italian, serving sharable plates of salumi and
nonna's meatball sliders plus heartier dishes such as grilled-to-
order veal lollipops; the stylish design includes a bar area with chandeliers and a more formal dining room with a cathedral ceiling and
Murano-glass sconces; P.S. it closed temporarily after a small fire.

Verona *Italian* | - | - | - | E |

Farmingdale | 1255 Melville Rd. (Smith St.) | 516-249-0000 |
www.veronafarmingdale.com

The husband-and-wife owners will greet you at the door of this
strip-mall Farmingdale Italian proffering classics such as veal sor-
rentino and chicken scarpariello; wall tapestries of Veronese court-
yards and street scenes plus a montage of family portraits add to the
warm, classic feel.

Vespa Cibobuono *Italian* | 22 | 18 | 20 | $49 |

Great Neck | 96 Northern Blvd. (bet. Buttonwood & Westminster Rds.) |
516-829-0005 | www.vespany.com

"When you need a break from red sauce", this "cute" Great Neck
Northern Italian offers a "terrific take" on "regional" fare from the

top of "The Boot" with its "delicious" renditions of Tuscan and Milanese specialties; "service is pleasant" if "slow at busy times", and even with highish prices, there's plenty of reason "it's caught on."

View 🅼 American/Continental   22 | 23 | 19 | $51

Oakdale | 3 Consuelo Pl. (Shore Dr.) | 631-589-2694 | www.viewoakdale.com

Thanks to new owner Lessing's Hospitality, this renamed and "re-modeled" Oakdale American-Continental "finally does justice" to its "breathtaking" Great South Bay vista with a "top-notch" menu and a "brighter", "updated dining room"; alfresco seating and "happy hour" "on the deck" are "what summer is all about", though some still view the service as unduly "slow."

Villa D'Aqua Italian   21 | 19 | 20 | $48

Bellmore | 2565 Bellmore Ave. (Public Hwy.) | 516-308-4900

Fans of this upscale, boat-accessible Bellmore Northern Italian "on the canal", from the folks behind Wantagh's Per Un' Angelo, tout the "very good" fare focusing on "fresh" seafood; the owners work hard to "make sure guests are satisfied", and though the "cozy" interior looks a bit "dated", the outdoor deck attracts "many locals."

Villa D'Este Italian   22 | 20 | 22 | $42

Floral Park | 186 Jericho Tpke. (bet. Flower & Tyson Aves.) | 516-354-1355 | www.villadesterestaurant.com

An "old favorite" in Floral Park, this "down-to-earth" Northern Italian is a "quiet" haven that's "always satisfying" for the "staples one would expect"; the "attentive staff" and "bargain" prix fixe menus for both lunch and dinner ensure the regulars "keep going back."

Village Lanterne German   ▽ 25 | 22 | 21 | $34

Lindenhurst | 143 N. Wellwood Ave. (bet. Auburn & Bristol Sts.) | 631-225-1690 | www.thevillagelanterne.com

The "party atmosphere" will "make you want to don your lederho-sen" at this "cozy" Lindenhurst hideaway, which delivers the "au-thentic German" experience with "*wunderbar*" grub – from "sauerbraten to die for" to desserts from partner Black Forest Bakery – and wall-to-wall Bavarian decor; *ja*, the going can be "slow", but with servers in "costumes", a "large beer menu" and "live music" on weekends, it's like "Oktoberfest all year."

Vincent's Clam Bar Italian   22 | 16 | 19 | $32

Carle Place | Carle Place Commons | 179 Old Country Rd. (Glen Cove Rd.) | 516-742-4577 | www.vincentsclambar.com

Typically "jam-packed", this slice of "Mulberry Street" in Carle Place is a local "institution" where marinara lovers "carbo-load" on "clas-sic" Italian dishes big enough to "feed a small Sicilian village"; you "can't beat the sauce" (though you can buy a bottle to go) or the easy-to-digest prices, but the "frenetic" scene and "unbearable noise level" drown out any intimate conversations, and live music on Sundays only "adds to the din"; P.S. reservations accepted for five or more (except Saturdays).

	FOOD	DECOR	SERVICE	COST

Vine Street Café *American*　　25 | 20 | 23 | $64

Shelter Island | 41 S. Ferry Rd. (Cartwright Rd.) | 631-749-3210 | www.vinestreetcafe.com

An "out-of-the-way oasis of culinary delights", this "quaint" Shelter Islander "consistently delivers" "on all counts" with a "market menu" of "superbly prepared" American fare, "timely" service and a "sweet little" "cottage" setting with a "porch in the back"; since "it's such a hot ticket" there may be "noise and tumult", but it's "definitely worth the ferry ride"; P.S. closed Tuesday and Wednesday in the winter.

Vine Wine Bar *Italian*　　- | - | - | M

Merrick | 2259 Merrick Rd. (bet. Fox Blvd. & Henry St.) | 516-812-7883 | www.thevinewinebar.com

This Merrick enoteca offers more than 50 wines by the glass and a moderately priced lineup of Italian bites including meats, cheeses and panini, with desserts like chocolate fondue to top things off; couches and a stylish back room add a loungey feel, while a helpful staff keeps the vibe unpretentious.

NEW Vinoco Wine Bar & Tapas *Eclectic*　　- | - | - | M

Mineola | 147 Mineola Blvd. (Harrison Ave.) | 516-307-8056 | www.vinocony.com

Small plates, skewers and midpriced entrees are on the menu at this vibrant Mineola hole-in-the-wall where globe-spanning tapas (with an emphasis on Spain and Latin America) are suited to sips from a 40-bottle wine list; nightly specials are scrawled on a chalkboard above the bar, and knowledgeable servers are quick to offer recommendations and top off your tempranillo.

Vintage Prime Steakhouse *Steak*　　25 | 21 | 23 | $67

St. James | 433 N. Country Rd. (Clinton Ave.) | 631-862-6440

Carnivores compliment the "phenomenal" steaks, "fabulous sides" and "extensive wine list" at this "pricey" St. James steakhouse with "quality" service; the Western "lodge atmosphere" isn't for everyone – some feel the vibe could be "cozier" and are bothered by "animals on the wall looking at" them – but the majority maintains they've "never had a bad meal" here.

Vitae Ⓜ *Continental*　　- | - | - | E

Huntington | 54 New St. (W. Carver St.) | 631-385-1919 | www.vitaeli.com
This classy Continental in the former Abel Conklin's space in Huntington features dark wood and big, semi-circular red leather booths as a plush surround for upscale fare such as the house veal chop and crab-crusted sole; a bluestone patio beckons in summer, hidden from the street by a high brick wall.

Vittorio's Restaurant & 　　25 | 22 | 25 | $48
Wine Bar *American/Italian*

Amityville | 184 Broadway (Greene Ave.) | 631-264-3333 | www.vittorios.biz

Amityville "locals" confirm this "charming" eatery-cum-enoteca is "always on the money", whether for "fabulous" American-Italian fare or "excellent" cuts of beef on the Wednesday "steak nights"; a 150-label wine list and "gracious" servers have loyalists "going back" despite the "slightly high price."

Viva Juan *Mexican*
∇ 21 | 16 | 19 | $28

Selden | 280 Middle Country Rd. (bet. New Ln. & Patchogue-Mt. Sinai Rd.) | 631-698-8172

The Mexican "comfort" chow is "decent", "filling and cheap" and the margarita-fueled "karaoke nights" are "so much fun" at this casual Selden cantina; then again, purists lament "Americanized" cooking that's "not even close to authentic."

Viva La Vida *Mexican/Spanish*
∇ 20 | 16 | 22 | $36

Oakdale | 1611 Montauk Hwy. (bet. Idlehour & Vanderbilt Blvds.) | 631-589-2300 | www.viva-la-vida.com

"Not your typical" south-of-the-border spot, this Oakdale outpost caters to compadres "willing to try" real-deal Spanish-Mexican cuisine via "very satisfying" traditional dishes ("the paella is especially great") accompanied by "housemade" sangria; a "super staff" that "aims to please" further confirms "this is a special place."

Voila! 🗷 *French*
24 | 22 | 26 | $48

St. James | 244 Lake Ave. (Woodlawn Ave.) | 631-584-5686 | www.voilathebistro.com

Habitués hope this St. James "sleeper" "stays a secret" so they can have the "superb" Provençal fare and "cute", homey setting all to themselves; with a chef-owner who "goes out of his way to please", "professional" service and a "bonus" no-corkage BYO policy (plus a full bar), this "special place" "holds its own against the best of LI."

Walk Street *American*
21 | 19 | 20 | $36

Garden City | 176 Seventh St. (Franklin Ave.) | 516-746-2592 | www.walkstreetgc.com

"Consistently good" New American "from burgers to fancy fish" puts a hop in the step of Garden City neighbors who rely on this "hangout" for "relaxed" weekday lunches and "solid" midpriced dinners; sidewalk seating and live music on Fridays make it more "enjoyable", though a few find the menu to be "quite stale."

Wall's Wharf *American/Seafood*
17 | 19 | 16 | $42

Bayville | 18 Greenwich Ave. (off Bayville Ave.) | 516-628-9696 | www.wallswharf.com

"Sit outside" and "enjoy a beautiful sunset" from the "awesome" split-level deck at this "beachfront" Bayville "standby" with a "spectacular" "up-close view of the Sound"; if the "simple" New American and seafood options are "only so-so" and service is "unorganized", followers still "look forward to going" for the "unbeatable" "scenery."

🗷 Waterzooi Belgian Bistro *Belgian*
24 | 19 | 21 | $42

Garden City | 850 Franklin Ave. (bet. 9th St. & Stewart Ave.) | 516-877-2177 | www.waterzooi.com

It's "mussel mania" at this "boisterous" Belgian bistro in Garden City that pots "plump, delicious" moules seemingly "by the ton", bathes them in "delectable" broths and matches them with an "unparalleled selection" of hard-to-find brews (more than 130 available); the vibe is "cool" and "convivial" with a "popping bar scene", and though it does get "loud", that's just the sound of everyone "raving" about the "fabulous frites" and clinking their Chimays.

Wave Seafood Kitchen *American*   19 | 23 | 19 | $47

Port Jefferson | Danfords Hotel & Marina | 25 E. Broadway (Main St.) | 631-928-5200 | www.danfords.com

It "made a huge comeback" after a complete makeover a few years back say Port Jeff guests about this New American in Danfords on the Sound with "fresh, beautiful" decor that complements the "unbelievable" harbor views; the food is still less impressive (ranging from "pretty good" to "decidedly average"), but that doesn't stop the "real bar scene" with "wonderful 'tenders" at "happy hour on Friday nights."

West East Bistro Ⓜ *Asian*   25 | 21 | 23 | $37

Hicksville | 758 S. Broadway (bet. Hazel St. & Oyster Bay Rd.) | 516-939-6618 | www.westeastbistro.com

Patrons praise the "extraordinary" Asian fusion fare at this "best-kept secret" hidden in a "practically deserted" Hicksville mall, saying the "varied", "city-caliber" menu "never disappoints"; a "hospitable" owner oversees "accommodating" service in the "sophisticated" dining room, and prices are "reasonable", so it's "worth seeking out."

Ⓩ West End Cafe *American*   25 | 20 | 22 | $43

Carle Place | Clocktower Shopping Ctr. | 187 Glen Cove Rd. (bet. Old Country Rd. & Westbury Ave.) | 516-294-5608 | www.westendli.com

Despite its "oddball" location in the back of a strip mall, the "crowds" have "discovered" this "exceptional" Carle Place bistro whose "imaginative" New American creations deliver a "fantastic" "culinary experience"; a "mature, well-trained" staff and "NYC ambiance" complete the picture, but since the "tight" space is in demand, be sure to reserve "weeks in advance" – and if you nab a seat for the early-bird, "you've scored a home run"; P.S. sibling Market Bistro has opened in Jericho.

Whale's Tale *Seafood*   ▽ 20 | 17 | 19 | $29

Northport | Brittania Yachting Ctr. | 81 Fort Salonga Rd. (Callahan's Beach Rd.) | East Northport | 631-651-8844 | www.brityacht.com

It's "quickly become a local favorite" say fans of this "publike" seasonal Northporter in the Brittania Yachting Center (from a former partner of Zim Zari and Mercato) that serves up "surprisingly good" seafood in a "casual waterfront setting"; "don't expect a gourmet meal, just a fun night out" (plastic forks and all) on a spacious patio in summer, or inside, where the fare "tastes better than the place looks"; P.S. arrive early for the "great sunsets."

Wild Fig *Mediterranean/Turkish*   19 | 15 | 18 | $28

Garden City | 829 Franklin Ave. (Stewart Ave.) | 516-739-1002
Glen Cove | 167 Glen St. (bet. Pearsall Ave. & Town Path) | 516-656-5645

(continued)

(continued)

Wild Fig

Syosset | 631 Jericho Tpke. (Cedar St.) | 516-558-7744
www.wildfigonline.com

The "endless menu" means there's "something for everyone" at this "casual" Med-Turkish triumvirate, "consistently" "solid" sources of both "staples" and "more adventurous" choices (e.g. "pizza-like *pides*"); sticklers are less wild about the "sparsely decorated" digs and "sometimes slow" service, but "ample portions" at "economical prices" keep them "relatively busy."

Wildfish *Seafood*   21 | 20 | 20 | $40

Freeport | 507 Guy Lombardo Ave. (Front St.) | 516-442-0565 |
www.wildfishli.com

Since "redoing the interior" the owners have made this Freeport seafooder much "more inviting", and the "innovative", "price-conscious" menu is "excellent" too; guests "love" to "sit outside" given the "beautiful views", and "helpful" service, "entertainment on weekends" and boat slips are further draws; P.S. hours vary by season.

Wild Ginger *Asian*   21 | 20 | 19 | $36

Great Neck | The Gdns. | 48 Great Neck Rd. (bet. Brompton & Middle Neck Rds.) | 516-487-8288 | www.wildgingerrestaurant.net
Rockville Centre | 424 Sunrise Hwy. (Forest Ave.) | 516-442-2225 |
www.wildginger424.com
East Northport | 3018 Jericho Tpke. (bet. Daly & Larkfield Rds.) |
631-858-1888 | www.wildgingerhuntington.com

With their "full-flavored dishes", "zippy" decor and "rocking" atmospherics, these "popular" Pan-Asians in Great Neck and East Northport rise "a cut above the usual neighborhood" options; but since the tables are "close", the "noise level's insane" at "peak times" and "service is so fast you can get whiplash", they're perhaps not the places to go "for a relaxing meal"; P.S. the Rockville Centre location was not surveyed.

Wild Honey Dining & Wine *American*   25 | 20 | 23 | $46

Oyster Bay | 1 E. Main St. (South St.) | 516-922-4690 |
www.wildhoneyrestaurant.com

Wild Honey on Main Ⓜ *American*

Port Washington | 172 Main St. (bet. Madison & Monroe Sts.) |
516-439-5324 | www.wildhoneyonmain.com

"Eclectic, flavorful" New American dishes "deliver a wallop" at this "delightful", upscale twosome: a "romantic little hideaway" with sidewalk seating and "SoHo" flair in Oyster Bay, and its "teeny-tiny" but "wonderful" Port Washington "sequel"; both benefit from "pleasant" service, and though they can get "hectic" and quite "noisy at times", they're still a top choice for "date night."

Willy Parkers *American*   - | - | - | E

Williston Park | 71 Hillside Ave. (bet. Nassau Blvd. & Willis Ave.) |
516-750-8125 | www.willyparkers.com

Named after the residents of Williston Park, this neighborhood American offers upscale comfort food from a new chef who worked in

FOOD DECOR SERVICE COST

top NYC kitchens; the simple setting features walls with maroon wainscoting and vintage photos as a backdrop for a lively local scene.

NEW Wobbly Olive *American*

`- | - | - | M`

Hauppauge | 160 Adams Ave. (bet. Arkay & Commerce Drs.) | 631-951-0026 | www.thewobblyolive.com

'Singing chef' Richard Desmond (ex Public House 49 in Patchogue) occasionally belts out opera at this Hauppauge gastropub situated in a tiny strip mall where the midpriced American menu offers the likes of sandwiches, burgers and fish 'n' chips; the setting includes high-top tables, a raised party room and a stage, and dancing to live music or a DJ some nights stokes the lively vibe.

World Pie ● *Pizza*

`19 | 15 | 17 | $37`

Bridgehampton | 2402 Montauk Hwy.
(bet. Bridgehampton-Sag Harbor Tpke. & Corwith Ave.) |
631-537-7999 | www.worldpiebh.com

"Choices abound" at this "gourmet" Bridgehampton pizza joint featuring a "gazillion" wood-fired pies with "unusual toppings" that keep "families, couples and even seniors" lining up to dine before the late-night "bar scene" gets cooking; it always works "in a pinch" or for "people-watching" on the patio, but even though moderate prices (for the Hamptons) leave some change in the pocket, crusty critics don't buy the "hype."

Xaga Sushi *Asian*

`- | - | - | M`

Hewlett | 1326 Broadway (bet. Everit & Piermont Aves.) | 516-295-4137
NEW Merrick | 217 Merrick Rd. (Chernucha Ave.) | 516-379-8888
www.xagasushi.com

Changing colored lights wash the high-ceilinged dining rooms of this Merrick and Hewlett duo of sushi–Asian fusion spots, where the theatrics sometimes extend to little flashing lights decorating plates of sushi and sashimi; the moderately priced menu also includes tempura, noodles and other hot dishes.

NEW XO Restaurant, Wine & Chocolate Lounge ●Ⓜ *American*

`- | - | - | E`

Huntington | 69 Wall St. (Central St.) | 631-549-7074 |
www.xowinebar.com

Chef Christopher Lano resurrected his Huntington restaurant and chocolate lounge which was destroyed by fire in 2011, in this larger, more elegant bi-level space (formerly Osteria Toscana), featuring a white-cloth dining room with an expensive New American menu of small and large plates; the upstairs lounge serves the restaurant menu from 5-11 PM, when it switches to chocolate-based drinks and a roster of chocolate desserts till 2 AM.

Yamaguchi Ⓜ *Japanese*

`25 | 14 | 21 | $39`

Port Washington | 63 Main St. (Herbert Ave.) | 516-883-3500

An "intimate" Port Washington "jewel" for "high-quality" sushi (rather than "contrived" rolls) and "top-notch" Japanese dishes, this "always crowded" "fixture" is a "home away from home" for many; the "generous" hosts "treasure" their customers ("regulars

FOOD DECOR SERVICE COST

get delicious extras"), but nitpickers pout over decor that "needs an update" and caution "make reservations or plan to wait a long time."

Yama Q ⬛Ⓜ *Japanese/Vegetarian* ▽ 23 | 15 | 19 | $44
Bridgehampton | 2393 Montauk Hwy. (bet. Ocean Rd. & School St.) | 631-537-0225
This "quiet" Bridgehampton "find" provides "fresh, healthy" Japanese dishes with an emphasis on sushi and vegetarian options and some "eclectic" global touches as well; the small, "quaint" space has an "almost private" feel, and while tabs are marked up with a slight Hamptons premium, the dishes are "worth it."

Yokohama *Japanese* 23 | 17 | 23 | $37
East Northport | 3082 Jericho Tpke. (Verleye Ave.) | 631-462-2464
"Fresh, well-prepared sushi is the priority" at this East Northport "go-to", "one of the best" around that pleases with "amazing" specialty rolls and Japanese cooking with "inventive" twists; the decor's "a little tired", but the "welcoming" owner "treats the locals right" and everything comes at a "fair price."

Yuki's Palette Too Ⓜ *Japanese* ▽ 24 | 17 | 22 | $31
Merrick | 151 Merrick Ave. (Loines Ave.) | 516-867-8738 | www.yukispalette.info
"Tender, delicious" sushi and "standout" rolls full of "exciting flavors" reel in regulars to this affordable Merrick Japanese with a "friendly" staff; the room itself is "not much to look at", but "it's the little touches", and often "stellar" quality, that "make it special" for fans.

Zim Zari *Californian/Mexican* 22 | 19 | 20 | $20
Massapequa Park | Southgate Shopping Ctr. | 4964 Merrick Rd. (Whitewood Dr.) | 516-809-6960 | www.zimzari.com
The folks behind Mercato, in the same Massapequa Park shopping center, have brought this "West Coast surfer shack to Long Island" where the "refreshing", beach-bum environs and "tasty", "cheap" "Cali-cool" Mex eats "cater to a young crowd" (and work for "families" too); despite sometimes "long waits for a table", there's "decent service" and deals like $2 "Taco Tuesdays rock."

Zorba the Greek *Greek* 19 | 13 | 19 | $25
Hicksville | 620 S. Oyster Bay Rd. (Old Country Rd.) | 516-932-9701
Port Jefferson Station | 572 Port Jefferson Plaza (Rte. 112) | 631-473-9220 | www.zorbathegreekpjs.com
"Consistent", "basic" Greek food for "super prices" satisfies customers at these separately owned "standbys" in Hicksville and Port Jefferson Station; most agree the decor "lacks a lot" and the service varies, but they're "quick, easy" choices for dinner and "even better for lunch", particularly with Port Jeff's "value" prix fixe.

176   Vote at zagat.com

INDEXES

Cuisines

Includes names, locations and Food ratings.

AFGHAN

Afghan Grill | **New Hyde Pk**	20
Ariana | **Huntington**	20
Kabul Afghani | **Huntington**	23

AMERICAN

NEW Alaine's | **Massapequa**	-
Amarelle | **Wading River**	25
Z American Hotel | **Sag Harbor**	25
NEW Andiamo | **Mineola**	-
NEW Angelina's Fireshack | **New Hyde Pk**	-
Argyle Grill | **Babylon**	22
Arthur Avenue | **Smithtown**	-
Z Atlantica | **Long Bch**	20
Z Barney's | **Locust Valley**	26
Bayview Inn | **S Jamesport**	22
Beacon | **Sag Harbor**	22
Bellport | **Bellport**	22
Birchwood | **Riverhead**	20
NEW Bistro Etc. | **Port Washington**	-
Bistro 44 | **Northport**	23
Bistro 72 | **Riverhead**	-
B.K. Sweeney's | **multi.**	18
Blackwells | **Wading River**	23
Bliss | **E Setauket**	22
Blond | **Miller Pl**	21
Blue | **Blue Pt**	22
Blue Point Bistro | **Blue Pt**	-
Bob's Rest. | **Floral Pk**	21
Brass Rail | **Locust Valley**	25
Bridgehampton Candy | **Bridgehampton**	15
Buckram Stables | **Locust Valley**	19
Bulldog Grille | **Amityville**	-
Butterfields | **Hauppauge**	20
Cafe Joelle | **Sayville**	22
Cafe Max | **E Hampton**	23
Café Red/Red | **multi.**	25
Canterbury | **Oyster Bay**	19
Catfish Max | **Seaford**	21
Cattlemen's | **Port Jefferson Station**	19
Cedar Creek | **Glen Cove**	-
Z Chachama | **E Patchogue**	27
Chadwicks | **Rockville Ctr**	22
Chalet Rest. | **Roslyn**	18
Z Cheesecake | **multi.**	20

Chequit Inn | **Shelter Is Hts**	19
Chop Shop | **Smithtown**	24
Cirella's | **Huntington Station**	21
City Cellar | **Westbury**	21
Claudio's | **Greenport**	16
Coach Grill | **Oyster Bay**	22
Coast Grill | **Southampton**	22
Cookroom | **Middle Island**	-
Cooperage Inn | **Baiting Hollow**	22
Z Country Hse. | **Stony Brook**	23
Crave 11025 | **Great Neck**	18
Crew Kit. | **Huntington**	24
Crossroads Cafe | **E Northport**	22
Dark Horse | **Riverhead**	-
Declan Quinn's | **Bay Shore**	19
Deco 1600 | **Plainview**	-
Desmond's | **Wading River**	20
Dish | **Water Mill**	27
Duke Falcon's | **Long Bch**	22
East/ Northeast | **Montauk**	21
NEW E. Hampton Grill | **E Hampton**	-
Z E. Hampton Pt. | **E Hampton**	19
E. B. Elliot's | **Freeport**	18
Estia's | **Sag Harbor**	23
Farm Country Kit. | **Riverhead**	23
F.H. Riley's | **Huntington**	23
Fifth Season | **Port Jefferson**	26
56th Fighter | **Farmingdale**	16
NEW 516 Amer. | **Syosset**	-
Fork & Vine | **Glen Head**	23
Four Food Studio | **Melville**	21
490 West | **Carle Pl**	-
NEW 420 North | **Great Neck**	-
Fresno | **E Hampton**	22
NEW Fusion 84 | **Sayville**	-
Garden Grill | **Smithtown**	21
George Martin | **Rockville Ctr**	22
George Martin's Grill | **multi.**	20
Georgica | **Wainscott**	18
Golden Pear Cafe | **multi.**	18
Gonzalo's | **Glen Cove**	21
Grasso's | **Cold Spring**	24
Grey Horse | **Bayport**	23
Grill/Pantigo | **E Hampton**	21
Grill Room | **Hauppauge**	21
Harbor Bistro | **E Hampton**	21
Harbor Grill | **E Hampton**	-
Harbor Mist | **Cold Spring**	19

Hemingway's | **Wantagh**	19
Hildebrandt's | **Williston Pk**	19
Honu Kit. | **Huntington**	22
Horace/Sylvia's | **Babylon**	20
Houston's | **Garden City**	22
H.R. Singleton's | **Bethpage**	18
Hudson's Mill | **Massapequa**	22
NEW Huntington Social | **Huntington**	–
Indian Wells | **Amagansett**	17
International Delight | **multi.**	18
Iron Skillet | **Mattituck**	–
Island Mermaid | **Ocean Beach**	20
Ivy Cottage | **Williston Pk**	23
Izumi | **Bethpage**	23
Jack Halyards | **Oyster Bay**	23
Jackson Hall | **E Islip**	–
NEW Jack's Shack | **Glen Head**	–
NEW Jake's Steak | **E Meadow**	–
Jamesport Country | **Jamesport**	23
Z Jamesport Manor | **Jamesport**	23
Jean Marie | **Great Neck**	22
NEW Jewel | **Melville**	–
Jonathan's | **Garden City Pk**	20
JT's Corner | **Nesconset**	23
Kyle's | **Shelter Is**	–
La Cocina/Marcia | **Freeport**	–
Z Lake Hse. | **Bay Shore**	28
NEW Lawson Pub | **Oceanside**	–
Library Cafe | **Farmingdale**	18
NEW Litttle Red | **Southampton**	–
NEW L.I.V.E. | **Seaford**	–
Living Rm. | **E Hampton**	25
Lola's Kit. | **Long Bch**	20
Love Ln. | **Mattituck**	23
Z Luce & Hawkins | **Jamesport**	25
Lucy's Café | **Babylon**	25
Ludlow Bistro | **Deer Park**	24
Maguire's | **Ocean Beach**	19
NEW Market Bistro | **Jericho**	–
Maureen/Daughers' | **Smithtown**	25
Maxwell's | **Islip**	–
Meeting Hse. | **Amagansett**	20
Mercato Kit. | **Massapequa Pk**	20
Met. Bistro | **Sea Cliff**	22
Michaels'/Maidstone | **E Hampton**	18
Milk & Sugar | **Bay Shore**	21
Milleridge Inn | **Jericho**	16
Mim's | **multi.**	20
Mirabelle Tavern | **Stony Brook**	21
NEW Mitch/Toni's | **Albertson**	–
Modern Snack | **Aquebogue**	18
Z Mosaic | **St. James**	28
Mother Kelly's | **multi.**	21
Muse | **Sag Harbor**	23
Navy Beach | **Montauk**	19
New Paradise | **Sag Harbor**	22
Nicholas James | **Merrick**	22
Nichol's | **E Hampton**	17
Z Noah's | **Greenport**	26
NEW North Fork Oyster | **Greenport**	–
Z North Fork Table | **Southold**	29
Oakland's/Sunday | **Hampton Bays**	18
Ocean Grill | **Freeport**	23
Old Fields | **Greenlawn**	–
Old Mill Inn | **Mattituck**	20
O'Mally's | **Southold**	18
Page One | **Glen Cove**	22
Z Palm Court | **E Meadow**	24
Park Place | **Floral Pk**	–
NEW Patio | **Freeport**	–
Patio/54 Main | **Westhampton Bch**	19
PeraBell | **Patchogue**	26
NEW Phoenix | **Seaford**	–
Z Piccolo | **Huntington**	27
Pine Island | **Bayville**	18
Post Office | **Babylon**	19
Post Stop | **Westhampton Bch**	17
Z Prime | **Huntington**	23
Public Hse. 49 | **Patchogue**	20
Race Lane | **E Hampton**	19
Rachel's Waterside | **Freeport**	20
Ram's Head | **Shelter Is**	20
Rare 650 | **Syosset**	24
Red Bar | **Southampton**	22
Red Fish | **Plainview**	23
Red Rooster | **Cutchogue**	16
Rein | **Garden City**	23
NEW Relish | **Kings Park**	–
NEW Riverhead Pjt. | **Riverhead**	–
Robinson's Tea | **Stony Brook**	23
Rockwell's B&G | **Smithtown**	22
Runyon's | **Seaford**	18
NEW Ruschmeyer's | **Montauk**	–
NEW Saffron | **Glen Head**	–
Sapsuckers | **Huntington**	–
Sarabeth's | **multi.**	20
Savanna's | **Southampton**	20
Scrimshaw | **Greenport**	23
Sea Grille | **Montauk**	21
Sea Levels | **Brightwaters**	22

ⓩ 1770 Hse. | **E Hampton**	25
Shagwong | **Montauk**	18
ⓩ Snaps | **Wantagh**	26
Southampton Publick | **Southampton**	18
NEW Southampton Social | **Southampton**	–
South Edison | **Montauk**	22
NEW Spiro's | **Rocky Pt**	–
NEW Spring Close | **E Hampton**	–
Squiretown | **Hampton Bays**	20
Star Confectionery | **Riverhead**	22
ⓩ Starr Boggs | **Westhampton Bch**	26
Stonewalls | **Riverhead**	23
Sugar | **Carle Pl**	–
Sugo | **Long Bch**	23
Sullivan's Quay | **Port Washington**	18
Surf Lodge | **Montauk**	19
Swallow | **Huntington**	–
Sweet Mama's | **Northport**	19
Taste 99 | **Farmingdale**	18
Tate's | **Nesconset**	26
NEW Tavern/Plaza | **Locust Valley**	–
388 Rest. | **Roslyn Hts**	20
Thyme | **Roslyn**	21
Tide Runners | **Hampton Bays**	16
Toast & Co. | **Huntington**	18
Top/Bay | **Cherry Grove**	–
Tricia's Café | **Babylon**	23
Trio | **Holbrook**	21
ⓩ Trumpets | **Eastport**	22
Tweeds | **Riverhead**	21
Varney's | **Brookhaven**	23
View | **Oakdale**	22
Vine Street | **Shelter Is**	25
Vittorio's | **Amityville**	25
Walk St. | **Garden City**	21
Wall's Wharf | **Bayville**	17
Wave Seafood | **Port Jefferson**	19
ⓩ West End | **Carle Pl**	25
Wild Honey | **multi.**	25
Willy Parkers | **Williston Pk**	–
NEW Wobbly Olive | **Hauppauge**	–
NEW XO | **Huntington**	–

ARGENTINEAN

Café Buenos Aires | **Huntington**	24

ASIAN

Asian Moon | **multi.**	23
Cho-Sen | **multi.**	19

NEW DoraNonnie | **Glen Head**	–
East/ Northeast | **Montauk**	21
Elaine's | **Great Neck**	22
Haiku Bistro/Sushi | **Woodbury**	24
Izumi | **Bethpage**	23
J&C 68 | **Farmingville**	–
Long River | **Kings Park**	21
Marco Polo's | **Westbury**	–
Matsulin | **Hampton Bays**	22
NEW Meridian | **Locust Valley**	–
NEW Mint | **Garden City**	–
MoCa Asian | **Hewlett**	18
NEW Monsoon | **Babylon**	–
Sensasian | **Levittown**	–
Sugar | **Carle Pl**	–
Sunset Beach | **Shelter Is Hts**	18
Taiko | **Rockville Ctr**	24
NEW Ten Ten Bistro | **Mount Sinai**	–
Thom Thom | **Wantagh**	20
ⓩ Toku | **Manhasset**	25
Tony's | **multi.**	19
West East | **Hicksville**	25
Wild Ginger | **multi.**	21

BAKERIES

Main St. Bakery | **Port Washington**	–
Roe's Casa Dolce | **Rockville Ctr**	24

BARBECUE

Big Daddy's | **Massapequa**	24
BobbiQue | **Patchogue**	21
NEW Cody's | **Riverhead**	–
Dixie's | **Kings Park**	–
Famous Dave's | **multi.**	19
Foody's | **Water Mill**	21
Harbor-Q | **Port Washington**	21
NEW Mara's | **Syosset**	–
ⓩ Smokin' Al's | **multi.**	23
Spare Rib | **Commack**	18
Spicy's BBQ | **multi.**	20
Swingbelly's | **Long Bch**	23
Townline | **Sagaponack**	19

BELGIAN

ⓩ Waterzooi | **Garden City**	24

BURGERS

American Burger | **Smithtown**	18
Bay Burger | **Sag Harbor**	21
Bobby's Burger | **multi.**	21
Buckram Stables | **Locust Valley**	19
Bulldog Grille | **Amityville**	–
Burger Spot | **Garden City**	–

Chalet Rest.	Roslyn	18
Downtown Burger	Sayville	-
Z Five Guys	multi.	21
George Martin's Grill	multi.	20
Gonzalo's	Glen Cove	21
Harbor Grill	E Hampton	-
NEW Jack's Shack	Glen Head	-
LT Burger	Sag Harbor	16
O'Mally's	Southold	18
Post Stop	Westhampton Bch	17
NEW Prime Burger	Albertson	-
Rowdy Hall	E Hampton	20
NEW Smashburger	Hicksville	-

CAJUN

Bayou	N Bellmore	23
Big Daddy's	Massapequa	24
Blackbirds' Grille	Sayville	20
B.Smith's	Sag Harbor	18
NEW Mara's	Syosset	-

CALIFORNIAN

NEW Left Coast	Merrick	-
Salsa Salsa	multi.	23
Zim Zari	Massapequa Pk	22

CARIBBEAN

Rumba	Hampton Bays	-
Tequila Jacks	Port Jefferson	18

CENTRAL AMERICAN

NEW La Casa Latina	Westbury	-

CHINESE

(* dim sum specialist)

Albert's Mandarin	Huntington	20
Ancient Ginger	St. James	21
Best Buffet	Huntington Station	18
Chi	Westbury	25
Dynasty/Pt. Wash.	Port Washington	20
Fortune Wheel*	Levittown	22
NEW Golden Temple	Syosset	-
Hunan Taste	Greenvale	22
Lotus East	multi.	21
Nanking	New Hyde Pk	19
Orchid	Garden City	23
Z Orient*	Bethpage	27
Pearl East	Manhasset	23
P.F. Chang's	Westbury	20
Tony's	Westhampton Bch	19
Uncle Dai's	Glen Cove	18

COFFEEHOUSES

Golden Pear Cafe	multi.	18
Hampton Coffee	multi.	19

COFFEE SHOPS/ DINERS

Bozena Polish	Lindenhurst	23
Bridgehampton Candy	Bridgehampton	15
International Delight	multi.	18
Star Confectionery	Riverhead	22
Sweet Mama's	Northport	19
Thomas's Eggery	Carle Pl	22
Tricia's Café	Babylon	23

COLOMBIAN

Chicken Coop	Valley Stream	-
Sabor a Colombia	Levittown	-

CONTINENTAL

Amicale	Huntington Station	25
Babylon Carriage	Babylon	21
Barolo	Melville	25
Bayview Inn	S Jamesport	22
Bellport	Bellport	22
Bulldog Grille	Amityville	-
Cafe Testarossa	Syosset	22
Chadwicks	Rockville Ctr	22
Chez Kama	Great Neck	25
Cirella's	Melville	21
Claudio's	Greenport	16
Cooperage Inn	Baiting Hollow	22
Crabtree's	Floral Pk	21
Z Dave's Grill	Montauk	27
Frederick's	Melville	23
Irish Coffee	E Islip	23
Koenig's	Floral Pk	19
La Gioconda	Great Neck	21
Le Chef	Southampton	22
NEW Meridian	Locust Valley	-
Meson Iberia	Island Pk	22
Oak Chalet	Bellmore	19
Z Palm Court	E Meadow	24
Palmer's	Farmingdale	21
Peppercorns	Hicksville	19
Ritz Cafe	Northport	19
Surfside Inn	Montauk	18
Z Trumpets	Eastport	22
View	Oakdale	22
Vitae	Huntington	-

CREOLE

Bayou	N Bellmore	23

CRÊPES

Fresco Crêperie	Williston Pk	23

CUBAN

Cafe Havana	Smithtown	18

DELIS

Ⓩ Ben's Deli | **multi.**	19
Deli King | **New Hyde Pk**	19
Pastrami King | **Merrick**	20

DESSERT

Bridgehampton Candy | **Bridgehampton**	15
Ⓩ Cheesecake | **multi.**	20
Fresco Crêperie | **Long Bch**	23
Hildebrandt's | **Williston Pk**	19

ECLECTIC

Babette's | **E Hampton**	20
Batata Café | **Northport**	21
Best Buffet | **Huntington Station**	-
Bistro 25 | **Sayville**	22
Cafe Joelle | **Sayville**	22
Cafe Max | **E Hampton**	23
Chalet Rest. | **Roslyn**	18
Chequit Inn | **Shelter Is Hts**	19
Chi | **Westbury**	25
Cirella's | **Huntington Station**	21
Dark Horse | **Riverhead**	-
Duke Falcon's | **Long Bch**	22
Frisky Oyster | **Greenport**	25
Grand Lux | **Garden City**	19
Hideaway | **Ocean Beach**	19
Inn Spot/Bay | **Hampton Bays**	19
NEW Jewel | **Melville**	-
Kyle's | **Shelter Is**	-
Ⓩ La Plage | **Wading River**	27
Legends | **New Suffolk**	23
Lola | **Great Neck**	24
Ⓩ Maroni Cuisine | **Northport**	28
Michael Anthony's | **Wading River**	24
Ⓩ Mirko's | **Water Mill**	26
New Paradise | **Sag Harbor**	22
NEW Page/63 Main | **Sag Harbor**	-
Page One | **Glen Cove**	22
Painters' | **Brookhaven Hamlet**	20
Pastrami King | **Merrick**	20
PeraBell | **Patchogue**	26
Ram's Head | **Shelter Is**	20
Salamander's | **Greenport**	24
Silver's | **Southampton**	23
Sip City | **Great Neck**	-
34 New St. | **Huntington**	18
Toast | **Port Jefferson**	24
Tula Kit. | **Bay Shore**	24
NEW Vinoco | **Mineola**	-

EUROPEAN

Brasserie 214 | **New Hyde Pk**	20

FONDUE

Melting Pot | **Farmingdale**	18
Simply Fondue | **Great Neck**	17
NEW XO | **Huntington**	-

FRENCH

Almond | **Bridgehampton**	20
Ⓩ American Hotel | **Sag Harbor**	25
Ⓩ Barney's | **Locust Valley**	26
Ⓩ Chez Noëlle | **Port Washington**	27
Fresco Crêperie | **multi.**	23
La Coquille | **Manhasset**	24
La Marmite | **Williston Pk**	24
Le Chef | **Southampton**	22
Ⓩ Le Soir | **Bayport**	27
Mirabelle, Rest. | **Stony Brook**	25
O's Food | **St. James**	22
Pierre's | **Bridgehampton**	21
Red Bar | **Southampton**	22
Sage Bistro | **Woodbury**	24
Ⓩ Stone Creek | **E Quogue**	26
Stonewalls | **Riverhead**	23

FRENCH (BISTRO)

Aperitif | **Rockville Ctr**	25
Bar Frites | **Greenvale**	18
Ⓩ Bistro Cassis | **Huntington**	24
Bistro Citron | **Roslyn**	21
Chat Noir | **Rockville Ctr**	21
Comtesse Thérèse Bistro | **Aquebogue**	-
Cuvée | **Greenport**	22
Ⓩ Kitchen A Bistro | **St. James**	27
La P'tite Framboise | **Port Washington**	22
Sage Bistro | **Bellmore**	24
Sunset Beach | **Shelter Is Hts**	18
Voila! | **St. James**	24

FRENCH (BRASSERIE)

Brasserie Cassis | **Plainview**	23
Brasserie Persil | **Oceanside**	25
Dark Horse | **Riverhead**	-

GASTROPUB

NEW Huntington Social | Amer. | **Huntington**	-
NEW Left Coast | Amer. | **Merrick**	-
Wobbly Olive | Amer. | **Hauppauge**	-

GERMAN

Koenig's | **Floral Pk**	19
Oak Chalet | **Bellmore**	19

Pumpernickels | **Northport** 21
Village Lanterne | **Lindenhurst** 25

GREEK

Alexandros | **Mount Sinai** 23
Athens Grill | **Riverhead** -
Chicken Kebab | **Roslyn Hts** 21
Ethos | **Great Neck** 21
Greek Village | **Commack** 19
Hellenic Snack | **E Marion** 20
Med. Snack | **Huntington** 22
NEW MP Taverna | **Roslyn** -
Souvlaki Palace | **Commack** 24
Surf 'N Turf | **Merrick** 24
Trata | **Water Mill** 22
Zorba/Greek | **multi.** 19

HEALTH FOOD

(See also Vegetarian)
Babette's | **E Hampton** 20
Sweet Tomato | **multi.** -

ICE CREAM PARLORS

Itgen's | **Valley Stream** -

INDIAN

Akbar | **Garden City** 22
Curry Club | **multi.** 20
Diwan | **multi.** 21
Dosa Diner | **Hicksville** 23
Hampton Chutney | **Amagansett** 22
House/Dosas | **Hicksville** 25
House/India | **Huntington** 21
Kiran Palace | **multi.** 24
Madras | **New Hyde Pk** 22
New Chilli/Curry | **Hicksville** 26
Rangmahal | **Hicksville** 23
Royal Bukhara Grill | **Hicksville** 22
NEW Southern Spice | -
  New Hyde Pk

IRISH

Irish Coffee | **E Islip** 23
Sullivan's Quay | **Port Washington** 18

ITALIAN

(N=Northern; S=Southern)
Absolutely Mario | **Farmingdale** 20
Allison's Amalfi | **Sea Cliff** 21
Almarco | **Huntington** 20
A Mano | **Mattituck** 24
NEW Andiamo | **Mineola** -
Angelina's | **multi.** 23
Anthony's Pizza | **multi.** -

NEW Antonette's | **Rockville Ctr** -
Arturo's | **Floral Pk** 22
Baby Moon | S | **Westhampton Bch** 18
Barolo | **Melville** 25
Basil Leaf Café | **Locust Valley** 21
Bellissimo Rist. | **Deer Park** 23
Benny's | N | **Westbury** 25
Bertucci's | **multi.** 17
Bevanda | N | **Great Neck** 22
Blue Moon | **Rockville Ctr** 20
Boccaccio | N | **Hicksville** 21
Bravo Nader!/Fish | S | 24
  Huntington
Brio | N | **Port Washington** 21
Z Butera's | **multi.** 21
Z Cafe Baci | **Westbury** 22
Café Capriccio | N | 24
  Port Washington
Café Formaggio | **Carle Pl** 20
Cafe La Strada | **Hauppauge** 23
Cafe Rustica | **Great Neck** 22
Cafe Toscano | **Massapequa** 21
La Bottega | **multi.** 21
Caffe Laguna | **Long Bch** 19
Caracalla | **Syosset** 23
Carnival | S | 22
  Port Jefferson Station
Carrabba's | **multi.** 19
Caruso's | **Rocky Pt** 23
Casa Rustica | **Smithtown** 25
Chefs of NY | **E Northport** 19
Ciao Baby | **multi.** 20
Cielo Rist. | N | **Rockville Ctr** 20
Cinelli's | **multi.** 18
Cipollini | **Manhasset** 21
Circa | **Mineola** 22
Cirella's | N | **Melville** 21
Ciro's | **multi.** 22
Cittanuova | N | **E Hampton** 20
Z Dario's | N | **Rockville Ctr** 26
Deco 1600 | **Plainview** -
Dee Angelo's | 19
  Westhampton Bch
DiMaggio's | **multi.** 19
Dodici | **Rockville Ctr** 24
NEW DoraNonnie | **Glen Head** -
Edgewater | **Hampton Bays** 22
NEW 18 Bay | **Shelter Is** -
El Parral | **Syosset** 21
Emilio's | **Commack** 23
Ernesto's East | **Glen Head** 22
Fanatico | **Jericho** 20
Franina | **Syosset** 26

Galleria Rist. | N | **Westbury**	26
Giulio Cesare | N | **Westbury**	25
Gulf Coast | N | **Montauk**	21
🏧 Harvest | N | **Montauk**	26
Iavarone Cafe | **New Hyde Pk**	21
Il Capuccino | **Sag Harbor**	19
Il Classico | N | **Massapequa Pk**	23
🏧 Il Mulino NY | N | **Roslyn Estates**	27
Il Villagio | **Malverne**	24
Intermezzo | **Ft Salonga**	23
NEW J. Michaels | **Northport**	-
Jonathan's Rist. | **Huntington**	24
King Umberto | **Elmont**	23
🏧 Kitchen A Tratt. | **St. James**	28
La Bussola | **Glen Cove**	23
La Famiglia | **multi.**	22
La Ginestra | S | **Glen Cove**	25
La Gioconda | S | **Great Neck**	21
La Marmite | N | **Williston Pk**	24
La Nonna Bella | **Garden City**	21
La Novella | N | **E Meadow**	19
La Pace/Chef Michael | N | **Glen Cove**	25
🏧 La Parma | S | **multi.**	23
La Parmigiana | **Southampton**	22
La Piazza | **multi.**	21
🏧 La Piccola | N | **Port Washington**	27
La Pizzetta | **E Norwich**	21
La Rotonda | **Great Neck**	19
La Spada | S | **Huntington Station**	21
La Strada | **Merrick**	20
La Tavola | **Sayville**	22
La Terrazza | **Cedarhurst**	22
La Viola | **Cedarhurst**	20
La Volpe | **Center Moriches**	23
NEW Lawson Pub | **Oceanside**	-
Lombardi's/Sound | **Port Jefferson**	21
Lucé | **E Norwich**	22
Luigi Q | **Hicksville**	23
Mama's | **multi.**	21
Mamma Lombardi's | S | **Holbrook**	23
Manucci's | **Montauk**	19
Marco Polo's | **Westbury**	-
Mario | N | **Hauppauge**	25
🏧 Maroni Cuisine | **Northport**	28
🏧 Matteo's | S | **multi.**	23
Mercato Kit. | **Massapequa Pk**	20
Mother Kelly's | **multi.**	21
Nello Summertimes | N | **Southampton**	16
🏧 Nick & Toni's | **E Hampton**	24
Nick's | **Rockville Ctr**	23
Nick's Tuscan | N | **Long Bch**	21
Nonnina | **W Islip**	25
Novitá Wine Bar & Trattoria | **Garden City**	23
Olive Oils | **Point Lookout**	20
NEW Orto | **Miller Pl**	-
Osteria da Nino | N | **Huntington**	24
Panini Café | **Roslyn**	23
Papa Razzi | N | **Westbury**	18
NEW Passione | **Carle Pl**	-
Pasta-eria | **Hicksville**	23
Pasta Pasta | **Port Jefferson**	25
Pentimento | **Stony Brook**	22
Pepe Rosso | **Port Washington**	-
Per Un Angelo | N | **Wantagh**	22
Piccola Bussola | **multi.**	23
🏧 Piccolo | **Huntington**	27
Piccolo's | N | **Mineola**	24
Pomodorino | **Huntington**	19
Porto Bello | **Greenport**	22
Porto Vivo | **Huntington**	22
NEW Primo Piatto | S | **Huntington**	-
Puglia's/Garden City | **Garden City**	-
Rachel's Cafe | **Syosset**	22
Ragazzi | **Nesconset**	-
NEW Red Tomato | S | **E Norwich**	-
Rialto | N | **Carle Pl**	26
Rist. Gemelli | **Babylon**	24
Rist. Italiano | **Port Washington**	24
Riviera Grill | **Glen Cove**	26
Robert's | **Water Mill**	25
Roe's Casa Dolce | **Rockville Ctr**	24
Ruvo | S | **multi.**	22
NEW Salumi Tapas | **Massapequa**	-
Sam's | **E Hampton**	18
🏧 San Marco | N | **Hauppauge**	26
Sant Ambroeus | N | **Southampton**	24
Scotto's | **Westbury**	20
Sea Basin | **Rocky Pt**	19
Sea Grille | **Montauk**	21
🏧 Sempre Vivolo | **Hauppauge**	27
Serafina | **E Hampton**	18
NEW Serata | **Oyster Bay**	-

Seventh Street Cafe | N | **Garden City**	20
75 Main | **Southampton**	18
Solé | **Oceanside**	26
Stella Rist. | **Floral Pk**	24
Steve's Piccola | **multi.**	24
Stresa | **Manhasset**	25
Sundried Tomato | **Nesconset**	21
Surf's Out | **Kismet**	17
NEW Tappo | **Glen Cove**	-
Tate's | **Nesconset**	26
Tesoro | **Westbury**	23
388 Rest. | **Roslyn Hts**	20
Torcellos | **E Northport**	21
Touch/Venice | N | **Cutchogue**	21
Tratt. Diane | N | **Roslyn**	25
Tratt. Di Meo | **Roslyn Hts**	21
Tuscan Hse. | **Southampton**	22
Tutto Il Giorno | **multi.**	25
Tutto Pazzo | **Huntington**	20
Umberto's | S | **multi.**	22
Uncle Bacala's | S | **multi.**	21
Venere | **Westbury**	20
Z Verace | **Islip**	26
Vero | **Amityville**	-
Verona | **Farmingdale**	-
Vespa | N | **Great Neck**	22
Villa D'Aqua | N | **Bellmore**	21
Villa D'Este | N | **Floral Pk**	22
Vincent's | **Carle Pl**	22
Vine Wine Bar | **Merrick**	-
Vittorio's | **Amityville**	25
World Pie | **Bridgehampton**	19

JAPANESE

(* sushi specialist)

Z Aji 53 | **multi.**	27
NEW Arata Sushi | **Syosset**	-
Azuma | **Greenlawn**	23
Benihana | **multi.**	19
Benkei* | **Northport**	23
Blue* | **Blue Pt**	22
Blue Fish | **Hicksville**	-
Bonbori Tiki* | **Huntington**	20
Bonsai* | **Port Washington**	22
Chez Kama | **Great Neck**	25
Daruma/Tokyo* | **Great Neck**	23
Domo Sushi | **E Setauket**	21
Fatty Fish | **Glen Cove**	22
Galangal* | **Syosset**	23
Gasho/Japan | **Hauppauge**	20
NEW Golden Temple | **Syosset**	-
Haiku* | **Riverhead**	-
Hinata | **Great Neck**	23
Homura Sushi* | **Williston Pk**	23
Hotoke | **Smithtown**	21
Imperial Seoul | **New Hyde Pk**	-
Kinha* | **Garden City**	-
Kiraku | **Glen Head**	26
Kiss'o* | **New Hyde Pk**	21
Z Kotobuki | **multi.**	27
Kumo Sushi | **Plainview**	25
Kura Barn* | **Huntington**	24
Kurofune* | **Commack**	23
NEW Legacy | **Huntington**	-
Matsuya* | **Great Neck**	21
Minado* | **Carle Pl**	21
Minami* | **Massapequa**	26
NEW Miraku* | **Great Neck**	-
Mitsui* | **Bay Shore**	24
Mumon | **Garden City**	22
Z Nagahama* | **Long Bch**	28
Nagashima* | **Jericho**	24
Nisen* | **multi.**	25
NEW Nobu/Capri* | **Southampton**	-
Onsen Sushi* | **Oakdale**	-
Osaka* | **Huntington**	24
Ozumo* | **Bethpage**	23
Robata* | **Plainview**	20
Sakaya | **Albertson**	-
Samurai | **Huntington**	24
Sapporo* | **Wantagh**	23
Sen* | **Sag Harbor**	21
Shiki (Babylon)* | **Babylon**	24
Shiki (E. Hampton)* | **E Hampton**	-
Shiro/Japan* | **Carle Pl**	22
Shogi* | **Westbury**	25
Show Win* | **multi.**	20
Suki Zuki* | **Water Mill**	24
Sushi Palace* | **Great Neck**	24
Sushi Ya* | **multi.**	21
Tai Show* | **multi.**	23
Takara* | **Islandia**	28
Tokyo* | **E Northport**	24
Tomo Hibachi* | **Huntington**	20
Tony's | **Westhampton Bch**	19
Xaga Sushi* | **multi.**	-
Yamaguchi* | **Port Washington**	25
Yama Q | **Bridgehampton**	23
Yokohama | **E Northport**	23
Yuki's Palette* | **Merrick**	24

KOREAN

Imperial Seoul | **New Hyde Pk**	-
Tokyo | **E Northport**	24

KOSHER/ KOSHER-STYLE

☑ Ben's Deli | **multi.**	19
Cho-Sen | **multi.**	19
Colbeh | **multi.**	21
Deli King | **New Hyde Pk**	19
Madras | **New Hyde Pk**	22

MEDITERRANEAN

Alexandros | **Mount Sinai**	23
Allison's Amalfi | **Sea Cliff**	21
Athens Grill | **Riverhead**	-
Ayhan's Shish | **multi.**	18
Ayhan's Trodos | **Westbury**	21
Azerbaijan | **multi.**	22
Backyard | **Montauk**	23
☑ Barrique Kit. | **Babylon**	24
Cafe Rustica | **Great Neck**	22
NEW Café Taka | **Bay Shore**	-
Crabtree's | **Floral Pk**	21
Fatfish | **Bay Shore**	21
☑ Harvest | **Montauk**	26
☑ Limani | **Roslyn**	26
NEW Martini Grill | **Speonk**	-
Med. Grill | **Hewlett**	21
Med. Snack | **Huntington**	22
Meeting Hse. | **Amagansett**	20
Miraj | **Williston Pk**	-
☑ Nick & Toni's | **E Hampton**	24
Pier 95 | **Freeport**	24
Pita House | **multi.**	22
NEW Saffron | **Glen Head**	-
☑ Stone Creek | **E Quogue**	26
Tulip B&G | **Great Neck**	19
Wild Fig | **multi.**	19

MEXICAN

NEW Agave | **Bridgehampton**	-
Baja Fresh | **New Hyde Pk**	18
Baja Grill | **multi.**	18
☑ Besito | **multi.**	24
NEW Caracara Mex. | **Farmingdale**	-
Chipotle | **multi.**	20
Cozymel's | **Westbury**	17
Goldmine Mex. | **Greenlawn**	21
Green Cactus | **multi.**	20
NEW K·Pacho | **New Hyde Pk**	-
La Panchita | **Smithtown**	22
Little Mexico | **Westbury**	-
Los Compadres | **Huntington Station**	23
Oaxaca Mex. | **Huntington**	23

Poco Loco | **Roslyn**	17
Quetzalcoatl | **Huntington**	20
Salsa Salsa | **multi.**	23
Viva Juan | **Selden**	21
Viva La Vida | **Oakdale**	20
Zim Zari | **Massapequa Pk**	22

NEW ENGLAND

Bigelow's | **Rockville Ctr**	24

NUEVO LATINO

Laguna Grille | **Woodbury**	20

PAKISTANI

Spice Village | **Huntington**	20

PAN-LATIN

NEW La Casa Latina | **Westbury**	-
Perfecto Mundo | **Commack**	24
Pollo Rico | **Centereach**	20

PERSIAN

Azerbaijan | **multi.**	22
Colbeh | **multi.**	21
Miraj | **Williston Pk**	-
Ravagh | **multi.**	22
Spice Village | **Huntington**	20

PERUVIAN

El Pio | **Glen Cove**	-
NEW Las Viñas | **Manhasset**	-

PIZZA

NEW Angelina's Fireshack | **New Hyde Pk**	-
Anthony's Pizza | **multi.**	-
Baby Moon | **Westhampton Bch**	18
Bertucci's | **multi.**	17
Blue Moon | **Rockville Ctr**	20
Chefs of NY | **E Northport**	19
Cirella's | **multi.**	21
California Pizza Kit. | **multi.**	17
Eddie's Pizza | **New Hyde Pk**	21
Emilio's | **Commack**	23
Foody's | **Water Mill**	21
Giaccone's Pizza | **Mineola**	-
Grimaldi's | **Garden City**	23
King Umberto | **Elmont**	23
La Piazza | **multi.**	21
La Pizzetta | **E Norwich**	21
La Rotonda | **Great Neck**	19
Manucci's | **Montauk**	19
Massa's | **Huntington Station**	23

Nick's | **Rockville Ctr**	23
Pasta-eria | **Hicksville**	23
Pie | **Port Jefferson**	21
Salvatore's | **multi.**	25
Pizza Place | **Bridgehampton**	24
NEW Red Tomato | **E Norwich**	-
Sam's | **E Hampton**	18
Scotto's | **Westbury**	20
Sundried Tomato | **Nesconset**	21
Torcellos | **E Northport**	21
Umberto's | **multi.**	22
World Pie | **Bridgehampton**	19

POLISH

Birchwood | **Riverhead**	20
Bozena Polish | **Lindenhurst**	23

PORTUGUESE

A Taberna | **Island Pk**	23
Churrasq. Bairrada | **Mineola**	25
Fado | **Huntington**	21
Heart/Portugal | **Mineola**	20
Lareira | **Mineola**	20
Luso | **Smithtown**	22

PUB FOOD

John Harvard's | **Lake Grove**	16
O'Mally's | **Southold**	18
Peppercorns | **Hicksville**	19
Post Office | **Babylon**	19
Rockwell's B&G | **Smithtown**	22
Rowdy Hall | **E Hampton**	20
Runyon's | **Seaford**	18
Southampton Publick | **Southampton**	18
Sullivan's Quay | **Port Washington**	18

SANDWICHES

(See also Delis)

Batata Café | **Northport**	21
Hampton Coffee | **multi.**	19
Lucy's Café | **Babylon**	25
Main St. Bakery | **Port Washington**	-
Panini Café | **Roslyn**	23
Pastrami King | **Merrick**	20
Press 195 | **Rockville Ctr**	-
NEW Roast | **Melville**	-
Sweet Tomato | **multi.**	-

SEAFOOD

NEW A Lure | **Southold**	-
Z Atlantica | **Long Bch**	20

Ayhan's Fish | **Port Washington**	19
NEW Beach Hse. | **E Hampton**	-
Bigelow's | **Rockville Ctr**	24
Black & Blue | **Huntington**	22
Z Blackstone Steak | **Melville**	24
Boathouse | **E Hampton**	19
Bostwick's | **E Hampton**	20
Bravo Nader!/Fish | **Huntington**	24
B.Smith's | **Sag Harbor**	18
Buoy One | **multi.**	23
Cafe Max | **E Hampton**	23
Canterbury | **Oyster Bay**	19
Catfish Max | **Seaford**	21
Chop Shop | **Smithtown**	24
Clam Bar | **Amagansett**	21
Claudio's | **Greenport**	16
Coast Grill | **Southampton**	22
Z Coolfish | **Syosset**	24
Crow's Nest | **Montauk**	19
Cull Hse. | **Sayville**	20
Cyril's Fish | **Amagansett**	18
Z Dave's Grill | **Montauk**	27
Dock B&G | **Montauk**	-
Dockers Waterside | **E Quogue**	20
Dockside B&G | **Sag Harbor**	21
Duryea's Lobster | **Montauk**	22
Fatfish | **Bay Shore**	21
Fishbar | **Montauk**	18
Fisherman's Catch | **Point Lookout**	20
Fishery | **multi.**	19
Fish Store | **Bayport**	-
Fulton Prime | **Syosset**	23
Gosman's Dock | **Montauk**	19
Harbor Crab | **Patchogue**	18
H2O Seafood | **Smithtown**	23
Hudson/McCoy | **Freeport**	18
Inlet Seafood | **Montauk**	21
Inn Spot/Bay | **Hampton Bays**	19
NEW Insignia | **Smithtown**	-
Island Mermaid | **Ocean Beach**	20
Jack Halyards | **Oyster Bay**	23
NEW Joe's Crab Shack | **Oceanside**	-
Jolly Fisherman | **Roslyn**	21
Z Kitchen A Bistro | **St. James**	27
Legal Sea Foods | **Huntington Station**	20
Z Limani | **Roslyn**	26
Lobster Roll | **Amagansett**	19
Lobster Roll N. | **Baiting Hollow**	20
Lombardi's/Bay | **Patchogue**	23
Louie's Oyster | **Port Washington**	17

NEW Mara's | **Syosset**	–
Matthew's | **Ocean Beach**	22
Mill Creek | **Bayville**	21
Mill Pond Hse. | **Centerport**	25
Nautilus Cafe | **Freeport**	24
NEW North Fork Oyster | **Greenport**	–
Oakland's/Sunday | **Hampton Bays**	18
Oar Steak | **Patchogue**	21
Ocean Grill | **Freeport**	23
NEW Oceans 5 | **Shoreham**	–
Off the Hook | **E Northport**	20
Old Mill Inn | **Mattituck**	20
Paddy McGees | **Island Pk**	18
Z Palm | **E Hampton**	26
Park Place | **Floral Pk**	–
NEW Patio | **Freeport**	–
Pier 95 | **Freeport**	24
Z Plaza Café | **Southampton**	26
Porters | **Bellport**	20
Prime Catch | **Rockville Ctr**	–
Rachel's Waterside | **Freeport**	20
Rare 650 | **Syosset**	24
Red Fish | **Plainview**	23
Z Riverbay | **Williston Pk**	23
Schooner | **Freeport**	17
Sea Basin | **Rocky Pt**	19
Sea Grille | **Montauk**	21
Sea Levels | **Brightwaters**	22
Shagwong | **Montauk**	18
Snapper Inn | **Oakdale**	18
Southfork | **Bridgehampton**	–
Southside Fish | **Lindenhurst**	20
Z Starr Boggs | **Westhampton Bch**	26
Surfside Inn | **Montauk**	18
Surf's Out | **Kismet**	17
Tequila Jacks | **Port Jefferson**	18
Thom Thom | **Wantagh**	20
Trata | **Water Mill**	22
NEW TR Rest. | **Hampton Bays**	–
Turquoise | **Great Neck**	21
Uncle Bacala's | **multi.**	21
Varney's | **Brookhaven**	23
Wall's Wharf | **Bayville**	17
Whale's Tale | **Northport**	20
Wildfish | **Freeport**	21

SMALL PLATES

(See also Spanish tapas specialist)

Z Barrique Kit. | Med. | **Babylon**	24
Brass Rail | Amer. | **Locust Valley**	25
Café Buenos Aires | Argent. | **Huntington**	24
NEW DoraNonnie | Asian/Italian | **Glen Head**	–
NEW España Tapas | Spanish | **St. James**	–
Fork & Vine | Amer. | **Glen Head**	23
Lola | Eclectic | **Great Neck**	24
Meeting Hse. | Amer./Med. | **Amagansett**	20
NEW Mitch/Toni's | Amer. | **Albertson**	–
NEW MP Taverna | Greek | **Roslyn**	–
Z Noah's | Amer. | **Greenport**	26
NEW Nobu/Capri | Japanese | **Southampton**	–
O's Food | Eclectic | **St. James**	22
NEW Phoenix | Amer. | **Seaford**	–
NEW Salumi Tapas | Italian/Spanish | **Massapequa**	–
Sugar | Amer./Asian | **Carle Pl**	–
Swallow | Amer. | **Huntington**	–
Toast | Eclectic | **Port Jefferson**	24
Z Verace | Italian | **Islip**	26
Vero | Italian | **Amityville**	–
Vine Wine Bar | Italian | **Merrick**	–
NEW Vinoco | Eclectic | **Mineola**	–

SOUTHERN

Blackbirds' Grille | **Sayville**	20
B.Smith's | **Sag Harbor**	18
LL Dent | **Carle Pl**	23

SOUTHWESTERN

RS Jones | **Merrick**	22

SPANISH

(* tapas specialist)

Bin 56* | **Huntington**	24
Casa Luis | **Smithtown**	22
Copa Wine* | **Bridgehampton**	20
El Parral | **Syosset**	21
NEW España Tapas* | **St. James**	–
La Cocina/Marcia | **Freeport**	–
La Panchita | **Smithtown**	22
Meson Iberia | **Island Pk**	22
NEW Salumi Tapas | **Massapequa**	–
Viva La Vida | **Oakdale**	20

STEAKHOUSES

NEW Beach Hse. | **E Hampton**	–
Benihana | **multi.**	19

Black & Blue | **Huntington** 22
Z Blackstone Steak | **Melville** 24
Blackwells | **Wading River** 23
Bobby Van's | **Bridgehampton** 22
Boulder Creek | **Hicksville** -
Brooks & Porter | **Merrick** 22
Z Bryant & Cooper | **Roslyn** 26
Burton & Doyle | **Great Neck** 24
Cattlemen's | **multi.** 19
Chop Shop | **Smithtown** 24
Cliff's | **multi.** 22
Clubhouse | **Huntington** 21
Dockers Waterside | **E Quogue** 20
Elbow East | **Southold** 19
Frank's Steaks | **multi.** 21
Fulton Prime | **Syosset** 23
Gasho/Japan | **Hauppauge** 20
George Martin's Steak | **Great River** -
NEW Grill 454 | **Commack** -
Hotoke | **Smithtown** 21
NEW Insignia | **Smithtown** -
NEW Jake's Steak | **E Meadow** -
Jimmy Hays | **Island Pk** 25
NEW J. Michaels | **Northport** -
Jolly Fisherman | **Roslyn** 21
Lombardi's/Bay | **Patchogue** 23
Mac's Steak | **Huntington** 23
Majors Steak | **multi.** 19
Mill Creek | **Bayville** 21
Mill Pond Hse. | **Centerport** 25
Z Morton's | **Great Neck** 25
Nautilus Cafe | **Freeport** 24
Oar Steak | **Patchogue** 21
Old Fields | **Greenlawn** -
1 North Steak | **Hampton Bays** 22
Pace's Steak | **multi.** 22
Z Palm | **E Hampton** 26
Peppercorns | **Hicksville** 19
Z Peter Luger | **Great Neck** 27
PG Steak | **Huntington** 22
Porters | **Bellport** 20
Rare 650 | **Syosset** 24
Z Rothmann's | **E Norwich** 25
Z Ruth's Chris | **Garden City** 25
Schooner | **Freeport** 17
NEW Spiro's | **Rocky Pt** -
Z Tellers | **Islip** 26
Thom Thom | **Wantagh** 20
Tomo Hibachi | **Huntington** 20
21 Main | **W Sayville** 23
Vintage Prime | **St. James** 25

TEAROOMS

Chat Noir | **Rockville Ctr** 21
Robinson's Tea | **Stony Brook** 23

TEX-MEX

Blue Parrot | **E Hampton** 15
NEW Del Fuego | **St. James** -
Pancho's | **Island Pk** 19

THAI

Bonbori Tiki | **Huntington** 20
Frankly Thai | **Franklin Sq** -
Galangal | **Syosset** 23
Lemonleaf Grill | **multi.** 22
Lemonleaf Thai | **multi.** 20
Nanking | **New Hyde Pk** 19
Onzon Thai | **Bellmore** 24
Phao | **Sag Harbor** 21
Sabai Thai | **Miller Pl** 22
Sarin Thai | **multi.** 24
Seeda Thai | **Valley Stream** 23
Z Siam Lotus | **Bay Shore** 28
Simply Thai | **Rockville Ctr** 21
Sripraphai | **Williston Pk** 25
Sri Thai | **Huntington** 22
Thai Gourmet | **Port Jefferson Station** 26
Thai Green Leaf | **multi.** 21
Thai Hse. | **Smithtown** 24
Thai Table | **Rockville Ctr** 23
Thai USA | **Huntington** 23
Tony's | **Westhampton Bch** 19

TURKISH

Ayhan's Fish | **Port Washington** 19
Ayhan's Shish | **multi.** 18
Azerbaijan | **multi.** 22
NEW Café Taka | **Bay Shore** -
Chicken Kebab | **Roslyn Hts** 21
Pita House | **multi.** 22
Surf 'N Turf | **Merrick** 24
Tulip B&G | **Great Neck** 19
Wild Fig | **multi.** 19

VEGETARIAN

Ariana | **Huntington** 20
Crave 11025 | **Great Neck** 18
Dosa Diner | **Hicksville** 23
House/Dosas | **Hicksville** 25
NEW L.I.V.E. | **Seaford** -
Madras | **New Hyde Pk** 22
Yama Q | **Bridgehampton** 23

Locations

Includes names, cuisines and Food ratings.

Nassau

ALBERTSON

NEW Mitch/Toni's | *Amer.*	-
NEW Prime Burger | *Burgers*	-
Sakaya | *Japanese*	-

BALDWIN

Ayhan's Shish | *Med./Turkish*	18

BAYVILLE

Mill Creek | *Seafood/Steak*	21
Pine Island | *Amer.*	18
Wall's Wharf | *Amer./Seafood*	17

BELLMORE

International Delight | *Amer./Diner*	18
Z Matteo's | *Italian*	23
Oak Chalet | *Continental/German*	19
Onzon Thai | *Thai*	24
Sage Bistro | *French*	24
Umberto's | *Italian/Pizza*	22
Villa D'Aqua | *Italian*	21

BETHPAGE

B.K. Sweeney's | *Amer.*	18
H.R. Singleton's | *Amer.*	18
Izumi | *Asian*	23
Z Orient | *Chinese*	27
Ozumo | *Japanese*	23

CARLE PLACE

Anthony's Pizza | *Pizza*	-
Z Ben's Deli | *Deli*	19
Café Formaggio | *Italian*	20
Chipotle | *Mex.*	20
490 West | *Amer.*	-
La Bottega | *Italian*	21
Lemonleaf Thai | *Thai*	20
LL Dent | *Southern*	23
Minado | *Japanese*	21
NEW Passione | *Italian*	-
Rialto | *Italian*	26
Shiro/Japan | *Japanese*	22
Sugar | *Amer./Asian*	-
Thomas's Eggery | *Diner*	22
Vincent's | *Italian*	22

Z West End | *Amer.*	25

CEDARHURST

La Terrazza | *Italian*	22
La Viola | *Italian*	20
Mother Kelly's | *Amer./Italian*	21

EAST MEADOW

Azerbaijan | *Mideast.*	22
NEW Jake's Steak | *Steak*	-
La Novella | *Italian*	19
Majors Steak | *Steak*	19
Z Palm Court | *Amer./Continental*	24

EAST NORWICH

Angelina's | *Italian*	23
La Pizzetta | *Italian*	21
Lucé | *Italian*	22
NEW Red Tomato | *Pizza*	-
Z Rothmann's | *Steak*	25

EAST ROCKAWAY

Fishery | *Seafood*	19

ELMONT

King Umberto | *Italian*	23

FARMINGDALE

Absolutely Mario | *Italian*	20
NEW Caracara Mex. | *Mex.*	-
Chipotle | *Mex.*	20
56th Fighter | *Amer.*	16
Library Cafe | *Amer.*	18
Melting Pot | *Fondue*	18
Palmer's | *Continental*	21
Taste 99 | *Amer.*	18
Verona | *Italian*	-

FLORAL PARK

Arturo's | *Italian*	22
Bob's Rest. | *Amer.*	21
Crabtree's | *Continental/Med.*	21
Koenig's | *Continental/German*	19
La Bottega | *Italian*	21
Park Place | *Amer./Seafood*	-
Stella Rist. | *Italian*	24
Umberto's | *Italian/Pizza*	22
Villa D'Este | *Italian*	22

FRANKLIN SQUARE

Cinelli's | *Italian*	18
Frankly Thai | *Thai*	-
La Bottega | *Italian*	21

FREEPORT

E. B. Elliot's | *Amer.*	18
Hudson/McCoy | *Seafood*	18
La Cocina/Marcia | *Amer./Spanish*	-
Nautilus Cafe | *Seafood/Steak*	24
Ocean Grill | *Amer./Seafood*	23
NEW Patio | *Amer./Seafood*	-
Pier 95 | *Med.*	24
Rachel's Waterside | *Amer./Seafood*	20
Schooner | *Seafood/Steak*	17
Wildfish | *Seafood*	21

GARDEN CITY

Akbar | *Indian*	22
Asian Moon | *Asian*	23
B.K. Sweeney's | *Amer.*	18
Bobby's Burger | *Burgers*	21
Burger Spot | *Burgers*	-
La Bottega | *Italian*	21
Grand Lux | *Eclectic*	19
Grimaldi's | *Pizza*	23
Houston's | *Amer.*	22
Kinha | *Japanese*	-
La Nonna Bella | *Italian*	21
NEW Mint | *Asian*	-
Mumon | *Japanese*	22
Novitá Wine Bar & Trattoria | *Italian*	23
Orchid | *Chinese*	23
Puglia's/Garden City | *Italian*	-
Rein | *Amer.*	23
Z Ruth's Chris | *Steak*	25
Sarabeth's | *Amer.*	20
Seventh Street Cafe | *Italian*	20
Sushi Ya | *Japanese*	21
Umberto's | *Italian/Pizza*	22
Walk St. | *Amer.*	21
Z Waterzooi | *Belgian*	24
Wild Fig | *Med./Turkish*	19

GARDEN CITY PARK

Green Cactus | *Mex.*	20
Jonathan's | *Amer.*	20
Uncle Bacala's | *Italian/Seafood*	21

GLEN COVE

Cedar Creek | *Amer.*	-
El Pio | *Peruvian*	-

Fatty Fish | *Japanese*	22
Gonzalo's | *Amer.*	21
La Bussola | *Italian*	23
La Ginestra | *Italian*	25
La Pace/Chef Michael | *Italian*	25
Page One | *Amer./Eclectic*	22
Riviera Grill | *Italian*	26
Sweet Tomato | *Sandwiches*	-
NEW Tappo | *Italian*	-
Uncle Dai's | *Chinese*	18
Wild Fig | *Med./Turkish*	19

GLEN HEAD

NEW DoraNonnie | *Asian/Italian*	-
Ernesto's East | *Italian*	22
Fishery | *Seafood*	19
Fork & Vine | *Amer.*	23
NEW Jack's Shack | *Amer./Burgers*	-
Kiraku | *Japanese*	26
NEW Saffron | *Amer./Med.*	-

GREAT NECK

Bevanda | *Italian*	22
Burton & Doyle | *Steak*	24
Cafe Rustica | *Italian/Med.*	22
Chez Kama | *Continental/Japanese*	25
Chipotle | *Mex.*	20
Cho-Sen | *Asian/Kosher*	19
Colbeh | *Persian*	21
Crave 11025 | *Amer./Veg.*	18
Daruma/Tokyo | *Japanese*	23
Elaine's | *Asian*	22
Ethos | *Greek*	21
NEW 420 North | *Amer.*	-
Hinata | *Japanese*	23
Jean Marie | *Amer.*	22
La Gioconda | *Continental/Italian*	21
La Rotonda | *Pizza*	19
Lola | *Eclectic*	24
Matsuya | *Asian*	21
NEW Miraku | *Japanese*	-
Z Morton's | *Steak*	25
Z Peter Luger | *Steak*	27
Simply Fondue | *Fondue*	17
Sip City | *Eclectic*	-
Sushi Palace | *Japanese*	24
Tulip B&G | *Med./Turkish*	19
Turquoise | *Seafood*	21
Vespa | *Italian*	22
Wild Ginger | *Asian*	21

GREENVALE

Bar Frites | *French*	18
Z Ben's Deli | *Deli*	19

| Hunan Taste | Chinese | 22 |
| Sarin Thai | Thai | 24 |

HEMPSTEAD
| Chipotle | Mex. | 20 |

HEWLETT
Med. Grill	Med.	21
MoCa Asian	Asian	18
Xaga Sushi	Asian	-

HICKSVILLE
Blue Fish	Japanese	-
Boccaccio	Italian	21
Boulder Creek	Steak	-
Chipotle	Mex.	20
Curry Club	Indian	20
Diwan	Indian	21
Dosa Diner	Indian/Veg.	23
☑ Five Guys	Burgers	21
House/Dosas	Indian/Veg.	25
Kiran Palace	Indian	24
Lemonleaf Grill	Thai	22
Luigi Q	Italian	23
New Chilli/Curry	Indian	26
Pasta-eria	Italian	23
Peppercorns	Continental	19
Rangmahal	Indian	23
Royal Bukhara Grill	Indian	22
NEW Smashburger	Burgers	-
West East	Asian	25
Zorba/Greek	Greek	19

ISLAND PARK
A Taberna	Portug.	23
Jimmy Hays	Steak	25
Meson Iberia	Continental/Spanish	22
Paddy McGees	Seafood	18
Pancho's	Tex-Mex	19
NEW Pop's Seafood	Seafood	-

JERICHO
Fanatico	Italian	20
Frank's Steaks	Steak	21
NEW Market Bistro	Amer.	-
Milleridge Inn	Amer.	16
Nagashima	Japanese	24

LAWRENCE
| Cho-Sen | Asian/Kosher | 19 |

LEVITTOWN
| ☑ Five Guys | Burgers | 21 |
| Fortune Wheel | Chinese | 22 |

Kiran Palace	Indian	24
Sabor a Colombia	Colombian	-
Sensasian	Asian	-
Tai Show	Japanese	23

LOCUST VALLEY
☑ Barney's	Amer./French	26
Basil Leaf Café	Italian	21
Brass Rail	Amer.	25
Buckram Stables	Amer.	19
NEW Meridian	Asian/Continental	-
NEW Tavern/Plaza	Amer.	-

LONG BEACH
☑ Atlantica	Amer./Seafood	20
Caffe Laguna	Italian	19
Duke Falcon's	Amer./Eclectic	22
☑ Five Guys	Burgers	21
Fresco Crêperie	French	23
George Martin's Grill	Burgers	20
Lola's Kit.	Amer.	20
☑ Nagahama	Japanese	28
Nick's Tuscan	Italian	21
Sugo	Amer.	23
Swingbelly's	BBQ	23

MALVERNE
| Il Villagio | Italian | 24 |

MANHASSET
Benihana	Japanese/Steak	19
Cipollini	Italian	21
La Coquille	French	24
NEW Las Viñas	Peruvian	-
Pearl East	Chinese	23
Sarabeth's	Amer.	20
Stresa	Italian	25
☑ Toku	Asian	25

MASSAPEQUA/
MASSAPEQUA PARK
NEW Alaine's	Amer.	-
Asian Moon	Asian	23
Big Daddy's	BBQ/Cajun	24
Cafe Toscano	Italian	21
Ciao Baby	Italian	20
Hudson's Mill	Amer.	22
Il Classico	Italian	23
Mercato Kit.	Amer./Italian	20
Minami	Japanese	26
NEW Salumi Tapas	Italian/Spanish	-

Smokin' Al's | *BBQ* — 23
Tai Show | *Japanese* — 23
Zim Zari | *Cal./Mex.* — 22

MERRICK

Brooks & Porter | *Steak* — 22
🅩 Five Guys | *Burgers* — 21
George Martin's Grill | *Burgers* — 20
La Piazza | *Pizza* — 21
La Strada | *Italian* — 20
NEW Left Coast | *Amer.* — -
Nicholas James | *Amer.* — 22
Pastrami King | *Deli/Sandwiches* — 20
RS Jones | *SW* — 22
Surf 'N Turf | *Greek/Turkish* — 24
Vine Wine Bar | *Italian* — -
Xaga Sushi | *Asian* — -
Yuki's Palette | *Japanese* — 24

MINEOLA

NEW Andiamo | *Amer./Italian* — -
Chipotle | *Mex.* — 20
Churrasq. Bairrada | *Portug.* — 25
Circa | *Italian* — 22
Giaccone's Pizza | *Pizza* — -
Heart/Portugal | *Portug.* — 20
Lareira | *Portug.* — 20
Lemonleaf Thai | *Thai* — 20
Piccola Bussola | *Italian* — 23
Piccolo's | *Italian* — 24
NEW Vinoco | *Eclectic* — -

NEW HYDE PARK

Afghan Grill | *Afghan* — 20
NEW Angelina's Fireshack | *Pizza* — -
Baja Fresh | *Mex.* — 18
Brasserie 214 | *Euro.* — 20
Deli King | *Deli* — 19
Eddie's Pizza | *Pizza* — 21
Iavarone Cafe | *Italian* — 21
Imperial Seoul | *Japanese/Korean* — -
Kiss'o | *Japanese* — 21
NEW K·Pacho | *Mex.* — -
Madras | *Indian/Veg.* — 22
Nanking | *Chinese/Thai* — 19
NEW Southern Spice | *Indian* — -
Sushi Ya | *Japanese* — 21
Umberto's | *Italian/Pizza* — 22

NORTH BELLMORE

Bayou | *Cajun/Creole* — 23

OCEANSIDE

Brasserie Persil | *French* — 25
Cinelli's | *Italian* — 18
NEW Joe's Crab Shack | *Seafood* — -
La Bottega | *Italian* — 21
🅩 La Parma | *Italian* — 23
NEW Lawson Pub | *Amer.* — -
Solé | *Italian* — 26

OYSTER BAY

Canterbury | *Amer./Seafood* — 19
Coach Grill | *Amer.* — 22
Jack Halyards | *Amer./Seafood* — 23
NEW Serata | *Italian* — -
Sweet Tomato | *Sandwiches* — -
Wild Honey | *Amer.* — 25

PLAINVIEW

Ayhan's Shish | *Med./Turkish* — 18
Brasserie Cassis | *French* — 23
Deco 1600 | *Amer./Italian* — -
Green Cactus | *Mex.* — 20
Kumo Sushi | *Japanese* — 25
La Bottega | *Italian* — 21
La Famiglia | *Italian* — 22
La Piazza | *Pizza* — 21
Red Fish | *Amer./Seafood* — 23
Robata | *Japanese* — 20

POINT LOOKOUT

Fisherman's Catch | *Seafood* — 20
Olive Oils | *Italian* — 20

PORT WASHINGTON

Ayhan's Fish | *Seafood/Turkish* — 19
Ayhan's Shish | *Med./Turkish* — 18
NEW Bistro Etc. | *Amer.* — -
Bonsai | *Japanese* — 22
Brio | *Italian* — 21
Café Capriccio | *Italian* — 24
🅩 Chez Noëlle | *French* — 27
DiMaggio's | *Italian* — 19
Diwan | *Indian* — 21
Dynasty/Pt. Wash. | *Chinese* — 20
Harbor-Q | *BBQ* — 21
🅩 La Parma | *Italian* — 23
🅩 La Piccola | *Italian* — 27
La P'tite Framboise | *French* — 22
Louie's Oyster | *Seafood* — 17
Main St. Bakery | *Bakery/Sandwiches* — -
Pepe Rosso | *Italian* — -
Rist. Italiano | *Italian* — 24

Salvatore's | *Pizza* 25
Sullivan's Quay | *Pub* 18
Wild Honey | *Amer.* 25
Yamaguchi | *Japanese* 25

ROCKVILLE CENTRE

NEW Antonette's | *Italian* -
Aperitif | *French* 25
Ayhan's Shish | *Med./Turkish* 18
Bigelow's | *New Eng./Seafood* 24
Blue Moon | *Italian/Pizza* 20
Chadwicks | *Amer./Continental* 22
Chat Noir | *French/Tea* 21
Cielo Rist. | *Italian* 20
Z Dario's | *Italian* 26
Dodici | *Italian* 24
Frank's Steaks | *Steak* 21
George Martin | *Amer.* 22
George Martin's Grill | *Burgers* 20
Green Cactus | *Mex.* 20
International Delight | *Amer./Diner* 18
La Bottega | *Italian* 21
Nick's | *Pizza* 23
Press 195 | *Sandwiches* -
Prime Catch | *Seafood* -
Roe's Casa Dolce | *Bakery/Italian* 24
Simply Thai | *Thai* 21
Taiko | *Asian* 24
Thai Table | *Thai* 23
Wild Ginger | *Asian* 21

ROSLYN/ ROSLYN HTS./ ROSLYN ESTATES

Z Besito | *Mex.* 24
Bistro Citron | *French* 21
Z Bryant & Cooper | *Steak* 26
Chalet Rest. | *Amer./Eclectic* 18
Chicken Kebab | *Greek/Turkish* 21
Colbeh | *Persian* 21
Green Cactus | *Mex.* 20
Z Il Mulino NY | *Italian* 27
Jolly Fisherman | *Seafood/Steak* 21
Z Kotobuki | *Japanese* 27
La Bottega | *Italian* 21
Z Limani | *Med./Seafood* 26
Z Matteo's | *Italian* 23
Mim's | *Amer.* 20
NEW MP Taverna | *Greek* -
Panini Café | *Sandwiches* 23
Poco Loco | *Mex.* 17
Ravagh | *Persian* 22
388 Rest. | *Amer./Italian* 20

Thyme | *Amer.* 21
Tratt. Diane | *Italian* 25
Tratt. Di Meo | *Italian* 21

SEA CLIFF

Allison's Amalfi | *Italian/Med.* 21
Met. Bistro | *Amer.* 22

SEAFORD

Z Butera's | *Italian* 21
Catfish Max | *Amer./Seafood* 21
NEW L.I.V.E. | *Veg.* -
NEW Phoenix | *Amer.* -
Runyon's | *Amer.* 18

SYOSSET

Angelina's | *Italian* 23
NEW Arata Sushi | *Japanese* -
Cafe Testarossa | *Continental* 22
Caracalla | *Italian* 23
Z Coolfish | *Seafood* 24
El Parral | *Italian/Spanish* 21
NEW 516 Amer. | *Amer.* -
Franina | *Italian* 26
Fulton Prime | *Seafood/Steak* 23
Galangal | *Japanese/Thai* 23
NEW Golden Temple | *Chinese/Japanese* -
NEW Mara's | *BBQ/Cajun* -
Mim's | *Amer.* 20
Mother Kelly's | *Amer./Italian* 21
Rachel's Cafe | *Italian* 22
Rare 650 | *Amer./Steak* 24
Steve's Piccola | *Italian* 24
Wild Fig | *Med./Turkish* 19

VALLEY STREAM

Chicken Coop | *Colombian* -
Itgen's | *Ice Cream* -
Seeda Thai | *Thai* 23

WANTAGH

Green Cactus | *Mex.* 20
Hemingway's | *Amer.* 19
Per Un Angelo | *Italian* 22
Sapporo | *Japanese* 23
Z Snaps | *Amer.* 26
Thom Thom | *Seafood/Steak* 20
Umberto's | *Italian/Pizza* 22

WESTBURY

Ayhan's Trodos | *Med.* 21
Azerbaijan | *Mideast.* 22

Benihana	*Japanese/Steak*	19
Benny's	*Italian*	25
Bertucci's	*Italian*	17
Z Cafe Baci	*Italian*	22
Z Cheesecake	*Amer.*	20
Chi	*Chinese/Eclectic*	25
City Cellar	*Amer.*	21
Cozymel's	*Mex.*	17
California Pizza Kit.	*Pizza*	17
Famous Dave's	*BBQ*	19
Galleria Rist.	*Italian*	26
Giulio Cesare	*Italian*	25
NEW La Casa Latina	*Pan-Latin*	-
Little Mexico	*Mex.*	-
Marco Polo's	*Asian/Italian*	-
Papa Razzi	*Italian*	18
P.F. Chang's	*Chinese*	20
Scotto's	*Italian/Pizza*	20
Shogi	*Japanese*	25
Steve's Piccola	*Italian*	24
Tesoro	*Italian*	23
Venere	*Italian*	20

WILLISTON PARK

Fresco Crêperie	*French*	23
Hildebrandt's	*Amer.*	19
Homura Sushi	*Japanese*	23
Ivy Cottage	*Amer.*	23
La Marmite	*French/Italian*	24
Z La Parma	*Italian*	23
Miraj	*Med./Persian*	-
Z Riverbay	*Seafood*	23
Sripraphai	*Thai*	25
Willy Parkers	*Amer.*	-

WOODBURY

Anthony's Pizza	*Pizza*	-
Z Ben's Deli	*Deli*	19
Z Butera's	*Italian*	21
Haiku Bistro/Sushi	*Asian*	24
Laguna Grille	*Nuevo Latino*	20
Majors Steak	*Steak*	19
Nisen	*Japanese*	25
Sage Bistro	*French*	24

Suffolk

AMAGANSETT

NEW Banzai Burger	*Burgers*	-
Clam Bar	*Seafood*	21
Cyril's Fish	*Seafood*	18
Hampton Chutney	*Indian*	22

Indian Wells	*Amer.*	17
Lobster Roll	*Seafood*	19
Meeting Hse.	*Amer./Med.*	20
Show Win	*Japanese*	20

AMITYVILLE

Bulldog Grille	*Amer./Continental*	-
Z Five Guys	*Burgers*	21
Vero	*Italian*	-
Vittorio's	*Amer./Italian*	25

AQUEBOGUE

Comtesse Thérèse Bistro	*French*	-
Modern Snack	*Amer.*	18

BABYLON/
NORTH BABYLON

Argyle Grill	*Amer.*	22
Babylon Carriage	*Continental*	21
Z Barrique Kit.	*Med.*	24
Green Cactus	*Mex.*	20
Horace/Sylvia's	*Amer.*	20
Z Kotobuki	*Japanese*	27
La Famiglia	*Italian*	22
Lucy's Café	*Amer.*	25
NEW Monsoon	*Asian*	-
Post Office	*Amer.*	19
Rist. Gemelli	*Italian*	24
Shiki (Babylon)	*Japanese*	24
Tricia's Café	*Amer.*	23

BAITING HOLLOW

Cooperage Inn	*Amer./Continental*	22
Lobster Roll N.	*Seafood*	20

BAYPORT

Fish Store	*Seafood*	-
Grey Horse	*Amer.*	23
Z Le Soir	*French*	27
Salsa Salsa	*Cal./Mex.*	23

BAY SHORE

Z Aji 53	*Japanese*	27
NEW Café Taka	*Med./Turkish*	-
Declan Quinn's	*Amer.*	19
Fatfish	*Med./Seafood*	21
Z Lake Hse.	*Amer.*	28
Milk & Sugar	*Amer.*	21
Mitsui	*Japanese*	24
Salvatore's	*Pizza*	25
Z Siam Lotus	*Thai*	28
Z Smokin' Al's	*BBQ*	23
Tula Kit.	*Eclectic*	24

BELLPORT

Bellport | *Amer./Continental*	22
Porters | *Seafood/Steak*	20
Spicy's BBQ | *BBQ*	20

BLUE POINT

Blue | *Amer.*	22
Blue Point Bistro | *Amer.*	-

BRIDGEHAMPTON

NEW Agave | *Mex.*	-
Almond | *French*	20
Bobby Van's | *Steak*	22
Bridgehampton Candy | *Diner*	15
Copa Wine | *Spanish*	20
Golden Pear Cafe | *Amer./Coffee*	18
Pierre's | *French*	21
Pizza Place | *Pizza*	24
Southfork | *Seafood*	-
World Pie | *Pizza*	19
Yama Q | *Japanese/Veg.*	23

BRIGHTWATERS

Sea Levels | *Amer./Seafood*	22

BROOKHAVEN HAMLET

Painters' | *Eclectic*	20

BROOKHAVEN/ ROCKY POINT

Caruso's | *Italian*	23
Sea Basin | *Italian/Seafood*	19
NEW Spiro's | *Steak*	-
Varney's | *Amer./Seafood*	23

CENTEREACH

Mama's | *Italian*	21
Pollo Rico | *Pan-Latin*	20

CENTER MORICHES

La Volpe | *Italian*	23

CENTERPORT

Mill Pond Hse. | *Seafood/Steak*	25

COLD SPRING HARBOR

Grasso's | *Amer.*	24
Harbor Mist | *Amer.*	19

COMMACK

Ciao Baby | *Italian*	20
Emilio's | *Pizza*	23

Z Five Guys | *Burgers*	21
Greek Village | *Greek*	19
NEW Grill 454 | *Steak*	-
Kiran Palace | *Indian*	24
Kurofune | *Japanese*	23
Nisen | *Japanese*	25
Perfecto Mundo | *Pan-Latin*	24
Souvlaki Palace | *Greek*	24
Spare Rib | *BBQ*	18

COPIAGUE

Thai Green Leaf | *Thai*	21

CUTCHOGUE

Red Rooster | *Amer.*	16
Touch/Venice | *Italian*	21

DEER PARK

Bellissimo Rist. | *Italian*	23
Chipotle | *Mex.*	20
Z Five Guys | *Burgers*	21
Ludlow Bistro | *Amer.*	24

EAST HAMPTON

Babette's | *Eclectic*	20
NEW Beach Hse. | *Seafood/Steak*	-
Blue Parrot | *Tex-Mex*	15
Boathouse | *Seafood*	19
Bostwick's | *Seafood*	20
Cafe Max | *Amer./Eclectic*	23
Cittanuova | *Italian*	20
NEW E. Hampton Grill | *Amer.*	-
Z E. Hampton Pt. | *Amer.*	19
Fresno | *Amer.*	22
Golden Pear Cafe | *Amer./Coffee*	18
Grill/Pantigo | *Amer.*	21
Harbor Bistro | *Amer.*	21
Harbor Grill | *Amer./Burgers*	-
Living Rm. | *Amer.*	25
Michaels'/Maidstone | *Amer.*	18
Nichol's | *Amer.*	17
Z Nick & Toni's | *Italian/Med.*	24
Z Palm | *Seafood/Steak*	26
Race Lane | *Amer.*	19
Rowdy Hall | *Pub*	20
Sam's | *Italian/Pizza*	18
Serafina | *Italian*	18
Z 1770 Hse. | *Amer.*	25
Shiki (E. Hampton) | *Japanese*	-
NEW Spring Close | *Amer.*	-

EAST MARION

Hellenic Snack | *Greek*	20

EAST MORICHES

Tony's | *Asian* — 19

EAST NORTHPORT

Baja Grill | *Mex.* — 18
Chefs of NY | *Italian/Pizza* — 19
Crossroads Cafe | *Amer.* — 22
Off the Hook | *Seafood* — 20
Thai Green Leaf | *Thai* — 21
Tokyo | *Japanese/Korean* — 24
Torcellos | *Italian* — 21
Wild Ginger | *Asian* — 21
Yokohama | *Japanese* — 23

EAST PATCHOGUE

Z Chachama | *Amer.* — 27

EASTPORT

Z Trumpets | *Amer./Continental* — 22

EAST SETAUKET

Bliss | *Amer.* — 22
Curry Club | *Indian* — 20
Domo Sushi | *Japanese* — 21
Pita House | *Med./Turkish* — 22
Tai Show | *Japanese* — 23

FARMINGVILLE

J&C 68 | *Asian* — ⌐

FIRE ISLAND

Hideaway | *Eclectic* — 19
Island Mermaid | *Amer./Seafood* — 20
Maguire's | *Amer.* — 19
Matthew's | *Seafood* — 22
Surf's Out | *Italian/Seafood* — 17
Top/Bay | *Amer.* — ⌐

FORT SALONGA

Intermezzo | *Italian* — 23

GREAT RIVER

George Martin's Steak | *Steak* — ⌐

GREENLAWN

Azuma | *Asian/Japanese* — 23
Goldmine Mex. | *Mex.* — 21
Old Fields | *Amer./Steak* — ⌐
Ruvo | *Italian* — 22

GREENPORT

Claudio's | *Amer./Continental* — 16
Cuvée | *French* — 22

Frisky Oyster | *Eclectic* — 25
Z Noah's | *Amer.* — 26
NEW North Fork Oyster | *Seafood* — ⌐
Porto Bello | *Italian* — 22
Salamander's | *Eclectic* — 24
Scrimshaw | *Amer.* — 23

HAMPTON BAYS

Edgewater | *Italian* — 22
Inn Spot/Bay | *Eclectic/Seafood* — 19
Matsulin | *Asian* — 22
Oakland's/Sunday | — 18
   Amer./Seafood
1 North Steak | *Steak* — 22
Rumba | *Carib.* — ⌐
Squiretown | *Amer.* — 20
Tide Runners | *Amer.* — 16
Tony's | *Asian* — 19
NEW TR Rest. | *Seafood* — ⌐

HAUPPAUGE

Bertucci's | *Italian* — 17
Butterfields | *Amer.* — 20
Cafe La Strada | *Italian* — 23
Chipotle | *Mex.* — 20
Ciro's | *Italian* — 22
Z Five Guys | *Burgers* — 21
Gasho/Japan | *Japanese/Steak* — 20
Grill Room | *Amer.* — 21
Z Kotobuki | *Japanese* — 27
Mario | *Italian* — 25
Pace's Steak | *Steak* — 22
Z San Marco | *Italian* — 26
Z Sempre Vivolo | *Italian* — 27
NEW Wobbly Olive | *Amer.* — ⌐

HOLBROOK

Mama's | *Italian* — 21
Mamma Lombardi's | *Italian* — 23
Trio | *Amer.* — 21

HUNTINGTON/ HUNTINGTON STATION

Albert's Mandarin | *Chinese* — 20
Almarco | *Italian* — 20
Amicale | *Continental* — 25
Ariana | *Afghan/Veg.* — 20
Z Besito | *Mex.* — 24
Best Buffet | *Chinese/Eclectic* — 18
Bin 56 | *Spanish* — 24
Z Bistro Cassis | *French* — 24
Black & Blue | *Seafood/Steak* — 22
Bonbori Tiki | *Japanese/Thai* — 20

Bravo Nader!/Fish	*Italian/Seafood*	24
Café Buenos Aires	*Argent.*	24
☑ Cheesecake	*Amer.*	20
Chipotle	*Mex.*	20
Cirella's	*Amer./Eclectic*	21
Clubhouse	*Steak*	21
California Pizza Kit.	*Pizza*	17
Crew Kit.	*Amer.*	24
Fado	*Portug.*	21
F.H. Riley's	*Amer.*	23
☑ Five Guys	*Burgers*	21
Green Cactus	*Mex.*	20
Honu Kit.	*Amer.*	22
House/India	*Indian*	21
NEW Huntington Social	*Amer.*	-
Jonathan's Rist.	*Italian*	24
Kabul Afghani	*Afghan*	23
Kura Barn	*Japanese*	24
☑ La Parma	*Italian*	23
La Spada	*Italian*	21
NEW Legacy	*Asian*	-
Legal Sea Foods	*Seafood*	20
Los Compadres	*Mex.*	23
Mac's Steak	*Steak*	23
Massa's	*Pizza*	23
☑ Matteo's	*Italian*	23
Med. Snack	*Greek/Med.*	22
Oaxaca Mex.	*Mex.*	23
Osaka	*Japanese*	24
Osteria da Nino	*Italian*	24
PG Steak	*Steak*	22
Piccola Bussola	*Italian*	23
☑ Piccolo	*Amer./Italian*	27
Pomodorino	*Italian*	19
Porto Vivo	*Italian*	22
☑ Prime	*Amer.*	23
NEW Primo Piatto	*Italian*	-
Quetzalcoatl	*Mex.*	20
Ravagh	*Persian*	22
Café Red/Red	*Amer.*	25
Samurai	*Japanese*	24
Sapsuckers	*Amer.*	-
Spice Village	*Pakistani/Persian*	20
Sri Thai	*Thai*	22
Swallow	*Amer.*	-
Thai USA	*Thai*	23
34 New St.	*Eclectic*	18
Toast & Co.	*Amer.*	18
Tomo Hibachi	*Japanese*	20
Tutto Pazzo	*Italian*	20
Vitae	*Continental*	-
NEW XO	*Amer.*	-

ISLANDIA

Takara	*Japanese*	28

ISLIP

(Including Central, East, West)

Carrabba's	*Italian*	19
Irish Coffee	*Continental/Irish*	23
Jackson Hall	*Amer.*	-
Maxwell's	*Amer.*	-
Nonnina	*Italian*	25
☑ Tellers	*Steak*	26
☑ Verace	*Italian*	26

JAMESPORT/ SOUTH JAMESPORT

Bayview Inn	*Amer./Continental*	22
Cliff's	*Steak*	22
Jamesport Country	*Amer.*	23
☑ Jamesport Manor	*Amer.*	23
☑ Luce & Hawkins	*Amer.*	25

KINGS PARK

Café Red/Red	*Amer.*	25
Ciro's	*Italian*	22
Dixie's	*BBQ*	-
Long River	*Asian*	21
NEW Relish	*Amer.*	-
Sarin Thai	*Thai*	24

LAKE GROVE

Bobby's Burger	*Burgers*	21
☑ Cheesecake	*Amer.*	20
California Pizza Kit.	*Pizza*	17
John Harvard's	*Pub*	16

LAUREL

Cliff's	*Steak*	22

LINDENHURST

Bozena Polish	*Polish*	23
Cattlemen's	*Steak*	19
Southside Fish	*Seafood*	20
Village Lanterne	*German*	25

MATTITUCK

A Mano	*Italian*	24
Iron Skillet	*Amer.*	-
Love Ln.	*Amer.*	23
Old Mill Inn	*Amer./Seafood*	20
Tony's	*Asian*	19

MELVILLE

Barolo	*Continental/Italian*	25
Bertucci's	*Italian*	17
☑ Blackstone Steak	*Steak*	24

Cirella's | *Continental/Italian* 21
Four Food Studio | *Amer.* 21
Frederick's | *Continental* 23
NEW Jewel | *Amer.* -
La Piazza | *Pizza* 21
NEW Roast | *Sandwiches* -

MIDDLE ISLAND

Cookroom | *Amer.* -

MILLER PLACE

Blond | *Amer.* 21
NEW Orto | *Italian* -
Sabai Thai | *Thai* 22

MONTAUK

Backyard | *Med.* 23
Crow's Nest | *Seafood* 19
☑ Dave's Grill | *Continental/Seafood* 27
Dock B&G | *Seafood* -
Duryea's Lobster | *Seafood* 22
East/ Northeast | *Amer./Asian* 21
Fishbar | *Seafood* 18
Gosman's Dock | *Seafood* 19
Gulf Coast | *Italian* 21
☑ Harvest | *Italian/Med.* 26
Inlet Seafood | *Seafood* 21
Manucci's | *Italian/Pizza* 19
Navy Beach | *Amer.* 19
NEW Ruschmeyer's | *Amer.* -
Sea Grille | *Amer./Italian* 21
Shagwong | *Amer./Seafood* 18
South Edison | *Amer.* 22
Surf Lodge | *Amer.* 19
Surfside Inn | *Continental/Seafood* 18

MOUNT SINAI

Alexandros | *Greek/Med.* 23
Lotus East | *Chinese* 21
NEW Ten Ten Bistro | *Asian* -

NESCONSET

JT's Corner | *Amer.* 23
Ragazzi | *Italian* -
Sundried Tomato | *Italian/Pizza* 21
Tate's | *Amer./Italian* 26

NEW SUFFOLK

Legends | *Eclectic* 23

NORTHPORT

Batata Café | *Eclectic* 21
Benkei | *Japanese* 23

Bistro 44 | *Amer.* 23
NEW J. Michaels | *Steak* -
☑ Maroni Cuisine | *Eclectic/Italian* 28
Pumpernickels | *German* 21
Ritz Cafe | *Continental* 19
Show Win | *Japanese* 20
Sweet Mama's | *Diner* 19
Whale's Tale | *Seafood* 20

OAKDALE

Green Cactus | *Mex.* 20
Mama's | *Italian* 21
Onsen Sushi | *Japanese* -
Snapper Inn | *Seafood* 18
Tai Show | *Japanese* 23
View | *Amer./Continental* 22
Viva La Vida | *Mex./Spanish* 20

PATCHOGUE

BobbiQue | *BBQ* 21
Harbor Crab | *Seafood* 18
Lombardi's/Bay | *Seafood/Steak* 23
Oar Steak | *Seafood/Steak* 21
PeraBell | *Amer./Eclectic* 26
Pita House | *Med./Turkish* 22
Public Hse. 49 | *Amer.* 20

PORT JEFFERSON/ PORT JEFFERSON STATION

Carnival | *Italian* 22
Cattlemen's | *Steak* 19
Fifth Season | *Amer.* 26
☑ Five Guys | *Burgers* 21
Lemonleaf Grill | *Thai* 22
Lombardi's/Sound | *Italian* 21
Pace's Steak | *Steak* 22
Pasta Pasta | *Italian* 25
Pie | *Pizza* 21
Ruvo | *Italian* 22
Salsa Salsa | *Cal./Mex.* 23
Tequila Jacks | *Carib./Seafood* 18
Thai Gourmet | *Thai* 26
Toast | *Eclectic* 24
Wave Seafood | *Amer.* 19
Zorba/Greek | *Greek* 19

QUOGUE/ EAST QUOGUE

Dockers Waterside | *Seafood/Steak* 20
☑ Stone Creek | *French/Med.* 26
Tony's | *Asian* 19

RIVERHEAD

Athens Grill	*Greek/Med.*	-
Birchwood	*Amer./Polish*	20
Bistro 72	*Amer.*	-
Buoy One	*Seafood*	23
Cliff's	*Steak*	22
NEW Cody's	*BBQ*	-
Dark Horse	*Amer./Eclectic*	-
Farm Country Kit.	*Amer.*	23
Haiku	*Japanese*	-
NEW Riverhead Pjt.	*Amer.*	-
Spicy's BBQ	*BBQ*	20
Star Confectionery	*Amer./Diner*	22
Stonewalls	*Amer./French*	23
Tweeds	*Amer.*	21

SAGAPONACK

Townline	*BBQ*	19

SAG HARBOR

Z American Hotel	*Amer./French*	25
Bay Burger	*Burgers*	21
Beacon	*Amer.*	22
B.Smith's	*Cajun/Southern*	18
Dockside B&G	*Seafood*	21
Estia's	*Amer.*	23
Golden Pear Cafe	*Amer./Coffee*	18
Il Capuccino	*Italian*	19
LT Burger	*Burgers*	16
Muse	*Amer.*	23
New Paradise	*Amer./Eclectic*	22
NEW Page/63 Main	*Eclectic*	-
Phao	*Thai*	21
Sen	*Japanese*	21
Tutto Il Giorno	*Italian*	25

SAYVILLE

Bistro 25	*Eclectic*	-
Blackbirds' Grille	*Cajun/Southern*	20
Z Butera's	*Italian*	21
Cafe Joelle	*Amer./Eclectic*	22
Cull Hse.	*Seafood*	20
Downtown Burger	*Amer./Burgers*	-
NEW Fusion 84	*Amer.*	-
La Tavola	*Italian*	22

SELDEN

Viva Juan	*Mex.*	21

SHELTER ISLAND/ SHELTER ISLAND HEIGHTS

Chequit Inn	*Amer./Eclectic*	19
NEW 18 Bay	*Italian*	-

Kyle's	*Amer.*	-
NEW La Maison Blanche	*French*	-
Ram's Head	*Amer./Eclectic*	20
Sunset Beach	*Asian/French*	18
Vine Street	*Amer.*	25

SHOREHAM

NEW Oceans 5	*Seafood*	-

SMITHTOWN

Z Aji 53	*Japanese*	27
American Burger	*Burgers*	18
Arthur Avenue	*Amer.*	-
Baja Grill	*Mex.*	18
Z Butera's	*Italian*	21
Cafe Havana	*Cuban*	18
Carrabba's	*Italian*	19
Casa Luis	*Spanish*	22
Casa Rustica	*Italian*	25
Chop Shop	*Amer.*	24
DiMaggio's	*Italian*	19
Famous Dave's	*BBQ*	19
Garden Grill	*Amer.*	21
Hotoke	*Japanese/Steak*	21
H2O Seafood	*Seafood*	23
NEW Insignia	*Seafood/Steak*	-
La Famiglia	*Italian*	22
La Panchita	*Mex./Spanish*	22
Luso	*Portug.*	22
Maureen/Daughers'	*Amer.*	25
Rockwell's B&G	*Amer.*	22
Salsa Salsa	*Cal./Mex.*	23
Thai Hse.	*Thai*	24
Uncle Bacala's	*Italian/Seafood*	21

SOUTHAMPTON

Coast Grill	*Amer./Seafood*	22
Golden Pear Cafe	*Amer./Coffee*	18
La Parmigiana	*Italian*	22
Le Chef	*Continental/French*	22
NEW Litttle Red	*Amer.*	-
Nello Summertimes	*Italian*	16
NEW Nobu/Capri	*Japanese*	-
Z Plaza Café	*Seafood*	26
Red Bar	*Amer./French*	22
Sant Ambroeus	*Italian*	24
Savanna's	*Amer.*	20
75 Main	*Italian*	18
Silver's	*Eclectic*	23
Southampton Publick	*Pub*	18
NEW Southampton Social	*Amer.*	-
Tuscan Hse.	*Italian*	22
Tutto Il Giorno	*Italian*	25

SOUTHOLD

NEW A Lure | *Seafood* -

Elbow East | *Steak* 19

Z North Fork Table | *Amer.* 29

O'Mally's | *Pub* 18

SPEONK

NEW Martini Grill | *Med.* -

ST. JAMES

Ancient Ginger | *Chinese* 21

NEW Del Fuego | *Tex-Mex* -

NEW España Tapas | *Spanish* -

Z Kitchen A Bistro | *French* 27

Z Kitchen A Tratt. | *Italian* 28

Lotus East | *Chinese* 21

Z Mosaic | *Amer.* 28

O's Food | *French* 22

Vintage Prime | *Steak* 25

Voila! | *French* 24

STONY BROOK

Z Country Hse. | *Amer.* 23

Green Cactus | *Mex.* 20

Mirabelle, Rest. | *French* 25

Mirabelle Tavern | *Amer.* 21

Pentimento | *Italian* 22

Robinson's Tea | *Tea* 23

WADING RIVER

Amarelle | *Amer.* 25

Blackwells | *Steak* 23

Desmond's | *Amer.* 20

Z La Plage | *Eclectic* 27

Michael Anthony's | *Eclectic* 24

WAINSCOTT

Georgica | *Amer.* 18

WATER MILL

Dish | *Amer.* 27

Foody's | *BBQ/Pizza* 21

Hampton Coffee | *Coffee* 19

Z Mirko's | *Eclectic* 26

Robert's | *Italian* 25

Suki Zuki | *Japanese* 24

Trata | *Greek/Seafood* 22

WESTHAMPTON/ WESTHAMPTON BEACH

Baby Moon | *Italian* 18

Buoy One | *Seafood* 23

Dee Angelo's | *Italian* 19

Hampton Coffee | *Coffee* 19

Patio/54 Main | *Amer.* 19

Post Stop | *Amer.* 17

Z Starr Boggs | *Amer./Seafood* 26

Tony's | *Asian* 19

WEST SAYVILLE

21 Main | *Steak* 23

LOCATIONS

Special Features

Listings cover the best in each category and include names, locations and Food ratings. Multi-location restaurants' features may vary by branch.

ADDITIONS

(Properties added since the last edition of the book)

Agave | **Bridgehampton**
Alaine's | **Massapequa**
A Lure | **Southold**
Andiamo | **Mineola**
Angelina's Fireshack | **New Hyde Pk**
Anthony's Pizza | **multi.**
Antonette's | **Rockville Ctr**
Arata Sushi | **Syosset**
Athens Grill | **Riverhead**
Banzai Burger | **Amagansett**
Beach Hse. | **E Hampton**
Bistro Etc. | **Port Washington**
Burger Spot | **Garden City**
Café Taka | **Bay Shore**
Caracara Mex. | **Farmingdale**
Cody's | **Riverhead**
Cookroom | **Middle Island**
Del Fuego | **St. James**
DoraNonnie | **Glen Head**
E. Hampton Grill | **E Hampton**
18 Bay | **Shelter Is**
El Pio | **Glen Cove**
España Tapas | **St. James**
516 Amer. | **Syosset**
420 North | **Great Neck**
Frankly Thai | **Franklin Sq**
Fusion 84 | **Sayville**
Golden Temple | **Syosset**
Grill 454 | **Commack**
Huntington Social | **Huntington**
Insignia | **Smithtown**
Iron Skillet | **Mattituck**
Itgen's | **Valley Stream**
Jack's Shack | **Glen Head**
Jake's Steak | **E Meadow**
Jewel | **Melville**
J. Michaels | **Northport**
Joe's Crab Shack | **Oceanside**
K·Pacho | **New Hyde Pk**
Kyle's | **Shelter Is**
La Casa Latina | **Westbury**
La Maison Blanche | **Shelter Is Hts**
Las Viñas | **Manhasset**

Lawson Pub | **Oceanside**
Left Coast | **Merrick**
Legacy | **Huntington**
Little Mexico | **Westbury**
Litttle Red | **Southampton**
L.I.V.E. | **Seaford**
Mara's | **Syosset**
Market Bistro | **Jericho**
Martini Grill | **Speonk**
Meridian | **Locust Valley**
Mint | **Garden City**
Miraku | **Great Neck**
Mitch/Toni's | **Albertson**
Monsoon | **Babylon**
MP Taverna | **Roslyn**
Nobu/Capri | **Southampton**
North Fork Oyster | **Greenport**
Oceans 5 | **Shoreham**
Orto | **Miller Pl**
Page/63 Main | **Sag Harbor**
Passione | **Carle Pl**
Patio | **Freeport**
Phoenix | **Seaford**
Pop's Seafood | **Island Pk**
Prime Burger | **Albertson**
Primo Piatto | **Huntington**
Ragazzi | **Nesconset**
Red Tomato | **E Norwich**
Relish | **Kings Park**
Riverhead Pjt. | **Riverhead**
Roast | **Melville**
Rumba | **Hampton Bays**
Ruschmeyer's | **Montauk**
Saffron | **Glen Head**
Salumi Tapas | **Massapequa**
Serata | **Oyster Bay**
Smashburger | **Hicksville**
Southampton Social | **Southampton**
Southern Spice | **New Hyde Pk**
Spiro's | **Rocky Pt**
Spring Close | **E Hampton**
Sweet Tomato | **multi.**
Tappo | **Glen Cove**
Tavern/Plaza | **Locust Valley**
Ten Ten Bistro | **Mount Sinai**
TR Rest. | **Hampton Bays**
Verona | **Farmingdale**

Vine Wine Bar | **Merrick**	⎤
Vinoco | **Mineola**	⎤
Willy Parkers | **Williston Pk**	⎤
Wobbly Olive | **Hauppauge**	⎤
Xaga Sushi | **multi.**	⎤
XO | **Huntington**	⎤

BOAT DOCKING FACILITIES

NEW A Lure | **Southold**	⎤
Boathouse | **E Hampton**	19⎤
B.Smith's | **Sag Harbor**	18⎤
Catfish Max | **Seaford**	21⎤
Claudio's | **Greenport**	16⎤
Coast Grill | **Southampton**	22⎤
Dockers Waterside | **E Quogue**	20⎤
☑ E. Hampton Pt. | **E Hampton**	19⎤
Fatfish | **Bay Shore**	21⎤
Fishbar | **Montauk**	18⎤
Fisherman's Catch | **Point Lookout**	20⎤
Gosman's Dock | **Montauk**	19⎤
Harbor Crab | **Patchogue**	18⎤
Louie's Oyster | **Port Washington**	17⎤
Maguire's | **Ocean Beach**	19⎤
Oakland's/Sunday | **Hampton Bays**	18⎤
Oar Steak | **Patchogue**	21⎤
Old Mill Inn | **Mattituck**	20⎤
Paddy McGees | **Island Pk**	18⎤
NEW Patio | **Freeport**	⎤
Pier 95 | **Freeport**	24⎤
NEW Pop's Seafood | **Island Pk**	⎤
☑ Prime | **Huntington**	23⎤
Rachel's Waterside | **Freeport**	20⎤
Ram's Head | **Shelter Is**	20⎤
Schooner | **Freeport**	17⎤
Scrimshaw | **Greenport**	23⎤
Snapper Inn | **Oakdale**	18⎤
Surf's Out | **Kismet**	17⎤
Tide Runners | **Hampton Bays**	16⎤
View | **Oakdale**	22⎤
Villa D'Aqua | **Bellmore**	21⎤
Wildfish | **Freeport**	21⎤

BREAKFAST

(See also Hotel Dining)

Ayhan's Shish | **Port Washington**	18⎤
Babette's | **E Hampton**	20⎤
Batata Café | **Northport**	21⎤
Bridgehampton Candy | **Bridgehampton**	15⎤
Buckram Stables | **Locust Valley**	19⎤

Cookroom | **Middle Island**	⎤
Cuvée | **Greenport**	22⎤
Estia's | **Sag Harbor**	23⎤
Golden Pear Cafe | **multi.**	18⎤
Hampton Coffee | **Water Mill**	19⎤
Hellenic Snack | **E Marion**	20⎤
International Delight | **multi.**	18⎤
Itgen's | **Valley Stream**	⎤
JT's Corner | **Nesconset**	23⎤
Lombardi's/Sound | **Port Jefferson**	21⎤
Love Ln. | **Mattituck**	23⎤
Maureen/Daughers' | **Smithtown**	25⎤
Post Stop | **Westhampton Bch**	17⎤
Robinson's Tea | **Stony Brook**	23⎤
Star Confectionery | **Riverhead**	22⎤
Sweet Mama's | **Northport**	19⎤
Thomas's Eggery | **Carle Pl**	22⎤
Toast | **Port Jefferson**	24⎤

BRUNCH

Ayhan's Shish | **multi.**	18⎤
☑ Bistro Cassis | **Huntington**	24⎤
Bistro Citron | **Roslyn**	21⎤
Bistro 25 | **Sayville**	⎤
Blackbirds' Grille | **Sayville**	20⎤
Bobby Van's | **Bridgehampton**	22⎤
B.Smith's | **Sag Harbor**	18⎤
Cafe Joelle | **Sayville**	22⎤
Cafe Max | **E Hampton**	23⎤
Canterbury | **Oyster Bay**	19⎤
☑ Cheesecake | **Westbury**	20⎤
Cooperage Inn | **Baiting Hollow**	22⎤
Desmond's | **Wading River**	20⎤
☑ E. Hampton Pt. | **E Hampton**	19⎤
56th Fighter | **Farmingdale**	16⎤
Garden Grill | **Smithtown**	21⎤
Gonzalo's | **Glen Cove**	21⎤
Hemingway's | **Wantagh**	19⎤
H.R. Singleton's | **Bethpage**	18⎤
☑ Jamesport Manor | **Jamesport**	23⎤
Jonathan's | **Garden City Pk**	20⎤
Library Cafe | **Farmingdale**	18⎤
☑ Limani | **Roslyn**	26⎤
Lombardi's/Sound | **Port Jefferson**	21⎤
Louie's Oyster | **Port Washington**	17⎤
Milleridge Inn | **Jericho**	16⎤
Paddy McGees | **Island Pk**	18⎤
Painters' | **Brookhaven Hamlet**	20⎤
☑ Palm Court | **E Meadow**	24⎤
Pierre's | **Bridgehampton**	21⎤

Pine Island | **Bayville**	18
Z Prime | **Huntington**	23
Rachel's Waterside | **Freeport**	20
Ram's Head | **Shelter Is**	20
Rein | **Garden City**	23
Ritz Cafe | **Northport**	19
Z Rothmann's | **E Norwich**	25
Snapper Inn | **Oakdale**	18
Southampton Publick | **Southampton**	18
Stonewalls | **Riverhead**	23
Z Trumpets | **Eastport**	22
Z Waterzooi | **Garden City**	24
Wild Ginger | **Great Neck**	21
World Pie | **Bridgehampton**	19

BUSINESS DINING

NEW A Lure | **Southold**	–
Amarelle | **Wading River**	25
Amicale | **Huntington Station**	25
NEW Andiamo | **Mineola**	–
Athens Grill | **Riverhead**	–
Z Atlantica | **Long Bch**	20
Benihana | **Manhasset**	19
Benny's | **Westbury**	25
Z Blackstone Steak | **Melville**	24
Bobby Van's | **Bridgehampton**	22
Z Bryant & Cooper | **Roslyn**	26
Burton & Doyle | **Great Neck**	24
Butterfields | **Hauppauge**	20
Café Capriccio | **Port Washington**	24
Caracalla | **Syosset**	23
Clubhouse | **Huntington**	21
NEW E. Hampton Grill | **E Hampton**	–
Z E. Hampton Pt. | **E Hampton**	19
NEW 18 Bay | **Shelter Is**	–
Fork & Vine | **Glen Head**	23
NEW 420 North | **Great Neck**	–
Franina | **Syosset**	26
Frederick's | **Melville**	23
Fulton Prime | **Syosset**	23
NEW Fusion 84 | **Sayville**	–
Giulio Cesare | **Westbury**	25
Z Il Mulino NY | **Roslyn Estates**	27
NEW Insignia | **Smithtown**	–
NEW Jake's Steak | **E Meadow**	–
Z Jamesport Manor | **Jamesport**	23
NEW Jewel | **Melville**	–
NEW J. Michaels | **Northport**	–
Jolly Fisherman | **Roslyn**	21
Jonathan's Rist. | **Huntington**	24
La Coquille | **Manhasset**	24

La Pace/Chef Michael | **Glen Cove**	25
Z La Piccola | **Port Washington**	27
Z Limani | **Roslyn**	26
Lola | **Great Neck**	24
Lombardi's/Sound | **Port Jefferson**	21
Z Luce & Hawkins | **Jamesport**	25
Mac's Steak | **Huntington**	23
Manucci's | **Montauk**	19
Mirabelle, Rest. | **Stony Brook**	25
NEW Mitch/Toni's | **Albertson**	–
NEW Monsoon | **Babylon**	–
Z Morton's | **Great Neck**	25
Muse | **Sag Harbor**	23
Nick's Tuscan | **Long Bch**	21
Nonnina | **W Islip**	25
NEW Orto | **Miller Pl**	–
Z Palm | **E Hampton**	26
Palmer's | **Farmingdale**	21
Patio/54 Main | **Westhampton Bch**	19
Z Peter Luger | **Great Neck**	27
Z Piccolo | **Huntington**	27
Z Plaza Café | **Southampton**	26
Z Prime | **Huntington**	23
Rare 650 | **Syosset**	24
Z Riverbay | **Williston Pk**	23
NEW Riverhead Pjt. | **Riverhead**	–
Robert's | **Water Mill**	25
Z Rothmann's | **E Norwich**	25
Z Ruth's Chris | **Garden City**	25
Sea Grille | **Montauk**	21
Z Sempre Vivolo | **Hauppauge**	27
Show Win | **Northport**	20
NEW Spiro's | **Rocky Pt**	–
NEW Spring Close | **E Hampton**	–
Z Stone Creek | **E Quogue**	26
Stresa | **Manhasset**	25
NEW Tappo | **Glen Cove**	–
Taste 99 | **Farmingdale**	18
Z Tellers | **Islip**	26
Touch/Venice | **Cutchogue**	21
Trio | **Holbrook**	21
Z Trumpets | **Eastport**	22
Tutto Il Giorno | **Southampton**	25
Verona | **Farmingdale**	–
Vespa | **Great Neck**	22
NEW XO | **Huntington**	–

BYO

Afghan Grill | **New Hyde Pk**	20
Almarco | **Huntington**	20
Amicale | **Huntington Station**	25

Angelina's | **Syosset**	23
Asian Moon | **Massapequa Pk**	23
⊠ Barney's | **Locust Valley**	26
Barolo | **Melville**	25
⊠ Barrique Kit. | **Babylon**	24
Bay Burger | **Sag Harbor**	21
Bayview Inn | **S Jamesport**	22
Bigelow's | **Rockville Ctr**	24
⊠ Bistro Cassis | **Huntington**	24
Bistro Citron | **Roslyn**	21
⊠ Blackstone Steak | **Melville**	24
Bob's Rest. | **Floral Pk**	21
Brasserie Persil | **Oceanside**	25
⊠ Bryant & Cooper | **Roslyn**	26
Burton & Doyle | **Great Neck**	24
Cafe Testarossa | **Syosset**	22
Caffe Laguna | **Long Bch**	19
⊠ Chez Noëlle | **Port Washington**	27
Ciao Baby | **Massapequa Pk**	20
Cipollini | **Manhasset**	21
Ciro's | **Kings Park**	22
Clubhouse | **Huntington**	21
Coach Grill | **Oyster Bay**	22
Colbeh | **Roslyn Estates**	21
⊠ Coolfish | **Syosset**	24
Crave 11025 | **Great Neck**	18
Crossroads Cafe | **E Northport**	22
Deli King | **New Hyde Pk**	19
Dish | **Water Mill**	27
Dockers Waterside | **E Quogue**	20
Dockside B&G | **Sag Harbor**	21
Dosa Diner | **Hicksville**	23
Duryea's Lobster | **Montauk**	22
East/ Northeast | **Montauk**	21
⊠ E. Hampton Pt. | **E Hampton**	19
Elbow East | **Southold**	19
Ernesto's East | **Glen Head**	22
Farm Country Kit. | **Riverhead**	23
Fork & Vine | **Glen Head**	23
Fresco Crêperie | **Williston Pk**	23
Frisky Oyster | **Greenport**	25
Fulton Prime | **Syosset**	23
Galleria Rist. | **Westbury**	26
George Martin's Steak | **Great River**	–
Gosman's Dock | **Montauk**	19
Grill/Pantigo | **E Hampton**	21
Haiku | **Riverhead**	–
Harbor Grill | **E Hampton**	–
⊠ Harvest | **Montauk**	26
Heart/Portugal | **Mineola**	20
Hellenic Snack | **E Marion**	20

Il Capuccino | **Sag Harbor**	19
Indian Wells | **Amagansett**	17
Inn Spot/Bay | **Hampton Bays**	19
International Delight | **multi.**	18
Jimmy Hays | **Island Pk**	25
Kiran Palace | **Levittown**	24
⊠ Kitchen A Bistro | **St. James**	27
⊠ Kitchen A Tratt. | **St. James**	28
La Pace/Chef Michael | **Glen Cove**	25
⊠ La Plage | **Wading River**	27
La P'tite Framboise | **Port Washington**	22
Le Chef | **Southampton**	22
Living Rm. | **E Hampton**	25
Main St. Bakery | **Port Washington**	–
Marco Polo's | **Westbury**	–
⊠ Maroni Cuisine | **Northport**	28
Massa's | **Huntington Station**	23
Matsulin | **Hampton Bays**	22
Meeting Hse. | **Amagansett**	20
NEW Meridian | **Locust Valley**	–
Michael Anthony's | **Wading River**	24
Michaels'/Maidstone | **E Hampton**	18
Nautilus Cafe | **Freeport**	24
New Chilli/Curry | **Hicksville**	26
Nichol's | **E Hampton**	17
⊠ Nick & Toni's | **E Hampton**	24
Nick's Tuscan | **Long Bch**	21
Nonnina | **W Islip**	25
Novitá Wine Bar & Trattoria | **Garden City**	23
Off the Hook | **E Northport**	20
Onzon Thai | **Bellmore**	24
O's Food | **St. James**	22
Osteria da Nino | **Huntington**	24
Pace's Steak | **multi.**	22
⊠ Palm | **E Hampton**	26
⊠ Palm Court | **E Meadow**	24
Patio/54 Main | **Westhampton Bch**	19
PeraBell | **Patchogue**	26
PG Steak | **Huntington**	22
Piccola Bussola | **multi.**	23
⊠ Piccolo | **Huntington**	27
Piccolo's | **Mineola**	24
Pie | **Port Jefferson**	21
Salvatore's | **Bay Shore**	25
Pierre's | **Bridgehampton**	21
Poco Loco | **Roslyn**	17
Porto Bello | **Greenport**	22
Porto Vivo | **Huntington**	22

Ram's Head | **Shelter Is**	20
Rare 650 | **Syosset**	24
Café Red/Red | **Huntington**	25
Red Fish | **Plainview**	23
Rein | **Garden City**	23
Rist. Gemelli | **Babylon**	24
Roe's Casa Dolce | **Rockville Ctr**	24
Sabai Thai | **Miller Pl**	22
Sakaya | **Albertson**	-
Salsa Salsa | **Smithtown**	23
☑ 1770 Hse. | **E Hampton**	25
NEW Southern Spice | **New Hyde Pk**	-
Sushi Palace | **Great Neck**	24
Taiko | **Rockville Ctr**	24
NEW Tappo | **Glen Cove**	-
Tate's | **Nesconset**	26
Thai Gourmet | **Port Jefferson Station**	26
Tratt. Diane | **Roslyn**	25
Trio | **Holbrook**	21
Turquoise | **Great Neck**	21
Vero | **Amityville**	-
Vespa | **Great Neck**	22
Vine Street | **Shelter Is**	25
Voila! | **St. James**	24
Walk St. | **Garden City**	21
West East | **Hicksville**	25
Wild Honey | **multi.**	25
World Pie | **Bridgehampton**	19

CATERING

Akbar | **Garden City**	22
Barolo | **Melville**	25
Bayou | **N Bellmore**	23
Bellport | **Bellport**	22
Big Daddy's | **Massapequa**	24
Blond | **Miller Pl**	21
Brio | **Port Washington**	21
Butterfields | **Hauppauge**	20
☑ Cafe Baci | **Westbury**	22
Café Capriccio | **Port Washington**	24
Cafe Joelle | **Sayville**	22
Cafe La Strada | **Hauppauge**	23
Cafe Toscano | **Massapequa**	21
Caffe Laguna | **Long Bch**	19
Casa Rustica | **Smithtown**	25
Ciao Baby | **multi.**	20
Colbeh | **Great Neck**	21
☑ Coolfish | **Syosset**	24
Curry Club | **E Setauket**	20
Cuvée | **Greenport**	22
☑ Dario's | **Rockville Ctr**	26

E. B. Elliot's | **Freeport**	18
Fresno | **E Hampton**	22
Galleria Rist. | **Westbury**	26
George Martin | **Rockville Ctr**	22
Golden Pear Cafe | **multi.**	18
Heart/Portugal | **Mineola**	20
House/Dosas | **Hicksville**	25
H.R. Singleton's | **Bethpage**	18
Iavarone Cafe | **New Hyde Pk**	21
Il Classico | **Massapequa Pk**	23
Ivy Cottage | **Williston Pk**	23
Jack Halyards | **Oyster Bay**	23
Jamesport Country | **Jamesport**	23
Kiran Palace | **Hicksville**	24
La Famiglia | **Smithtown**	22
La Gioconda | **Great Neck**	21
Laguna Grille | **Woodbury**	20
La Piazza | **multi.**	21
☑ La Plage | **Wading River**	27
La Terrazza | **Cedarhurst**	22
Lemonleaf Grill | **Hicksville**	22
Lemonleaf Thai | **Carle Pl**	20
Lombardi's/Sound | **Port Jefferson**	21
Lotus East | **multi.**	21
Mamma Lombardi's | **Holbrook**	23
☑ Maroni Cuisine | **Northport**	28
Mirabelle, Rest. | **Stony Brook**	25
Mother Kelly's | **Cedarhurst**	21
Nagashima | **Jericho**	24
Nicholas James | **Merrick**	22
Nick's | **Rockville Ctr**	23
Nisen | **Commack**	25
Orchid | **Garden City**	23
O's Food | **St. James**	22
Pace's Steak | **multi.**	22
Page One | **Glen Cove**	22
☑ Palm Court | **E Meadow**	24
Pasta-eria | **Hicksville**	23
Pasta Pasta | **Port Jefferson**	25
Pastrami King | **Merrick**	20
Piccola Bussola | **multi.**	23
Pita House | **Patchogue**	22
☑ Plaza Café | **Southampton**	26
Rachel's Waterside | **Freeport**	20
Rangmahal | **Hicksville**	23
RS Jones | **Merrick**	22
Salamander's | **Greenport**	24
Salsa Salsa | **multi.**	23
☑ San Marco | **Hauppauge**	26
Sapporo | **Wantagh**	23
Shiki (Babylon) | **Babylon**	24

☑ Siam Lotus | **Bay Shore**	28
☑ Smokin' Al's | **Bay Shore**	23
☑ Snaps | **Wantagh**	26
Solé | **Oceanside**	26
Southside Fish | **Lindenhurst**	20
Spare Rib | **Commack**	18
☑ Stone Creek | **E Quogue**	26
Stresa | **Manhasset**	25
Sundried Tomato | **Nesconset**	21
Taiko | **Rockville Ctr**	24
Tai Show | **multi.**	23
Tesoro | **Westbury**	23
Thai Gourmet | **Port Jefferson Station**	26
Thai Table | **Rockville Ctr**	23
Thyme | **Roslyn**	21
Umberto's | **New Hyde Pk**	22
Uncle Dai's | **Glen Cove**	18
Venere | **Westbury**	20
Viva La Vida | **Oakdale**	20
Voila! | **St. James**	24
Walk St. | **Garden City**	21
☑ West End | **Carle Pl**	25
World Pie | **Bridgehampton**	19

CELEBRITY CHEFS

Starr Boggs
☑ Starr Boggs | **Westhampton Bch**	26

Joe Bonacore
NEW Lawson Pub | **Oceanside**	⎤

Philippe Corbet
O's Food | **St. James**	22

George Echeverria
NEW Andiamo | **Mineola**	⎤

Massimo Fedozzi
Vero | **Amityville**	⎤

Bobby Flay
Bobby's Burger | **multi.**	21

Claudia Fleming/Gerry Hayden
☑ North Fork Table | **Southold**	29

Danny Gagnon
NEW DoraNonnie | **Glen Head**	⎤

Nader Gebrin
Bravo Nader!/Fish | **Huntington**	24

Chris Gerdes
Blackwells | **Wading River**	23

Michael Ginor
Lola | **Great Neck**	24

Doug Gulija
☑ Plaza Café | **Southampton**	26

Joe Isidori
Southfork | **Bridgehampton**	⎤

Todd Jacobs
☑ Atlantica | **Long Bch**	20

Paul LaBue
Navy Beach | **Montauk**	19

Christopher Lee
NEW Huntington Social | **Huntington**	⎤

Eric Lomando
☑ Kitchen A Bistro | **St. James**	27
☑ Kitchen A Tratt. | **St. James**	28
NEW Orto | **Miller Pl**	⎤

Keith Luce
☑ Luce & Hawkins | **Jamesport**	25

Michael Maroni
☑ Maroni Cuisine | **Northport**	28

Nobu Matsuhisa
NEW Nobu/Capri | **Southampton**	⎤

Michael Meehan
H2O Seafood | **Smithtown**	23

Todd Mitgang
South Edison | **Montauk**	22

Kent Monkan
Brass Rail | **Locust Valley**	25

Michael Psilakis
NEW MP Taverna | **Roslyn**	⎤

Guy Reuge
Mirabelle, Rest. | **Stony Brook**	25
Mirabelle Tavern | **Stony Brook**	21

Rosa Ross
Scrimshaw | **Greenport**	23

Tom Schaudel
NEW A Lure | **Southold**	⎤
A Mano | **Mattituck**	24
☑ Coolfish | **Syosset**	24
NEW Jewel | **Melville**	⎤

Mitchell SuDock
NEW Mitch/Toni's | **Albertson**	⎤

Sam Talbot
Surf Lodge | **Montauk**	19

Laurent Tourondel
LT Burger | **Sag Harbor**	16

Jason Weiner
Almond | **Bridgehampton**	20

CHILD-FRIENDLY

(Alternatives to the usual fast-food places; * children's menu available)
Albert's Mandarin | **Huntington**	20
Angelina's | **E Norwich**	23

SPECIAL FEATURES

Argyle Grill* | **Babylon**	22
Ayhan's Fish* | **Port Washington**	19
Ayhan's Shish* | **multi.**	18
Babylon Carriage* | **Babylon**	21
Baby Moon | **Westhampton Bch**	18
Baja Fresh* | **New Hyde Pk**	18
Baja Grill* | **multi.**	18
Bellport | **Bellport**	22
Benihana* | **multi.**	19
Big Daddy's* | **Massapequa**	24
Bigelow's* | **Rockville Ctr**	24
Bliss* | **E Setauket**	22
Boccaccio | **Hicksville**	21
Bonsai | **Port Washington**	22
Bostwick's | **E Hampton**	20
Boulder Creek* | **Hicksville**	-
Bozena Polish* | **Lindenhurst**	23
Bridgehampton Candy | **Bridgehampton**	15
🄩 Butera's* | **Woodbury**	21
Butterfields* | **Hauppauge**	20
🄩 Cafe Baci* | **Westbury**	22
Café Capriccio | **Port Washington**	24
Cafe La Strada | **Hauppauge**	23
Cafe Rustica | **Great Neck**	22
Cafe Toscano | **Massapequa**	21
Caffe Laguna | **Long Bch**	19
Canterbury* | **Oyster Bay**	19
Carrabba's* | **Smithtown**	19
Casa Luis | **Smithtown**	22
🄩 Cheesecake | **Westbury**	20
Chefs of NY | **E Northport**	19
Churrasq. Bairrada | **Mineola**	25
Cirella's* | **Huntington Station**	21
Cooperage Inn* | **Baiting Hollow**	22
🄩 Country Hse. | **Stony Brook**	23
Crossroads Cafe* | **E Northport**	22
Curry Club* | **E Setauket**	20
DiMaggio's* | **Port Washington**	19
Dodici* | **Rockville Ctr**	24
Duke Falcon's | **Long Bch**	22
Eddie's Pizza | **New Hyde Pk**	21
Emilio's* | **Commack**	23
Estia's | **Sag Harbor**	23
🄩 Five Guys* | **multi.**	21
Frank's Steaks | **multi.**	21
Frederick's | **Melville**	23
Galleria Rist.* | **Westbury**	26
George Martin's Grill* | **Rockville Ctr**	20
Golden Pear Cafe* | **multi.**	18
Goldmine Mex. | **Greenlawn**	21
Gonzalo's* | **Glen Cove**	21
Gosman's Dock* | **Montauk**	19
Green Cactus | **multi.**	20
Grimaldi's | **Garden City**	23
Hampton Chutney* | **Amagansett**	22
Hellenic Snack | **E Marion**	20
House/Dosas | **Hicksville**	25
Il Capuccino* | **Sag Harbor**	19
Jamesport Country* | **Jamesport**	23
Jolly Fisherman* | **Roslyn**	21
Kiran Palace | **Hicksville**	24
Kiss'o | **New Hyde Pk**	21
Kurofune | **Commack**	23
La Bussola | **Glen Cove**	23
La Famiglia | **Smithtown**	22
Laguna Grille* | **Woodbury**	20
🄩 La Parma | **multi.**	23
La Parmigiana | **Southampton**	22
La Pizzetta | **E Norwich**	21
Legal Sea Foods* | **Huntington Station**	20
Lobster Roll* | **Amagansett**	19
Lobster Roll N.* | **Baiting Hollow**	20
Lombardi's/Sound* | **Port Jefferson**	21
Los Compadres | **Huntington Station**	23
Louie's Oyster* | **Port Washington**	17
Lucy's Café | **Babylon**	25
Mamma Lombardi's* | **Holbrook**	23
🄩 Matteo's | **multi.**	23
Maureen/Daughers' | **Smithtown**	25
Med. Snack | **Huntington**	22
Mim's* | **multi.**	20
Minado | **Carle Pl**	21
Mirabelle, Rest.* | **Stony Brook**	25
Modern Snack* | **Aquebogue**	18
🄩 Nagahama | **Long Bch**	28
Nagashima | **Jericho**	24
Nautilus Cafe* | **Freeport**	24
Nicholas James* | **Merrick**	22
Nick's | **Rockville Ctr**	23
Oaxaca Mex. | **Huntington**	23
O'Mally's* | **Southold**	18
Orchid | **Garden City**	23
O's Food* | **St. James**	22
Ozumo* | **Bethpage**	23
Pace's Steak* | **multi.**	22
Page One* | **Glen Cove**	22
Painters'* | **Brookhaven Hamlet**	20
Pancho's* | **Island Pk**	19

Pasta-eria | **Hicksville**	23
Pentimento | **Stony Brook**	22
Per Un Angelo | **Wantagh**	22
Pier 95 | **Freeport**	24
Pita House | **Patchogue**	22
Poco Loco* | **Roslyn**	17
Pomodorino* | **Huntington**	19
Post Stop* | **Westhampton Bch**	17
Pumpernickels* | **Northport**	21
Rangmahal | **Hicksville**	23
Red Fish* | **Plainview**	23
Rein* | **Garden City**	23
Rist. Gemelli* | **Babylon**	24
☑ Riverbay | **Williston Pk**	23
RS Jones | **Merrick**	22
Salamander's | **Greenport**	24
Salsa Salsa* | **multi.**	23
Sam's* | **E Hampton**	18
Sapporo* | **Wantagh**	23
Seeda Thai | **Valley Stream**	23
Shiki (Babylon)* | **Babylon**	24
Shogi | **Westbury**	25
☑ Siam Lotus | **Bay Shore**	28
☑ Smokin' Al's* | **Bay Shore**	23
☑ Snaps* | **Wantagh**	26
Solé* | **Oceanside**	26
Spare Rib* | **Commack**	18
Spicy's BBQ | **multi.**	20
Star Confectionery | **Riverhead**	22
Steve's Piccola | **Westbury**	24
Sundried Tomato* | **Nesconset**	21
Sushi Ya* | **Garden City**	21
Taiko | **Rockville Ctr**	24
Tai Show* | **Massapequa**	23
Tesoro | **Westbury**	23
Thai Gourmet | **Port Jefferson Station**	26
Thai Table | **Rockville Ctr**	23
34 New St.* | **Huntington**	18
Thomas's Eggery* | **Carle Pl**	22
Thom Thom* | **Wantagh**	20
Thyme* | **Roslyn**	21
Tutto Pazzo* | **Huntington**	20
Umberto's | **New Hyde Pk**	22
Uncle Dai's | **Glen Cove**	18
Venere* | **Westbury**	20
Villa D'Este | **Floral Pk**	22
Voila! | **St. James**	24
World Pie | **Bridgehampton**	19

DANCING

Arthur Avenue | **Smithtown**	-
Bellport | **Bellport**	22

Black & Blue | **Huntington**	22
Blue | **Blue Pt**	22
Butterfields | **Hauppauge**	20
E. B. Elliot's | **Freeport**	18
56th Fighter | **Farmingdale**	16
Hudson/McCoy | **Freeport**	18
Island Mermaid | **Ocean Beach**	20
NEW Left Coast | **Merrick**	-
Oakland's/Sunday | **Hampton Bays**	18
Oar Steak | **Patchogue**	21
Phao | **Sag Harbor**	21
Prime Catch | **Rockville Ctr**	-
Puglia's/Garden City | **Garden City**	-
Sea Grille | **Montauk**	21
75 Main | **Southampton**	18
Snapper Inn | **Oakdale**	18
Sugar | **Carle Pl**	-
Tulip B&G | **Great Neck**	19
View | **Oakdale**	22
NEW Wobbly Olive | **Hauppauge**	-

DELIVERY/TAKEOUT

(D=delivery, T=takeout)

Albert's Mandarin | T | **Huntington**	20
Angelina's | T | **multi.**	23
Ayhan's Shish | D, T | **Port Washington**	18
Baby Moon | T | **Westhampton Bch**	18
Baja Grill | T | **multi.**	18
Big Daddy's | T | **Massapequa**	24
Bigelow's | T | **Rockville Ctr**	24
Bliss | T | **E Setauket**	22
Blond | T | **Miller Pl**	21
Bonbori Tiki | T | **Huntington**	20
Bonsai | D, T | **Port Washington**	22
Bridgehampton Candy | T | **Bridgehampton**	15
Brio | D | **Port Washington**	21
Buckram Stables | T | **Locust Valley**	19
☑ Butera's | T | **Woodbury**	21
Cafe La Strada | T | **Hauppauge**	23
Cafe Toscano | T | **Massapequa**	21
Caffe Laguna | D | **Long Bch**	19
Chicken Kebab | T | **Roslyn Hts**	21
Churrasq. Bairrada | D, T | **Mineola**	25
Cirella's | T | **multi.**	21
Clam Bar | T | **Amagansett**	21

Curry Club | T | **E Setauket**	20
Cyril's Fish | T | **Amagansett**	18
DiMaggio's | T | **Port Washington**	19
Duryea's Lobster | T | **Montauk**	22
Dynasty/Pt. Wash. | D | **Port Washington**	20
Eddie's Pizza | T | **New Hyde Pk**	21
Emilio's | T | **Commack**	23
Fortune Wheel | T | **Levittown**	22
Frederick's | T | **Melville**	23
Fresco Crêperie | T | **Long Bch**	23
Galangal | T | **Syosset**	23
Golden Pear Cafe | D, T | **multi.**	18
Goldmine Mex. | T | **Greenlawn**	21
Gonzalo's | D, T | **Glen Cove**	21
Green Cactus | T | **multi.**	20
Grimaldi's | T | **Garden City**	23
Hampton Chutney | T | **Amagansett**	22
Hampton Coffee | T | **Water Mill**	19
Hellenic Snack | T | **E Marion**	20
Hinata | D | **Great Neck**	23
Iavarone Cafe | D | **New Hyde Pk**	21
Intermezzo | D | **Ft Salonga**	23
Kiran Palace | D, T | **Hicksville**	24
Kiss'o | T | **New Hyde Pk**	21
Kura Barn | T | **Huntington**	24
Kurofune | T | **Commack**	23
Laguna Grille | T | **Woodbury**	20
☑ La Parma | T | **multi.**	23
La Parmigiana | T | **Southampton**	22
La Pizzetta | T | **E Norwich**	21
La Viola | D | **Cedarhurst**	20
Lemonleaf Grill | D | **Hicksville**	22
Lemonleaf Thai | D | **Carle Pl**	20
Lobster Roll | T | **Amagansett**	19
Lobster Roll N. | T | **Baiting Hollow**	20
Lombardi's/Sound | T | **Port Jefferson**	21
Long River | T | **Kings Park**	21
Los Compadres | T | **Huntington Station**	23
Lucy's Café | T | **Babylon**	25
☑ Maroni Cuisine | T | **Northport**	28
Matsuya | D | **Great Neck**	21
☑ Matteo's | T | **multi.**	23
Maureen/Daughers' | T | **Smithtown**	25
Med. Snack | T | **Huntington**	22
Mim's | T | **multi.**	20
Minami | T | **Massapequa**	26
Modern Snack | T | **Aquebogue**	18
Mother Kelly's | D | **Cedarhurst**	21
☑ Nagahama | D, T | **Long Bch**	28
Nagashima | T | **Jericho**	24
Nautilus Cafe | T | **Freeport**	24
Nicholas James | T | **Merrick**	22
Nick's | T | **Rockville Ctr**	23
O'Mally's | T | **Southold**	18
Onzon Thai | T | **Bellmore**	24
Orchid | T | **Garden City**	23
O's Food | T | **St. James**	22
Ozumo | T | **Bethpage**	23
Pace's Steak | T | **multi.**	22
Pancho's | T | **Island Pk**	19
Pasta-eria | T | **Hicksville**	23
Pasta Pasta | T | **Port Jefferson**	25
Pearl East | D, T | **Manhasset**	23
Pita House | T | **Patchogue**	22
Pomodorino | T | **Huntington**	19
Post Stop | T | **Westhampton Bch**	17
Pumpernickels | T | **Northport**	21
Rangmahal | D, T | **Hicksville**	23
Ravagh | D, T | **Roslyn Hts**	22
Red Fish | T | **Plainview**	23
Rowdy Hall | T | **E Hampton**	20
RS Jones | T | **Merrick**	22
Salamander's | T | **Greenport**	24
Salsa Salsa | T | **multi.**	23
Sam's | T | **E Hampton**	18
☑ San Marco | T | **Hauppauge**	26
Sant Ambroeus | T | **Southampton**	24
Sapporo | T | **Wantagh**	23
Sarin Thai | T | **Greenvale**	24
Seeda Thai | T | **Valley Stream**	23
Shagwong | T | **Montauk**	18
Shogi | T | **Westbury**	25
Show Win | D, T | **Northport**	20
☑ Siam Lotus | T | **Bay Shore**	28
Silver's | T | **Southampton**	23
☑ Smokin' Al's | T | **Bay Shore**	23
☑ Snaps | T | **Wantagh**	26
Southampton Publick | T | **Southampton**	18
Southside Fish | T | **Lindenhurst**	20
Spicy's BBQ | D, T | **multi.**	20
Star Confectionery | T | **Riverhead**	22
Suki Zuki | T | **Water Mill**	24
Sushi Ya | T | **Garden City**	21

Taiko | T | **Rockville Ctr**	24
Tai Show | T | **multi.**	23
Tesoro | T | **Westbury**	23
Thai Gourmet | T | **Port Jefferson Station**	26
Thai Green Leaf | D, T | **E Northport**	21
Thai Table | T | **Rockville Ctr**	23
Thai USA | T | **Huntington**	23
34 New St. | D, T | **Huntington**	18
Thomas's Eggery | T | **Carle Pl**	22
Thom Thom | T | **Wantagh**	20
Thyme | T | **Roslyn**	21
Tokyo | T | **E Northport**	24
Tony's | D | **E Quogue**	19
Tratt. Di Meo | T | **Roslyn Hts**	21
Tutto Pazzo | T | **Huntington**	20
Umberto's | T | **New Hyde Pk**	22
Uncle Dai's | D, T | **Glen Cove**	18
Venere | T | **Westbury**	20
Wild Ginger | D, T | **Great Neck**	21
World Pie | T | **Bridgehampton**	19
Yamaguchi | T | **Port Washington**	25

DINING ALONE

(Other than hotels and places with counter service)

Babette's | **E Hampton**	20
🄩 Ben's Deli | **multi.**	19
Bliss | **E Setauket**	22
Bridgehampton Candy | **Bridgehampton**	15
🄩 Coolfish | **Syosset**	24
NEW 18 Bay | **Shelter Is**	-
Estia's | **Sag Harbor**	23
Frisky Oyster | **Greenport**	25
Golden Pear Cafe | **multi.**	18
Hampton Chutney | **Amagansett**	22
NEW Jack's Shack | **Glen Head**	-
NEW J. Michaels | **Northport**	-
Kyle's | **Shelter Is**	-
NEW Litttle Red | **Southampton**	-
Lobster Roll N. | **Baiting Hollow**	20
NEW Monsoon | **Babylon**	-
NEW Page/63 Main | **Sag Harbor**	-
Panini Café | **Roslyn**	23
Salamander's | **Greenport**	24
Sen | **Sag Harbor**	21
Show Win | **Northport**	20
Star Confectionery | **Riverhead**	22

Sushi Ya | **Garden City**	21
Townline | **Sagaponack**	19

DRAMATIC INTERIORS

🄩 American Hotel | **Sag Harbor**	25
🄩 Atlantica | **Long Bch**	20
Chi | **Westbury**	25
City Cellar | **Westbury**	21
Claudio's | **Greenport**	16
🄩 Country Hse. | **Stony Brook**	23
E. B. Elliot's | **Freeport**	18
56th Fighter | **Farmingdale**	16
Fisherman's Catch | **Point Lookout**	20
Four Food Studio | **Melville**	21
Garden Grill | **Smithtown**	21
Honu Kit. | **Huntington**	22
NEW Insignia | **Smithtown**	-
🄩 Jamesport Manor | **Jamesport**	23
NEW Jewel | **Melville**	-
NEW K·Pacho | **New Hyde Pk**	-
NEW Legacy | **Huntington**	-
Library Cafe | **Farmingdale**	18
🄩 Limani | **Roslyn**	26
🄩 Luce & Hawkins | **Jamesport**	25
Ludlow Bistro | **Deer Park**	24
Milleridge Inn | **Jericho**	16
NEW Mint | **Garden City**	-
NEW Monsoon | **Babylon**	-
Mumon | **Garden City**	22
Nanking | **New Hyde Pk**	19
Nisen | **multi.**	25
Nonnina | **W Islip**	25
Novità Wine Bar & Trattoria | **Garden City**	23
🄩 Palm Court | **E Meadow**	24
Porto Vivo | **Huntington**	22
Ram's Head | **Shelter Is**	20
Café Red/Red | **Huntington**	25
Rist. Gemelli | **Babylon**	24
Robert's | **Water Mill**	25
🄩 1770 Hse. | **E Hampton**	25
Taste 99 | **Farmingdale**	18
🄩 Tellers | **Islip**	26
Thom Thom | **Wantagh**	20
🄩 Toku | **Manhasset**	25
Tula Kit. | **Bay Shore**	24
Tweeds | **Riverhead**	21
View | **Oakdale**	22
Wave Seafood | **Port Jefferson**	19
Xaga Sushi | **multi.**	-

SPECIAL FEATURES

ENTERTAINMENT

(Call for days and times of performances)

Babette's | jazz | **E Hampton**	20
Backyard | DJ | **Montauk**	23
Bayou | bands | **N Bellmore**	23
Big Daddy's | live music | **Massapequa**	24
Bistro 25 | acoustic guitar | **Sayville**	-
Blackbirds' Grille | live music | **Sayville**	20
Blond | jazz | **Miller Pl**	21
Blue | DJ/live music | **Blue Pt**	22
Bulldog Grille | rock bands | **Amityville**	-
Café Capriccio | piano | **Port Washington**	24
Chequit Inn | rock | **Shelter Is Hts**	19
Ciao Baby | vocals | **multi.**	20
🔁 Coolfish | varies | **Syosset**	24
Curry Club | varies | **E Setauket**	20
Dockers Waterside | varies | **E Quogue**	20
🔁 E. Hampton Pt. | reggae | **E Hampton**	19
E. B. Elliot's | karaoke | **Freeport**	18
Fatfish | acoustic rock | **Bay Shore**	21
Fishery | varies | **E Rockaway**	19
Galleria Rist. | piano | **Westbury**	26
Gosman's Dock | jazz | **Montauk**	19
Grasso's | jazz | **Cold Spring**	24
Grey Horse | live music | **Bayport**	23
Grill Room | live music | **Hauppauge**	21
H2O Seafood | live music | **Smithtown**	23
Hudson/McCoy | live music | **Freeport**	18
Irish Coffee | Irish folk/piano | **E Islip**	23
Jack Halyards | live music | **Oyster Bay**	23
Kabul Afghani | belly dancing | **Huntington**	23
La Coquille | harpist | **Manhasset**	24
Library Cafe | varies | **Farmingdale**	18
Lobster Roll N. | guitar | **Baiting Hollow**	20
Lombardi's/Sound | varies | **Port Jefferson**	21
Milleridge Inn | piano | **Jericho**	16
Mill Pond Hse. | piano | **Centerport**	25
Nisen | DJ; varies | **Woodbury**	25
Oakland's/Sunday | varies | **Hampton Bays**	18
Oar Steak | varies | **Patchogue**	21
Pace's Steak | live music | **Port Jefferson**	22
Paddy McGees | DJ | **Island Pk**	18
Painters' | bands | **Brookhaven Hamlet**	20
🔁 Palm Court | varies | **E Meadow**	24
Patio/54 Main | varies | **Westhampton Bch**	19
Per Un Angelo | varies | **Wantagh**	22
🔁 Piccolo | piano | **Huntington**	27
Pierre's | jazz | **Bridgehampton**	21
Pollo Rico | guitar/harp | **Centereach**	20
Post Office | live music | **Babylon**	19
Ram's Head | jazz | **Shelter Is**	20
RS Jones | varies | **Merrick**	22
Sea Grille | DJ/karaoke | **Montauk**	21
Snapper Inn | piano | **Oakdale**	18
Southampton Publick | DJ | **Southampton**	18
Swingbelly's | acoustic | **Long Bch**	23
Taste 99 | varies | **Farmingdale**	18
Tide Runners | bands | **Hampton Bays**	16
Tulip B&G | belly dancing/live music | **Great Neck**	19
Tweeds | piano | **Riverhead**	21
21 Main | live music | **W Sayville**	23
View | bands | **Oakdale**	22
Village Lanterne | folk | **Lindenhurst**	25
Walk St. | live band | **Garden City**	21

FIREPLACES

Absolutely Mario | **Farmingdale**	20
Amarelle | **Wading River**	25
🔁 American Hotel | **Sag Harbor**	25
Amicale | **Huntington Station**	25
Angelina's | **Syosset**	23
Babylon Carriage | **Babylon**	21
Baby Moon | **Westhampton Bch**	18
🔁 Barney's | **Locust Valley**	26

Basil Leaf Café	**Locust Valley**	21
Bayview Inn	**S Jamesport**	22
Bellport	**Bellport**	22
Bertucci's	**Hauppauge**	17
Birchwood	**Riverhead**	20
Bistro 72	**Riverhead**	-
Blackbirds' Grille	**Sayville**	20
⛔ Blackstone Steak	**Melville**	24
Blackwells	**Wading River**	23
Blue	**Blue Pt**	22
Boathouse	**E Hampton**	19
Bob's Rest.	**Floral Pk**	21
Brasserie 214	**New Hyde Pk**	20
Brooks & Porter	**Merrick**	22
⛔ Bryant & Cooper	**Roslyn**	26
Burton & Doyle	**Great Neck**	24
Cafe Havana	**Smithtown**	18
Casa Rustica	**Smithtown**	25
Chalet Rest.	**Roslyn**	18
Chequit Inn	**Shelter Is Hts**	19
Cielo Rist.	**Rockville Ctr**	20
Circa	**Mineola**	22
Cooperage Inn	**Baiting Hollow**	22
⛔ Country Hse.	**Stony Brook**	23
Cozymel's	**Westbury**	17
Crossroads Cafe	**E Northport**	22
Cuvée	**Greenport**	22
Dark Horse	**Riverhead**	-
Deco 1600	**Plainview**	-
E. B. Elliot's	**Freeport**	18
Famous Dave's	**multi.**	19
56th Fighter	**Farmingdale**	16
Fisherman's Catch	**Point Lookout**	20
Franina	**Syosset**	26
Garden Grill	**Smithtown**	21
George Martin's Steak	**Great River**	-
Harbor Mist	**Cold Spring**	19
Heart/Portugal	**Mineola**	20
Hemingway's	**Wantagh**	19
Honu Kit.	**Huntington**	22
Horace/Sylvia's	**Babylon**	20
H.R. Singleton's	**Bethpage**	18
Hudson/McCoy	**Freeport**	18
Il Classico	**Massapequa Pk**	23
⛔ Insignia	**Smithtown**	-
Irish Coffee	**E Islip**	23
⛔ Jamesport Manor	**Jamesport**	23
Jimmy Hays	**Island Pk**	25
⛔ J. Michaels	**Northport**	-
Jolly Fisherman	**Roslyn**	21
Jonathan's	**Garden City Pk**	20
⛔ Lake Hse.	**Bay Shore**	28
La Pace/Chef Michael	**Glen Cove**	25
Legends	**New Suffolk**	23
Living Rm.	**E Hampton**	25
Lobster Roll N.	**Baiting Hollow**	20
⛔ Luce & Hawkins	**Jamesport**	25
Maguire's	**Ocean Beach**	19
Majors Steak	**multi.**	19
Mamma Lombardi's	**Holbrook**	23
Mario	**Hauppauge**	25
Milk & Sugar	**Bay Shore**	21
Mill Creek	**Bayville**	21
Milleridge Inn	**Jericho**	16
Mirabelle, Rest.	**Stony Brook**	25
Mirabelle Tavern	**Stony Brook**	21
⛔ Mirko's	**Water Mill**	26
Nello Summertimes	**Southampton**	16
Nichol's	**E Hampton**	17
Nonnina	**W Islip**	25
⛔ North Fork Oyster	**Greenport**	-
⛔ North Fork Table	**Southold**	29
Oak Chalet	**Bellmore**	19
Old Mill Inn	**Mattituck**	20
1 North Steak	**Hampton Bays**	22
O's Food	**St. James**	22
⛔ Palm	**E Hampton**	26
⛔ Palm Court	**E Meadow**	24
Papa Razzi	**Westbury**	18
⛔ Patio	**Freeport**	-
Per Un Angelo	**Wantagh**	22
Piccolo's	**Mineola**	24
Pierre's	**Bridgehampton**	21
⛔ Plaza Café	**Southampton**	26
Porto Bello	**Greenport**	22
Post Office	**Babylon**	19
⛔ Prime	**Huntington**	23
Puglia's/Garden City	**Garden City**	-
Race Lane	**E Hampton**	19
Ram's Head	**Shelter Is**	20
Rein	**Garden City**	23
Rist. Gemelli	**Babylon**	24
⛔ Riverhead Pjt.	**Riverhead**	-
Robert's	**Water Mill**	25
⛔ Rothmann's	**E Norwich**	25
Rowdy Hall	**E Hampton**	20
Runyon's	**Seaford**	18
⛔ 1770 Hse.	**E Hampton**	25
Seventh Street Cafe	**Garden City**	20
Snapper Inn	**Oakdale**	18

SPECIAL FEATURES

NEW Southampton Social | **Southampton**	-_
Southfork | **Bridgehampton**	-_
NEW Spiro's | **Rocky Pt**	-_
☑ Starr Boggs | **Westhampton Bch**	26
☑ Stone Creek | **E Quogue**	26
Sullivan's Quay | **Port Washington**	18
Surfside Inn | **Montauk**	18
Taste 99 | **Farmingdale**	18
Tesoro | **Westbury**	23
388 Rest. | **Roslyn Hts**	20
Thyme | **Roslyn**	21
Tratt. Di Meo | **Roslyn Hts**	21
☑ Trumpets | **Eastport**	22
Tutto Il Giorno | **Sag Harbor**	25
Tutto Pazzo | **Huntington**	20
Tweeds | **Riverhead**	21
21 Main | **W Sayville**	23
Umberto's | **New Hyde Pk**	22
Venere | **Westbury**	20
View | **Oakdale**	22
Vintage Prime | **St. James**	25
Wall's Wharf | **Bayville**	17

GREEN/LOCAL/ ORGANIC

A Mano | **Mattituck**	24
Amarelle | **Wading River**	25
☑ Atlantica | **Long Bch**	20
Babette's | **E Hampton**	20
Backyard | **Montauk**	23
Bistro 72 | **Riverhead**	-_
Bistro 25 | **Sayville**	-_
Coast Grill | **Southampton**	22
Comtesse Thérèse Bistro | **Aquebogue**	-_
Cuvée | **Greenport**	22
☑ Dave's Grill | **Montauk**	27
Dish | **Water Mill**	27
Farm Country Kit. | **Riverhead**	23
Fifth Season | **Port Jefferson**	26
Gosman's Dock | **Montauk**	19
Grey Horse | **Bayport**	23
Inlet Seafood | **Montauk**	21
Jamesport Country | **Jamesport**	23
☑ Jamesport Manor | **Jamesport**	23
NEW L.I.V.E. | **Seaford**	-_
Living Rm. | **E Hampton**	25
Love Ln. | **Mattituck**	23
☑ Luce & Hawkins | **Jamesport**	25
Michael Anthony's | **Wading River**	24

☑ Mirko's | **Water Mill**	26
☑ Nick & Toni's | **E Hampton**	24
☑ Noah's | **Greenport**	26
☑ North Fork Table | **Southold**	29
Old Mill Inn | **Mattituck**	20
1 North Steak | **Hampton Bays**	22
Scrimshaw | **Greenport**	23
South Edison | **Montauk**	22
Southfork | **Bridgehampton**	-_
☑ Starr Boggs | **Westhampton Bch**	26
Touch/Venice | **Cutchogue**	21
Vine Street | **Shelter Is**	25

HISTORIC PLACES

(Year opened; * building)

1647 | Nello Summertimes* | **Southampton**	16
1663 | 1770 Hse.* | **E Hampton**	25
1672 | Milleridge Inn* | **Jericho**	16
1699 | Palm* | **E Hampton**	26
1700 | Living Rm.* | **E Hampton**	25
1710 | Country Hse.* | **Stony Brook**	23
1751 | Mirabelle, Rest.* | **Stony Brook**	25
1800 | Spring Close* | **E Hampton**	-_
1821 | Old Mill Inn* | **Mattituck**	20
1826 | Garden Grill* | **Smithtown**	21
1842 | Chalet Rest.* | **Roslyn**	18
1846 | American Hotel* | **Sag Harbor**	25
1850 | Bistro 44* | **Northport**	23
1850 | 18 Bay* | **Shelter Is**	-_
1850 | Farm Country Kit.* | **Riverhead**	23
1857 | Inn Spot/Bay* | **Hampton Bays**	19
1863 | Kyle's* | **Shelter Is**	-_
1863 | Luce & Hawkins* | **Jamesport**	25
1865 | Babylon Carriage* | **Babylon**	21
1870 | Claudio's | **Greenport**	16
1872 | Chequit Inn* | **Shelter Is Hts**	19
1888 | View* | **Oakdale**	22
1891 | 21 Main* | **W Sayville**	23
1896 | Tweeds* | **Riverhead**	21
1898 | Ayhan's Fish* | **Port Washington**	19
1900 | Brasserie 214* | **New Hyde Pk**	20

1900 | O's Food* | **St. James** 22

1900 | Porters* | **Bellport** 20

1902 | Silver's* | **Southampton** 23

1902 | Wild Honey* | 25
Oyster Bay

1903 | Spicy's BBQ* | **Riverhead** 20

1904 | La Marmite* | 24
Williston Pk

1905 | Louie's Oyster | 17
Port Washington

1906 | Mill Pond Hse.* | 25
Centerport

1907 | Main St. Bakery* | -
Port Washington

1907 | Rothmann's* | **E Norwich** 25

1910 | Ariana* | **Huntington** 20

1911 | Star Confectionery* | 22
Riverhead

1914 | Post Stop* | 17
Westhampton Bch

1915 | Duryea's Lobster* | 22
Montauk

1920 | Alexandros* | 23
Mount Sinai

1920 | Ayhan's Shish* | 18
Port Washington

1926 | Bridgehampton Candy | 15
Bridgehampton

1926 | Tellers* | **Islip** 26

1927 | Hildebrandt's | 19
Williston Pk

1927 | Shagwong* | **Montauk** 18

1928 | Post Office* | **Babylon** 19

1929 | Backyard* | **Montauk** 23

1929 | Birchwood* | **Riverhead** 20

1929 | Gulf Coast* | **Montauk** 21

1929 | Jimmy Hays | **Island Pk** 25

1929 | Ram's Head* | **Shelter Is** 20

1929 | Snapper Inn | **Oakdale** 18

1934 | Southside Fish | 20
Lindenhurst

1935 | Red Bar* | **Southampton** 22

1936 | Maguire's | **Ocean Beach** 19

1937 | Blue Moon* | 20
Rockville Ctr

1938 | Declan Quinn's* | 19
Bay Shore

1939 | Bigelow's | **Rockville Ctr** 24

1941 | Eddie's Pizza | 21
New Hyde Pk

1943 | Gosman's Dock | 19
Montauk

1944 | Koenig's | **Floral Pk** 19

1945 | Fulton Prime | **Syosset** 23

1945 | Wall's Wharf | **Bayville** 17

1946 | Thomas's Eggery | 22
Carle Pl

1947 | Sam's | **E Hampton** 18

1950 | Harbor Grill* | -
E Hampton

1950 | Modern Snack | 18
Aquebogue

1950 | 1 North Steak* | 22
Hampton Bays

1950 | Pier 95* | **Freeport** 24

1955 | Carnival | 22
Port Jefferson Station

1956 | Dockers Waterside* | 20
E Quogue

1956 | Dockside B&G* | 21
Sag Harbor

1957 | Jolly Fisherman | **Roslyn** 21

1958 | Cliff's | **Jamesport** 22

1960 | Peter Luger | **Great Neck** 27

1960 | Stella Rist. | **Floral Pk** 24

1961 | Arturo's | **Floral Pk** 22

1962 | Clubhouse | **Huntington** 21

HOTEL DINING

Allegria Hotel
  🟥 Atlantica | **Long Bch** 20

American Hotel
  🟥 American Hotel | **Sag Harbor** 25

Andrew Hotel
  Colbeh | **Great Neck** 21

Bayview Inn
  Bayview Inn | **S Jamesport** 22

Capri
  NEW Nobu/Capri | -
  Southampton

Chequit Inn
  Chequit Inn | **Shelter Is Hts** 19

c/o The Maidstone
  Living Rm. | **E Hampton** 25

Danfords Hotel & Marina
  Wave Seafood | **Port Jefferson** 19

Days Inn
  Blue Fish | **Hicksville** -

Freeport Inn & Marina
  NEW Patio | **Freeport** -

Garden City Hotel
  Rein | **Garden City** 23

Gurney's Inn
  Sea Grille | **Montauk** 21

Hotel Indigo
  Bistro 72 | **Riverhead** -

Housers Hotel, Fire Island
  Hideaway | **Ocean Beach** 19

Huntting Inn	
Ƶ Palm | E Hampton	26
Inn at East Wind	
Desmond's | **Wading River**	20
Inn at New Hyde Park	
Brasserie 214 | **New Hyde Pk**	20
Jedediah Hawkins Inn	
Ƶ Luce & Hawkins | Jamesport	25
Jones Beach Hotel	
Per Un Angelo | **Wantagh**	22
Kenny's Tipperary Inn	
Manucci's | **Montauk**	19
La Maison Blanche Hotel	
NEW La Maison Blanche | Shelter Is Hts	–
Montauk Yacht Club Resort	
Gulf Coast | **Montauk**	21
Nello Summertimes	
Nello Summertimes | **Southampton**	16
North Fork Table & Inn	
Ƶ North Fork Table | Southold	29
Ram's Head Inn	
Ram's Head | **Shelter Is**	20
Ruschmeyer's Resort	
NEW Ruschmeyer's | Montauk	–
1770 House	
Ƶ 1770 Hse. | E Hampton	25
Solé East	
Backyard | **Montauk**	23
Stone Lion Inn	
East/ Northeast | **Montauk**	21
Sunset Beach Hotel	
Sunset Beach | **Shelter Is Hts**	18
Surf Lodge	
Surf Lodge | **Montauk**	19
Surfside Inn	
Surfside Inn | **Montauk**	18
Three Village Inn	
Mirabelle, Rest. | **Stony Brook**	25
Mirabelle Tavern | **Stony Brook**	21
Viana Hotel & Spa	
Marco Polo's | **Westbury**	–

LATE DINING

(Weekday closing hour)

Arthur Avenue | varies | **Smithtown**	–
Bin 56 | 12 AM | **Huntington**	24
Bulldog Grille | 12 AM | **Amityville**	–
Carnival | 12 AM | **Port Jefferson Station**	22
Chalet Rest. | 12 AM | **Roslyn**	18
Copa Wine | 11:30 PM | **Bridgehampton**	20
E. B. Elliot's | 4 AM | **Freeport**	18
Eddie's Pizza | varies | **New Hyde Pk**	21
Inn Spot/Bay | 12 AM | **Hampton Bays**	19
NEW Joe's Crab Shack | 1 AM | Oceanside	–
Library Cafe | 1 AM | **Farmingdale**	18
NEW L.I.V.E. | 12 AM | Seaford	–
Maxwell's | varies | **Islip**	–
Muse | 2 AM | **Sag Harbor**	23
O'Mally's | 12 AM | **Southold**	18
O's Food | 12 AM | **St. James**	22
Porto Vivo | 12 AM | **Huntington**	22
Post Office | varies | **Babylon**	19
Serafina | 12 AM | **E Hampton**	18
75 Main | 12 AM | **Southampton**	18
Swingbelly's | 12:30 AM | **Long Bch**	23
Trata | 12 AM | **Water Mill**	22
World Pie | 12 AM | **Bridgehampton**	19
NEW XO | 12 AM | Huntington	–

LOCAL FAVORITES

Almond | **Bridgehampton**	20
Angelina's | **multi.**	23
Arturo's | **Floral Pk**	22
Azuma | **Greenlawn**	23
Bellport | **Bellport**	22
Benny's | **Westbury**	25
Bigelow's | **Rockville Ctr**	24
Ƶ Bistro Cassis | Huntington	24
B.K. Sweeney's | **Garden City**	18
Blackbirds' Grille | **Sayville**	20
Blue Moon | **Rockville Ctr**	20
Brass Rail | **Locust Valley**	25
Bravo Nader!/Fish | **Huntington**	24
Bridgehampton Candy | **Bridgehampton**	15
Buckram Stables | **Locust Valley**	19
Bulldog Grille | **Amityville**	–
Cafe Toscano | **Massapequa**	21
Canterbury | **Oyster Bay**	19
Ciao Baby | **Commack**	20
Cliff's | **multi.**	22
Coast Grill | **Southampton**	22

Cookroom | **Middle Island** | -
Cooperage Inn | **Baiting Hollow** | 22
Crossroads Cafe | **E Northport** | 22
Curry Club | **E Setauket** | 20
☑ Dario's | **Rockville Ctr** | 26
☑ Dave's Grill | **Montauk** | 27
Duke Falcon's | **Long Bch** | 22
Duryea's Lobster | **Montauk** | 22
East/ Northeast | **Montauk** | 21
Eddie's Pizza | **New Hyde Pk** | 21
NEW 18 Bay | **Shelter Is** | -
Emilio's | **Commack** | 23
Fork & Vine | **Glen Head** | 23
Hellenic Snack | **E Marion** | 20
Hemingway's | **Wantagh** | 19
Hildebrandt's | **Williston Pk** | 19
Il Capuccino | **Sag Harbor** | 19
Iron Skillet | **Mattituck** | -
Itgen's | **Valley Stream** | -
Ivy Cottage | **Williston Pk** | 23
Jamesport Country | **Jamesport** | 23
Jimmy Hays | **Island Pk** | 25
JT's Corner | **Nesconset** | 23
☑ Kotobuki | **multi.** | 27
Kyle's | **Shelter Is** | -
La Parmigiana | **Southampton** | 22
La Piazza | **multi.** | 21
NEW Lawson Pub | **Oceanside** | -
Legends | **New Suffolk** | 23
Little Mexico | **Westbury** | -
Lobster Roll | **Amagansett** | 19
Lobster Roll N. | **Baiting Hollow** | 20
Love Ln. | **Mattituck** | 23
Ludlow Bistro | **Deer Park** | 24
NEW Market Bistro | **Jericho** | -
Maureen/Daughers' | **Smithtown** | 25
NEW Meridian | **Locust Valley** | -
Michaels'/Maidstone | **E Hampton** | 18
Mill Creek | **Bayville** | 21
Mim's | **multi.** | 20
Modern Snack | **Aquebogue** | 18
NEW MP Taverna | **Roslyn** | -
☑ Nagahama | **Long Bch** | 28
Nichol's | **E Hampton** | 17
Orchid | **Garden City** | 23
NEW Orto | **Miller Pl** | -
Page One | **Glen Cove** | 22
Panini Café | **Roslyn** | 23
Pierre's | **Bridgehampton** | 21
Rachel's Cafe | **Syosset** | 22
Red Bar | **Southampton** | 22

NEW Relish | **Kings Park** | -
NEW Roast | **Melville** | -
Rowdy Hall | **E Hampton** | 20
Ruvo | **Port Jefferson** | 22
Sage Bistro | **Bellmore** | 24
Salsa Salsa | **Smithtown** | 23
Salvatore's | **Port Washington** | 25
Sam's | **E Hampton** | 18
Sen | **Sag Harbor** | 21
Shagwong | **Montauk** | 18
☑ Siam Lotus | **Bay Shore** | 28
Silver's | **Southampton** | 23
☑ Smokin' Al's | **Bay Shore** | 23
Southampton Publick | **Southampton** | 18
Star Confectionery | **Riverhead** | 22
Surfside Inn | **Montauk** | 18
Sweet Tomato | **multi.** | -
Taiko | **Rockville Ctr** | 24
Tesoro | **Westbury** | 23
Thai Gourmet | **Port Jefferson Station** | 26
Thomas's Eggery | **Carle Pl** | 22
Umberto's | **New Hyde Pk** | 22
Varney's | **Brookhaven** | 23
Wall's Wharf | **Bayville** | 17
☑ West End | **Carle Pl** | 25
Wild Honey | **Oyster Bay** | 25

MEET FOR A DRINK

NEW Agave | **Bridgehampton** | -
NEW A Lure | **Southold** | -
Amarelle | **Wading River** | 25
☑ Atlantica | **Long Bch** | 20
Babylon Carriage | **Babylon** | 21
Backyard | **Montauk** | 23
NEW Banzai Burger | **Amagansett** | -
Bar Frites | **Greenvale** | 18
Bayou | **N Bellmore** | 23
Bayview Inn | **S Jamesport** | 22
NEW Beach Hse. | **E Hampton** | -
☑ Besito | **Huntington** | 24
Bin 56 | **Huntington** | 24
Birchwood | **Riverhead** | 20
Bistro 25 | **Sayville** | -
B.K. Sweeney's | **Garden City** | 18
☑ Blackstone Steak | **Melville** | 24
Blackwells | **Wading River** | 23
Boathouse | **E Hampton** | 19
Bobby Van's | **Bridgehampton** | 22
Brass Rail | **Locust Valley** | 25
B.Smith's | **Sag Harbor** | 18

Bulldog Grille | **Amityville**	-﹚
Burton & Doyle | **Great Neck**	24﹚
Café Buenos Aires | **Huntington**	24﹚
Canterbury | **Oyster Bay**	19﹚
Cattlemen's | **Port Jefferson Station**	19﹚
Cedar Creek | **Glen Cove**	-﹚
Chalet Rest. | **Roslyn**	18﹚
Chi | **Westbury**	25﹚
Cipollini | **Manhasset**	21﹚
Cittanuova | **E Hampton**	20﹚
City Cellar | **Westbury**	21﹚
Claudio's | **Greenport**	16﹚
Clubhouse | **Huntington**	21﹚
Coach Grill | **Oyster Bay**	22﹚
Coast Grill | **Southampton**	22﹚
NEW Cody's | **Riverhead**	-﹚
Z Coolfish | **Syosset**	24﹚
Copa Wine | **Bridgehampton**	20﹚
Cuvée | **Greenport**	22﹚
Cyril's Fish | **Amagansett**	18﹚
NEW E. Hampton Grill | **E Hampton**	-﹚
Z E. Hampton Pt. | **E Hampton**	19﹚
E. B. Elliot's | **Freeport**	18﹚
Fatfish | **Bay Shore**	21﹚
F.H. Riley's | **Huntington**	23﹚
Fishery | **E Rockaway**	19﹚
Fork & Vine | **Glen Head**	23﹚
NEW 420 North | **Great Neck**	-﹚
NEW Fusion 84 | **Sayville**	-﹚
George Martin's Grill | **Rockville Ctr**	20﹚
Grand Lux | **Garden City**	19﹚
Grey Horse | **Bayport**	23﹚
NEW Grill 454 | **Commack**	-﹚
Hemingway's | **Wantagh**	19﹚
Hideaway | **Ocean Beach**	19﹚
Honu Kit. | **Huntington**	22﹚
Horace/Sylvia's | **Babylon**	20﹚
Houston's | **Garden City**	22﹚
Hudson/McCoy | **Freeport**	18﹚
Hunan Taste | **Greenvale**	22﹚
NEW Huntington Social | **Huntington**	-﹚
Indian Wells | **Amagansett**	17﹚
NEW Insignia | **Smithtown**	-﹚
NEW Jake's Steak | **E Meadow**	-﹚
NEW Jewel | **Melville**	-﹚
NEW K·Pacho | **New Hyde Pk**	-﹚
Z La Piccola | **Port Washington**	27﹚
NEW Left Coast | **Merrick**	-﹚
Legends | **New Suffolk**	23﹚
Z Limani | **Roslyn**	26﹚
NEW Litttle Red | **Southampton**	-﹚
Mac's Steak | **Huntington**	23﹚
Maguire's | **Ocean Beach**	19﹚
NEW Market Bistro | **Jericho**	-﹚
Matthew's | **Ocean Beach**	22﹚
Maxwell's | **Islip**	-﹚
NEW Mint | **Garden City**	-﹚
Mirabelle Tavern | **Stony Brook**	21﹚
NEW Monsoon | **Babylon**	-﹚
Z Morton's | **Great Neck**	25﹚
NEW MP Taverna | **Roslyn**	-﹚
Muse | **Sag Harbor**	23﹚
Navy Beach | **Montauk**	19﹚
Nello Summertimes | **Southampton**	16﹚
Z Nick & Toni's | **E Hampton**	24﹚
Nick's Tuscan | **Long Bch**	21﹚
NEW Nobu/Capri | **Southampton**	-﹚
Nonnina | **W Islip**	25﹚
Novitá Wine Bar & Trattoria | **Garden City**	23﹚
Old Mill Inn | **Mattituck**	20﹚
Painters' | **Brookhaven Hamlet**	20﹚
NEW Patio | **Freeport**	-﹚
Pine Island | **Bayville**	18﹚
NEW Pop's Seafood | **Island Pk**	-﹚
Porto Vivo | **Huntington**	22﹚
Post Office | **Babylon**	19﹚
Z Prime | **Huntington**	23﹚
Public Hse. 49 | **Patchogue**	20﹚
Race Lane | **E Hampton**	19﹚
Café Red/Red | **Huntington**	25﹚
Rein | **Garden City**	23﹚
NEW Riverhead Pjt. | **Riverhead**	-﹚
Rockwell's B&G | **Smithtown**	22﹚
Z Rothmann's | **E Norwich**	25﹚
Rowdy Hall | **E Hampton**	20﹚
Rumba | **Hampton Bays**	-﹚
NEW Ruschmeyer's | **Montauk**	-﹚
Sakaya | **Albertson**	-﹚
Serafina | **E Hampton**	18﹚
NEW Serata | **Oyster Bay**	-﹚
Sip City | **Great Neck**	-﹚
Southampton Publick | **Southampton**	18﹚
NEW Southampton Social | **Southampton**	-﹚
Southfork | **Bridgehampton**	-﹚
NEW Spiro's | **Rocky Pt**	-﹚
Sugar | **Carle Pl**	-﹚
Sunset Beach | **Shelter Is Hts**	18﹚

Surf Lodge	Montauk	19
Surfside Inn	Montauk	18
Taste 99	Farmingdale	18
Tide Runners	Hampton Bays	16
☑ Toku	Manhasset	25
Townline	Sagaponack	19
Trata	Water Mill	22
☑ Verace	Islip	26
Vero	Amityville	-
Verona	Farmingdale	-
Vine Wine Bar	Merrick	-
Wall's Wharf	Bayville	17
☑ Waterzooi	Garden City	24
Willy Parkers	Williston Pk	-
NEW Wobbly Olive	Hauppauge	-
NEW XO	Huntington	-

OFFBEAT

Ariana	Huntington	20
Baby Moon	Westhampton Bch	18
Backyard	Montauk	23
Benihana	multi.	19
Big Daddy's	Massapequa	24
Bliss	E Setauket	22
Chalet Rest.	Roslyn	18
Cookroom	Middle Island	-
Cuvée	Greenport	22
Cyril's Fish	Amagansett	18
NEW Del Fuego	St. James	-
NEW DoraNonnie	Glen Head	-
Farm Country Kit.	Riverhead	23
Hampton Chutney	Amagansett	22
House/Dosas	Hicksville	25
Iron Skillet	Mattituck	-
Itgen's	Valley Stream	-
Kyle's	Shelter Is	-
LL Dent	Carle Pl	23
Los Compadres	Huntington Station	23
Melting Pot	Farmingdale	18
New Paradise	Sag Harbor	22
Nichol's	E Hampton	17
Painters'	Brookhaven Hamlet	20
Poco Loco	Roslyn	17
RS Jones	Merrick	22
Samurai	Huntington	24
☑ Smokin' Al's	Bay Shore	23
Spicy's BBQ	multi.	20
Sunset Beach	Shelter Is Hts	18
Surfside Inn	Montauk	18
Swingbelly's	Long Bch	23

Toast	Port Jefferson	24
Tomo Hibachi	Huntington	20
Townline	Sagaponack	19
Tula Kit.	Bay Shore	24
Tweeds	Riverhead	21

OUTDOOR DINING

(G=garden; P=patio; S=sidewalk; T=terrace)

NEW A Lure	P	Southold	-
A Mano	P	Mattituck	24
Amarelle	P	Wading River	25
Babette's	S	E Hampton	20
Backyard	T	Montauk	23
Bay Burger	P	Sag Harbor	21
NEW Beach Hse.	P	E Hampton	-
Beacon	T	Sag Harbor	22
Bistro Citron	T	Roslyn	21
Blue	P	Blue Pt	22
Blue Parrot	P	E Hampton	15
Boathouse	P	E Hampton	19
B.Smith's	P	Sag Harbor	18
Chequit Inn	P	Shelter Is Hts	19
Cipollini	P	Manhasset	21
Cittanuova	P, S	E Hampton	20
Clam Bar	P	Amagansett	21
Crew Kit.	T	Huntington	24
Cyril's Fish	P	Amagansett	18
Dee Angelo's	P	Westhampton Bch	19
Dockers Waterside	T	E Quogue	20
Duryea's Lobster	T	Montauk	22
☑ E. Hampton Pt.	P, T	E Hampton	19
Fishbar	P	Montauk	18
Fishery	T	E Rockaway	19
Fork & Vine	G	Glen Head	23
Fresno	P	E Hampton	22
Gosman's Dock	P	Montauk	19
☑ Harvest	G, P	Montauk	26
Hellenic Snack	P	E Marion	20
Hideaway	T	Ocean Beach	19
Inlet Seafood	T	Montauk	21
Inn Spot/Bay	T	Hampton Bays	19
NEW Insignia	P	Smithtown	-
Island Mermaid	T	Ocean Beach	20
NEW Jewel	P	Melville	-
NEW La Maison Blanche	P	Shelter Is Hts	-
Living Rm.	G	E Hampton	25

Lombardi's/Sound | T | Port Jefferson | 21
Louie's Oyster | T | Port Washington | 17
🅉 Maroni Cuisine | P | Northport | 28
Mill Pond Hse. | P | Centerport | 25
NEW Mint | Garden City | -
🅉 Mirko's | P | Water Mill | 26
Mumon | T | Garden City | 22
Navy Beach | P | Montauk | 19
Nello Summertimes | P, T | Southampton | 16
New Paradise | T | Sag Harbor | 22
Nichol's | P | E Hampton | 17
🅉 Nick & Toni's | G | E Hampton | 24
🅉 Noah's | S | Greenport | 26
NEW Nobu/Capri | P | Southampton | -
NEW North Fork Oyster | P | Greenport | -
Oakland's/Sunday | T | Hampton Bays | 18
Old Mill Inn | T | Mattituck | 20
NEW Orto | P | Miller Pl | -
🅉 Palm Court | P | E Meadow | 24
NEW Patio | P | Freeport | -
Pine Island | T | Bayville | 18
Poco Loco | P | Roslyn | 17
NEW Pop's Seafood | P | Island Pk | -
Post Stop | T | Westhampton Bch | 17
Ram's Head | T | Shelter Is | 20
NEW Riverhead Pjt. | P | Riverhead | -
Rumba | T | Hampton Bays | -
Sant Ambroeus | S | Southampton | 24
Savanna's | G | Southampton | 20
Scrimshaw | P | Greenport | 23
Sea Grille | P | Montauk | 21
NEW Southampton Social | G | Southampton | -
🅉 Starr Boggs | P | Westhampton Bch | 26
Stonewalls | P | Riverhead | 23
Sunset Beach | T | Shelter Is Hts | 18
Surf Lodge | P | Montauk | 19
Surfside Inn | P | Montauk | 18
Surf's Out | P, T | Kismet | 17
Taste 99 | P | Farmingdale | 18
Tide Runners | T | Hampton Bays | 16
Touch/Venice | P | Cutchogue | 21
Trio | P | Holbrook | 21

🅉 Trumpets | T | Eastport | 22
Tutto Il Giorno | P | multi. | 25
🅉 Verace | P, S | Islip | 26
Villa D'Aqua | P | Bellmore | 21
Vine Street | T | Shelter Is | 25
🅉 Waterzooi | P | Garden City | 24
World Pie | G, P | Bridgehampton | 19

PEOPLE-WATCHING

Almond | Bridgehampton | 20
NEW A Lure | Southold | -
🅉 American Hotel | Sag Harbor | 25
Amicale | Huntington Station | 25
🅉 Atlantica | Long Bch | 20
Babette's | E Hampton | 20
Babylon Carriage | Babylon | 21
Backyard | Montauk | 23
Bar Frites | Greenvale | 18
🅉 Barney's | Locust Valley | 26
Boathouse | E Hampton | 19
Bobby Van's | Bridgehampton | 22
B.Smith's | Sag Harbor | 18
Burton & Doyle | Great Neck | 24
Cipollini | Manhasset | 21
Cittanuova | E Hampton | 20
Clam Bar | Amagansett | 21
🅉 Coolfish | Syosset | 24
Copa Wine | Bridgehampton | 20
🅉 E. Hampton Pt. | E Hampton | 19
Grill Room | Hauppauge | 21
Hudson/McCoy | Freeport | 18
NEW Huntington Social | Huntington | -
🅉 Il Mulino NY | Roslyn Estates | 27
NEW Insignia | Smithtown | -
NEW Jewel | Melville | -
NEW K·Pacho | New Hyde Pk | -
NEW Legacy | Huntington | -
🅉 Limani | Roslyn | 26
Lobster Roll | Amagansett | 19
🅉 Luce & Hawkins | Jamesport | 25
Mill Pond Hse. | Centerport | 25
Mirabelle Tavern | Stony Brook | 21
NEW Monsoon | Babylon | -
🅉 Morton's | Great Neck | 25
NEW MP Taverna | Roslyn | -
Muse | Sag Harbor | 23
Navy Beach | Montauk | 19
Nello Summertimes | Southampton | 16
🅉 Nick & Toni's | E Hampton | 24
Nisen | Woodbury | 25

NEW Nobu/Capri | Southampton	⌐
Orto | Miller Pl	⌐
▣ Palm | E Hampton	26
▣ Peter Luger | Great Neck	27
NEW Pop's Seafood | Island Pk	⌐
Porto Vivo | Huntington	22
Red Bar | Southampton	22
Rein | Garden City	23
NEW Riverhead Pjt. | Riverhead	⌐
Robert's | Water Mill	25
NEW Ruschmeyer's | Montauk	⌐
Sant Ambroeus | Southampton	24
Savanna's | Southampton	20
NEW Serata | Oyster Bay	⌐
▣ 1770 Hse. | E Hampton	25
75 Main | Southampton	18
NEW Southampton Social | Southampton	⌐
Southfork | Bridgehampton	⌐
▣ Starr Boggs | Westhampton Bch	26
▣ Stone Creek | E Quogue	26
Stresa | Manhasset	25
Sunset Beach | Shelter Is Hts	18
Surf Lodge | Montauk	19
▣ Toku | Manhasset	25
Trata | Water Mill	22
Tratt. Diane | Roslyn	25
Tutto Il Giorno | multi.	25
▣ Verace | Islip	26
Vero | Amityville	⌐
▣ Waterzooi | Garden City	24
World Pie | Bridgehampton	19

POWER SCENES

▣ American Hotel | Sag Harbor	25
Amicale | Huntington Station	25
▣ Barney's | Locust Valley	26
Barolo | Melville	25
▣ Blackstone Steak | Melville	24
Bobby Van's | Bridgehampton	22
▣ Bryant & Cooper | Roslyn	26
Burton & Doyle | Great Neck	24
Crew Kit. | Huntington	24
▣ E. Hampton Pt. | E Hampton	19
Franina | Syosset	26
▣ Il Mulino NY | Roslyn Estates	27
NEW Insignia | Smithtown	⌐
NEW Jake's Steak | E Meadow	⌐
NEW Jewel | Melville	⌐
La Coquille | Manhasset	24
▣ Limani | Roslyn	26

Mac's Steak | Huntington	23
Mirabelle, Rest. | Stony Brook	25
NEW Monsoon | Babylon	⌐
▣ Morton's | Great Neck	25
▣ Nick & Toni's | E Hampton	24
▣ Palm | E Hampton	26
▣ Palm Court | E Meadow	24
▣ Peter Luger | Great Neck	27
▣ Plaza Café | Southampton	26
Porto Vivo | Huntington	22
▣ Prime | Huntington	23
▣ Ruth's Chris | Garden City	25
▣ 1770 Hse. | E Hampton	25
▣ Stone Creek | E Quogue	26
Stresa | Manhasset	25
▣ Tellers | Islip	26
▣ Toku | Manhasset	25

PRIVATE ROOMS

(Restaurants charge less at off times; call for capacity)

▣ American Hotel | Sag Harbor	25
Amicale | Huntington Station	25
Babylon Carriage | Babylon	21
Barolo | Melville	25
Basil Leaf Café | Locust Valley	21
Birchwood | Riverhead	20
Blackwells | Wading River	23
Blue Moon | Rockville Ctr	20
Boccaccio | Hicksville	21
B.Smith's | Sag Harbor	18
Burton & Doyle | Great Neck	24
Café Capriccio | Port Washington	24
Cafe La Strada | Hauppauge	23
Carnival | Port Jefferson Station	22
Casa Rustica | Smithtown	25
Chi | Westbury	25
Coast Grill | Southampton	22
Cooperage Inn | Baiting Hollow	22
▣ Country Hse. | Stony Brook	23
Crabtree's | Floral Pk	21
Curry Club | E Setauket	20
Dodici | Rockville Ctr	24
Dynasty/Pt. Wash. | Port Washington	20
▣ E. Hampton Pt. | E Hampton	19
E. B. Elliot's | Freeport	18
Emilio's | Commack	23
Fisherman's Catch | Point Lookout	20
Frank's Steaks | Rockville Ctr	21
Frederick's | Melville	23
Galleria Rist. | Westbury	26

George Martin | **Rockville Ctr** 22
Giulio Cesare | **Westbury** 25
Gosman's Dock | **Montauk** 19
Grasso's | **Cold Spring** 24
Heart/Portugal | **Mineola** 20
H2O Seafood | **Smithtown** 23
Iavarone Cafe | **New Hyde Pk** 21
Il Capuccino | **Sag Harbor** 19
Il Classico | **Massapequa Pk** 23
Inn Spot/Bay | **Hampton Bays** 19
Irish Coffee | **E Islip** 23
Jimmy Hays | **Island Pk** 25
Jolly Fisherman | **Roslyn** 21
Kiss'o | **New Hyde Pk** 21
La Marmite | **Williston Pk** 24
☒ La Plage | **Wading River** 27
Lareira | **Mineola** 20
☒ Limani | **Roslyn** 26
Lombardi's/Sound | 21
    Port Jefferson
Louie's Oyster | 17
    Port Washington
Lucé | **E Norwich** 22
Mamma Lombardi's | **Holbrook** 23
Mario | **Hauppauge** 25
☒ Maroni Cuisine | **Northport** 28
Mill Pond Hse. | **Centerport** 25
Mim's | **Roslyn Hts** 20
Minado | **Carle Pl** 21
☒ Morton's | **Great Neck** 25
Mother Kelly's | **Cedarhurst** 21
Nagashima | **Jericho** 24
Nicholas James | **Merrick** 22
Nonnina | **W Islip** 25
Orchid | **Garden City** 23
☒ Orient | **Bethpage** 27
O's Food | **St. James** 22
Pace's Steak | **multi.** 22
Pasta Pasta | **Port Jefferson** 25
Peppercorns | **Hicksville** 19
Per Un Angelo | **Wantagh** 22
Piccola Bussola | **Mineola** 23
☒ Piccolo | **Huntington** 27
Piccolo's | **Mineola** 24
Pierre's | **Bridgehampton** 21
Pine Island | **Bayville** 18
Porto Vivo | **Huntington** 22
Ram's Head | **Shelter Is** 20
Rare 650 | **Syosset** 24
Rialto | **Carle Pl** 26
☒ Riverbay | **Williston Pk** 23
Robert's | **Water Mill** 25
☒ Rothmann's | **E Norwich** 25

☒ Ruth's Chris | **Garden City** 25
☒ San Marco | **Hauppauge** 26
Sea Grille | **Montauk** 21
☒ 1770 Hse. | **E Hampton** 25
Seventh Street Cafe | 20
    Garden City
Shiki (Babylon) | **Babylon** 24
Solé | **Oceanside** 26
Southampton Publick | 18
    Southampton
Southside Fish | **Lindenhurst** 20
☒ Stone Creek | **E Quogue** 26
Sundried Tomato | **Nesconset** 21
Sunset Beach | **Shelter Is Hts** 18
☒ Tellers | **Islip** 26
Tesoro | **Westbury** 23
Thom Thom | **Wantagh** 20
Thyme | **Roslyn** 21
Touch/Venice | **Cutchogue** 21
Tratt. Diane | **Roslyn** 25
Trio | **Holbrook** 21
Umberto's | **New Hyde Pk** 22
Vespa | **Great Neck** 22
Villa D'Este | **Floral Pk** 22
Vintage Prime | **St. James** 25
World Pie | **Bridgehampton** 19

PRIX FIXE MENUS

(Call for prices and times)
Albert's Mandarin | **Huntington** 20
Amicale | **Huntington Station** 25
Angelina's | **Syosset** 23
Argyle Grill | **Babylon** 22
Arturo's | **Floral Pk** 22
Azerbaijan | **Westbury** 22
Babylon Carriage | **Babylon** 21
☒ Barney's | **Locust Valley** 26
Bayou | **N Bellmore** 23
Bellport | **Bellport** 22
Benny's | **Westbury** 25
Big Daddy's | **Massapequa** 24
Bistro Citron | **Roslyn** 21
Bistro 44 | **Northport** 23
Bobby Van's | **Bridgehampton** 22
Bob's Rest. | **Floral Pk** 21
Brasserie 214 | **New Hyde Pk** 20
Brio | **Port Washington** 21
Butterfields | **Hauppauge** 20
Café Capriccio | 24
    Port Washington
Cafe Max | **E Hampton** 23
Cafe Rustica | **Great Neck** 22
Caracalla | **Syosset** 23

Casa Rustica | **Smithtown**	25
Z Chachama | **E Patchogue**	27
Z Chez Noëlle | **Port Washington**	27
Cho-Sen | **multi.**	19
Z Coolfish | **Syosset**	24
Z Country Hse. | **Stony Brook**	23
Crossroads Cafe | **E Northport**	22
Declan Quinn's | **Bay Shore**	19
Desmond's | **Wading River**	20
Dish | **Water Mill**	27
Duke Falcon's | **Long Bch**	22
Elaine's | **Great Neck**	22
Fifth Season | **Port Jefferson**	26
Fisherman's Catch | **Point Lookout**	20
Fork & Vine | **Glen Head**	23
Fortune Wheel | **Levittown**	22
Fresno | **E Hampton**	22
Garden Grill | **Smithtown**	21
George Martin's Grill | **multi.**	20
Hemingway's | **Wantagh**	19
Hudson's Mill | **Massapequa**	22
Z Jamesport Manor | **Jamesport**	23
Jolly Fisherman | **Roslyn**	21
Jonathan's Rist. | **Huntington**	24
La Coquille | **Manhasset**	24
La Tavola | **Sayville**	22
Le Chef | **Southampton**	22
Z Limani | **Roslyn**	26
Living Rm. | **E Hampton**	25
Lola's Kit. | **Long Bch**	20
Mama's | **Centereach**	21
Z Maroni Cuisine | **Northport**	28
Matsulin | **Hampton Bays**	22
Michaels'/Maidstone | **E Hampton**	18
Milleridge Inn | **Jericho**	16
Mill Pond Hse. | **Centerport**	25
Mirabelle, Rest. | **Stony Brook**	25
Nicholas James | **Merrick**	22
Page One | **Glen Cove**	22
Z Palm Court | **E Meadow**	24
Pearl East | **Manhasset**	23
Peppercorns | **Hicksville**	19
Pierre's | **Bridgehampton**	21
Z Plaza Café | **Southampton**	26
Café Red/Red | **Huntington**	25
Red Bar | **Southampton**	22
Rist. Gemelli | **Babylon**	24
RS Jones | **Merrick**	22
Runyon's | **Seaford**	18

Ruvo | **multi.**	22
Schooner | **Freeport**	17
Sea Levels | **Brightwaters**	22
Z 1770 Hse. | **E Hampton**	25
Shagwong | **Montauk**	18
Z Snaps | **Wantagh**	26
Southampton Publick | **Southampton**	18
Z Stone Creek | **E Quogue**	26
Stresa | **Manhasset**	25
Z Tellers | **Islip**	26
34 New St. | **Huntington**	18
Thyme | **Roslyn**	21
Tratt. Diane | **Roslyn**	25
Uncle Bacala's | **Garden City Pk**	21
Villa D'Este | **Floral Pk**	22
Voila! | **St. James**	24
Wild Honey | **Oyster Bay**	25

QUIET CONVERSATION

Allison's Amalfi | **Sea Cliff**	21
NEW Antonette's | **Rockville Ctr**	–
Ariana | **Huntington**	20
Athens Grill | **Riverhead**	–
Basil Leaf Café | **Locust Valley**	21
Bayview Inn | **S Jamesport**	22
Bevanda | **Great Neck**	22
Cafe Max | **E Hampton**	23
Caracalla | **Syosset**	23
Chat Noir | **Rockville Ctr**	21
Z Chez Noëlle | **Port Washington**	27
NEW E. Hampton Grill | **E Hampton**	–
E. B. Elliot's | **Freeport**	18
NEW 18 Bay | **Shelter Is**	–
Ernesto's East | **Glen Head**	22
Estia's | **Sag Harbor**	23
Franina | **Syosset**	26
Garden Grill | **Smithtown**	21
Haiku | **Riverhead**	–
Hampton Chutney | **Amagansett**	22
Inn Spot/Bay | **Hampton Bays**	19
Itgen's | **Valley Stream**	–
NEW J. Michaels | **Northport**	–
Jonathan's Rist. | **Huntington**	24
Kura Barn | **Huntington**	24
Kyle's | **Shelter Is**	–
La Coquille | **Manhasset**	24
NEW La Maison Blanche | **Shelter Is Hts**	–
La Pace/Chef Michael | **Glen Cove**	25

SPECIAL FEATURES

La Plage | **Wading River** | 27
La Spada | **Huntington Station** | 21
Living Rm. | **E Hampton** | 25
Z Luce & Hawkins | **Jamesport** | 25
Mac's Steak | **Huntington** | 23
NEW Martini Grill | **Speonk** | -
Michaels'/Maidstone | **E Hampton** | 18
Mill Pond Hse. | **Centerport** | 25
Mirabelle, Rest. | **Stony Brook** | 25
Z Mirko's | **Water Mill** | 26
Z Mosaic | **St. James** | 28
NEW North Fork Oyster | **Greenport** | -
Osteria da Nino | **Huntington** | 24
Page One | **Glen Cove** | 22
Patio/54 Main | **Westhampton Bch** | 19
Ram's Head | **Shelter Is** | 20
Robert's | **Water Mill** | 25
Robinson's Tea | **Stony Brook** | 23
Sant Ambroeus | **Southampton** | 24
Sarin Thai | **Greenvale** | 24
Z 1770 Hse. | **E Hampton** | 25
Stonewalls | **Riverhead** | 23
Stresa | **Manhasset** | 25
NEW Tappo | **Glen Cove** | -
Thai Green Leaf | **E Northport** | 21
Tratt. Diane | **Roslyn** | 25
Z Trumpets | **Eastport** | 22
Vespa | **Great Neck** | 22
NEW XO | **Huntington** | -

RAW BARS

Z Aji 53 | **Bay Shore** | 27
Z Atlantica | **Long Bch** | 20
Bistro 25 | **Sayville** | -
Z Blackstone Steak | **Melville** | 24
Blue | **Blue Pt** | 22
Boathouse | **E Hampton** | 19
Bonbori Tiki | **Huntington** | 20
Brasserie Persil | **Oceanside** | 25
Brass Rail | **Locust Valley** | 25
Buoy One | **multi.** | 23
Café Formaggio | **Carle Pl** | 20
Caffe Laguna | **Long Bch** | 19
Canterbury | **Oyster Bay** | 19
Claudio's | **Greenport** | 16
Z E. Hampton Pt. | **E Hampton** | 19
Hudson/McCoy | **Freeport** | 18
NEW Insignia | **Smithtown** | -
NEW Jewel | **Melville** | -
Kinha | **Garden City** | -

Legal Sea Foods | **Huntington Station** | 20
Louie's Oyster | **Port Washington** | 17
NEW Mara's | **Syosset** | -
Mill Pond Hse. | **Centerport** | 25
Z Noah's | **Greenport** | 26
NEW North Fork Oyster | **Greenport** | -
Oar Steak | **Patchogue** | 21
NEW Oceans 5 | **Shoreham** | -
Paddy McGees | **Island Pk** | 18
Porters | **Bellport** | 20
Prime Catch | **Rockville Ctr** | -
Z Riverbay | **Williston Pk** | 23
Sage Bistro | **Bellmore** | 24
Sensasian | **Levittown** | -
Snapper Inn | **Oakdale** | 18
South Edison | **Montauk** | 22
Southside Fish | **Lindenhurst** | 20
Squiretown | **Hampton Bays** | 20
Tai Show | **Massapequa** | 23
Z Tellers | **Islip** | 26
Z Toku | **Manhasset** | 25
Tony's | **Westhampton Bch** | 19
View | **Oakdale** | 22
Vincent's | **Carle Pl** | 22
Wildfish | **Freeport** | 21

ROMANTIC PLACES

Amarelle | **Wading River** | 25
Z American Hotel | **Sag Harbor** | 25
NEW Antonette's | **Rockville Ctr** | -
Athens Grill | **Riverhead** | -
Z Atlantica | **Long Bch** | 20
Z Barney's | **Locust Valley** | 26
Benny's | **Westbury** | 25
Blackwells | **Wading River** | 23
Bliss | **E Setauket** | 22
Cafe Joelle | **Sayville** | 22
Caffe Laguna | **Long Bch** | 19
Caracalla | **Syosset** | 23
NEW Caracara Mex. | **Farmingdale** | -
Casa Rustica | **Smithtown** | 25
Chadwicks | **Rockville Ctr** | 22
Z Chez Noëlle | **Port Washington** | 27
Comtesse Thérèse Bistro | **Aquebogue** | -
Cooperage Inn | **Baiting Hollow** | 22
Z Country Hse. | **Stony Brook** | 23
E. B. Elliot's | **Freeport** | 18
NEW 18 Bay | **Shelter Is** | -

Elaine's | **Great Neck** `22`

`NEW` Fusion 84 | **Sayville** `-`

Grasso's | **Cold Spring** `24`

`Z` Jamesport Manor | **Jamesport** `23`

`NEW` J. Michaels | **Northport** `-`

Kura Barn | **Huntington** `24`

La Coquille | **Manhasset** `24`

`Z` Lake Hse. | **Bay Shore** `28`

`NEW` La Maison Blanche | **Shelter Is Hts** `-`

La Pace/Chef Michael | **Glen Cove** `25`

`Z` La Plage | **Wading River** `27`

La Spada | **Huntington Station** `21`

`Z` Le Soir | **Bayport** `27`

Living Rm. | **E Hampton** `25`

Lola | **Great Neck** `24`

Lombardi's/Sound | **Port Jefferson** `21`

Lucé | **E Norwich** `22`

`Z` Luce & Hawkins | **Jamesport** `25`

Mac's Steak | **Huntington** `23`

Mill Pond Hse. | **Centerport** `25`

Mirabelle, Rest. | **Stony Brook** `25`

`Z` Mirko's | **Water Mill** `26`

Navy Beach | **Montauk** `19`

`Z` North Fork Table | **Southold** `29`

`NEW` Orto | **Miller Pl** `-`

`Z` Palm Court | **E Meadow** `24`

Per Un Angelo | **Wantagh** `22`

`Z` Piccolo | **Huntington** `27`

Pine Island | **Bayville** `18`

`Z` Plaza Café | **Southampton** `26`

Ram's Head | **Shelter Is** `20`

Rist. Gemelli | **Babylon** `24`

Robert's | **Water Mill** `25`

`NEW` Saffron | **Glen Head** `-`

Sant Ambroeus | **Southampton** `24`

`Z` Sempre Vivolo | **Hauppauge** `27`

`Z` 1770 Hse. | **E Hampton** `25`

`NEW` Spring Close | **E Hampton** `-`

`Z` Stone Creek | **E Quogue** `26`

Stresa | **Manhasset** `25`

Taste 99 | **Farmingdale** `18`

Tratt. Diane | **Roslyn** `25`

Trio | **Holbrook** `21`

`Z` Trumpets | **Eastport** `22`

21 Main | **W Sayville** `23`

Vespa | **Great Neck** `22`

Villa D'Aqua | **Bellmore** `21`

`NEW` XO | **Huntington** `-`

SENIOR APPEAL

Afghan Grill | **New Hyde Pk** `20`

Basil Leaf Café | **Locust Valley** `21`

Café Capriccio | **Port Washington** `24`

Cafe Max | **E Hampton** `23`

Cafe Rustica | **Great Neck** `22`

Itgen's | **Valley Stream** `-`

Jolly Fisherman | **Roslyn** `21`

Le Chef | **Southampton** `22`

Lombardi's/Sound | **Port Jefferson** `21`

Med. Snack | **Huntington** `22`

Michaels'/Maidstone | **E Hampton** `18`

Milleridge Inn | **Jericho** `16`

Modern Snack | **Aquebogue** `18`

Nicholas James | **Merrick** `22`

Page One | **Glen Cove** `22`

Pastrami King | **Merrick** `20`

Schooner | **Freeport** `17`

Sea Grille | **Montauk** `21`

Sweet Mama's | **Northport** `19`

Villa D'Este | **Floral Pk** `22`

Zorba/Greek | **Hicksville** `19`

SINGLES SCENES

Almond | **Bridgehampton** `20`

`NEW` A Lure | **Southold** `-`

Argyle Grill | **Babylon** `22`

Babylon Carriage | **Babylon** `21`

Backyard | **Montauk** `23`

B.K. Sweeney's | **Garden City** `18`

Blue Parrot | **E Hampton** `15`

Boathouse | **E Hampton** `19`

`Z` Bryant & Cooper | **Roslyn** `26`

Bulldog Grille | **Amityville** `-`

Burton & Doyle | **Great Neck** `24`

Cafe Testarossa | **Syosset** `22`

Cipollini | **Manhasset** `21`

`NEW` Cody's | **Riverhead** `-`

Copa Wine | **Bridgehampton** `20`

Cyril's Fish | **Amagansett** `18`

`NEW` E. Hampton Grill | **E Hampton** `-`

`Z` E. Hampton Pt. | **E Hampton** `19`

Four Food Studio | **Melville** `21`

`NEW` Fusion 84 | **Sayville** `-`

George Martin's Grill | **Rockville Ctr** `20`

`NEW` Grill 454 | **Commack** `-`

Hudson/McCoy | **Freeport** `18`

`NEW` Huntington Social | **Huntington** `-`

SPECIAL FEATURES

NEW Insignia | **Smithtown**	_–_
NEW Jewel | **Melville**	_–_
NEW K·Pacho | **New Hyde Pk**	_–_
NEW Left Coast | **Merrick**	_–_
Legal Sea Foods | **Huntington Station**	20
Legends | **New Suffolk**	23
Library Cafe | **Farmingdale**	18
Z Limani | **Roslyn**	26
Melting Pot | **Farmingdale**	18
NEW Mint | **Garden City**	_–_
NEW Monsoon | **Babylon**	_–_
Nisen | **Woodbury**	25
NEW Nobu/Capri | **Southampton**	_–_
Oakland's/Sunday | **Hampton Bays**	18
NEW Patio | **Freeport**	_–_
NEW Pop's Seafood | **Island Pk**	_–_
Porto Vivo | **Huntington**	22
Post Office | **Babylon**	19
Public Hse. 49 | **Patchogue**	20
NEW Riverhead Pjt. | **Riverhead**	_–_
Rockwell's B&G | **Smithtown**	22
Z Rothmann's | **E Norwich**	25
NEW Ruschmeyer's | **Montauk**	_–_
NEW Serata | **Oyster Bay**	_–_
Sip City | **Great Neck**	_–_
Southampton Publick | **Southampton**	18
NEW Southampton Social | **Southampton**	_–_
Sugar | **Carle Pl**	_–_
Sunset Beach | **Shelter Is Hts**	18
Surf Lodge | **Montauk**	19
Z Tellers | **Islip**	26
Tide Runners | **Hampton Bays**	16
Z Toku | **Manhasset**	25
Trata | **Water Mill**	22
Z Verace | **Islip**	26
Wall's Wharf | **Bayville**	17
Z Waterzooi | **Garden City**	24
Wild Ginger | **Great Neck**	21
Willy Parkers | **Williston Pk**	_–_
NEW Wobbly Olive | **Hauppauge**	_–_

SLEEPERS

(Good food, but little known)

Backyard | **Montauk**	23
Bellissimo Rist. | **Deer Park**	23
Benkei | **Northport**	23
Bin 56 | **Huntington**	24
Bozena Polish | **Lindenhurst**	23
Chi | **Westbury**	25

Cuvée | **Greenport**	22
Dish | **Water Mill**	27
Il Villagio | **Malverne**	24
Izumi | **Bethpage**	23
La Terrazza | **Cedarhurst**	22
Los Compadres | **Huntington Station**	23
Madras | **New Hyde Pk**	22
Matthew's | **Ocean Beach**	22
Met. Bistro | **Sea Cliff**	22
Mumon | **Garden City**	22
Ocean Grill | **Freeport**	23
Osaka | **Huntington**	24
Panini Café | **Roslyn**	23
Perfecto Mundo | **Commack**	24
Pizza Place | **Bridgehampton**	24
Ravagh | **multi.**	22
Rist. Italiano | **Port Washington**	24
Rockwell's B&G | **Smithtown**	22
Roe's Casa Dolce | **Rockville Ctr**	24
Royal Bukhara Grill | **Hicksville**	22
Sabai Thai | **Miller Pl**	22
Salamander's | **Greenport**	24
Samurai | **Huntington**	24
Shiki (Babylon) | **Babylon**	24
Shogi | **Westbury**	25
South Edison | **Montauk**	22
Star Confectionery | **Riverhead**	22
Surf 'N Turf | **Merrick**	24
Sushi Palace | **Great Neck**	24
Takara | **Islandia**	28
Tate's | **Nesconset**	26
Tokyo | **E Northport**	24

TASTING MENUS

Amicale | **Huntington Station**	25
NEW Andiamo | **Mineola**	_–_
Z Barney's | **Locust Valley**	26
Bin 56 | **Huntington**	24
Bistro 72 | **Riverhead**	_–_
Bob's Rest. | **Floral Pk**	21
Cafe Rustica | **Great Neck**	22
Chadwicks | **Rockville Ctr**	22
Z Coolfish | **Syosset**	24
Crew Kit. | **Huntington**	24
Crossroads Cafe | **E Northport**	22
Daruma/Tokyo | **Great Neck**	23
NEW 18 Bay | **Shelter Is**	_–_
Fork & Vine | **Glen Head**	23
Z Kitchen A Tratt. | **St. James**	28
Lola | **Great Neck**	24
Z Maroni Cuisine | **Northport**	28
Mirabelle, Rest. | **Stony Brook**	25

☑ Mosaic | **St. James**	28
1 North Steak | **Hampton Bays**	22
O's Food | **St. James**	22
Café Red/Red | **Huntington**	25
☑ Snaps | **Wantagh**	26
Voila! | **St. James**	24

TEEN APPEAL

Baby Moon | **Westhampton Bch**	18
Bigelow's | **Rockville Ctr**	24
Blackbirds' Grille | **Sayville**	20
Bobby's Burger | **multi.**	21
☑ Five Guys | **multi.**	21
Green Cactus | **multi.**	20
Grimaldi's | **Garden City**	23
NEW Jack's Shack | **Glen Head**	-
La Pizzetta | **E Norwich**	21
LT Burger | **Sag Harbor**	16
Melting Pot | **Farmingdale**	18
Salsa Salsa | **Port Jefferson**	23
NEW Smashburger | **Hicksville**	-
☑ Smokin' Al's | **Bay Shore**	23
Southside Fish | **Lindenhurst**	20

TRENDY

☑ Aji 53 | **Bay Shore**	27
Almond | **Bridgehampton**	20
NEW A Lure | **Southold**	-
Amicale | **Huntington Station**	25
Babette's | **E Hampton**	20
Babylon Carriage | **Babylon**	21
Backyard | **Montauk**	23
Bar Frites | **Greenvale**	18
☑ Barney's | **Locust Valley**	26
☑ Besito | **Huntington**	24
Blue Parrot | **E Hampton**	15
Boathouse | **E Hampton**	19
☑ Bryant & Cooper | **Roslyn**	26
B.Smith's | **Sag Harbor**	18
Burton & Doyle | **Great Neck**	24
Chi | **Westbury**	25
Cipollini | **Manhasset**	21
Cittanuova | **E Hampton**	20
☑ Coolfish | **Syosset**	24
Copa Wine | **Bridgehampton**	20
East/ Northeast | **Montauk**	21
Fork & Vine | **Glen Head**	23
Four Food Studio | **Melville**	21
Frisky Oyster | **Greenport**	25
Georgica | **Wainscott**	18
Honu Kit. | **Huntington**	22
Hudson/McCoy | **Freeport**	18

NEW Huntington Social | **Huntington**	-
☑ Il Mulino NY | **Roslyn Estates**	27
NEW Insignia | **Smithtown**	-
NEW Jewel | **Melville**	-
NEW K·Pacho | **New Hyde Pk**	-
NEW Legacy | **Huntington**	-
☑ Limani | **Roslyn**	26
Ludlow Bistro | **Deer Park**	24
Minado | **Carle Pl**	21
NEW Monsoon | **Babylon**	-
☑ Morton's | **Great Neck**	25
NEW MP Taverna | **Roslyn**	-
Navy Beach | **Montauk**	19
Nello Summertimes | **Southampton**	16
☑ Nick & Toni's | **E Hampton**	24
Nisen | **Woodbury**	25
NEW Nobu/Capri | **Southampton**	-
Novitá Wine Bar & Trattoria | **Garden City**	23
☑ Peter Luger | **Great Neck**	27
NEW Phoenix | **Seaford**	-
☑ Piccolo | **Huntington**	27
NEW Pop's Seafood | **Island Pk**	-
Porto Vivo | **Huntington**	22
Red Bar | **Southampton**	22
Rein | **Garden City**	23
NEW Riverhead Pjt. | **Riverhead**	-
NEW Ruschmeyer's | **Montauk**	-
Savanna's | **Southampton**	20
Sen | **Sag Harbor**	21
Serafina | **E Hampton**	18
NEW Serata | **Oyster Bay**	-
NEW Southampton Social | **Southampton**	-
South Edison | **Montauk**	22
NEW Spiro's | **Rocky Pt**	-
☑ Starr Boggs | **Westhampton Bch**	26
☑ Stone Creek | **E Quogue**	26
Sugar | **Carle Pl**	-
Sunset Beach | **Shelter Is Hts**	18
Surf Lodge | **Montauk**	19
☑ Toku | **Manhasset**	25
Trata | **Water Mill**	22
Tratt. Diane | **Roslyn**	25
Tutto Il Giorno | **Southampton**	25
Vero | **Amityville**	-
Vitae | **Huntington**	-
☑ Waterzooi | **Garden City**	24
Wild Ginger | **multi.**	21
Xaga Sushi | **multi.**	-

SPECIAL FEATURES

VALET PARKING

Akbar | **Garden City**	22
NEW Antonette's | **Rockville Ctr**	–
Arthur Avenue | **Smithtown**	–
Arturo's | **Floral Pk**	22
🯄 Atlantica | **Long Bch**	20
Bistro Citron | **Roslyn**	21
🯄 Blackstone Steak | **Melville**	24
Blue | **Blue Pt**	22
Bob's Rest. | **Floral Pk**	21
Brasserie 214 | **New Hyde Pk**	20
Brio | **Port Washington**	21
Brooks & Porter | **Merrick**	22
🯄 Bryant & Cooper | **Roslyn**	26
Burton & Doyle | **Great Neck**	24
Café Capriccio | **Port Washington**	24
Café Formaggio | **Carle Pl**	20
Cafe La Strada | **Hauppauge**	23
Cafe Testarossa | **Syosset**	22
Casa Rustica | **Smithtown**	25
Cedar Creek | **Glen Cove**	–
Chi | **Westbury**	25
Cielo Rist. | **Rockville Ctr**	20
Circa | **Mineola**	22
Cirella's | **Melville**	21
Clubhouse | **Huntington**	21
Coach Grill | **Oyster Bay**	22
Crabtree's | **Floral Pk**	21
Crew Kit. | **Huntington**	24
🯄 Dario's | **Rockville Ctr**	26
Desmond's | **Wading River**	20
Fatfish | **Bay Shore**	21
Fisherman's Catch | **Point Lookout**	20
Four Food Studio | **Melville**	21
Franina | **Syosset**	26
Frank's Steaks | **Rockville Ctr**	21
Frederick's | **Melville**	23
Hudson/McCoy | **Freeport**	18
🯄 Il Mulino NY | **Roslyn Estates**	27
NEW Insignia | **Smithtown**	–
NEW Jewel | **Melville**	–
Jimmy Hays | **Island Pk**	25
NEW J. Michaels | **Northport**	–
Jolly Fisherman | **Roslyn**	21
NEW K·Pacho | **New Hyde Pk**	–
La Bussola | **Glen Cove**	23
La Famiglia | **multi.**	22
La Marmite | **Williston Pk**	24
La Pace/Chef Michael | **Glen Cove**	25
🯄 La Parma | **multi.**	23
NEW Left Coast | **Merrick**	–
🯄 Limani | **Roslyn**	26
Living Rm. | **E Hampton**	25
Lombardi's/Bay | **Patchogue**	23
Lombardi's/Sound | **Port Jefferson**	21
Luigi Q | **Hicksville**	23
Mac's Steak | **Huntington**	23
Marco Polo's | **Westbury**	–
Mario | **Hauppauge**	25
🯄 Matteo's | **multi.**	23
Mill Pond Hse. | **Centerport**	25
Mim's | **multi.**	20
🯄 Morton's | **Great Neck**	25
NEW MP Taverna | **Roslyn**	–
Nautilus Cafe | **Freeport**	24
Nello Summertimes | **Southampton**	16
Nonnina | **W Islip**	25
Pace's Steak | **Hauppauge**	22
Paddy McGees | **Island Pk**	18
🯄 Palm | **E Hampton**	26
🯄 Palm Court | **E Meadow**	24
NEW Passione | **Carle Pl**	–
NEW Patio | **Freeport**	–
Pearl East | **Manhasset**	23
Per Un Angelo | **Wantagh**	22
🯄 Peter Luger | **Great Neck**	27
Piccola Bussola | **multi.**	23
Pine Island | **Bayville**	18
Porto Bello | **Greenport**	22
Porto Vivo | **Huntington**	22
🯄 Prime | **Huntington**	23
Puglia's/Garden City | **Garden City**	–
Rare 650 | **Syosset**	24
Rein | **Garden City**	23
Rist. Gemelli | **Babylon**	24
🯄 Riverbay | **Williston Pk**	23
Robert's | **Water Mill**	25
Rumba | **Hampton Bays**	–
🯄 Ruth's Chris | **Garden City**	25
🯄 San Marco | **Hauppauge**	26
Savanna's | **Southampton**	20
Schooner | **Freeport**	17
Sea Grille | **Montauk**	21
NEW Serata | **Oyster Bay**	–
Solé | **Oceanside**	26
NEW Southampton Social | **Southampton**	–
Steve's Piccola | **Westbury**	24
🯄 Stone Creek | **E Quogue**	26
Sugar | **Carle Pl**	–

Surfside Inn | **Montauk**	18
NEW Tappo | **Glen Cove**	-
Z Tellers | **Islip**	26
388 Rest. | **Roslyn Hts**	20
Thyme | **Roslyn**	21
Tratt. Diane | **Roslyn**	25
Tratt. Di Meo | **Roslyn Hts**	21
Tutto Pazzo | **Huntington**	20
21 Main | **W Sayville**	23
Uncle Bacala's | **multi.**	21
Vespa | **Great Neck**	22
View | **Oakdale**	22
Wall's Wharf | **Bayville**	17

VIEWS

NEW A Lure | **Southold**	-
Amarelle | **Wading River**	25
Z Atlantica | **Long Bch**	20
Beacon | **Sag Harbor**	22
Blackwells | **Wading River**	23
Boathouse | **E Hampton**	19
B.Smith's | **Sag Harbor**	18
Catfish Max | **Seaford**	21
Chequit Inn | **Shelter Is Hts**	19
Claudio's | **Greenport**	16
Coast Grill | **Southampton**	22
Dockers Waterside | **E Quogue**	20
Duryea's Lobster | **Montauk**	22
East/ Northeast | **Montauk**	21
Z E. Hampton Pt. | **E Hampton**	19
E. B. Elliot's | **Freeport**	18
Edgewater | **Hampton Bays**	22
Farm Country Kit. | **Riverhead**	23
Fatfish | **Bay Shore**	21
Fishbar | **Montauk**	18
Fisherman's Catch | **Point Lookout**	20
Fishery | **E Rockaway**	19
Georgica | **Wainscott**	18
Gosman's Dock | **Montauk**	19
Harbor Bistro | **E Hampton**	21
Harbor Mist | **Cold Spring**	19
Z Harvest | **Montauk**	26
Hideaway | **Ocean Beach**	19
Hudson/McCoy | **Freeport**	18
Inlet Seafood | **Montauk**	21
Inn Spot/Bay | **Hampton Bays**	19
Island Mermaid | **Ocean Beach**	20
Jolly Fisherman | **Roslyn**	21
Z Lake Hse. | **Bay Shore**	28
Lombardi's/Bay | **Patchogue**	23
Lombardi's/Sound | **Port Jefferson**	21

Louie's Oyster | **Port Washington**	17
Maguire's | **Ocean Beach**	19
Matthew's | **Ocean Beach**	22
Meeting Hse. | **Amagansett**	20
Mill Pond Hse. | **Centerport**	25
Muse | **Sag Harbor**	23
Nautilus Cafe | **Freeport**	24
Navy Beach | **Montauk**	19
Oakland's/Sunday | **Hampton Bays**	18
Oar Steak | **Patchogue**	21
Ocean Grill | **Freeport**	23
Old Mill Inn | **Mattituck**	20
NEW Patio | **Freeport**	-
Pine Island | **Bayville**	18
NEW Pop's Seafood | **Island Pk**	-
Porto Bello | **Greenport**	22
Z Prime | **Huntington**	23
Ram's Head | **Shelter Is**	20
Rumba | **Hampton Bays**	-
NEW Ruschmeyer's | **Montauk**	-
Schooner | **Freeport**	17
Scrimshaw | **Greenport**	23
Sea Grille | **Montauk**	21
Snapper Inn | **Oakdale**	18
Stonewalls | **Riverhead**	23
Sunset Beach | **Shelter Is Hts**	18
Surf Lodge | **Montauk**	19
Surfside Inn | **Montauk**	18
Surf's Out | **Kismet**	17
Thyme | **Roslyn**	21
Tide Runners | **Hampton Bays**	16
Top/Bay | **Cherry Grove**	-
Touch/Venice | **Cutchogue**	21
Trio | **Holbrook**	21
Z Trumpets | **Eastport**	22
View | **Oakdale**	22
Villa D'Aqua | **Bellmore**	21
Wall's Wharf | **Bayville**	17
Wave Seafood | **Port Jefferson**	19
Whale's Tale | **Northport**	20

WATERSIDE

NEW A Lure | **Southold**	-
Z Atlantica | **Long Bch**	20
Beacon | **Sag Harbor**	22
Bistro Citron | **Roslyn**	21
Boathouse | **E Hampton**	19
B.Smith's | **Sag Harbor**	18
Catfish Max | **Seaford**	21
Claudio's | **Greenport**	16
Coast Grill | **Southampton**	22
Dockers Waterside | **E Quogue**	20

Duryea's Lobster | **Montauk**	22
East/ Northeast | **Montauk**	21
☑ E. Hampton Pt. | **E Hampton**	19
E. B. Elliot's | **Freeport**	18
Fatfish | **Bay Shore**	21
Fishbar | **Montauk**	18
Fisherman's Catch | **Point Lookout**	20
Fishery | **E Rockaway**	19
Georgica | **Wainscott**	18
Gosman's Dock | **Montauk**	19
Gulf Coast | **Montauk**	21
Harbor Bistro | **E Hampton**	21
Harbor Crab | **Patchogue**	18
☑ Harvest | **Montauk**	26
Hideaway | **Ocean Beach**	19
Inlet Seafood | **Montauk**	21
Inn Spot/Bay | **Hampton Bays**	19
Island Mermaid | **Ocean Beach**	20
☑ Lake Hse. | **Bay Shore**	28
Lombardi's/Sound | **Port Jefferson**	21
Louie's Oyster | **Port Washington**	17
Maguire's | **Ocean Beach**	19
Matthew's | **Ocean Beach**	22
Mill Pond Hse. | **Centerport**	25
Nautilus Cafe | **Freeport**	24
Navy Beach | **Montauk**	19
Oakland's/Sunday | **Hampton Bays**	18
Oar Steak | **Patchogue**	21
Old Mill Inn | **Mattituck**	20
Paddy McGees | **Island Pk**	18
NEW Patio | **Freeport**	-
Pier 95 | **Freeport**	24
Pine Island | **Bayville**	18
NEW Pop's Seafood | **Island Pk**	-
Porto Bello | **Greenport**	22
☑ Prime | **Huntington**	23
Rachel's Waterside | **Freeport**	20
Rumba | **Hampton Bays**	-
Schooner | **Freeport**	17
Scrimshaw | **Greenport**	23
Sea Grille | **Montauk**	21
Snapper Inn | **Oakdale**	18
Sunset Beach | **Shelter Is Hts**	18
Surf Lodge | **Montauk**	19
Surf's Out | **Kismet**	17
Tide Runners | **Hampton Bays**	16
Top/Bay | **Cherry Grove**	-
☑ Trumpets | **Eastport**	22
View | **Oakdale**	22
Wall's Wharf | **Bayville**	17
Wildfish | **Freeport**	21

WINNING WINE LISTS

Allison's Amalfi | **Sea Cliff**	21
NEW A Lure | **Southold**	-
☑ American Hotel | **Sag Harbor**	25
Amicale | **Huntington Station**	25
Arturo's | **Floral Pk**	22
☑ Barney's | **Locust Valley**	26
Barolo | **Melville**	25
☑ Blackstone Steak | **Melville**	24
Blackwells | **Wading River**	23
☑ Bryant & Cooper | **Roslyn**	26
Burton & Doyle | **Great Neck**	24
Butterfields | **Hauppauge**	20
Cafe La Strada | **Hauppauge**	23
Cafe Max | **E Hampton**	23
Caracalla | **Syosset**	23
☑ Chez Noëlle | **Port Washington**	27
City Cellar | **Westbury**	21
☑ Coolfish | **Syosset**	24
Crew Kit. | **Huntington**	24
Cuvée | **Greenport**	22
Dodici | **Rockville Ctr**	24
East/ Northeast | **Montauk**	21
NEW E. Hampton Grill | **E Hampton**	-
☑ E. Hampton Pt. | **E Hampton**	19
Fork & Vine | **Glen Head**	23
Franina | **Syosset**	26
Fresno | **E Hampton**	22
Galleria Rist. | **Westbury**	26
☑ Harvest | **Montauk**	26
☑ Il Mulino NY | **Roslyn Estates**	27
NEW Insignia | **Smithtown**	-
Jack Halyards | **Oyster Bay**	23
Jamesport Country | **Jamesport**	23
NEW Jewel | **Melville**	-
Jonathan's Rist. | **Huntington**	24
La Coquille | **Manhasset**	24
La Marmite | **Williston Pk**	24
La Pace/Chef Michael | **Glen Cove**	25
☑ La Piccola | **Port Washington**	27
☑ La Plage | **Wading River**	27
Legal Sea Foods | **Huntington Station**	20
☑ Le Soir | **Bayport**	27
☑ Limani | **Roslyn**	26
Lucé | **E Norwich**	22
☑ Luce & Hawkins | **Jamesport**	25
Mac's Steak | **Huntington**	23
Melting Pot | **Farmingdale**	18
Mill Pond Hse. | **Centerport**	25

Mirabelle, Rest. | **Stony Brook** 25

🇿 Mirko's | **Water Mill** 26

🇿 Morton's | **Great Neck** 25

🇿 Nick & Toni's | **E Hampton** 24

Novitá Wine Bar & Trattoria |
  Garden City 23

Pace's Steak | **multi.** 22

🇿 Palm Court | **E Meadow** 24

Pentimento | **Stony Brook** 22

🇿 Piccolo | **Huntington** 27

🇿 Plaza Café | **Southampton** 26

🇿 Prime | **Huntington** 23

Ram's Head | **Shelter Is** 20

Rare 650 | **Syosset** 24

Café Red/Red | **Huntington** 25

Red Bar | **Southampton** 22

🇿 Riverbay | **Williston Pk** 23

Robert's | **Water Mill** 25

🇿 Rothmann's | **E Norwich** 25

🇿 Ruth's Chris | **Garden City** 25

🇿 San Marco | **Hauppauge** 26

🇿 Sempre Vivolo | **Hauppauge** 27

🇿 1770 Hse. | **E Hampton** 25

🇿 Starr Boggs |
  Westhampton Bch 26

🇿 Stone Creek | **E Quogue** 26

Stresa | **Manhasset** 25

🇿 Tellers | **Islip** 26

Tratt. Diane | **Roslyn** 25

🆕 Vinoco | **Mineola** –

Vintage Prime | **St. James** 25

🆕 XO | **Huntington** –

WORTH A TRIP

Babylon
  🇿 Kotobuki 27
  🆕 Monsoon –

Bayport
  🇿 Le Soir 27

Bay Shore
  🇿 Lake Hse. 28

East Hampton
  🇿 Nick & Toni's 24
  🇿 1770 Hse. 25

East Patchogue
  🇿 Chachama 27

East Quogue
  🇿 Stone Creek 26

Garden City
  Mumon 22

Hauppauge
  🇿 Kotobuki 27

Jamesport
  🇿 Luce & Hawkins 25

Locust Valley
  🇿 Barney's 26

Melville
  🆕 Jewel –

New Hyde Park
  🆕 K·Pacho –

Northport
  🇿 Maroni Cuisine 28

Roslyn
  🇿 Limani 26
  🆕 MP Taverna –

Roslyn Estates
  🇿 Il Mulino NY 27

Sag Harbor
  🇿 American Hotel 25

Smithtown
  🆕 Insignia –

Southold
  🇿 North Fork Table 29

St. James
  🇿 Kitchen A Bistro 27
  🇿 Kitchen A Tratt. 28

Wading River
  🇿 La Plage 27

Water Mill
  🇿 Mirko's 26

West Islip
  Nonnina 25

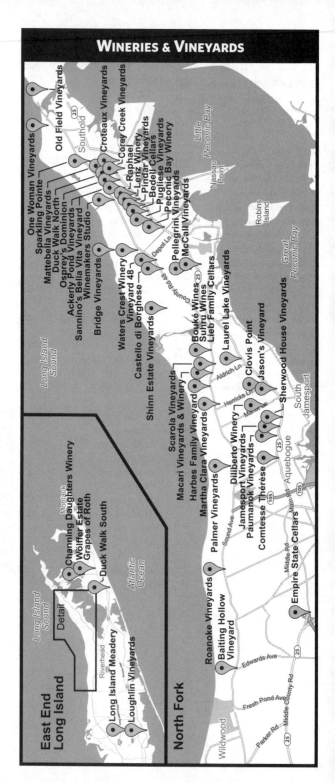

WINERIES & VINEYARDS

East End
Long Island

North Fork

One Woman Vineyards
Old Field Vineyards
Sparkling Pointe
Mattebella Vineyards
Duck Walk North
Osprey's Dominion
Ackerly Pond Vineyards
Sannino's Bella Vita Vineyard
Winemakers Studio

Croteaux Vineyards
Corey Creek Vineyards
Raphael
Lenz Winery
Pindar Vineyards
Bedell Cellars
Pugliese Vineyards
Peconic Bay Winery

Pellegrini Vineyards
McCall Vineyards

Bridge Vineyards
Waters Crest Winery
Vineyard 48
Castello di Borghese

Bouké Wines
Suhru Wines
Lieb Family Cellars
Laurel Lake Vineyards
Clovis Point
Jason's Vineyard
Sherwood House Vineyards

Shinn Estate Vineyards
Scarola Vineyards
Macari Vineyards & Winery
Harbes Family Vineyard
Martha Clara Vineyards

Diliberto Winery
Jamesport Vineyards
Paumanok Vineyards
Comtesse Thérèse

Palmer Vineyards

Roanoke Vineyards
Baiting Hollow Vineyard

Empire State Cellars

Channing Daughters Winery
Wölffer Estate
Grapes of Roth
Duck Walk South

Long Island Meadery
Loughlin Vineyards

Long Island Sound
Atlantic Ocean
Little Peconic Bay
Great Peconic Bay
Nassau Point
Robins Island
Southold
South Jamesport
Aquebogue
Riverhead
Montauk
Wildwood
Detail

Depot Ln.
County Rd 48
Aldrich Ln.
Herricks Ln.
Manor Ln.
Sound Ave
Edwards Ave
Fresh Pond Ave
Parker Rd
Middle Rd
Main Rd
Middle County Rd

Wineries & Vineyards

Ackerly Pond Vineyards
1375 Peconic Ln. | Peconic | 631-765-6861 |
www.ackerlypondvineyards.com

Baiting Hollow Farm Vineyard
2114 Sound Ave. | Baiting Hollow | 631-369-0100 |
www.baitinghollowfarmvineyard.com

Bedell Cellars
36225 Main Rd./Rte. 25 | Cutchogue | 631-734-7537 |
www.bedellcellars.com

Bouké Wines
35 Cox Neck Rd. | Mattituck | 877-877-0527 | www.boukewines.com

Bridge Vineyards
8850 Bridge Ln. | Cutchogue | 917-439-6592 | www.bridgevineyards.com

Castello di Borghese
17150 County Rd. | Cutchogue | 631-734-5111 |
www.castellodiborghese.com

Channing Daughters Winery
1927 Scuttlehole Rd. | Bridgehampton | 631-537-7224 |
www.channingdaughters.com

Clovis Point
1935 Main Rd. | Jamesport | 631-722-4222 | www.clovispointwines.com

Comtesse Thérèse
Union Ave./Rte. 105 | Aquebogue | 631-765-6404 |
www.comtessetherese.com

Corey Creek Vineyards
45470 Main Rd./Rte. 25 | Southold | 631-765-4168 |
www.bedellcellars.com

Croteaux Vineyards
1450 S. Harbor Rd. | Southold | 631-765-6099 | www.croteaux.com

Diliberto Winery
250 Manor Ln. | Jamesport | 631-722-3416 | www.dilibertowinery.com

Duck Walk North
44535 Main Rd./Rte. 25 | Southold | 631-765-3500 | www.duckwalk.com

Duck Walk South
231 Montauk Hwy. | Water Mill | 631-726-7555 |
www.duckwalk.com

Empire State Cellars
308 Tanger Mall Dr. | Riverhead | 631-369-3080 |
www.empirestatecellars.com

Grapes of Roth
P.O. Box 114 | Sag Harbor | 631-725-7999 |
www.thegrapesofroth.com

Harbes Family Vineyard
715 Sound Ave. | Mattituck | 631-298-0700 | www.harbesfamilyfarm.com

Jamesport Vineyards
1216 Main Rd./Rte. 25 | Jamesport | 631-722-5256 |
www.jamesportvineyards.com

Jason's Vineyard
1785 Main Rd./Rte. 25 | Jamesport | 631-238-5801 |
www.jasonsvineyard.com

Laurel Lake Vineyards
3165 Main Rd./Rte. 25 | Laurel | 631-298-1420 | www.llwines.com

Lenz Winery, The
Main Rd./Rte. 25 | Peconic | 631-734-6010 | www.lenzwine.com

Lieb Family Cellars
35 Cox Neck Rd. | Mattituck | 631-734-1100 | www.liebcellars.com

Long Island Meadery
1347 Lincoln Ave. | Holbrook | 631-285-7469 | www.limeadery.com

Loughlin Vineyards
S. Main St. | Sayville | 631-589-0027 | www.loughlinvineyard.com

Macari Vineyards & Winery
150 Bergen Ave. | Mattituck | 631-298-0100 | www.macariwines.com

Martha Clara Vineyards
6025 Sound Ave. | Riverhead | 631-298-0075 |
www.marthaclaravineyards.com

Mattebella Vineyards
46005 Main Rd. | Southold | 631-655-9554 |
www.mattebellavineyards.com

McCall Vineyards
22600 Main Rd. | Cutchogue | 404-274-2809 |
www.mccallwines.com

Old Field Vineyards, The
59600 Main Rd./Rte. 25 | Southold | 631-765-0004 |
www.theoldfield.com

One Woman Vineyards
5195 Old North Rd. | Southold | 631-765-1200 |
www.onewomanwines.com

Osprey's Dominion
44075 Main Rd./Rte. 25 | Peconic | 631-765-6188 |
www.ospreysdominion.com

Palmer Vineyards
108 Sound Ave./Rte. 48 | Aquebogue | 631-722-9463 |
www.palmervineyards.com

Paumanok Vineyards
1074 Main Rd./Rte. 25 | Aquebogue | 631-722-8800 |
www.paumanok.com

WINERIES & VINEYARDS

Peconic Bay Winery
31320 Main Rd./Rte. 25 | Cutchogue | 631-734-7361 |
www.peconicbaywinery.com

Pellegrini Vineyards
23005 Main Rd./Rte. 25 | Cutchogue | 631-734-4111 |
www.pellegrinivineyards.com

Pindar Vineyards
37645 Main Rd./Rte. 25 | Peconic | 631-734-6200 |
www.pindar.net

Pugliese Vineyards
34515 Main Rd./Rte. 25 | Cutchogue | 631-734-4057 |
www.pugliesevineyards.com

Raphael
39390 Main Rd./Rte. 25 | Peconic | 631-765-1100 |
www.raphaelwine.com

Roanoke Vineyards
3543 Sound Ave. | Riverhead | 631-727-4161 |
www.roanokevineyards.com

Sannino Bella Vita Vineyard
1375 Peconic Ln. | Peconic | 631-734-8282 | sanninovineyard.com

Scarola Vineyards
4850 Sound Ave. | Mattituck | 631-335-4199 |
www.scarolawines.com

Sherwood House Vineyards
1291 Main Rd./Rte. 25 | Jamesport | 631-779-2817
2600 Oregon Rd. | Mattituck | 631-298-1396
www.sherwoodhousevineyards.com

Shinn Estate Vineyards
2000 Oregon Rd. | Mattituck | 631-804-0367 |
www.shinnestatevineyards.com

Sparkling Pointe
39750 Rte. 48 | Southold | 631-765-0200 |
www.sparklingpointe.com

Suhru Wines
35 Cox Neck Rd. | Mattituck | 631-603-8127 | www.suhruwines.com

Vineyard 48
18910 Rte. 48 | Cutchogue | 631-734-5200 | www.vineyard48.net

Waters Crest Winery
22355 Rte. 48 | Cutchogue | 631-734-5065 |
www.waterscrestwinery.com

Winemaker Studio
2885 Peconic Ln. | Peconic | 774-641-7488 |
www.anthonynappawines.com

Wölffer Estate
139 Sagg Rd. | Sagaponack | 631-537-5106 | www.wolffer.com

Wine Vintage Chart

This chart is based on a 30-point scale. The ratings (by U. of South Carolina law professor **Howard Stravitz**) reflect vintage quality and the wine's readiness to drink. A dash means the wine is past its peak or too young to rate. Loire ratings are for dry whites.

Whites

	95	96	97	98	99	00	01	02	03	04	05	06	07	08	09	10
France:																
Alsace	24	23	23	25	23	25	26	22	21	22	23	21	26	26	23	26
Burgundy	27	26	22	21	24	24	23	27	23	26	26	25	26	25	25	-
Loire Valley	-	-	-	-	-	-	-	25	20	22	27	23	24	24	24	25
Champagne	26	27	24	25	25	25	21	26	21	-	-	-	-	-	-	-
Sauternes	21	23	25	23	24	24	29	24	26	21	26	25	27	24	27	-
California:																
Chardonnay	-	-	-	-	22	21	24	25	22	26	29	24	27	23	27	-
Sauvignon Blanc	-	-	-	-	-	-	-	-	-	25	24	27	25	24	25	-
Austria:																
Grüner V./Riesl.	22	-	25	22	26	22	23	25	25	24	23	26	25	24	25	-
Germany:	22	26	22	25	24	-	29	25	26	27	28	26	26	26	26	-

Reds

	95	96	97	98	99	00	01	02	03	04	05	06	07	08	09
France:															
Bordeaux	25	25	24	25	24	29	26	24	26	25	28	24	24	25	27
Burgundy	26	27	25	24	27	22	23	25	25	23	28	24	24	25	27
Rhône	26	22	23	27	26	27	26	-	26	25	27	25	26	23	27
Beaujolais	-	-	-	-	-	-	-	-	-	27	25	24	23	28	25
California:															
Cab./Merlot	27	24	28	23	25	-	27	26	25	24	26	24	27	26	25
Pinot Noir	-	-	-	-	-	-	26	25	24	25	26	24	27	24	26
Zinfandel	-	-	-	-	-	-	25	24	26	24	23	21	26	23	25
Oregon:															
Pinot Noir	-	-	-	-	-	-	-	26	24	25	24	25	24	27	24
Italy:															
Tuscany	25	24	29	24	27	24	27	-	24	27	25	26	25	24	-
Piedmont	21	27	26	25	26	28	27	-	24	27	26	26	27	26	-
Spain:															
Rioja	26	24	25	22	25	24	28	-	23	27	26	24	24	25	26
Ribera del Duero/ Priorat	25	26	24	25	25	24	27	-	24	27	26	24	25	27	-
Australia:															
Shiraz/Cab.	23	25	24	26	24	24	26	26	25	25	26	21	23	26	24
Chile:	-	-	-	-	24	22	25	23	24	24	27	25	24	26	24
Argentina:															
Malbec	-	-	-	-	-	-	-	-	-	25	26	27	26	26	25

MILL NECK MANOR

UNDERHILL BURYING GROUNDS

MILL SWAMP

OYSTER BAY

* BEAVER BROOK ROADS

ZAGAT
Long Island Map

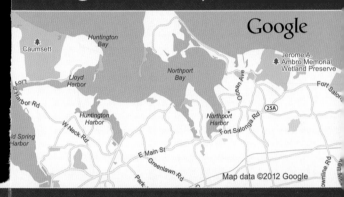

Most Popular Restaurants

Map coordinates follow each name. For chains, only flagship or central locations are plotted. Sections A-G show places in Nassau and Suffolk Counties (see adjacent map). Sections H-N focus on the East End (see reverse side of map).

1. Peter Luger (D-1)
2. Besito (B-4, C-2)
3. Kotobuki† (C-7)
4. Bryant & Cooper (C-2)
5. West End Cafe (D-2)
6. North Fork Table (I-5)
7. Il Mulino NY (D-1)
8. Cheesecake Factory† (D-2)
9. Kitchen A Bistro (B-7)
10. Smokin' Al's BBQ (E-6, F-4)
11. American Hotel (J-6)
12. Waterzooi (E-2)
13. Butera's† (C-4)
14. Blackstone Steak (D-4)
15. Prime (B-4)
16. Bistro Cassis (B-4)
17. Lake House (E-6)
18. Tellers Chophouse (E-7)
19. Coolfish (C-3)
20. Maroni (B-5)
21. Morton's (D-1)
22. Ruth's Chris (E-2)
23. Cafe Baci (D-2)
24. Matteo's† (C-4)
25. La Parma† (C-4)

26. Palm (J-6)
27. Riverbay (D-2)
28. Limani (C-2)
29. Sage Bistro (C-4, F-3)
30. Nick & Toni's (J-6)
31. Ben's Kosher Deli† (C-4)
32. Rothmann's Steak (C-3)
33. Harvest/Ft. Pond (J-7)
34. 1770 House (J-6)
35. Stone Creek (K-5)
36. Five Guys† (E-3)
37. Legal Sea Foods (C-4)
38. Mirabelle (A-7)
39. Umberto's† (E-1)
40. Solé (F-2)
41. H2O Seafood (B-7)
42. Ayhan's Shish† (C-1)
43. Chachama Grill (K-3)
44. Piccolo* (B-4)
45. Bobby Van's (J-6)
46. Jimmy Hays* (G-2)
47. City Cellar (E-2)
48. Jolly Fisherman (C-2)
49. Wild Ginger (C-5, D-1)
50. Millpond House (B-5)

*Indicates tie with above   † Indicates multiple branches

New London

Essex

Groton

Old Lyme

Westbrook

Fishers Island Sound

95

Clinton

Block Isla Sound

Greenport

Gardiners Bay

6

Southold

33

Montauk

Sag Harbor

11

30

Napeague

attituck

26

34

45

North Sea

East Hampton

Bridgehampton

Sunrise Hwy

Southampton

Hampton Bays

t

ue

Map data ©2012 Google, Sanborn